MARX, DURKHEIM, WEBER

MARX, DURKHEIM, WEBER

Formations of Modern
Social Thought

KEN MORRISON

SAGE Publications
London • Thousand Oaks • New Delhi

ISBN 0-8039-7562-7 (hbk)
ISBN 0-8039-7563-5 (pbk)
© Kenneth Morrison 1995
First published 1995
Reprinted 1996, 1997, 1998, 2000, 2001 (twice), 2002, 2003 (twice),
2004, 2005

SAGE Publications Ltd
1 Oliver's Yard
55 City Road
London EC1Y 1SP

SAGE Publications Inc
2455 Teller Road
Thousand Oaks
California 91320

SAGE Publications India Pvt. Ltd
B–42 Panchsheel Enclave
PO Box 4109
New Delhi 110 017

British Library Cataloguing in Publication data
A catalogue record for this book is available from the British Library

Library of Congress Control Number: 95071354

Printed on paper from sustainable sources

Typeset by Mayhew Typesetting, Rhayader, Powys
Printed and bound in Great Britain by
Cromwell Press Limited, Trowbridge, Wiltshire

To the memory of my mother
Gertrude Morrison

Contents

Preface

This book has been written with four central objectives in mind. First, I have tried to outline the main ideas and theoretical perspectives of Marx, Durkheim and Weber in the most comprehensive manner possible. In this regard, special consideration has been given to the treatment of central concepts which have generally been omitted or abbreviated by other commentators or traditions of commentary. Second, I have provided a general background of European social history preceding the great social movements of the modern era and the formation of modern social thought itself. Here, I have tried to provide discussion of the political and economic foundations of feudalism and capitalism in England and France, but only so far as it advances an understanding of the changes taking place in the economic and political spheres of society. Third, where possible I have examined the theoretical contributions of the writings of Marx, Durkheim and Weber in the light of philosophical traditions which, in one way or another, could be directly traced to developments in social thought in the nineteenth and twentieth centuries. These include schools of thought such as idealism and empiricism in its classical and modern form. Fourth, I have tried to furnish some understanding of the social and political foundations of theoretical writing itself. In this endeavor, the texts of Marx, Durkheim and Weber have played a central role in forming the spirit of the book. The discussion of their work has been written in the light of an appreciation of traditions of writing and argument long since past, but which have come down to us as an inexhaustible source of discussion.

Acknowledgments

During the seven years in which this book was written, I have built up considerable debt and owe gratitude to many. Among those I would like to thank are my wife Susan and my son Frank, for their unconditional support and belief in me; Samuel Jedwab and Martin Fischer, who gave me positive encouragement; Dorothy Smith and James Heap of the Ontario Institute for Studies in Education, for their unfailing support which I would like to acknowledge publicly. John O'Neill, of York University, whose friendship I have valued for three decades, I thank for passing on the love of social theory and book culture. To Jeff Ross, Rita Kanarek and Corey Gillingham, all students of mine at York University during the turbulent years of 1986–88, I owe a debt of thanks for convincing me that a book of this nature would be worth writing.

Finally, I would like to thank my colleagues in the Department of Sociology and Anthropology at Wilfrid Laurier University for their support while writing this book and for the opportunity to work in a congenial environment.

1

Introduction

The Origins of Modern Social Theory: 1750–1920

Modern social theory first emerged during the period of what is often called the 'great transformation,' a term used by Karl Polanyi to describe the massive social change which took place in Europe between 1750 and 1920.[1] In practical terms, it is possible to outline some of the steps leading to these developments by looking at three geographical centers in European society: France, Germany and England. Generally, the story begins in France in the decade of the 1780s as France approaches the revolution. The French Revolution of 1789 was one of the most decisive determinants leading to the development of a theory of society which was officially separate from philosophy. By the time the revolution had ended, it had delivered three distinct blows against society, history and politics. First, in asserting the reality of individual freedom and rights, the revolution shook the political and social foundations of individuals. Second, the economic and political consequences of the revolution rocked the foundations of feudal society in its social and economic existence. Third, the political and social changes of the revolution shook the framework of philosophy in its inward-looking and introspective existence.[2] These blows to society, history and politics set the stage for the development of an autonomous social theory by creating a division in philosophy along two distinct lines of development. In the first place, it necessitated a break with the philosophic tendency to look inward in favor of a direct encounter with reality and history. As Herbert Marcuse points out, this tended to bring philosophy into the sphere of history.[3] In the second place, all of the philosophic concepts which had been preoccupied with abstraction began to pattern themselves after social and historical content. By 1800, historical concepts had been brought more fully into the sphere of philosophy and these came fundamentally to rest in the subject matter of society and history. This had a profound effect on the development of social theory since all of the economic and political theorizing which had been packed

1 Karl Polanyi, *The Great Transformation: The Political and Economic Origins of our Time*, Boston: Beacon Press, 1957. See also, E.J. Hobsbawm, *The Age of Revolution*, New York: Dover, 1938.
2 H. Marcuse, *Reason and Revolution: Hegel and the Rise of Social Theory*, New York: Humanities Press, 1954, pp. 251–60.
3 Ibid., p. 253.

into the philosophic mind since Plato and Aristotle had become externally manifest in the social and historical world as a consequence of the revolution in France.

By 1810, the impact of historical developments on philosophy was fully realized in the work of Georg Hegel. It was Hegel who, in 1806, responded to the events of the French Revolution in his writings and, despite their philosophic language, his works were extremely forward-looking in their focus on society and history.[4] Hegel's response to the revolution not only changed philosophy and history, it also led to the development of an autonomous social theory distinct from philosophy itself. Hegel brought this about in several ways. First, he took the view that the French Revolution fundamentally changed the way thought understood reality and history. Previously, history had been seen as fixed in its political and social existence. The rapid decline of French society led Hegel to observe that one form of social and political existence was replacing another and this led to the view that history itself changes from one form to another. This made it evident that economy and politics were obviously linked to society and history, a point which had not been stated in precisely this way before. It was Hegel, therefore, who was the first to understand that historical change took a social form and this manifested itself in terms of distinct stages of development. Second, in showing a direct line of political development from slavery to the modern democratic state, Hegel was able to make political functions the focus of historical development. This step made it clear that philosophy could only understand history by adopting social concepts and that history was, in fact, social in nature. Third, Hegel's philosophy was forward-looking in its focus on individual freedom and self-realization. In making the individual part of historical development, Hegel was one of the first to make individual experience the subject matter of historical and social analysis, which became fully developed in the work of Marx. Fourth, to the extent Hegel believed that history was marked by stages of development, each of the stages represented actual ways of thinking and being which could be separately investigated in terms of distinct social and political functions of societies.

By 1844–45, many of the developments in Hegel's philosophy were consolidated in the writings of Marx and Engels, and as a result the philosophical and historical concepts changed once again. With Marx and Engels, the critical elements of Hegel's philosophy began to turn more distinctly into social theory. But, where Hegel had used philosophic concepts, Marx used economic ones to explain historical and social development.[5] Where the French Revolution had shaped Hegel's historical philosophy, it was the economic and industrial changes in England which shaped Marx's and Engels' thinking. Where Hegel had absorbed society and history into philosophy, Marx was absorbing philosophy into history

---

4 J.N. Findlay, *Hegel: A Re-Examination*, London: George Allen & Unwin, 1958.
5 Marcuse, *Reason and Revolution*, pp. 251–7.

and economy and this led to the use of economic categories to understand society and social existence. This shift from philosophy to economy necessitated the second critical transition of philosophic concepts to the sphere of political economy and the study of capitalism.

Parallel to these developments, enormous changes were under way in Europe and in Britain. These took place on several different fronts. First, by 1830 industrial capitalism had replaced the early agrarian economies of the preceding centuries and Adam Smith had laid the foundations for the first study of capitalism, making him the founder of modern political economy. Second, the mechanical discoveries necessary for industrial production had made England the 'workshop of the world.' This began to dissolve the old agrarian economy and led to rapid developments in commerce, science and industry. Agricultural land began to be used for commercial purposes, and landholders began to evict tenant farmers from their agricultural holdings leaving them without the means of economic livelihood. Third, economic changes occurring in land and labor necessitated the rise of a new working class of wage laborers who were separated from the land as a primary means of economic survival.[6] At this stage, the migration of philosophic concepts into history and social theory had become more complete and, by the time Marx had published Volume 1 of *Capital* in 1867, they were fully incorporated into social thought.

In France, there were comparable developments. French social theory was being shaped by thinkers such as Saint-Simon (1760–1825), Auguste Comte (1798–1857) and Emile Durkheim (1858–1917) who were grappling with the themes of social progress and industrial change. Comte and Durkheim, for their part, founded a school of social theory which was largely shaped by the themes of science, by a conservative response to the French Revolution and by a rejection of philosophy as a basis of social inquiry. By 1830, an important step was taken with the appearance of Comte's *Positive Philosophy*.[7] For his part, Comte had described the age primarily in terms of the development of scientific reasoning which he wanted to extend to the study of society. The impact of Comte's positivism was felt throughout Europe and eventually led to a worldwide movement to segregate the theory of society from speculative philosophy.[8] In France, this began a period of reaction against speculative philosophy culminating in the work of Durkheim, who wanted to found a scientific social theory. With the work of Durkheim, who generally conceived of sociology as a description of the objective facts of society, there was a third transition in the development of social theory which changed the concepts once again. Durkheim's assertion that social theory was separable from philosophy

---

6 For a thorough account of this period see Maurice Dobb, *Studies in the Development of Capitalism*, New York: International Publishers, 1947.

7 Auguste Comte, *Cours de Philosophie Positive*, Paris: Bachelier, 1830–42.

8 D.G. Charlton, *Positive Thought in France*, London: Verso, 1979; W.M. Simon, *European Positivism in the Nineteenth Century*, New York: Cornell, 1963.

meant that all the philosophic and critical language of Hegel and Marx was to be converted into investigative concepts. Observation, description and classification replaced the search for historical laws and the underlying themes of economic development. The scientific movement created by positivism was thus a force in its own right, leaving the study of society to be treated as any other field of scientific investigation.

In Germany, the work of Max Weber (1864–1920) represented a third shift in the direction of modern social theory. Though he was born in 1864, Weber did not make his first theoretical contribution until 1903 when he put forward a theory of capitalism. Weber's investigative insights into capitalist economies established the study of capitalism as a central subject matter of modern social theory.[9] Overall, Weber's theoretical work was largely in response to the themes of late modern society and, in this sense, many of his writings pursued studies of civilization processes and historical change in the West. Along with Weber's broad historical works on ancient economies, feudalism, bureaucracy, household organization, religion and law, his economic studies were among the first to challenge Marx's view regarding the primacy of economic forces. In looking at society from the perspective of what he called the overlapping social spheres of religion, economy, politics and law, Weber asserted that a theory of society could be derived only by looking at the causal influences of various social spheres, rather than restricting analysis to economic factors as Marx had done. Weber developed the concept of the 'social sphere' into a methodological tool which is evident in his discussion of the legal and political influences on modern social classes and the development of the bureaucratic state. The fundamental insight by Weber, that society could be understood in terms of the role played by overlapping social spheres, cannot be overestimated. He thought that the variation in the political, economic and legal spheres of society redefined the nature of social life in changes occurring after Marx. This led him to re-examine the underlying conditions of social class and the nature of capitalist economies.

In addition to this was Weber's methodological work and the role it played in the development of the social sciences. More than Durkheim or Marx, Weber challenged the validity of adopting a methodology in the social sciences which was drawn exclusively from the natural sciences. It was within this framework that Weber put forward a general theory of social action which he outlined in *Economy and Society* and this was to establish his difference from Durkheim.[10] Whereas Durkheim's writings were in reaction to speculative philosophy, Weber's writing was in reaction to science and scientific methodology. In his methodological essays, Weber

9 Weber wrote two theories of capitalism, *The Protestant Ethic and The Spirit of Capitalism*, New York: Scribner, 1958 and *General Economic History*, New York: Collier Books, 1961.

10 Max Weber, *Economy and Society*, Vol. 1, Berkeley: University of California Press, 1978.

drew the distinction between the subject matter of the social and natural sciences, and this led him to focus on human 'social acts' which he thought were fundamentally different from the 'acts' of physical phenomena. Weber believed that 'evaluation' and 'judgment' underlie human social acts and this led him to pursue the dimension of human 'inner states' by propounding a theory of social action. To the extent that Weber's work called into question the investigative focus on external social facts, the concepts changed once again. Weber's stress on the role played by values and judgment in human social action, shifted the investigative focus from external social rules or 'outer states' to the 'inner states' of actors and the necessity of integrating human inner states into a theory of society.

Modern Social Theory Defined

The term modern social theory grew out of the framework of European social thought beginning in the nineteenth century and began to take shape in a more definitive form with the transition to modern times, the growth of industrialized economies, modern political systems and scientific thought. As a formal response to the changes of modernism, the writings of Marx, Durkheim and Weber led to the development of large-scale explanatory perspectives on society and history. Social theory implies two broad areas of investigation. First is the focus on the description of societies, past and present, and their historical development. In itself, this interest takes the form of a historical comparison between different kinds of societies including the forms of political authority, means of economic production, development of legal rules, forms of religious beliefs, the role played by large-scale social institutions, the growth of individualism and the development of capitalism.[11] This investigative focus takes the form of accumulating factual knowledge of different societies and endeavors to understand their social, political and economic change by applying the explanatory perspectives of Marx, Durkheim and Weber to particular historical circumstances, and by looking for the origins and causes of these circumstances.[12]

A second broad area of investigation in social theory relates to the way of looking at society and history. This focus deals primarily with the explanatory framework of social theory and its underlying foundation in the history of social thought. It is this latter focus which establishes the connection between theory and society. For all practical purposes, this focus is based on three interrelated assumptions about society. First is the belief that underlying the factual world of experience is a system of values, standards, ethics and politics which derives from societies in the past and

11 See Leo Strauss and Joseph Cropsey (eds), *History of Political Philosophy*, Chicago: Rand McNally & Co., 1963.
12 Sheldon Wolin, *Politics and Vision: Continuity and Innovation in Western Political Thought*, Boston: Little Brown, 1960.

acts as a common condition of action in the present. These social and political values, so to speak, form the underlying basis of society and act as common conditions of human social action. Second is the belief that, since values and standards often manifest themselves in a system of politics and ethics, they may be employed to describe societies past and present, to look for underlying patterns of development and the effects of this development on human social groups. Third is the view which holds that, since all human experience is in some way related to the social world, a theory of society cannot be divorced from a theory of politics, economics, ethics and social values. Under these circumstances, these 'social things' form a class of events which are distinct from 'physical things' and as such are to be studied in their own right forming a body of knowledge separate from knowledge of the physical or natural world.

This takes us directly to the question of subject matter in social theory. Generally, the subject matter of social theory encompasses three broad dimensions of social change and development. These are: (i) the political changes brought about by the French Revolution; (ii) the economic development leading to the growth of modern society and the emergence of capitalism; and (iii) the rise of individualism. The story begins in the decade of the 1780s, a period of the most far-reaching political, social and economic upheaval. Taken collectively, these changes fragmented social life, segmented social institutions, accelerated social crises and differentiated peoples and collectivities.

The Central Subject Matter of Social Theory

1 Political Change and the Revolution in France

The events leading to the French Revolution began to be shaped in the decade of the 1780s and came to a turbulent conclusion in July and August of 1789. By 1791, a whole way of political and economic life had been replaced by new social and political conditions. In order to understand these developments, it will be necessary to look more closely at the social and political arrangements in France in the last half of the eighteenth century.

In the eighteenth century, remnants of feudalism were evident in French society. Feudalism may be defined as a system of land holding used primarily for agricultural purposes.[13] The feudal order began in France during the ninth century and comprised a total way of economic and political life. The feudal economy was entirely rural, land was used solely for agricultural purposes, and there was a complete absence of towns and town life. Predicated on the allotment of large parcels of land to a political aristocracy, feudal estates were managed by an aristocratic class who used

13 Georges Duby, *Rural Economy and Country Life in the Medieval West*. Columbia, S.C.: University of South Carolina Press, 1968.

the land as a source of economic livelihood. The principal activity of the estate was agricultural production. Estates were politically and legally autonomous and comprised a total way of life including a parish, village and various branches of rural economy.[14]

At the center of feudal society was the production of a food supply, a production highlighted by the relation between the landholder and the peasant cultivator. Peasants occupied agricultural holdings comprised of small undertakings in which they cultivated land and produced their economic livelihood. While the landholder was the legal and political head of the estate, a complex system of obligations and customary rights linked the peasant to the lord.[15] Among these, four distinct social bonds stand out as significant. (i) First, were a series of economic obligations imposed upon the serf by the lord, and chief among these were the corvée system of labor rights.[16] The corvée right, which was so central to feudal economy, goes back as far as Roman law and can be defined as a legal privilege of the landholder to compel or requisition work from a serf or a slave. Corvée rights allowed landholders to compel unpaid labor service from the serf in the form of work on the lord's agricultural holdings or labor within the manor. On average, labor service could amount to one week in four. Under these circumstances, serfs were the direct producers of physical labor and while serfs produced for the landholder, the landholder did not produce for them.

(ii) Serfs were legitimately subordinated to the lord through a system of legal and social distinction. While resting formally on physical coercion, the subordination of the serf was mediated by a complex system of prerogatives and obligations supported by political, legal and religious distinctions. In many respects, the social relation between the lord and serf duplicated the coercive mechanism of slavery, even though the social fabric of feudal society was such as to link individuals by obligations and customary rights.[17]

(iii) A third right inherent in feudal society was the system of economic exactions. These took the form of taxes, dues and fees levied by lords upon the serf.[18] In many instances, the principal economic resources of the aristocracy consisted in levying dues and fees on the peasant population. In some cases these took the form of charges imposed upon serfs to grind corn in the lord's mill or to use presses involved in wine production. In other cases a system of payments, usually rendered in the form of labor service, existed in the form of taxation, dues and economic fees payable by the serf to the lord. In still other cases, economic exactions took the

14 Perry Anderson, *Passages From Antiquity to Feudalism*, London: Verso, 1978.

15 Ibid., pp. 182–96.

16 Georges Duby, *Rural Economy*.

17 Alexis De Tocqueville, *The Old Régime and the French Revolution*, New York: Anchor Books, [1856] 1955.

18 Anderson, *Passages from Antiquity*, p. 193; and Albert Soboul, *The French Revolution 1787–1799*, Vol. 1, London: NLB, 1974, pp. 33–67.

form of the right of the lord to control the agricultural production of the serf.[19]

(iv) A fourth characteristic of feudal society was its fixed social hierarchy and system of social distinctions, backed up by legal and religious sanctions. Wide variations existed within the social structure of the manor and between the lord and the serf. These ranged from individual serfs who worked small holdings and paid rents by surrendering part of their agricultural production, to serfs whose crop production was to go directly to the lord. Others were obligated to perform labor service directly on the lord's manor.

In the years preceding the revolution, France retained the political and economic characteristics of feudal society: rigid social hierarchy, social and economic inequality, a system of taxation on peasants and mandatory unpaid labor. By 1780, France began to show signs of economic distress and, in the years preceding the revolution, tenant farmers found it difficult to maintain their livelihoods while paying excessive dues and taxes. Eventually, poor crops, rising prices and economic mismanagement led to a crisis calling for economic and political reform. As the crisis deepened, demands for reform became more urgent and antagonism between peasants and aristocracy grew. By 1787, members of the middle class began to form a revolutionary committee and drew up a set of demands which were submitted to the central authority of the French state, the Estates General – a 300-year-old political body comprised of three main orders of society: the aristocracy, clergy and peasants.[20] The demands, or grievances as they were called, became the central political focus of reform and received extraordinary philosophical sanction by upholding human rights, equality and liberty.

The Fall of Feudalism and the Elimination of Social Distinctions By September of 1789, the Revolutionary Committee challenged the authority of the King who, in response, called a meeting of the Estates General, hoping that the aristocracy and clergy would outvote the peasants and avoid a crisis. But by the time the Estates General had assembled, the loyalties of the clergy had shifted in support of the peasants and a turbulent debate broke out over voting procedure. Members of the aristocracy favored a vote canvassing the three Estates, while representatives of the people demanded a vote by head. On June 17, 1789, the Third Estate had split off from the Estates General, proclaiming a new political body called the National Assembly.[21] On June 27 the King backed down from the confrontation, leaving the National Assembly as the party of social and political reform. Between June and July of 1789, riots swept

19 Soboul, *The French Revolution*, pp. 86–8.

20 Georges Lefebvre, *The French Revolution From its Origins to 1793*, London: Routledge, 1962.

21 Soboul, *The French Revolution*.

France and troops appeared in Paris. In July, after an armed mob stormed the Bastille – a military garrison on the outskirts of the city – the revolution had become a political reality.

Shortly after these events, the National Assembly drafted the 'Declaration of the Rights of Man,' a central political document defining human rights and setting out demands for reform. The rights and freedoms proclaimed by the 'Declaration' were so wide-ranging in their human emancipation that it set the standard for social and political thinking, and formed the central rallying point of the revolution. The 'Declaration' stated at the outset that all human beings were born free and equal in their political rights and proceeded to set up a system of constitutional principles based on liberty, security and resistance to oppression. With philosophical authority, the 'Declaration' proclaimed that all individuals had the prerogative to exercise their 'natural right' and that the law rather than the monarch was the expression of the common interest.[22] By August, the National Assembly began to deal directly with political and legal reforms, first by eliminating feudal dues and corvée privileges and then by abolishing serfdom. Second, by compelling the church to give up the right to tithes, the National Assembly altered the hierarchical authority of the clergy. Third, in declaring that 'all citizens, without distinction, can be admitted to all ecclesiastical, civil and military posts and dignities' it proclaimed an end to all feudal social distinctions.

As the criticism of social and political inequalities spread throughout society, there was a widespread critique of economic inequality and this led to 'the putting into question of all other forms of subordination.'[23] With this came the idea that human beings, without distinctions, were the bearers of natural rights – a concept which had a corrosive effect on all forms of inequality. Finally, from the assertions inherent in the 'Declaration of Rights,' a new category of social person came into being which came fundamentally to rest in the concept of the 'citizen,' whose social and political rights were brought within the framework of the state.

2 Economic Changes and the Development of Capitalism

Another dimension of change was the wide-sweeping economic development of the eighteenth and nineteenth centuries. Though confined largely to England and the rural economy in the early stages, economic change eventually spread throughout Europe and transformed the economic and political structure of society. There was large-scale social disruption leading ultimately to a total transformation of the way of life which had been based on agricultural production. While change was occurring at various levels of society, the center of change was in the economic system, which eventually led to the transition from feudalism to capitalism. In

22 Lefebvre, *The French Revolution*.
23 E. Laclau and C. Mouffe, *Hegemony and Socialist Strategy*, London: Verso, 1985, p. 156.

order to understand the impact of these changes, it is important that we look closely at the feudal economy in England.

Earlier we used the term 'feudalism' to refer to a period of social and economic organization beginning in the ninth century. A feudal society was defined as a self-sufficient system of estates which were economically and politically autonomous. Political power derived from a class of land-holders who used tenant cultivators to produce and maintain their liveli-hoods. Landholders drew their social and political powers from links to aristocratic classes which conferred rights centering upon land holdings and economic prerogatives centering on powers over tenant serfs. Land-holdings involved large bodies of land, used primarily for purposes of agricultural production, and formed independent economies and auton-omous legal jurisdictions.[24]

In the early stages of feudal society the rural way of life was universal. There was an absence of towns and the production of a food supply dominated everyday life.[25] Individuals were attached to the land by a system of obligations resting on customary rights rather than explicit legal rules. Obligations set out the social relations between lord and serf and formed an elaborate system of privilege which defined the feudal way of life. In exchange for the use of land, serfs performed labor service on the lord's estate and gave up part of their agricultural production. In addition, a system of customary rights defined the role of the landholder and the serf in relation to the use of land. These manifested themselves, in the first place, in the absence of private property in land. Landholders held jurisdiction and assumed entitlements, but they did not own land outright as private property. In the place of private property was an elaborate system of obligations, linking individuals to each other and to the land. Within the scope of these rights existed distinction in the kinds and uses of land. First were estate lands, which included the lord's agricultural holdings.[26] Second was the distinction in arable land called 'open fields,' land directly used by peasants to grow crops and provide economic livelihood. Third was the distinction in land referred to as 'common fields,' which was the name given to lands on which no tenant claim existed but which were used generally for purposes of grazing domestic animals. In exchange for the use of land, serfs were obligated to pay 'labor rent' – an entitlement of the lord which placed a claim upon the serf payable in the form of labor service on the lord's holdings.

Depopulation and the Enclosure Movement   By the middle of the sixteenth century, however, economic changes began to have an impact on the feudal economy as a whole and these manifested themselves in four broad dimensions of change. First was the gradual enclosing of estate lands,

---

24 Anderson, *Passages from Antiquity*, pp. 16–22.
25 R.H. Hilton, *The English Peasantry in the Later Middle Ages*, Oxford: Clarendon, 1975.
26 Eric Kerridge, *The Agricultural Revolution*, New York: Augustus Kelly, 1968.

leading to the removal of peasants from their holdings. This brought about the disappearance of customary rights in land and hastened the sale and purchase of land as a commodity subject to the right of private property.[27] Second was the emergence of town economies, which began to replace the agrarian economy of the countryside and facilitate capitalist development. Third was the decline in the power of trade guilds to contain capitalist expansion, which led to large-scale capitalist development. Fourth were the wide-ranging economic and social effects of capitalist economies and the introduction of a system of exchange. Since no complete understanding of the scale of change is possible without discussing these developments, let us consider them in greater detail.

The first signs of change manifested themselves in the form of land enclosures which began to appear as early as 1560.[28] Essentially, the enclosure movement can be described as a system whereby tenant holdings in feudal land became enclosed and made available for private use. As a result, peasant families were evicted from their holdings and thrown off the land. Many of the first enclosures were initiated by landlords in order to appropriate tenant holdings, in most cases for sheep pasture. But by 1710 the first Enclosure Bill appeared which legalized the enclosure of tenant holdings by parliamentary Acts.[29] With parliamentary approval, enclosures could proceed at an advanced rate and eventually became commonplace by the mid-seventeenth century. By 1850, 4000 parliamentary Acts had been passed and in excess of 6 million acres of land enclosed.[30]

In practice, enclosures became a society-wide depopulation movement fueled by mass evictions and foreclosures which coercively removed peasants from the land. Under such circumstances, landlords were able to assert rights of modern private property over lands to which they held only feudal title. As these operations intensified, it hastened the transformation of land into a commercial commodity, first by subjecting it to buying and selling, and second by extending its capacity to produce money rent.[31] Under these circumstances, all customary rights and obligations began to be forcibly dissolved, and with these went the bonds connecting peasants to the land through hereditary tenure and leasehold. As soon as money rents replaced labor rent, peasants were forced to focus their attention on their own holdings, making money rent a precondition

27 R.H. Tawney, *The Agrarian Problem in the Sixteenth Century*, New York: Harper & Row, 1967.

28 William Lazonick, 'Karl Marx and Enclosures in England,' *Review of Radical Political Economics*, 6, 2, 1974, pp. 1–58. Kerridge, *The Agricultural Revolution*, pp. 19–24; J.D. Chambers and G.E. Mingay, *The Agricultural Revolution 1750–1880*, London: Batsford, 1966.

29 Tawney, *The Agrarian Problem*, New York: Harper & Row, 1967.

30 Lazonick, 'Karl Marx and Enclosures in England,' p. 10.

31 See J.D. Chambers, 'Enclosure and the Labour Supply in The Industrial Revolution,' *Economic History Review 2nd Series*, Vol. V, 1953, pp. 319–43; Eric Kerridge, 'The Movement of Rent, 1540–1640,' *Economic History Review 2nd Series*, Vol. VI, 1953, pp. 17–34.

to economic survival. Those who were unable to pay were ruined.[32] As soon as rent for land began to be expressed in money, it became possible to place an economic value on the land itself. As land became a commercial commodity subject to buying and selling, the economic balance between serfs and landlords was upset and feudal obligations in land and livelihood began to deteriorate. The disintegration of feudal obligation in land began to subject peasants to new forces of social differentiation. Peasants became detached from the land as a means of economic survival as they were placed at the disposal of the new forces of production, and were transformed into a landless class whose labor was to be bought and sold in the emerging industrial centers.

Capitalist Development and the Decline of the Guild System   A second dimension of change was the growth of town economies and the role towns played in capitalist development. In the early stages of feudal society there were no towns as such. Existence was confined to the rural economy and the production of a food supply. Gradually, towns began to develop and by the fourteenth century the town was put into economic competition with the rural economy of the countryside.[33] This had the effect of dissolving the economic boundaries of the feudal estates and promoting more open economies. By the seventeeth century, towns began to gain an economic foothold due to the growth of concentrated skills and crafts and, as towns gained the upper hand, small-scale production in textiles and weaving began to operate independently of the feudal economy. Though they were not capitalist enterprises by any means, the development of new production techniques, the level and intensity of commodity production and the division of labor were sufficient to add to the productive push to establish manufacturing in towns, making them the center of economic life rather than rural economies.

A third dimension of change was the transformation of the role which had been played by the handicraft guilds and the guild system in economic life. The guild system may be defined as a professional association of craftsmen whose basic function was to protect and regulate work relating to trades.[34] Trades included all goods and services produced by persons who were skilled and who had served a period of training under a master. During the sixteenth and seventeenth centuries, guilds played a dominant role in economic life by restricting capitalist development. Chief among the functions of guilds was the practice of restricting access into trades by the system of apprenticeship and by controlling entry through restrictive

32 Rodney Hilton develops this line of argument in his 'Capitalism: What's in a Name?,' *Past and Present*, 1, 1952, pp. 32–43.

33 For discussion on the development of towns and the competition between rural and town economies, see A.B. Hibbert, 'The Origins of the Medieval Town Patriciate,' *Past and Present*, 3, 1953, pp. 15–27.

34 See Antony Black, *Guilds and Civil Society in European Political Thought from the Twelfth Century to the Present*, London: Methuen and Co., 1984.

practices such as licensing. In addition, guilds regulated prices of goods and restricted competition among workshops by controlling rival markets.[35] Of all the restrictive functions performed by guilds, the regulation of the expansion of workshops was the most significant. Guilds, in effect, were opposed to the development of large-scale enterprises and capitalist expansion. By restricting the number of employees and the kinds of labor used in shops, guilds prevented existing workshops from turning into large-scale enterprises. By discouraging the intermingling of trades, guilds were able to thwart the development of a complex division of labor, thus blocking the development of specialization necessary for full-blown capitalist production and manufacture.

By 1800, guild regulations began to lose their influence over selected workshops, giving way to concentrations of capital and free wage labor. Production in England began to focus almost wholly on cloth and woolen goods and this gradually began to be influenced by the overall economic expansion, leading to growth in commercial markets and in world trade. This put the pressure of expansion on the centers of production and, as the demand for woolen goods increased, some workshops began to be infiltrated by non-guild labor and gradually guild regulation broke down altogether.

By mid century, the transition from feudalism to capitalism was more or less complete. Peasants were forcibly cleared from the land, feudal obligations in land were dissolved and the rights of private property asserted, there was development of towns and town economies, and the decline in the guild system led to the expansion of capitalist enterprise.[36] As a result, peasants were wrenched from their roles as agricultural producers and formed a large class of landless laborers who were forced to seek their livelihoods in the new industrial centers.[37] The serf of feudal economy had been transformed into the wage laborer of a capitalist economy. Accordingly, a whole series of economic changes were set into motion creating a fourth dimension of change. This was as a result of the large-scale development of a capitalist economy and its effects on the labor process and the system of exchange.

3 The Rise of Individualism

From the large-scale change in the political and economic foundations of society there emerged a third significant development. This concerned the individual's relation to society as a whole and to its collective unity. This theme, so central to the development of social theory, is called the process

---

35 See Maurice Dobb, *Studies in the Development of Capitalism*, New York: International Pub., 1947, p. 90.

36 Paul Mantoux, *The Industrial Revolution in the Eighteenth Century*, London: Methuen, 1907.

37 E.P. Thompson, *The Making of the English Working Class*, Harmondsworth: Penguin, 1968.

of individualism.[38] The term 'individualism' grew out of the framework of European social thought which emerged during the Enlightenment and the French Revolution. Thinkers such as Joseph de Maistre and Henri Saint-Simon were the first to use the term to criticize the glorification of the individual over the dominance of social institutions which arose after the French Revolution.[39] Since no complete understanding of social theory is possible without looking at the relationship between the individual and society, let us look at this relationship more closely.

Within the context of European social thought, the maintenance of society was thought to depend on the preservation of the large-scale social powers of the church, monarchy and state. Within this tradition, individuals were thought to participate in society and social life only as members of larger social groups. These groups asserted collective rights over individuals and acted as corporate bodies which exercised proprietary powers over them and, to a large extent, determined their place in society. In addition to this, group affiliation in large social institutions determined the legal rights and social obligations of individuals that acted to define their place within society as a whole. Large collective bodies, such as the guilds, church and feudal estates functioned as corporate entities whose authority, prerogative and proprietary powers over individuals were spelled out by state government. Generally, these large political bodies dominated social life, controlled trades and regulated occupations. Here, individuals participated in society only as members of these large groups.[40] Many were unable to practice occupations except as members of corporate bodies and only as members of these bodies did individuals participate in the wider society. Under these circumstances, the rights and purposes of collective bodies always exceeded the rights and purposes of individuals.

Individualism, then, is the name given to the overall process leading to the political, social and economic separation of individuals from larger social wholes. Two basic forces were at work to bring these changes about: (i) After the French Revolution the legal rights assigned to individuals began to dissolve the proprietary powers inherent in corporate bodies.[41] (ii) As a result of the changes wrought by the Revolution, all groups such as estates and guilds were abolished and their powers, rights and prerogatives assigned as legal entitlement to individuals. What had been corporate and collective in nature was suddenly centered on the individual.

38 Steven Lukes, *Individualism*, Oxford: Basil Blackwell, 1973; C.D. Macpherson, *The Political Theory of Possessive Individualism*, London: Oxford University, 1962; K.W. Swart, 'Individualism in the Mid-Nineteenth Century (1826–1860),' *Journal of the History of Ideas*, 23, 1962, pp. 77–90. R.R. Palmer, 'Man and Citizen: Applications of Individualism in the French Revolution,' in Milton R. Konvitz and Arthur E. Murphy (eds), *Essays in Political Theory*, New York: Kennikat Press, 1972, pp. 130–52; A.D. Lindsay, 'Individualism,' *Encyclopedia of the Social Sciences*, 7, 1930–33, pp. 674–80.
39 Swart, 'Individualism,' pp. 77–90.
40 Lukes, *Individualism*, p. 21.
41 See R.R. Palmer, 'Man and Citizen,' pp. 130–52.

Later in the nineteenth century, the term 'individualism' began to be used to designate the themes of egoism and autonomy, which were thought to have been brought about as the overt links connecting individuals to larger groups began to dissolve. Many thinkers believed that the progressive focus on the individual evident in expanded rights and freedoms automatically jeopardized the greater collective interests of society, and, for some, this meant the collapse of social unity and the dissolution of society. In French social thought, individualism was seen as a threat to aggregate social maintenance and many believed that it would undermine the political and economic order of society.[42] In France, where the concept of society had been premised on individual interest, individualism was looked upon as the social and political equivalent of a crisis. It threatened to atomize society and destroy collective unity. At every level of society, it signified autonomy, freedom and lack of restraint from collective social rules.

By 1840, individualism was supported by an economic doctrine and then a political doctrine.[43] As an economic doctrine, individualism had been outlined in Adam Smith's defense of the development of private enterprise found in *The Wealth of Nations* published in 1776.[44] In this work, Smith set out the fundamental principle of private enterprise by stating that each individual is free to compete among their fellows and pursue their self-interest in the form of private economic gain. While this may not seem extraordinary in itself, the effects of universal competition based on the private acts of individuals cut deeply into the social fabric. Where individuals had once been linked by common obligation and economic bonds, these were suddenly replaced by the independent pursuit of self-interest and private gain. Seen from this perspective, society was little more than an association of autonomous individuals acting on the principle of exchange and economic self-interest.

What was extraordinary about Smith's proposal of the pursuit of private interest was its conception of the collective whole and community of individuals. It was Smith's idea that the individual was a member of the social fabric only through his or her individual pursuit of private gain, and only through this gain did individuals contribute to the common prosperity of society.[45] According to this view, individuals are 'free agents' able to make contracts and enter into economic interchanges without

---

42 Durkheim's reaction to the individualist trend in society is evident in his study of *Suicide*, New York: The Free Press, [1897], 1951 and in his discussion of individuals in 'Individualism and the Intellectuals' (trans. S. and J. Lukes), *Political Studies*, 17, [1898], 1969, pp. 14–30. Gregory Claeys, 'Individualism, Socialism and Social Science: Further Notes on a Process of Conceptual Formation 1800–1850,' *Journal of the History of Ideas*, 33, 1986, pp. 81–93.

43 A.D. Lindsay, 'Individualism,' pp. 674–80.

44 Adam Smith, *The Wealth of Nations*, London: Dent & Sons, [1776], 1910.

45 See Jacob Viner, 'Adam Smith and Laissez Faire,' in J.M. Clark and P.H. Douglas et al., *Adam Smith 1776–1926*, New York: Augustus Kelly, 1966.

obligation to the larger society. Conceived of in this way, social relations between individuals are reduced to a set of commercial transactions and the idea of the common authority of society reduced to the norm of economic self-interest.

Adam Smith's economic justification of private enterprise and individual competition was ingenious. Through a crude appeal to the collective good conceived in terms of a 'fiscal well being,' Smith pronounced his rationale for individual competition: 'By pursuing his own self-interest,' wrote Smith, 'the individual promotes the greater good of society by contributing to its national wealth' and this he does 'more effectively than when he really intends to promote it.'[46] Essentially, by conceiving of the unity of society as a 'common economic prosperity,' Smith was able to reduce the maintenance of society to collective forces of self-interest and economic competition. Accordingly, the functions of society shrank to the role of protecting private rights of individuals to engage in the pursuit of economic gain.

The Two Philosophies of Knowledge: Idealism and Empiricism

No complete understanding of the period in which Marx, Durkheim and Weber worked is possible without some discussion of the philosophies which dominated debate at the time. Let us briefly turn our attention to some of the issues which were uppermost as the social sciences were becoming established in England and Europe during the nineteenth century.

By the end of the nineteenth century, two dominant philosophies had come to the forefront in the social sciences: 'idealism' and 'empiricism.' Both these viewpoints influenced the development of social thought and had an enormous impact on nineteenth-century social theory as a whole.

Classical Idealism

Philosophical idealism originated in 380 BC with the writings of Socrates and Plato who were among the first to set out principles of thought which acted as guidelines for investigating the existence of a realm of ideas thought to be beyond the physical world. As a philosophic perspective, idealism gets its name from a branch of investigation which believed that the most important task of philosophy was to inquire into a realm whose existence could only be grasped by theoretical activity rather than by straightforward observation.

The growth of idealist philosophy is best understood in the context of Greek philosophical thought. In fact, Western philosophical investigation essentially began in Greece during the sixth century BC.[47] One of the first investigative interests of the early philosophers was in the origin of the

---

46 Smith, *Wealth of Nations*, p. 423.
47 Ernest Barker, *Greek Political Theory*, London: Methuen, 1918.

natural world. Among the first to put forward a rudimentary theory of nature were philosophers who believed only in the ultimate reality of the physical world. The claims put forward by these philosophers included the idea that the natural world was primarily made up of physical matter and that, according to this view, the object of philosophy was to explain how change took place in reality and in the physical world itself.

The tradition of philosophic idealism, therefore, can best be understood as a direct response to the very straightforward philosophic view which insisted that reality was to be regarded as nothing more than what can be determined by the senses. By 430 BC, Socrates was among the first to advance an idealist doctrine urging that beneath the basic physical structure of reality was some greater fundamental reality giving purpose and meaning to existence and that, without this, individual being made little sense. It was Socrates, therefore, who first put forward the view that a more enduring pattern or purpose must underlie the apparent physical reality of experience and that this pattern was not subject to change but was eternal and unchanging.[48]

This disagreement in philosophy over the appropriate subject matter of investigation – between 'physical matter,' on the one hand, and 'ideals' on the other – led to the formation of two distinct schools of thought; in fact, two distinct tendencies in knowledge. The first of these perspectives took the view that only the world of physical reality exists and that knowledge of these realities can only be apprehended and brought to light by the senses. The second perspective, however, took the view that only the realities which involve the good of the social and political community are the proper object of philosophical investigation, since these bear on human and political things in contrast to physical or material things. This distinction between things 'physical' and things 'human' is the central starting point of Greek political philosophy and the focusing of philosophy on human political questions. In contrast to physical reality, therefore, those things studied by the branch of philosophy concerned with the human political community could not be known by sense perception since they involve principles, standards, ideas and ethics not directly grasped by the senses. According to this view, social and political things form a class of objects by themselves and, therefore, should be studied separately from physical things.

The absolute starting place for social and political thought is Plato's *Republic*. The central discussion in this work relates to the importance of social and political ideals or standards for collective life. While many believe that Plato's *Republic* is a political fantasy, others take the view that Plato had a more serious purpose in mind. In fact, the *Republic* is one of the first sustained philosophic conversations about the 'ideal' state and in it the view is put forward that the state is founded on two primary functions. The first of these concerned practical matters such as the

48 A.E. Taylor, *Elements of Metaphysics*, London: Methuen, 1956.

division of labor, food supply, a system of education, and the conditions of safety and security.[49] These functions of the state served practical ends and relate to securing the material well-being of individuals. But Socrates believed that a second group of things – formally defined as 'ideal' functions – involves principles, practices and standards of the state which relate to the system of human conduct, and thus involves the social and political good.[50] In contrast to the practical functions, these are organized in reference to human and political things. In these terms, the 'ideal,' then, can be described simply as anything relating to the human political community which strives for what is beyond the functional or practical and which promotes the well-being of the human community. As far as the ancients were concerned, practical things had a utilitarian sanction, while those things relating to purposes or standards of the state were given an 'extraordinary ethical sanction.'[51] Plato believed that the leap from the practical to the ideal was, in fact, ethical in nature and it was this that formed the basis of Greek political philosophy. Social and political theory, therefore, was an instrument first used to make the ethical questions seem compelling and important, a necessary social and political good. Since everything depends on the system of ethics and values of the society we live in, the first social and political thinkers believed that a special branch of philosophic thought should be dedicated to things political and human, and this branch of thinking got its name in direct contrast to the body of thought which studied material reality.

It was Plato, then, who was among the first to make the ideal realm an object of discussion in his dialogues, and to assume that knowledge was attainable only by making the distinction between the 'ideal' and the 'material' realms. The first of these realms, Plato thought, is the sense world, the world of everyday material existence – the most immediate and first level of experience. But here, the objects of the material world are in a constant state of change and, therefore, cannot be known absolutely since when in a state of change no object maintains its form over time. Rather, objects constantly come into being and then cease to exist. Plato reasoned, therefore, that since the world of immediate experience was constantly changing, any absolute knowledge of it was impossible.

The second realm recognized by Plato was made up of what have been called 'universals,' sometimes referred to as 'absolutes' or 'essences.' Basically, this dimension gets its name from a set of ideas which the Greeks believed were permanent and unchanging because they were related to human things and applied universally to all social and historical circumstances.[52] These absolutes get their name from a set of ideas which

49 Richard Nettleship, *Lectures on the Republic of Plato*, London: Macmillan, 1958.

50 Taylor, *Elements of Metaphysics*, pp. 18–22.

51 The distinction between utilitarian and ethical sanctions is developed by Laszlo Versenyi, *Socratic Humanism*, New Haven: Yale, 1963, pp. 79–98.

52 Barker, *Greek Political Theory*, pp. 282–3.

were thought to supersede time and place and thus surpass all historical situations. So far as they did, they were believed to be universally applicable to human existence, and were thus called 'universals,' 'essences' or 'forms.' But, what is the sphere of ideals that Plato is talking about? Simply stated, Plato believed that the ideal realm included concepts such as reason, justice, virtue, equality and goodness. These were considered to be 'absolute' to the extent that they were unchanging in nature, not subject to decay and thus universally valid for all human societies in representing a standard of human action. In the main, the ideal realm derived its philosophical force from the concept that universals structure human action and are 'ethical' in nature because they promote political good. Classical idealism may therefore be described as the first philosophic investigation into the sphere of ideals which shaped human action in terms of a standard of political life.[53]

At least three distinct characteristics of idealism as a branch of philosophical investigation can be identified. (i) The reliance on a conception of philosophy as a body of thought aimed at understanding existence by means of universals which cannot be known by sense perception or experience. (ii) The implied philosophic relation between the universals and the structure of human social action along some norm or standard on which is to be founded a political community based on reasoned action. (iii) The attempt to develop knowledge about universals and human nature which stands in contrast to the natural sciences which seek to develop knowledge of the natural world.[54]

Hegelian Idealism

A second stream of philosophical idealism emerged in Germany with the writings of Georg Hegel (1770–1831). Hegel is best known for developing a complete system of idealist philosophy. By the early nineteenth century, Hegel's writings had become the dominant philosophic framework in European universities. He pioneered theoretical investigations into history, existence, consciousness, aesthetics, and social and political theory. In order to understand the impact of his work on the development of idealism and social theory, we must look more closely at some of his views.

Hegel was born in 1770 in Stuttgart and he studied theology and philosophy at Tübingen University. In 1806, when at the University of Jena, Hegel wrote his first major philosophical work entitled *Phenomenology of Spirit*. Hegel's philosophic writings were central in several respects. First, he forced philosophy to confront historical and social questions, thus shifting philosophic concepts into social and historical ones.[55] Second, Hegel's work

53 Plato's *Republic* (509d–511e), in Hamilton and Huntington (eds) *The Collected Dialogues of Plato*, Princeton: The University Press, 1961.

54 Nettleship, *Lectures*.

55 Marcuse, *Reason and Revolution*; Findlay, *Hegel: A Re-Examination*; Sidney Hook, *From Hegel to Marx*, London: Victor Gollancz, 1936.

acted as a theoretical background to Marx and Engels' economic and political theories. Third, it was Hegel's philosophical idealism which later shaped Comte's critique of philosophy known as 'positivism,' eventually leading to widespread opposition to idealism.

In order to put Hegel's work in perspective, it will be helpful to understand his contribution by placing it in the context of classical idealism. As we noted earlier, classical idealism had taken the view that the physical world could not be known with direct certainty because its material existence was always changing. According to this view, the fundamental task of philosophy was to study the realm of absolute truths whose existence could be relied upon as objects of investigation. Hegel, however, began by arguing that the tendency to draw such a sharp distinction between the material and ideal world ultimately split human experience into two spheres and this, he thought, canceled out the study of experience. Hegel's main theoretical influence was Aristotle.[56] What interested Hegel in Aristotle's work was his rejection of Plato's doctrine of the transcendent realm of absolutes which tended to stand above the material world of experience. Aristotle maintained that Plato's separation of the material and ideal realm was unnecessary, and he took the view that both the ideal and the material world were in fact immanent in human experience, and thus fundamentally belonged together and should be treated as a philosophic unity.[57]

For Hegel, this was a key philosophic step since it took the view that the principles of human and social development worked implicitly toward ultimate ends and that the process of development was implicit in all matter. As a result, the focal point of philosophical and theoretical activity shifted from an investigation of a realm of 'ideals' to one of explaining the process of historical development. Aristotle had asserted that the natural and social world acted according to ultimate purposes or ends which are actualized in the principle of development. The name Aristotle gave to this process was 'teleology,' a concept which took the view that the ideal and material realm were fused together in a process of development. This process, Aristotle reasoned, must be implicit in the natural and social world and is manifested in the underlying principle of the development of matter. Aristotle believed that all matter was, in effect, self-actualizing and that this was manifest in the process of development toward greater and more explicit stages of growth and existence. In this view, human and material things ultimately act according to ends or purposes in the process of development and the function of theory is to explain these processes.

Drawing from Aristotle, Hegel attempted to pioneer a system of thinking which endeavored to explain existence as a process of development. Simply stated, Hegel believed that the 'ideal' and 'material' realm belonged together and were fundamentally rooted in the structure of

56 Findlay, *Hegel: A Re-Examination.*
57 Ibid.

reality and history.[58] This step was of central philosophic importance because it tied essence into existence rather than placing it above experience as classical idealist philosophy had done. Hegel's idealism was thus founded upon a theory of history and development. But what does this mean in the context of his philosophy and social theory? To answer this question, we have to consider these issues in greater detail.

In his early works, Hegel began by stating that human perception of individual experience appears to be unrelated, diverse and even disconnected in terms of past, present and future. Hegel's aim was focused on building a system which would show how our various experiences of past and present are, in fact, linked together to form totalities or meaningful wholes which can be explained by philosophical analysis. He pursued this investigation in one of his most famous studies, *Phenomenology of Spirit*, the structure of which actually etches out individual life in relation to the development of parallel totalities that are connected to a central concept Hegel used in his work called 'spirit' or *'geist.'*

Though we cannot explicitly define the concept of the spirit, we can sketch out how Hegel used the term in his philosophical system. To explain the concept of 'spirit,' Hegel began with the simple focal point of the individual subject. We can, he said, begin with the particular subject and add on characteristics which emphasize the fixed nature of the subject's experience and circumstance. We can focus, for instance, on spatial location, on place in history, on consciousness, on particular being and on specific circumstances.[59] All of these fixed locations tie the individual to a position in time and space and to an empirical circumstance. But, at the same time that we are linked to empirical circumstances, Hegel believed that the power of abstract thought gives the individual the ability to think beyond immediate concrete circumstances and location.[60] This ability to abstract from a fixed position or physical circumstance, Hegel maintains, connects the individual to the universal or spiritual; that is, to the larger totalities of history and humanity. Hegel believed that this unifying capacity of thought to abstract from the particular to the universal meant that thought itself was a form of self-actualizing activity. According to this view, human nature has two distinct manifestations: the particular or empirical, and the universal or spiritual.

Stated simply, Hegel believed that the concept of spirit was the active principle of universal development.[61] In this sense, spirit is a 'unifying pattern' which confers order and meaning on the material and ethical world. Hegel went on to reason that even while human beings are confined by circumstance to the here and now, they have conscious reason which enables them to connect with the universal through thought. Hegel

58 Hook, *From Hegel to Marx*; Findlay, *Hegel: A Re-Examination.*
59 Findlay, *Hegel: A Re-Examination.*
60 Marcuse, *Reason and Revolution.*
61 See Findlay, *Hegel: A Re-Examination.*

asserted that this capacity to remove ourselves from the boundaries of immediate circumstance by conscious thought establishes our ultimate spiritual identity.[62] He maintained that thought performs this function in two distinct ways: (i) it provides the power to lift the individual beyond immediate circumstances by inherently placing the individual outside the boundaries provided by empirical limitations.[63] In this way, thought links the individual to the indeterminate and universal. (ii) Thought provides the capacity of abstraction, and this gives the individual the power to use the objective world as a 'medium' of development beyond concrete limitations and circumstances.[64] Hegel's assertion regarding the role of the 'spirit' established two key links between philosophy and history: (i) it made 'spirit' as real as the concrete world of experience; and (ii) it made the universal a part of history by showing that human history was subject to laws of development.

Hegel's Theory of Development   Hegel's theory of development is perhaps the core of his social and political thought. In 1812, Hegel had worked out a theory of dialectics in a work called *The Science of Logic*. First and foremost, Hegel used dialectical principles to expound a theory of development and change. The theory of the dialectic begins by taking the view that all things are in a continuous state of motion and change and that the general laws of motion are intrinsic to the development of nature, history and thought. In these terms, Hegel viewed the world, existence and being in terms of processes in which all things were seen as interconnected and related to one another rather than existing separately by themselves.

The central principle of Hegel's dialectical thinking is the concept of relation or interconnection.[65] Viewed from the perspective of inter-connectedness, the world and others appear as a vast set of interrelations in which everything is related in terms of the past, present and future.[66] Under these circumstances, Hegel believed it is possible to visualize these interconnections when we picture ourselves, the world and others in terms of what he called 'relational' concepts. These include terms such as humanity, history, experience, existence, etc. Viewed from this perspective, no individual is an isolated being but rather is part of a larger whole. The idea that the existence of one thing was tied up with that of another led Hegel to look for the principle by means of which separate things were integrated into larger totalities of being. The key concepts which Hegel used to understand this principle of integration were the categories 'history,' 'spirit,' 'consciousness,' 'reason,' and so on.

---

62 Marcuse, *Reason and Revolution*, pp. 30–91.

63 Ibid.

64 Ibid.

65 See Z.A. Jordan, *The Evolution of Dialectical Materialism*, New York: St. Martin's Press, 1967.

66 Frederick Engels, *Anti-Dühring*, Peking: Foreign Languages Press, [1878] 1976.

The doctrine that all things were interconnected to larger wholes or unities later became the theoretical basis of the dialectical view of reality which led to important developments at the level of historical analysis by Marx and Engels. According to this perspective, no individual is independent or separate of others since each is connected in ways which define their being and consciousness in a relation to the social world, to others, and to the system of beliefs and values which are already in existence.

Empiricism and the View from Science

While idealism had attained philosophical dominance as a historical perspective during the first quarter of the nineteenth century, it was clear that by 1850 a serious critical attack had begun to be mounted against idealism, and in order to understand these developments we need to look at the history of empiricism.

The term 'empiricism' derives from the Greek word *empereiria*, meaning experience. Empiricism can be defined as the general name given to the doctrine in philosophy which holds that knowledge of the world must be based on observation and sense perception. Aristotle (320 BC) is believed to be the founder of empiricism by his straightforward attempt to integrate experience into a theory of development. In contrast to idealism, the fundamental tenet of empiricism is the belief that knowledge is the product of a straightforward perceptual encounter with the natural world. Historically, empiricism attained its place in Western thought because of its relation to modern science and the emphasis it placed on substantiating statements by recourse to observation and fact.[67] As successes in the natural sciences began to mount up in the nineteenth century, there was universal acceptance of empirical methods in the sciences and these became standardized in disciplines such as history, social science, psychology and anthropology.

One of the principal qualities of empiricism is its reliance on sense perception. This is expressed in a number of key assumptions which characterize the empirical standpoint. The first assumes that objects in the material world remain the same over time and are subject to observation and description. Second, empiricist methodologies assume that a division exists between an 'outer world' of things and an 'inner world' of the mind which is capable of apprehending objects in the outer world. In this view, knowledge is the straightforward grasping of the object in the material world. Third, empirical methods assume that accounts must be given about the operations and procedures performed to obtain knowledge of things in the outer world. Where no account can be given, claims may not be validated. Fourth, empirical methodologies assume that certainty lies in the methods of measurement used to obtain reliable knowledge from the

67 Paul K. Feyerabend, *Problems of Empiricism*, London: Cambridge University Press, 1981.

physical world and believe that these methods are a reliable means of representing the consistency of the natural world. Fifth, empiricism assumes that the tendency to commit error in our knowledge of the material world can only be reduced by increased reliance on the senses, through such methods as observation and measurement.[68]

The Development of Positivism

The critical attack on idealism did not fully emerge until the middle of the nineteenth century when a scientific movement called positivism was under way. Primarily a philosophic doctrine associated with the work of Auguste Comte, positivism sustained one of the most thoroughgoing critiques of idealist philosophy. Comte published his work on positive philosophy in 1830, and subsequently it became a worldwide movement when it announced that the age of 'speculation' and 'intuition' in philosophy was at an end.[69]

Comte believed that all speculative philosophy would be replaced by the methods of the natural sciences. Essentially, he took the view that positivism was the highest stage in the development of knowledge and tended to equate positivism with progress and social reform. As a scientific doctrine, positivism emphasized two key points of departure from idealist philosophy: (i) it stressed the reliability of observation as a basis for a theory of knowledge; and (ii) it placed an emphasis on the search for factual regularities which Comte thought would lead to the formation of general laws. Positivism thus constituted a key shift in the philosophy of knowledge since it insisted that the search for meaning and ultimate causes be abandoned and replaced with the ultimate stress on observation and description.

The influence of positivism on nineteenth-century European society was dramatic.[70] Generally, there were two pivotal assertions which made positivism so influential. First, Comte developed what he called the 'law of three stages,' which, while not extraordinary in and of itself, had the effect of essentially equating science with historical development. Second, Comte developed a system for classifying the sciences by arranging them in terms of a definite order and by hierarchically organizing the sciences in relation to their complexity.[71] Though Comte's law of three stages was very straightforward, its social impact was considerable. It argued that the human mind develops in three distinct and unalterable phases: the theological stage, in which human beings explain causes in terms of the will of anthropomorphic gods; the metaphysical stage, in which causes are explained in terms of abstract speculative ideas; and the positive stage, in which causes are explained in terms of scientific laws. What proved to be

68 Ibid.
69 Auguste Comte, *A General View of Positivism*, London: Routledge, 1908.
70 Simon, *European Positivism*, pp. 4–18.
71 Ibid.

so controversial about Comte's assertion was its claim that the replacement of the speculative by the positive stage was inevitable and, therefore, a fact of historical development.

In essence, this meant that positivism became associated in the minds of many with progress and social reform. Under these circumstances, it suddenly became a matter of historical urgency for all disciplines to develop from the speculative to the positive stage, thereby marking their scientific stature. In this sense, positive philosophy did nothing less than mark the end of speculative thought.

Positivism, in this respect, was clearly distinct from empiricism. Whereas empiricism was the general philosophical view that reality was to be equated with the physical world and sense perception, positivism may be described as a social movement which pronounced the demise of speculative philosophy by promising to resolve the 'intellectual anarchy' which was thought to be present in the philosophic sciences.[72] Even though it had adopted empiricist principles, exemplified by its stress on observation and sense perception, positivism gained its historical significance by proclaiming that the age of speculative philosophy was at an end.

By 1890, positivism had become a dominant social force advocating scientific change and social reform and had adopted methods premised on the natural sciences.[73] The key characteristics of positivism may be outlined as follows. (i) Positivism was premised on the assumption that a search for universal truths or ideals be abandoned in favor of a search for law-like regularities. (ii) It took the view that the only legitimate objects of investigation were those subject to observation, observation having become the central criterion of verification. Since verification was preparatory to the formulation of general laws, laws must be subject to the test of facts. (iii) With its stress on observation, positivism equated knowledge with the experience of facts and this greatly reduced the role reason had played in theory formation. (iv) Positivism's straightforward acceptance of the physical sciences as a model of certainty and exactness put other disciplines on notice that the methods of the natural sciences were to be the ultimate goal of all the disciplines. (v) Positivism upheld the view that progress and social reform depended on an orientation to facts.

It is important to remember that in advocating positivism Comte was responding to two particular challenges which he felt represented a threat on the threshold of a new scientific age. The first of these was the social and political anarchy which had been caused by the social revolution in France. Second was the perceived anarchy of philosophical speculation which had prevailed since the dominance of Hegel's idealism in European

---

72 See Marcuse, *Reason and Revolution*, pp. 323–60.

73 For discussion of the social and political reforms of positivism see, D.G. Charlton, *Positivist Thought in France During the Second Empire: 1852–70*, Oxford: Clarendon Press, 1959.

thought. Comte took the view that the new science of positive philosophy would serve two specific functions: it would make French society whole again by examining it scientifically and it would pronounce the end of speculative philosophy and its mystical view of nature and history.[74] Viewed from this perspective, positivism may be defined as a scientific outlook on the world which departs from the anarchy of speculative philosophy by abandoning the search for ultimate, final or first causes or truths.

We now turn our attention to the works of Marx, Durkheim and Weber. The chapters which follow begin with a discussion of the historical context of the works of each of the central thinkers. An extensive discussion of their writings is undertaken with the aim of providing a detailed and explicit transmission of concepts not outlined in earlier traditions of commentary.

74 On this point see, D.G. Charlton, *Secular Religions in France 1815–1870*, London: Oxford University Press, 1963.

2

Karl Marx

The Historical Context of Karl Marx's Work

Karl Marx was born on May 5, 1818 in Trier, a small city situated in the southern part of the German Rhineland. He grew up in a middle class Jewish family which had converted to Protestantism to escape the social difficulty suffered by Jews in German society. Marx's father, a lawyer, played a major role in his life acting as both his advisor and friend. Marx corresponded with him regularly until he died. By contrast with his father, little is known of Marx's mother or the role she played in his life. In 1835, at the age of 17 Marx entered the University of Bonn as a law student and shortly thereafter left Bonn for the University of Berlin. It was in Berlin that Marx first read the works of Georg Hegel, whose theoretical influence remained with him throughout his life. In April 1841, Marx received his doctorate and headed back to Bonn to search for work in the University. Unable to find academic employment, Marx tried to earn a living as a journalist and during that time met Arnold Ruge, the editor of a popular periodical called the *Deutsche Jahrbücher*. Ruge invited Marx to contribute and in 1842 Marx published his first work in the *Jahrbücher*.[1] Thereafter, Ruge helped Marx publish a series of critical articles. Later, in 1843 Marx moved to Cologne where he studied the works of Ludwig Feuerbach. During this period of his life, Marx's work was shaped by his criticism of Hegel and Hegel's dominance in German philosophy. In 1843 Marx produced two major writings criticizing Hegel's conception of the state, *A Critique of Hegel's Philosophy of Right* and 'On the Jewish Question.'[2] Immediately following these critiques, he began to develop an outline of a theory of history and economic life – a theory which was later to become one of Marx's most important contributions.

In October 1843, Marx moved to Paris where he took up the study of political economy by reading the works of Adam Smith and David Ricardo. While Marx was in Paris, social and political questions began to become more pressing and he became involved in the socialist movement. By May of 1844, Marx had drafted some notes related to classical

---

1 M. Rubel and M. Manale, *Marx Without Myth: A Chronological Study of His Life and Work*, New York: Harper & Row, 1975.

2 Karl Marx, *A Critique of Hegel's Philosophy of Right*, J. O'Malley (ed.), Cambridge, University Press, [1843] 1970; R.C. Tucker, *Marx-Engels Reader*, New York: W.W. Norton, 1978.

economics and alienated labor entitled the *Economic and Philosophic Manuscripts,* one of his most famous writings. It was this work which led him into a formal study of political economy and economic questions. Parallel to these developments, Europe was grappling with the effects of industrialization which had brought poverty and social distress to the working classes. Low wages, long hours and poor working conditions led to growing social unrest and, eventually, social revolution in France in 1848. As a result, Marx became more involved in economic issues and an open criticism of society. While working on these problems, Marx read Frederick Engels' work, *The Condition of the Working Class in England,* and as a consequence became aware of the scale of the misery endured by industrial workers. In the same year, Engels went to Paris to visit Marx and, as a result, struck up a friendship and collaboration that was to last a lifetime.

In 1845, Marx left Paris for Brussels where his work with Engels grew more frequent. One of the first products of their collaboration was *The Holy Family,* a polemical writing which attacked the Young Hegelians for their conservative view of society and the state.[3] Later Marx and Engels collaborated on a manuscript entitled *The German Ideology,* which laid out the conditions of the break with German philosophy and outlined what later became the materialist theory of history, another of Marx's most important contributions.[4]

Near the end of his stay in Brussels, Marx became more involved in the workers' movement and this took him further into economic questions. It is against this background that, in 1848, the Communist League asked Marx and Engels to draw up a workers' charter. This led to *The Communist Manifesto* of 1848, which had an enormous impact on the workers' movement throughout Europe. In 1849 Marx left Brussels to settle in London where he pursued economic questions and began work on a detailed analysis of capitalism. By 1859, he had published *A Contribution to the Critique of Political Economy,* the famous preface of which is one of the most frequently quoted excerpts from his writings.[5] Over the next 10 years, Marx devoted himself to writing and preparing his most famous work, Volume 1 of *Capital,* which was published in 1867. Eighteen years later, Marx died in London at the age of 65.

Rejection of Hegel and the Shift to Materialism

No complete understanding of Marx's work is possible without some discussion of his life-long fascination with the work of Georg Hegel.

3 K. Marx and F. Engels, *The Holy Family, or Critique of Critical Criticism,* Moscow: Progress Publishers, [1845] 1956.

4 K. Marx and F. Engels, *The German Ideology,* New York: International Publishers, [1846] 1947.

5 K. Marx, *A Contribution to the Critique of Political Economy,* Moscow: Progress Publishers [1859] 1977.

Philosophically, Hegel was by far the most dominant thinker in Europe. By 1815, he had written several powerful books which advanced a broad theory of existence which was both philosophical and historical in its orientation. Without question, Hegel was the dominant philosopher during the time in which Marx worked and, even though Hegel had died in 1831, the legacy of his writings was extremely important to the intellectual and social background in which Marx lived. In fact, a great deal of Marx's early writings can only be understood in relation to Hegel's thinking. Hegel was the originator of one of the most far-reaching philosophical doctrines of the nineteenth century referred to as philosophical idealism. Idealism can be defined as a philosophic perspective which put forward the idea that the ultimate conditions of human existence and development can be arrived at only through the examination of abstract philosophic categories. As a philosophical perspective, idealism had claimed that the fundamental task of philosophy and social thought was to understand human existence by an examination of abstract categories such as being, reason, history and spirit. The importance of Hegel's observation was that it viewed the world, existence and being in terms of interrelated processes rather than seeing individuals and history as separate, free-standing entities. The terms Hegel used to denote the interconnectedness between the human and historical realms were spirit, reason, being and history.

While a student at the University of Berlin, Marx had read Hegel and this marked a turning point in his intellectual career as it had for many students.[6] Hegel was intoxicating for a generation of thinkers because of the radical form of his philosophy and the method he adopted to explain broad aspects of historical and individual development. In essence, Hegel assumed that the abstract categories of 'history,' 'spirit' and 'reason' were the ultimate subject matter of philosophic investigation. This led to the view that the world of everyday experience was not an object of philosophic contemplation. Marx's rejection of Hegel's philosophic viewpoint was thus central to his thinking because it called into question the whole basis of philosophy and the role it played in explaining human existence. Marx's attack on Hegel is evident in an early work – *The Holy Family* – where, speaking of Hegel's system, he wrote:

> the whole destructive work results in the most conservative philosophy because it thinks it has overcome the objective world merely by transforming it into a 'thing of thought.' [Hegel thus] stands the world on its head and can therefore dissolve in the head all the limitations which naturally remain in existence. If, from real apples, pears and strawberries, I form the general idea 'Fruit,' if I go further and imagine that my abstract idea 'Fruit,' derived from real fruit, is an entity existing outside me, is indeed the true essence of the pear, the apple, etc., then, in the language of [Hegelian] philosophy I am declaring that 'Fruit' is the 'Substance' of the pear, the apple etc. I am saying, therefore, that to be a pear is not essential to the pear, that to be an apple is not essential to the apple; that

---

6 David McLellan, *Karl Marx: His Life and Thought*, New York: Harper & Row, 1973, pp. 28–32.

what is essential to these things is not their real being, perceptible to the senses, but the essence that I have extracted from them and then foisted on them, the essence of my idea – 'Fruit.'[7]

In his own work, Marx was moving more in the direction of developing an understanding of reality and history. This led him to focus his attention on issues of social existence and economic necessity and, in order to develop a body of thought consistent with it, Marx went on to outline the conditions of the break with philosophical idealism by resting his rejection of Hegel on four central theoretical premises. First, Marx objected to the role Hegel had assigned to philosophy and social theory. Hegel had asserted that the fundamental task of philosophy was to examine the role played by the abstract categories of history and spirit in human development. Marx took the position that Hegel's idealist framework led to a fundamental misunderstanding of human existence because it led to the conclusion that only philosophic categories are real. Marx felt that this was a major oversight since it assigned reality to abstract forces rather than human agents.[8] If, as Hegel had reasoned, only history is real and individuals are abstract, then the philosopher's duty is to concentrate on abstract processes rather than on individuals. Marx felt that this was a fundamental distortion, since to understand history as a series of categories was equivalent to reducing human experience to abstract processes. In fact, Marx took the view that the categories put forward by idealist philosophers referred neither to concrete human activity nor to physical reality, but only to abstract processes grasped as ideas. This ultimate distortion, Marx thought, consisted of raising the categories to the level of existence, as if they had 'natures,' 'processes' and, ultimately, 'needs' of their own. In addition, Marx believed that to place such emphasis on an abstract conception of history only mystified human experience and in doing so it made the real questions of human life abstract as well. Marx believed that when the existence of human beings is understood only as 'ideas and thoughts,' the more real and practical problems of individual lives are overlooked.

Second, Marx disagreed with Hegel over the role of ideas in history.[9] Hegel had stated that ideas were paramount in understanding social and historical development because they acted as causes. Marx took the view that Hegel's ultimate stress on the reality of abstract ideas led him to misrepresent the essential nature of human social life as well as the forces which gave rise to it. Whereas Hegel had believed that human reason was the highest good, Marx thought that individuals have physical needs and requirements which sustain their life and well-being, and these needs come before intellectual needs and can only be filled by direct productive activity

7 Marx and Engels, *The Holy Family*, p. 72.

8 See Nathan Rotenstreich, *Basic Problems of Marx's Philosophy*, Indianapolis: Bobbs-Merrill, 1965.

9 See Lucio Colletti, *Marxism and Hegel*, London: Verso, 1979.

in the world. Moreover, he thought that these needs are so central to human life that, in fact, they precede intellectual needs and are of greater importance than those which Hegel had assigned to the philosophic categories. Marx took the position that, in and of themselves, 'ideas' do not live or act nor do they have needs – only human beings do. In this respect, Marx reasoned that the most significant fact about human beings is that they must satisfy their material needs in order to live and that these needs must be met on a daily and hourly basis, otherwise there is no life or material existence. Thus where Hegel had stressed the centrality of reason in human history and had placed theoretical emphasis on the category of the 'ideal' and raised it to the level of an abstraction, Marx thought that the single most important aspect of human life was the fact of material well-being, which could only be brought about by the satisfaction of material needs. Hence materialism, for Marx, stands in opposition to idealism.

A third basis of disagreement relates to Hegel's view of the ultimate role of society and the state. Hegel's philosophical perspective took a politically conservative view of history and society. Hegel thought that society and the state had developed out of what he called the forces of the spirit in history and 'the actualization of the ethical.'[10] This meant that the state was synonymous with processes of development based on ethical and moral categories which were realized through historical process rather than individual acts. This led to the view that the state was, in essence, a theological embodiment of the spirit of human beings. In this way, Hegel had empowered the state with a kind of 'eternal' quality which meant that its activities were unalterable. Marx rejected this view by stating that Hegel had created the illusion that inequality and human hardship were natural outcomes (or actualities) of history rather than resulting from social disadvantages and historical social inequalities of society. This illusion sustained by Hegel's philosophy resulted, in part, from his view that human history can only be seen as part of an overall eternal and ever-lasting process.

The fourth point of disagreement concerns Hegel's understanding of human hardship and social inequality itself. Hegel had claimed that hardship and suffering stem from a kind of consciousness existing in the minds of individuals rather than in the form of material obstacles which exist in reality and hinder individual freedom. The classic representation of this process is Hegel's discussion of the master-slave relationship in *The Phenomenology of Mind*, published in 1807. In it, Hegel basically understands the slave's subjection to the master as an inner dialogue which takes place in the slave's consciousness. Hegel believed that the condition of slavery originated in the capacity of slaves to see themselves as subjects of others. Freedom can only come, Hegel argued, when slaves see themselves in another light and change their consciousness. He therefore reasoned

10 G.W.F. Hegel, *Philosophy of Right*, Oxford: Clarendon Press, 1958, p. 218.

that, in relation with others and society, the primary form of oppression is self-imposed.[11] While Hegel's classic example of the relationship between master and slave was the philosophic prototype of the class struggle, Marx could not disagree more. For Marx, the answer to social inequality and human hardship lay not in abstract forces of the development of consciousness, but rather in the concrete material conditions which make it necessary for one class of persons to be dominant over others. In Marx's view, it is economic necessity, not abstract conscious relations, that binds the slave to the master. While Hegel believed that freedom from oppression exists when individuals change their consciousness, Marx asserted that suppression stems from the system of social relations which arise from economic inequalities rather than the other way round. Marx believed, therefore, that idealist philosophy mistakenly assumes that individual hardship is a product of consciousness, when in fact it derives from material conditions which give rise to economic inequalities. While Hegel had asserted that individual freedom ultimately comes from changing individual consciousness, Marx made it clear that such a view amounts to asking individuals to interpret reality in a different way, when, in fact, they can only become free by altering their social conditions.

Materialism as a Theoretical Perspective

What was decisive about Marx's criticism of German idealism was that it put forward a new interpretive framework for understanding history – the materialist perspective. Marx introduced materialism in order to overcome the problems posed by idealist philosophy and its abstraction of society and social life. But what did Marx mean by 'materialism' in this context? Simply stated, materialism is a theoretical perspective which looks at human problems by studying the real conditions of human existence, especially those related to the satisfaction of simple economic needs. It is the most basic premise of materialism that the very first thing human beings must do is satisfy their material needs of food, shelter and clothing. It goes on to assume that society and history are created from the sequence of productive acts which are designed to fulfill these needs. Materialism, therefore, may be defined as a theoretical perspective which takes as its starting place the view that, before anything else, human beings must satisfy their everyday economic needs through their physical labor and practical productive activity.[12] What was so important about this perspective was its attempt to devise a social theory of society and existence from the starting point of practical human needs and economic production.

The distinction Marx makes between the 'material' and the 'ideal' is

---

11 This discussion can be found in *The Phenomenology of Mind*, New York: Harper & Row, [1807] 1967, pp. 229–40. The passage on 'Lordship and Bondage' should be read by modern readers for its psychological insights.

12 Marx and Engels, *German Ideology*, p. 16.

therefore central to his thinking in several respects. First, by anchoring theoretical activity in material reality, Marx put theory in the service of human experience and made this a formal requirement for theoretical work. Up to this time, all philosophic reasoning had merely interpreted history in various ways, whereas Marx believed it was the aim of theory to change history.[13] Second, by beginning with actual experience and practical activity rather than its representative philosophic categories, Marx separated the aims of philosophy from materialist social theory, outlining the conditions of the break with speculative philosophy. What made this position so unique was that it marked a turning point in social thought itself. Whereas almost all philosophy had been based on the idea that the subject matter of philosophic investigation was to be found lying above the realm of everyday experience, materialism had taken as its starting point the most basic human act – economic production.

The German Ideology

The German Ideology was written between 1845 and 1846 while Marx was living in Brussels.[14] It was completed in the summer of 1846, but eventually abandoned as a manuscript due to critical attacks directed at its polemical sections. In its original form, *The German Ideology* was divided into three volumes totaling more than 500 pages. By far the most important part of the work is the section entitled 'Feuerbach' which contains the most substantive discussion of Marx's and Engels' theory of history. Made up of only 70 pages, the first section begins with a critical attack on Feuerbach. After criticizing their philosophical contemporaries, Marx and Engels turned their attention to outlining a framework for developing the materialist theory of history, and this forms the central subject matter of the work.

Written as a collaborative work by Marx and Engels, *The German Ideology* had essentially two aims. First, to outline the conditions of the break with German speculative philosophy and to 'settle accounts' with the Young Hegelians. In setting out the conditions of the break with philosophy, Marx and Engels criticized the Young Hegelians for their failure to take part in political and social reforms and for promoting the 'illusion' that political change comes about when 'true ideas' replace prevailing ones. The second aim of *The German Ideology* was to develop and expound the materialist conception of history by setting out the views of materialism in opposition to Hegelian philosophy. Because of its broad historical outlook and far-reaching interpretation of history, this section of

13 This is found in the eleventh thesis on Feuerbach which states 'The philosophers have only interpreted the world differently, the point is to change it.' See *German Ideology*, International Edition, 1947, p. 199.

14 Rubel and Manale, *Marx Without Myth*, pp. 58–63; and for a discussion of the writing of *German Ideology*, see David McLellan, *Marx: His Life and Thought*, pp. 137–77.

the work had much deeper theoretical impact. In order to understand the perspective put forward by Marx, we must examine the argument more closely.

To begin with, Marx and Engels started with a criticism of German speculative philosophy, and moved directly to a criticism of Feuerbach. The focal point of their criticism was Feuerbach's uncritical reliance on Hegelian thinking, and his putting forward of a theory of religion. According to Marx, Feuerbach's treatment of religion is rooted in the philosophy of Hegel and this means that, like Hegel, Feuerbach represents religious ideas as if they had independent existence.[15] Marx maintained that the philosophical criticism of Hegel – and therefore of Feuerbach – fundamentally misunderstands human existence because it begins with abstract premises, assuming that 'ideas' are products of history rather than of human action. According to this view, human limitations and hardships are nothing but the products of consciousness and, instead of changing social circumstances, self-change is recommended. Marx captured this tendency toward abstraction when he wrote:

> the Young Hegelians consider conceptions, thoughts, ideas, in fact all the products of consciousness, to which they attribute an independent existence, as the real chains of human beings. Since, according to their fantasy, the relationships of human beings, all their doings, their chains and their limitations are products of their consciousness, the Young Hegelians logically put to them the moral postulate of exchanging their present consciousness for human, critical or egoistic consciousness, and thus of removing their limitations. This demand to change consciousness amounts to a demand to interpret reality in another way.[16]

The Young Hegelians therefore believe that hardship can be resolved by 'interpreting reality in another way,' and by substituting one set of conceptions for another. This, according to Marx, shows that German philosophy deals in 'illusions' and 'abstract conceptions.'

The Materialist Theory of History

After laying out the conditions of the break with speculative philosophy, Marx and Engels turned their attention to developing a framework for the materialist theory of history. Perhaps the most important element in Marx's social thought, the materialist theory of history is the cornerstone of his social and political thinking and remains one of the most thoroughgoing perspectives on historical and economic processes ever devised. First developed in its most comprehensive form in *The German Ideology*, Marx outlined the materialist theory of history with Engels. Let us begin by looking at the three main premises which shaped Marx's understanding of society and history.

15 L. Feuerbach, *The Essence of Christianity*, Buffalo, N.Y.: Prometheus, 1989, pp. xiii–xxiv.

16 Marx and Engels, *German Ideology*, pp. 5–6; and Tucker, *Marx-Engels Reader*, p. 149.

As we said earlier, Marx put forward three basic propositions which were to guide his own thinking in identifying the materialist perspective. First, Marx believed that, before anything else, human beings must be in a position to obtain food, shelter and clothing in order to live.[17] Thus, the first and most important historical act, is the act of production of the means to satisfy human economic needs.[18] Second, human beings actually distinguish themselves from animals to the extent that they produce the means to satisfy their primary material needs.[19] In this respect, human beings are different from animals because they must produce their means of subsistence and because they enter into a conscious relation with nature in order to survive. Third, the way in which human beings produce depends on what they find in nature and what they must produce to survive. How they exist and how they live thus tends to 'coincide with what they produce and how they produce, and the nature of individuals depends on the material conditions determining their production.'[20] On the basis of these premises, the materialist outlook took up the task of understanding historical and social processes from the perspective of human economic activity.

As discussed earlier, historical materialism is the term used to describe Marx's main theoretical perspective for understanding society and history. In order to look more closely at the premises and scope of the theory, it will be useful to quote from the 1859 preface of Marx's *A Contribution to the Critique of Political Economy*; it is one of the most incisive summaries of his theory ever written. Marx wrote:

> In the social production which men carry on they enter into definite relations that are indispensable and independent of their will. These relations of production correspond to a definite stage of the development of their material forces of production. The totality of these relations of production constitutes the economic structure of society, which is the real foundation on top of which arises a legal and political superstructure to which correspond definite forms of social consciousness. It is not the consciousness of men, therefore, that determines their existence, but instead their social existence determines their consciousness. At a certain stage of their development, the material forces of production in society come in conflict with the existing relations of production, or – what is but a legal expression of the same thing – with the property relations within which they had been at work before. From forms of development of the forces of production these relations turn into their fetters. Then occurs a period of social revolution. With the change of the economic foundation the entire immense superstructure is more or less rapidly transformed.[21]

17 Marx and Engels, *German Ideology*, pp. 7–9.
18 Ibid., p. 16. Marx states: 'The first premise of all human existence, and therefore of all history, is that human beings must be in a position to live in order to be able to "make history." But, life involves before everything eating, drinking, a habitation, clothing and many other things. The first act is thus the production of the means to satisfy these needs, the production of material life itself.'
19 Ibid., p. 7.
20 Ibid., p. 7.
21 Marx, *Contribution to the Critique*, pp. 20–1.

From this passage, we can derive four fundamental concepts central to the materialist theory of history: (i) means of production; (ii) relations of production; (iii) mode of production; and (iv) forces of production. Taken together, these make up the core of the materialist theory of history and, in order to see how they relate theoretically, let us begin by looking at the concept of means of production.

Means of Production   Marx asserted that in every stage of history, human beings have at their disposal certain productive forces such as land, animals, tools, machinery, etc., which are necessary to produce the means of their survival: food, shelter and clothing. These are called the means of production.[22] According to Marx, the means of production refer to any-thing in the external world that is used to produce material needs and maintain existence. For instance, the way jobs are used to produce wages and land to produce food and fuel constitutes the means of production. It is important to note that material needs and economic necessities cannot be produced privately on one's own, but rather only when we employ the means of production. All human beings, according to Marx, must employ the means of production in order to meet their basic economic needs. But, stated Marx, what we observe historically is that only one class of persons have owned or monopolized the means of production. This condition of ownership over the means of production is the single most fundamental fact of the materialist theory of history since it is this that leads to the division of society into economic classes.[23] The key division, Marx reasoned, is between owners and non-owners of the means of production. This is a central distinction, since the existence of these classes denotes that only one class are owners of the means of production, while the other is subject to those who rule over them.[24] Marx referred to the class of non-owners as the direct producers of physical labor, and the most distinguishing characteristic of this class is their inability to obtain unhindered access to the means of production for purposes of satisfying their material needs.

Relations of Production   The second concept in the materialist theory of history is the existence of relations of production. These are of central importance since it is the relations of production which economically bind one class to another. One of the clearest ways, perhaps, of understanding the relations of production is to remember that Marx used the term 'relations' repeatedly in his writings to indicate the connection between the way a society produces and the social roles allotted to individuals in

22 See Maurice Cornforth, *Dialectical Materialism: An Introduction*, London: Lawrence & Wishart, 1953.

23 *German Ideology*, pp. 8–13.

24 Ibid., p. 9. The various stages in the development of history, says Marx, 'is just so many different forms of ownership.'

production. Marx believed the roles individuals assume in production are directly related to the system of social class arising from the fact that ownership tends to be concentrated only in one class of society. Marx thought that the tendency for ownership to reside in one class created two distinct social roles in production: producers and non-producers of physical labor.

The role played by the relations of production, therefore, becomes clear when we look at the result of class relations in historical terms. Marx thought that these could be outlined by noting two essential characteristics. First, non-owners are compelled to enter into relations of production in order to satisfy their own economic needs and, as a result, they are subordinated to the class who are dominant over them. Second, since historically non-owners tend to be subordinate to a class who rule over them, they are compelled to perform the economic maintenance of the dominant class. This subordination in productive roles gives rise to several key consequences of the relations of production outlined by Cohen in his useful book on Marx.[25] First, non-owners produce for others who do not produce for them; second, the livelihoods of the non-owners depend on their relations with their superiors; third, the dominant classes have direct rights over the economic product of the producer; fourth, the owners of the means of production always receive more from the production process than the producer; and fifth, non-owners are subject to the authority of their superiors.[26]

A second major feature of the relations of production is their tendency to govern the way non-owners use the means of production to satisfy their material needs and create a livelihood. In this case, non-owners are unable freely to produce the means of their existence since they do not have unobstructed access to the means of production. This can be elucidated if we look at feudal society. In a feudal system of production, the relations of production are between lord and serf who are respectively owners and non-owners of the means of production. Marx reasoned that in order for serfs to put the means of production to work, they are compelled to enter into a relation of production with the landholder, giving the landholder the right over the labor of the serf and the right over the serf's agricultural production.[27] Marx thought that the relations of production created three central elements which make them conceptually key to the materialist theory of history. First is their ability to be transformed into relations of domination; second is their ability to become physical and economic fetters for one class and an economic advantage for the other;[28] and third

---

25 G.A. Cohen, *Karl Marx's Theory of History*, New Jersey: Princeton University, 1978.
26 Ibid., pp. 69–70.
27 Marx and Engels, *German Ideology*, pp. 11–13.
28 Marx, *Contribution to the Critique*, Marx states: 'these relations turn into their fetters.' p. 21.

is their ability to be backed up by coercive sanctions, legitimated by the political and legal structure of society.[29]

A third feature of the relations of production is their tendency to appear in all societies. Marx maintained that different relations of production manifest themselves at definite stages of economic development and these always seem to coincide with the way societies produce. The name given to these various relations of production, in each of these stages, corresponds to the stage of economic development. For instance, patrician and slave are the names given to the relations of production in ancient societies, based on a system of production in which a class of military rulers enslave populations who produce directly for those who rule over them. Lord and serf, on the other hand, are the names given to the relations of production in feudal society, where economic production is based on an aristocratic class of landholders who rely on an enserfed peasantry to perform necessary labor. Finally, capitalist and wage laborer are the names given to relations of production in capitalist societies, where production is based on a large class of wage laborers who produce surplus value (profit) for the class which rules over them.

Mode of Production, Forces of Production   A third concept in the materialist theory of history is the mode of production. While Marx never completely elucidated the term, he did leave various references to it throughout his writings. In one of these he states that 'social relations are closely bound up with productive forces. In acquiring new productive forces human beings change their mode of production; and in changing their mode of production they change their way of earning their living and all their social relations. The handmill gives you a society with the feudal lord; the steam mill, a society with the industrial capitalist.'[30] 'In broad outline,' wrote Marx, 'we can designate the asiatic, ancient, feudal and the modern bourgeois modes of production as so many epochs in the process of the economic formation of society.'[31]

Initially, the term 'mode of production' is used by Marx to identify the primary elements of a given historical stage of production by showing how its economic base shapes its social relations. In this sense, the way people actually produce and enter into social relationships with one another is called a mode of production and this comprises a total way of life of society, its social activities and its social institutions. But, in and of itself, this does not give us a clear understanding of the term and so we must look more closely.

In order to reach a clearer understanding of what Marx meant by a mode of production, we have to distinguish between 'forces of production'

29 Ibid., pp. 192–3.
30 K. Marx, *The Poverty of Philosophy*, New York: International Publishers, [1847] 1982, p. 109.
31 Marx, *Contribution to the Critique*, p. 21.

and 'relations of production' since together these define the mode of production.[32] As discussed earlier, forces of production may be taken to mean the instruments, equipment, land, tools, etc. which are put to work for purposes of producing a livelihood. As such, forces of production only have capacities to be put to work. But these forces can only be put into operation, so to speak, when people in society enter into the relations of production. The relations of production, therefore, are always about how the forces of production are to be used in order to produce, and one key idea stemming from the relations of production is that one class is the proprietor over these forces, the other being subject to them.

This being the case, two key conditions of the relations of production can be highlighted: first, the right of proprietors to control the labor of the producer; second, the right of proprietors to control the products of the laborer. This can be shown directly when we look at the modes of production. For instance, in an ancient mode of production the dominant classes preside over the forces of production in such a way that the relations of production entered into by the producer transform them into slaves. This gives the dominant classes direct control over all the labor of the producer and complete control over the product. In a feudal mode of production, on the other hand, the landholder directly presides over the forces of production and has rights to control a portion of the serfs' labor as well as rights over the serfs' agricultural production. In a capitalist mode of production, by contrast, the capitalist has direct ownership over the forces of production including the land, machinery and materials, and exercises a right over the disposition of the product of labor but does not exercise direct control over the laborer, as in the case of slavery or serfdom. Rather, the capitalist has control only over the portion of labor time sold to him by the laborer during the working day. In capitalism, it should be noted that the control existing in the dominant classes to exercise rights over labor and over the product migrates to the wage-form, where the capitalist pays out in wages sufficiently less than the amount of wealth created by the worker.[33]

Another characteristic of the mode of production is its ability to determine the system of social relations arising from it. For instance, the primary way of producing economic necessities in feudal society is by cultivation. This produces food crops, domestic animals, shelter and clothing. From this way of producing material needs arises a system of social relations (lord and serf) which tends to govern how the means of production are used. Since landholder and serf became the central economic institutions of feudal society, Marx would argue that they do so only because they reflect the unequal relations of production arising out of the fact that one class of persons tends to preside over the forces of

32 For discussion of the distinction between 'forces' and 'relations,' see Maurice Cornforth, *Historical Materialism*, London: Lawrence & Wishart, 1962, p. 36.

33 Marx and Engels, *German Ideology*, p. 12.

production. The concept of mode of production allowed Marx to identify the primary economic elements of a historical period by showing how its economic base directly shaped its system of social relations.

Marx believed that the division of society into owners and non-owners of the means of production is a law of historical development. To prove this he divided history into three essential parts or stages: ancient, feudal and capitalist. Each of these stages has three central tendencies: (i) they perpetuate the division of society into classes, in which one class is dominant over another; (ii) they perpetuate economic, political and social inequality; and (iii) in each society, unequal social relations are supported by religion, law, and the political structure.

Laws of Historical Development: Ancient, Feudal and Capitalist Forms of Ownership   So far we have seen that the materialist perspective is, above all, a theory of historical development which explains human existence in terms of a series of economic stages. After laying out the basic framework for the materialist conception of history, Marx began to turn his attention toward evidence that would confirm his thesis that the historical development of society tends to be economic in nature. He went on to conceive of history as different forms of ownership which he thought could be expressed in four separate stages or epochs: tribal, ancient, feudal and capitalist modes of production. This broad conceptualization of history in terms of stages of economic development was central in two key respects. First, it constituted what some scholars believe to be a 're-periodization' of history in that it substituted dominant views of historical time marked by religious epochs, with a development of economic stages.[34] Second, in focusing on the sequence of economic stages, it reconceptualized historical development by concentrating on the 'system of production' which was characteristic of all societies. In addition, Marx went on to point out that each of the stages of historical development has three characteristics: (i) a system of production and division of labor; (ii) forms of property ownership; and (iii) a system of class relations.

As was noted earlier, Marx saw world history in terms of 'different forms of ownership,' and essentially he thought there were four distinct forms or stages: tribal, ancient, feudal and capitalistic.[35] The first type of ownership Marx called tribal. This encompasses a rudimentary system of production in which people live together principally by hunting and gathering. The division of labor is rudimentary, there is no development of private property and the social structure is derived from the family and kinship group. Because property is communal, there is no developed system of class relations, although there is incipient exploitation within the

34 L. Althusser and E. Balibar, *Reading Capital*, London: Verso, 1979, pp. 102–3.
35 Marx and Engels, *German Ideology*, pp. 9–13; and in Karl Marx, *Pre-Capitalist Economic Formations*, New York: International Publishers, [1857–58] 1984, pp. 67–120; and Marx, *Contribution to the Critique*, p. 21.

family system. This tribal form of association originates from a productive system which is largely based on kinship and on a communal orientation to production. This leads to a society that is classless, and a system of production which is egalitarian in the sense that individual members cooperatively produce the means of subsistence collectively. As a result, no exploitative relations arise.

The second form of ownership is found in ancient society. This form of social organization develops from an association of tribes who form an organization of city states, giving rise to a political and civil structure. The productive system is largely agrarian with rudimentary industry and a system of trade and commerce.[36] In contrast to tribal society, there is private property and a system of class relations develops from property ownership. The relation between owners of property and producers of physical labor has formed itself into a class system of citizen and slave. Unlike tribal society, the division into classes has crystallized and the primary form of labor is slave labor. Societies of this type occupy vast territories and the productive system has an extensive division of labor. In addition, a civil, political and military authority arises as an adjunct to the productive system. The ancient Graeco-Roman world is a historical example of productive systems where labor is in the form of slavery.[37]

In addition to these characteristics, a state ownership emerges from 'the union of several tribes into a city by agreement or by conquest.'[38] Ownership of the means of production is in the hands of a small class of military élite who live by conquering territories whose lands are seized and the population turned into slaves.[39] The dominant classes maintain their economic existence by searching for ever-widening means of production, resulting in a political organization combining conquered lands to form new political territories. Rome's march into Brittany in the first century is an example of development of this type. The division of society into patricians and slaves grows directly from the productive system. As populations of slaves die off, they are replaced by newly-acquired slaves from other territories. The prevailing relations of production are between élites and slave laborers, and élites draw their wealth from the class of slaves who act as the direct producers.

A third form of ownership identified by Marx is that of feudal society. This system of production is agricultural in origin and the major means of producing food is concentrated on the land. The focal point of production is the countryside, agriculture is widespread, there is no industry and town life is not developed.[40] Unlike tribal or ancient society, ownership is concentrated in an aristocratic class who act as the sole proprietors over

---

36 Marx and Engels, *German Ideology*, p. 9.

37 Ibid., p. 10.

38 Marx, *Pre-Capitalist Economic Formations*, New York: International Publishers, 1984, p. 71.

39 Marx and Engels, *German Ideology*, p. 9; Marx, *Pre-Capitalist Social Formations*, p. 72.

40 Marx and Engels, *German Ideology*, pp. 11–13.

the land. Though private property is not developed as such, there is a system by which aristocratic classes and the class of enserfed peasants use land 'in common.' The chief form of property is landed property, with a developed class system emerging between enserfed peasants who perform physical labor and an aristocratic class who have social and political prerogatives giving them power over serfs.[41] Feudal societies were dominant throughout Europe and England between the ninth and the seventeenth centuries. The social and political power of the landholder was backed up by legal and political institutions which provided landholders with the powers of coercion over the class of serfs.

The fourth form of ownership is found in capitalist society. The development of capitalist society presupposes the destruction of a feudal mode of production and a transformation of production from the countryside to the town. During the destruction of feudal society, the class of peasant serfs are coercively separated from the land as a means of livelihood and, as a result, are turned into a class of wage laborers who must sell their labor to meet their economic needs. The productive system is based on an advanced division of labor, with developed trade and commercial activity. In a capitalist mode of production, the town has become the center of economic life, the productive system has shifted from agriculture to industry, and there is fully developed political and civil life. There is widespread emergence of private property and a developed class system of capitalists, who are the owners of the means of production, and wage laborers, who are producers of physical labor.[42] The means of production have become diversified and largely consist of machinery, technology and the factory system of production. Ownership is over economic resources such as machines, manufactories, tools and other productive materials. The capitalist classes draw their wealth from the class of wage laborers who function as the primary producers, and wage labor is the prevailing form of exploitation.

After a capitalist mode of production, the next stage begins, according to Marx, when the economic contradictions inherent in the class system become so great that the majority of workers form a class constituting the potential for revolutionary change – and this starts the transition from capitalism to socialism. As Marx wrote, 'at a certain stage of development, the material forces of production in society come in conflict with the existing relations of production, or – what is but a legal expression of the same thing – with the property relations within which they had been at work before. From forms of development of the forces of production these relations turn into their fetters. Then occurs a period of social revolution. With the change of the economic foundation the entire immense superstructure is more or less rapidly transformed.'[43] Just as the strains

41 Ibid., p. 12.
42 Ibid., pp. 43–78.
43 Marx, *Contribution to the Critique*, pp. 20–21.

emerging within the class system of feudal society brought about the transition from a feudal to a capitalist mode of production, so the strains within the capitalist class system bring about the transition to the next stage of development.

Marx's Theory of Ideology

History of the Term in Hegel and Marx Marx developed his general theory of ideology with Frederick Engels between 1845 and 1846. The theory of ideology follows directly from the materialist conception of history, and the discussion takes place in the first section of *The German Ideology*, entitled 'Feuerbach.'[44] As we saw earlier, the title of the work was initially intended as a critical attack against a circle of thinkers Marx and Engels called the central 'ideologists' of German society who promoted mistaken conceptions of reality by espousing philosophical views of history. The circle of Young Hegelians, including figures such as David Strauss, Max Stirner and Bruno Bauer, attracted the attention of various groups in Germany during the 1840s by critically attacking Christianity, the state and the central authorities.[45] As Hegelians, they put forward their criticism of society and religion by drawing on the precepts of idealist philosophy which advocated the view that objective reality was nothing more than the manifestation of the internal will of the individual, actualized historically in what Hegel called the 'spirit.' In their ruthless criticism of everything authoritative, the Young Hegelians believed that historical change was nothing more than a manifestation of the 'spirit' in world historical progress, and this ultimately led to the view that the origin of all thought and ideas had to be found in the development of the spirit in history.

It is in this context that Marx and Engels wrote *The German Ideology* and directed its polemic against the philosophical views of the Young Hegelians.[46] The primary focus of Marx's and Engels' attack was the stress which the Hegelians had placed on philosophy as a way of analyzing historical and political problems. At the root of this view was Hegel's belief that 'ideas' were manifestations of the 'spirit,' and that social and historical problems could be analyzed by looking at the role ideas played in social and political life. For Hegel, ideas were nothing less than effective forces in history, a view which was evident in his account of the French Revolution which, he thought, was a manifestation of the 'freedom idea' in history.

44 Marx's full discussion of Ideology can be found in Marx and Engels, *German Ideology*, pp. 13–14, 39–43; and K. Marx and F. Engels, *The German Ideology: Collected Works*, Vol. 5, New York: International Publishers, 1975, pp. 35–7, 59–62.

45 For an extended discussion of the influence of the 'Young Hegelians' and the nature of their work, see L.S. Stepelevich, *The Young Hegelians: An Anthology*, Cambridge: University Press, 1983, pp. 1–15.

46 Ibid., p. 4; Rubel and Manale, *Marx without Myth*, pp. 56–62.

Marx criticized this approach for its abstract conception of historical forces, and went on to attack Hegel and the Young Hegelians in a number of ways. First, he objected to the role Hegel had assigned to ideas. For Hegel, not only were ideas first but they were seen as real historical causes. Marx felt this was a fundamental error since it concluded that abstractions were real forces and thus had material existence. Second, Marx felt that Hegel's position led to a major distortion of reality by philosophy. This pinpointed an oversight in the philosophical understanding of reality which showed that it tended to misrepresent empirical reality by 'turning it upside down,' which is to say, it represented reality from the abstract rather than practical side. If, as Hegel had reasoned, only ideas are real and individuals are abstract, then philosophy itself can only be a distortion of reality since it actively misrepresents it by 'turning reality upside down.'[47]

Marx took the view that philosophy itself must be the ultimate distortion of reality since it tended to elevate 'ideas' to the level of existence, as if they had 'forces' and 'characteristics' of their own. Marx thought that to place such an emphasis on the abstract side of the idea only abstracted the understanding of social life and, in doing so, made the real questions of human existence abstract as well. Marx went on to urge that when the real existence of human beings is understood only as 'ideas and thoughts' – as so many philosophic categories – then the more real and practical problems of individual lives are overlooked.

The Four Building Blocks of a Theory of Ideology   There are at least two primary motives Marx had in putting forward a theory of ideology. The first was to show that ideas had a material origin and arose from practical activity, rather than the other way round. In this respect, Marx wanted to show that ideas were in fact expressions of material relationships and, thus, demonstrate once and for all that Hegel had misunderstood the origin of ideas. Second, Marx wanted to show that he could provide a coherent link between ideas and material activity so that he could break with the philosophic tradition of ideology as an abstract representation of the idea. The importance of this point cannot be overestimated. In contrast to Hegelian thought that ideas came first historically, Marx took the view that ideas were historical outcomes of economic activity. From this standpoint, we can look more closely at the theory of ideology, but in order to understand how Marx developed the argument, four broad building blocks of ideology will be discussed: (i) the relationship between ideas and material activity in society; (ii) the relationship between the concept of ideology and a theory of perception; (iii) the relationship between ideology and the dominant classes; and (iv) the functions of ideology.

The first building block of a theory of ideology is the link between ideas

---

47 Marx and Engels, *German Ideology*, p. 14.

and the material base of society. As we stated, Marx thought that ideas have their origin in the material base of society and that 'the production of ideas is directly interwoven with material activity.'[48] In order to show Marx's reasoning here, we return briefly to the basic premises of the materialist theory of history which is as follows. The first thing that human beings do is produce the material means of their existence. This production is so central to their well-being that the subsequent shape of society always coincides with the way they produce. The manner in which this production is carried out determines the system of social relations which tend to arise from it, so much so that it creates the division of society into classes, one of which is dominant because it presides over the means of production, the other subordinate, because it is subject to the will of those who rule over them. The assertion that the shape of society always coincides with the way individuals produce derives its force from the simple fact that the first act of individuals is always economic, because human beings must produce to live. From this simple starting place, we can see that the system of social relations always reflects the social relations of production. Two important conclusions can be drawn from this: (i) the act of economic production shapes social relations and, therefore, the structure of society; and (ii) economic production gives rise to a system of ideas and beliefs which come to represent the productive relations that stand as 'conscious images in mental life.'[49] Marx therefore reasoned that the ideas individuals have are related to the way they produce and the class relations they form in the system of production.

A second broad building block of the theory of ideology concerns the way ideas alter the individual's internal perception of the outer world. This takes us to the next step, which is Marx's definition of the concept of ideology. There are two definitions we shall deal with. The first states: 'if in all ideology human beings and their relations appear upside down as in a camera obscura, this phenomenon arises just as much from their historical life processes as the inversion of objects on the retina does from their physical life processes.'[50] The second definition states: 'if in their imagination [individuals] turn reality upside down, then this in turn is the result of their limited material mode of activity and their limited social relations arising from it.'[51] From these two quotations we can draw out two key points about ideology. First and foremost, ideology is a system of attitudes, conceptions, ideas and beliefs which are capable of: (i) making circumstances 'appear upside down'; and (ii) 'inverting' our perception of reality. These two essential features of ideology are most important since they have the power to alter our perception of the outer world, or

---

48 Ibid.

49 Marx and Engels, *German Ideology*, pp. 14–16.

50 Marx and Engels, *The German Ideology: Collected Works*, Vol. 5, p. 36; Marx and Engels, *German Ideology* International edn, p. 14.

51 Marx and Engels, *Collected Works*, Vol. 5, p. 36. This passage was crossed out in the original manuscript.

objective social reality. But, exactly what did Marx mean by this? Essentially it is at this point that Marx's theory of ideology becomes a theory of perception, having to do with how ideas affect our grasp or apprehension of the outer world. In order to put this in perspective, we must look more closely.

To begin with, Marx believed that we do not perceive reality directly but rather through prevailing ideas and conceptions. To this extent, the prevailing ideas and conceptions act as distorting lenses or filters through which we come to perceive reality, and this raises two central questions: first, how does society distort our perception of reality by making social relations appear upside down; and second, in what way does society deceive individuals into thinking that these perceptions are acceptable substitutes for reality?[52] In order to develop these two points, it will be necessary to discuss how Marx understood the individual's relation to society more generally.

One of the central precepts of Marx's theory of ideology is the idea that individuals produce history and social relations, and that, for Marx, society is always to be thought of as a historical product of human actors. In these terms, the social world is always related to individuals as the object of their own production. This means that society and social relations – and by extension reality – are human products so far as individuals produce their own material circumstances in the act of production. In that individuals are actively related to history through their material activity, consciousness, according to Marx, must be a social product. Marx's repeated reference to consciousness, especially in his phrase 'social existence determines consciousness,' attempts to convey the thought that the way we come to perceive reality is ultimately dependent upon the conceptions and ideas of those who rule over the means of production. If only one class is dominant throughout history, this means that their ideas become the dominant ideas in the sense that, as a class, they rule over those who are subject to them. The central methodological premise at work here is that individual perception of reality is not only tied to material conditions but to consciousness as well.

Marx's theory of perception hinges on the assertion that, in ideology, everything appears upside down and actively turns things upside down in imagination.[53] In this view, ideology has the extraordinary power to (i) shape reality and (ii) alter the perception of reality. But how is this possible? Marx thought individuals perceive reality indirectly, through the filters of prevailing conceptions, ideas, and attitudes of the dominant classes. This active turning of reality upside down in perception is directly linked to the fact that dominant conceptions always reflect the dominant material relationships, and this happens, Marx thought, when the ideas

---

52 J. Larrain, *Marxism and Ideology*, London: Macmillan Press, 1983; and Dorothy Smith, 'The Ideological Practice of Sociology,' *Catalyst*, 8, 1974, 39–54.
53 Marx and Engels, *Collected Works*, Vol. 5, p. 36.

and beliefs reflect only the wills, intentions and interests of the dominant classes.[54]

So far, we have been able to show that: (i) 'ideas' have a material base so far as they reflect the wills and interests of the dominant classes; and (ii) ideas stem from the dominant material relationships in society, since 'the class which has the means of material production at its disposal, has control over the means of mental production, so that, generally speaking, the ideas of those who lack the means of mental production are subject to it.'[55]

Another way to understand how ideas can distort reality is to look at the distinction, which Marx employed often enough in his own work, between appearance and reality. Historically, the distinction between reality and appearance goes back to the earliest times of social and political thought and was used by Plato to draw attention to the difference between the way things 'appear' on the surface and an underlying essence or reality. As we have said, one of the first and most basic precepts of ideology is that we do not perceive the world directly, but rather see it through the distorting lenses of our conceptions, attitudes and ideas arising from material relationships. This is already clear enough. But, Marx believed that these ideas have the power to transform the real empirical conditions of reality into what he called their 'appearance forms.'[56] In this manner, reality presents itself in a distorted way and appears to be other than it actually is.

On a larger scale, the distinction between reality and appearance stressed the idea that the perceptible world is often contradictory to some underlying pattern, truth or reality and this signifies a split between what something appears to be and that which it is in reality. While Marx believed that appearance and reality never really coincide, he stressed the view that reality is not distorted by itself, but rather is distorted because our ideas and beliefs grow out of our social relations, which in turn arise from economic production.[57] It is these material relations that act as distorting lenses through which we perceive reality.[58]

Immanuel Kant's view on how we come to know the external world will be useful in illustrating Marx's point. Kant wrote an important philosophical treatise in the eighteenth century, the *Critique of Pure Reason*, which put forward a theory of how the human mind is capable of grasping external reality. Kant maintained that we can never know the external

---

54 Marx and Engels, *German Ideology*, pp. 39–40.

55 Ibid.

56 Ibid., p. 30.

57 Many commentators refer to ideology as 'false consciousness,' but Marx himself never used the term to describe ideological functions. It was Engels who originally used the term in a letter written to Franz Mehring in 1893. Later, the term was appropriated by Georg Lukács and used in his *History and Class Consciousness* to describe ideological practices.

58 Norman Geras, 'Essence and Appearance: Aspects of Fetishism in Marx's *Capital*,' *New Left Review*, 65, 1971, pp. 69–85.

world as it is in reality because the knower always contributes something to the perception of reality. In Kant's view, what the knower contributes is the main perceptual categories of space and time, and this subjectively alters reality. According to Kant, we are always forced to alter reality in the act of apprehending it. Kant's position was that we misperceive reality because we alter it through the categories of space and time, reason and consciousness. Marx, however, went one step further by showing that our economic production, in fact, shapes the way we come to understand reality itself. But, how could this be possible? The short answer to this question is: because we see the world through a position allotted to us within a social class. According to this reasoning, our apprehension of the world is shaped by our membership in a social class and how – through our class membership in society – we come to use the means of production. For Marx, the perception of reality is altered by the system of production since the social relations which exist within it turn reality upside down in our imaginations. This point may seem obscure, but the process it refers to is simple. Marx believed that our apprehension of the real world is always conditioned by the terms under which we produce and the roles we play in economic production. More specifically, the terms under which we work for our livelihoods condition our perception of the world, and this means that our apprehension of reality is conditioned by our location in a social class. This lived aspect of reality makes our apprehension of life always concrete and consequential. While these relations should reflect human qualities, they often do not and instead appear as relations between things. But, precisely, why? In order to answer this question we need to look at Marx's third building block of the theory of ideology which is its basis in class relations.

The third building block in the theory of ideology is the relationship between ideology and the interests of the dominant classes. Marx wrote:

> The ideas of the ruling class are in every epoch the ruling ideas: i.e., the class, which is the ruling material force of society, is at the same time its ruling intellectual force. The class which has the means of material production at its disposal, has control at the same time over the means of mental production, so that thereby generally speaking, the ideas of those who lack the means of mental production are subject to it. The ruling ideas are nothing more than the ideal expression of the dominant material relationships, the dominant material relationships grasped as ideas; hence of the relationship which makes the one class the ruling one, therefore the *ideas* of its dominance.[59]

This capacity of ideas to invert reality stems, Marx believed, from the fact that they represent the economic interests and dominance of one class of persons over another. Two specific questions remain: (i) what is the specific link between the dominant classes and the ruling ideas; and (ii) how do ideas come to turn reality upside down and rule over our perception? There are many clues in the above quotation: first, the class

59 Marx and Engels, *German Ideology*, p. 39.

which presides over the means of material production 'controls the means of mental production.'[60] This means that with each period of history, the dominance of one class leads to a group of persons who act as 'ideologists,' that is persons or agents who disseminate ideas and beliefs which represent the dominant economic interests of the ruling classes. For example, during the time when an aristocracy was dominant, the conceptions of honour, fealty and allegiance were dominant and so were the categories of submission and belief that went with them. By contrast, during the time capitalism is dominant, the conceptions of 'freedom' and 'equality' are prevalent.[61] What happens during this period of dominance, Marx believed, is that the conceptions and the ideas 'take on the form of universality,' meaning that they disseminate throughout the wider society and take on a life of their own.[62] Then, the dominant classes represent their interests as the common interest and this interest takes on the character of an 'ideal form,' and 'represents them as the only universally valid ideas.'[63] The final step, according to Marx, takes place when the ideologists turn everything upside down. Simply stated, this means that the real relations are represented by conceptions which 'assume an independent existence over and against' individuals and appear to them to be the legitimate system of ideas and social relations. This happens when the ideas and beliefs (the distillates) reflect only the will and interests of a dominant class – specifically the economic and legal ideas of the dominant social class. In realizing the interests of only one class, these social relations stand in a contradictory relation to the class of workers. In this sense, ideology legitimates and justifies the reality of one class. The theory of ideology, therefore, is about how reality comes to be set up in opposition to individuals who are economically outside the dominant ideas.

Having said that the theory of ideology hinges on its capacity to alter our perception of reality – to turn it upside down in the imagination – these ideological distortions can be directly illustrated by drawing on Marx's own examples. A first distortion takes place at the level of value. Marx pointed out that in a society in which exchange is the dominant social relation, value appears to be part of the physical substance of a commodity. This makes commodities appear as if they have intrinsic values and powers when in reality they only have use values. This distortion leads to the fetishism of the commodities, where the commodity appears to have powers which in reality it does not have. Marx would say that in reality objects have no powers, only individuals do. A second distortion occurs at the level of social relations. In a commodity economy, according to Marx, society itself appears to take on a form which reflects economic transactions, with everything being subject to buying and selling.

60 Ibid., p. 39.
61 Ibid., p. 39.
62 Ibid., p. 39.
63 Ibid., pp. 40–1.

This means that in our social relations we confront each other as possessors of commodities, as buyers and sellers, when in reality society is a series of relations between human beings. Under these circumstances, society is reduced to relations of exchange between things having economic value when in reality it is a relationship between human beings who are valuable in themselves.

The Functions of Ideology   The fourth building block of a theory of ideology concerns the functions performed by ideological arrangements in society. So far, we have said that ideology may be defined as any set of beliefs, ideas, conceptions and attitudes whose main function is to conceal class distinctions by making existing social relations appear legitimate. Under these circumstances, ideology has several explicit functions which can be enumerated as follows. First, ideology serves to conceal social contradictions emanating from class distinctions. Second, ideology works to resolve the contradictions in favour of the dominant classes and their interests. Third, ideology serves to legitimate the system of domination by making the contradictions appear as if they were based on natural rather than social distinctions. Fourth, ideology makes appearances take a form directly opposite to actual relations by making it appear as if economic exchange is the sole object and aim of social relations.

Explaining Contradictions   No discussion of ideology would be complete without providing a clear understanding of the concept of contradictions.[64] A contradiction may be thought of as a way of denoting the social, economic and political distinctions between social classes. Marx stated: 'society has hitherto always developed within the framework of a contradiction between free men and slaves; in the Middle Ages, that between nobility and serfs, and in modern times between the bourgeoisie and the proletariat.'[65] For Marx it is clear that the first contradictions emerged in class distinctions and, therefore, classes are the original site of contradictions. To this extent, one of the primary functions of ideology is to make class distinctions, specifically the material differences between classes, appear legitimate rather than contradictory. A contradiction, in this sense, is a concept used by Marx to understand how social distinctions come about due to the existence of social class and how they exist, side by side, in society. Contradictions therefore have their roots in class inequalities and, thus, always reflect the fact that social relations are based on unequal class divisions. The job of ideology is to manage the contradictions by: (i) making them appear as legitimate; and (ii) by explaining the contradictions away by assigning their causes to sources other than social inequalities and class differences.

---

64 See, J. Larrain, *The Concept of Ideology*, Athens, Georgia: University of Georgia Press, 1979, Chapters 1 and 2; and Larrain, *Marxism and Ideology*, Chapter 4.
65 Marx and Engels, *German Ideology*, p. 42.

*Stages of Capitalist Development: Shift from the Economy of the
Country to the Town*

In *The German Ideology* Marx turned his attention to outlining two broad
stages of capitalist development. While it is almost impossible to isolate
the specific conditions leading to the development of capitalism, some of
the historical and economic circumstances which facilitate its emergence
can be pinpointed. In his discussion, Marx restricted himself to pinpointing the development of capitalism in Britain between 1475 and 1850.
The British Empire was the birthplace of the economic revolution and by
1830 had become the 'workshop of the world.' Marx believed that the
beginning of capitalist development coincides with a number of key social
transformations which are rooted in a number of social processes.
Essential to this development is the transition from feudalism to capitalism
which Marx believed is played out in the growing conflict between what he
called the economy of the country and the economy of the town.

By capitalist development, Marx was referring to the shift which took
place from a rural economy to a town economy. Simply stated, this shift
marked the beginning of capitalist society. The process of development
began, Marx pointed out, in the fifteenth century with the dissolution of
the feudal way of life. 'The greatest division of material and mental
labours,' wrote Marx, 'is the separation between town and country.'[66]
Basically, Marx identified two stages of capitalist development. The first
pertained to the growth and expansion of towns and town economies; the
second, to the loss of control by guilds over capitalist expansion. To have
a clear grasp of the changes, it is necessary to develop an understanding of
the conditions existing before capitalism.

In the early stages of feudal society, the rural way of life was dominant.
There were no towns, the economy was entirely agrarian and the productive
system was geared to creating a food supply.[67] Under these circumstances,
industry was mainly confined to weaving in which small producers relied on
hereditary customers. At this stage, wealth was primarily in landed property
and hereditary resources.[68] As the first towns began to develop, they
remained under feudal jurisdiction and almost no independent commercial
life evolved beyond the agricultural economy.[69] Life was lived primarily in
the countryside, commerce between towns was restricted, work was regulated
by guilds, populations at a minimum and communication was limited.

Then, according to Marx, the division of labor began to develop
creating a 'separation between production and commerce.'[70] This led to

66 Ibid., p. 43.
67 R.H. Hilton, *The English Peasantry in the Later Middle Ages*, Oxford: Clarendon, 1975.
68 Marx and Engels, *German Ideology*, p. 47.
69 For further comments on the development of towns, see Perry Anderson, *Passages
From Antiquity to Feudalism*, London: Verso, 1978; and A.B. Hibbert, 'The Origins of the
Medieval Town Patriciate,' *Past and Present*, 3, Feb. 1953, pp. 15–27.
70 Marx and Engels, *German Ideology*, p. 47.

the formation of a new class of merchants who were independent of feudal economies and who began to take on new commercial enterprises which, for the first time, rose above feudal considerations and the old restrictions of tariffs and travel existing between feudal jurisdictions. Towns began to grow and became less dependent on rural economies. Communications between towns began to increase, sparking new development, greater accessibility and a state of order and security between localities.[71]

As these changes took place, there began a period of trade beyond the boundaries of towns, creating further interaction between 'production and commerce.'[72] As a consequence, towns entered into new relations with one another, and exchanged information and methods of production. After some time, this gave rise to an increase in the division of labor which led to some towns becoming dominant over others in specialized branches of industry. By 1750, the remaining feudal restrictions on commerce began to disappear and the common interests of the commercial class began to assert themselves, giving rise to common conditions between localities. As towns gained the upper hand over rural economies, small-scale production in textiles, weaving and potteries began to operate entirely independently of the feudal economy. Though these were not capitalist enterprises as such, the development of new productive techniques and the level and intensity of the division of labor were sufficient to add to the productive push to establish workshops and industries in towns. As a result, towns with trade skills and concentrated crafts began to gain economic and political autonomy by the fifteenth and sixteenth centuries.[73]

A second stage of capitalist development pointed out by Marx is related to the role played by the guild system in economic life, and the consequences of the loss of guild controls over trades and crafts. During the fifteenth and sixteenth centuries, guilds were dominant in economic life. They functioned as professional associations designed to protect and regulate work relating to trades.[74] Chief among their functions was the restriction of competition among workshops and the regulation of expansion and markets.[75] By restricting the number of employees and the kinds of labor which could be put into shops, guilds prevented existing work environments from turning into capitalist enterprises. In effect, guilds opposed capitalist development by blocking specialization and the division of labor necessary for full-scale capitalist production and manufacture. Gradually, however, the power exerted by guilds began to erode and as a result different branches of production began to escape the restrictions of

71 Ibid., pp. 48–9.

72 Ibid., pp. 48–9.

73 Hibbert, 'Medieval Town Patriciate,' pp. 20–4; Anderson, *Passages From Antiquity*, pp. 191–6.

74 Antony Black, *Guilds and Civil Society in European Political Thought from the Twelfth Century to the Present*, London: Methuen and Co., 1984.

75 Maurice Dobb, *Studies in the Development of Capitalism*, New York: International Publishers, 1947, p. 90.

guild regulation altogether. As soon as guilds lost control over trades, regulation began to relax and capitalist expansion increased. Weaving, once regulated by guilds, was one of the first branches of industry to develop. At first, weaving was carried on in the countryside by peasants as a 'secondary occupation,'[76] but, as commercial activity grew and the demand for woolen material increased, the growth of populations and the mobilization of capital resources created further expansion of commerce and this took 'weaving out of the first stage of production in which it existed.'[77] As weaving began to be concentrated in the town, it became subject to a division of labor – setting up forces of social differentiation pushing weaving from rural localities into industrial towns. Under these circumstances, customs and traditions associated with the rural economy began to give way to the commercial practices of the town, leading to the dissolution of the feudal way of life.

In addition to these developments, there was a shift in property relations. At first there was the emergence of private property which had not existed in feudal times. With the creation of private property, there was a money price for land and this hastened the sale and purchase of land as a commodity.[78] As a result of the growth of private property, landholders were able to evict peasant cultivators from the land, making larger and more productive farms commonplace. The production of wool became subject to capitalist enterprise and this led to a period of enclosing lands, advanced agricultural techniques and increased production related to woolen trades. As the pressure between town and country increased, it placed peasant farmers under new forces of social differentiation. As enclosures of land accelerated, seizures of property became common, and peasants were detached from the land as a means of economic livelihood. Eventually, the peasant classes were unable to meet their basic economic needs and were placed at the disposal of the new forces of production, making them a landless class who moved toward the industrial towns to sell their labor in exchange for a wage. By this time, town economies had become dominant over the rural economy.

The second major phase of capitalist development outlined by Marx began in the late seventeenth century and continued to the end of the eighteenth. During this time, development was marked by the convergence of the forces of commerce, navigation and colonization.[79] This led to the universalization of commercial practices and a worldwide economic order based on production and exchange. The existence of colonies led to the opening of new markets, which increased trade, perfected finance and promoted manufacturing. As a consequence, commercial towns began to

76 Marx and Engels, *German Ideology*, pp. 50–1.

77 Ibid., p. 50.

78 Previously, there was no private property in the modern sense of the term since feudal land was subject to a web of obligations and customary rights existing between the landholder and the serf.

79 Marx and Engels, *German Ideology*, p. 54.

take on the appearance of large cities whose standards of life were the outcome of intense commercial enterprises. This led to an established banking system, paper money, stocks and speculation due to the worldwide demand for manufactured products.

Marx believed that the new concentration of productive forces – including manufacturing, capital, free labor, world markets and a growing division of labor – surpassed the old productive forces tied to the land. Large industrial undertakings and universal competition increased communication, giving birth to modern world markets and this 'transformed all [natural] capital into industrial capital.'[80] This gave rise to universal competition forcing 'all individuals to strain their energy to the utmost.'[81] For the first time, this 'produced world history and made all civilized nations and every individual member of them dependent for the satisfaction of their wants on trade and commerce thus destroying the natural exclusiveness of separate nations. Where the natural town once was, in its place there are large industrial cities.'[82] At this stage, Marx believed that the triumph of the commercial town over the countryside was complete. The development and concentration of the productive forces brought the development of one class with a universal interest. At this stage, 'life activity began to coincide with material acquisition and the casting off of all natural relationships.'[83] In conjunction with this, wrote Marx, 'a class is called forth which has to bear all the burdens of society without enjoying any of the advantages. This class is ousted from society and antagonistically opposed to it.'[84]

Marx's Economic Works

Marx's economic writings make up one of the most comprehensive contributions to his social thought. His first major economic work entitled *A Contribution to the Critique of Political Economy* was written in 1859. While this work served as an outline of his major economic study of capitalism, the most comprehensive contribution was the three volume work on the origin and history of capitalist society entitled *Capital*. At the center of Marx's economic contribution, therefore, is his study of capitalist society. While Marx had tackled some of the major elements of capitalist development in *The German Ideology* (co-written with Engels), there are three distinct kinds of issue that Marx wanted to outline in his study of capitalism. First, he wanted to look at the historical emergence of commerce as a dominant way of life. Second, he wanted to outline the framework of the historical changes taking place in the conditions of

80 Ibid., p. 57.
81 Ibid., p. 57.
82 Ibid., p. 57.
83 Ibid., p. 57.
84 Ibid., p. 57.

ownership and use of land and labor that accompanies capitalism. Third, Marx wanted to lay out the fundamental changes taking place in the system of social relations as capitalism began to become established.

Marx, Capital *and the* Critique of Political Economy

It is almost impossible to deal substantively with Marx's economic writings without looking into the history of political economy and the criticism Marx leveled against the political economists and the methods they used to describe capitalist society. First and foremost, the term 'political economy' is used by Marx to refer to a body of work developed by two prominent thinkers, Adam Smith and David Ricardo. More explicitly, political economy is the name given to a school of thought whose thinkers put forward a branch of economic theory which attempted to explain the structural characteristics of capitalist economies. Since economics was not yet an established discipline, political economy was the name given to nineteenth century economic theory.

Both Smith and Ricardo had written powerful books. For his part, Smith was one of the first to outline the basic laws of capitalist development in a work entitled *The Wealth of Nations*, published in 1776 – a work which became one of the most important economic documents ever written. Along with Smith, David Ricardo's *Principles of Political Economy*, published in 1817, became the standard economic theory of the day.[85] Marx's critique of Smith and Ricardo took up a number of central questions related to a theory of capitalism. Let us examine these more closely.

In Volume 1 of *Capital*, Marx engaged the political economists almost as forcefully as he had Hegel. In fact, just as Marx's philosophic side can be understood in relation to Hegel, so his economic aspect can be understood in relation to classical political economy. Marx's critique of the political economists is leveled at Smith's and Ricardo's inability to see how economic laws were the effects of much broader historical and social processes.

Marx attacked political economy on five separate fronts. First he disagreed with Smith's and Ricardo's conception of capitalist society as governed by immutable laws and economic functions. Second, he criticized their tendency to conceive of the common good of society as consisting of the private pursuit of economic gain and their conception of society as an interchange between free merchants who exchange labor and wages in the market. Third, he criticized their work for being totally indifferent to the economic inequalities inherent in acts of exchange. Fourth, he rejected the claim by Smith and Ricardo that value was a 'substance' inherent in commodities. Fifth, Marx criticized the political economists for their theoretical methods and their use of abstract categories, which tended to

---

85 A. Smith, *The Wealth of Nations* and D. Ricardo, *On the Principles of Political Economy and Taxation*, London: Dent, [1817] 1973.

view economic activity as existing above the practical acts of individuals. Let us look at what Marx had to say on four of these central points.

(i) First is Marx's criticism of Smith's and Ricardo's conception of society as a set of fixed economic laws.[86] Smith had put forward an elegant theory of capitalist development in which he stated that the nature of capitalist competition, production and exchange were governed by un-changeable laws of economic activity. Smith had argued that the rela-tionship between commodities, price, wages and profit paralleled natural laws which were self-regulating. If economic laws were unalterable, as Smith had suggested, this meant that the low wages and poverty of the working classes were unalterable as well. Marx criticized these views in several ways. First, he thought that money and commodities alone do not make capitalism. Rather, money and commodities have to be transformed into a system of social relations based on a division between social classes. Second, Marx argued that capitalism is not a system of fixed eternal laws which has existed for all time, but rather came into being at a certain stage of historical development and thus must be looked upon as a historical phenomenon. Third, while political economists essentially described capitalism from the standpoint of scientific functions, Marx saw capitalist society as a system of social relations based on the dominance of one class over another and criticized class inequality from the perspective of historical functions. Fourth, Marx criticized Smith's claim that the main economic categories of capitalism such as commodities, wages, production and labor were universally valid for all societies. Marx thought that they had validity only under particular historical circumstances and were thus tied to a specific mode of production. In his view, political economy had failed to see the social and historical determinants lying behind the transition from one mode of production to the other and thus had failed to see how this transition altered the economic categories. In this case, Marx was able to show that economic categories are derived from historical circumstances and were not expressions of fixed laws. He demonstrated this by looking at the transition from feudalism to capitalism, and by showing that the category 'labor' had been transformed from the labor of the serf to the labor of wages. As far as Marx was concerned, this meant that economic categories were ultimately derived from historical social relations rather than existing as fixed attributes of a given economic system.[87]

In response to Smith's assertion that a capitalist economy was auton-omous and self-regulating, Marx thought that Smith had failed to see the interconnections between human activity and economic life. He therefore criticized Smith's thesis that the economic order was independent of human activity. Wealth, for Marx, was not something independently

86 K. Marx, *Grundrisse: Foundations of the Critique of Political Economy*, Middlesex, England: Penguin, [1953] 1973, pp. 100–11.
87 For Marx's discussion of the methods of political economy, see ibid., pp. 100–8.

produced outside of a mode of production, but was rather inherent in the activity of human labor. By showing that wealth was not some abstract product of economic laws, Marx drew attention to the social relation between labor and capital. Whereas Smith thought that labor and capital were separate, Marx maintained they were interconnected and that, in order to understand capitalism, we had first to understand the underlying basis of the interconnection between the two and their relationship in a mode of production.

(ii) Marx criticized Smith and Ricardo for their tendency to conceive of the common good of society as consisting of the pursuit of private economic gain and for their conception of individuals as free merchants engaged in acts of buying and selling. Smith had stated that in pursuing their self-interest, individuals contribute to the overall good of society by increasing the national prosperity. 'It is not,' wrote Smith, 'through the benevolence of the butcher, the brewer or the baker that we expect our dinner, but from their regard for their own self interest.'[88] In Smith's view, each individual has a duty to pursue monetary gain since it is their self-interest which contributes to the common prosperity of society. Smith went on to reason that, in and of itself, this makes each individual a 'merchant' to the extent that they live by exchange and meet in the market as buyers and sellers of commodities.[89]

In response to this, Marx criticized Smith for being totally indifferent to the economic inequalities inherent in acts of exchange. In response to Smith's assertion that capital and labor meet in the market as equal merchants who freely exchange different commodities (one labor; the other wages), Marx thought that Smith failed to recognize that their 'exchange' was in fact conditioned by their social class. Looked at from this standpoint, the drama between these 'free agents' who are buyers and sellers of labor takes on an entirely different light. Wrote Marx, 'he who is the money-owner strides out in front as a capitalist; the possessor of labor-power follows as his worker. The one smirks self-importantly and is intent on business; the other timid and holds back, like someone who has brought his own hide to market and now has nothing else to expect but a tanning.'[90]

(iii) Third is Marx's criticism of the way political economists conceive of value. Smith had put forward the view that labor adds value to the commodity and this value forms part of the substance of the commodity. In this case, Smith argued that value increases the wealth of society and emerges as commodities exchange for a price on the market. But in this view, value is an attribute of commodities and inheres in it as a 'substance.'[91] This position has come to be known as the labor theory of

88 Smith, *Wealth of Nations*, p. 13.

89 Ibid., p. 24.

90 K. Marx, *Capital: A Critique of Political Economy*, Vol. 1, Middlesex, England: Penguin, [1867] 1976, p. 280.

91 R. Meek, *Studies in the Labour Theory of Value*, London: Lawrence & Wishart, 1973, p. 62.

value, since it takes the view that value is conferred on the commodity by the act of labor.

In response to Smith's claim that value emerges from the interaction of commodities, Marx believed that Smith had failed to see that value was part of a social framework and therefore a historical phenomenon. Marx rejected this view by stating, in the first place, that value is not an independent economic phenomenon, but is in fact related to a whole sequence of social relations which come into being only in a capitalist society. In demonstrating that value is a historical creation, rather than an independent economic phenomenon, Marx was able to shift the dispute from a quantitative argument focusing on price, to a qualitative argument focusing on social relations.[92] One way he had of showing this was to demonstrate that the concept of value as something inherent in a commodity arises only in societies whose system of production is based on exchange and whose commodities are produced for exchange. In this way, Marx was able to show that exchange value was historical. In demonstrating that an active system of commodity production only comes into being in capitalist society, the concept of value became linked to the mode of production rather than being a fixed law of economic activity. This could be directly shown by the example of feudal societies where the products of labor are directly consumed, do not enter into the medium of exchange and, therefore, have only use value.

(iv) Marx criticized Smith and Ricardo for their claim that the economic activities of production, consumption and exchange could be studied as if they were independent economic categories, operating above social and political life. He argued that political economy had failed to consider the fundamental connection between human social life and economic categories. This was shown in Smith's straightforward assumption that production and consumption were independent economic acts. Marx, on the other hand, thought they were fundamentally related to each other and felt they could only be understood as a system of social relations. This is nowhere more evident than in his example of production and consumption. Marx stated that we cannot think of the product as a vague indeterminate object without the concept of consumption, and consumption cannot be thought of without visualizing the active subject. 'A dress,' Marx wrote, 'becomes really a dress only by being worn' and thus, 'a product is a product, not because it is materialized activity, but only in so far as it is an object for the active subject.'[93]

Marx went on to assert that the economic categories of Smith and Ricardo were products of a one-sided theoretical perspective. The fact that their methods looked at only one side in the relation of economic categories was fundamental for Marx, since he looked at these categories

92 Ibid., pp. 63–4.
93 Marx, *Contribution to the Critique*, p. 196.

from the vantage point of their interconnectedness. Drawing upon the concept of the social relation, Marx argued that economic categories are not separate but interconnected and, thus, there are always two sides in any social relationship. In addition, when political economy considered economic phenomena, it did so only from what Marx called the 'non-active side' in the relation – from the side of capital rather than labor. To illustrate, Marx used the example of wealth. He maintained that wealth was not something independently produced outside of a mode of production but was inherent in the activity of human labor. By showing that wealth was not some abstract product of economic laws, Marx drew attention to the social relation between labor and capital. Under these circumstances, Marx thought that political economy was a bourgeois science in two major respects: (i) because it did not look beneath appearances to underlying social relations; and (ii) because it mistook production, consumption and exchange for the reality of economic life when, as far as Marx was concerned, the essence of capitalism was the system of social relations in which everyone is interconnected. Political economy, in this sense, was the science of appearances.[94]

Marx's Study of Capitalism: Capital

Marx's three-volume work *Capital* is the centerpiece of his economic writings. He wrote the first volume of *Capital* between 1855 and 1867, and it made its first appearance in the winter of 1867. A wide-ranging study comprising 33 chapters, *Capital* is a scholarly work grounded in the history of the nineteenth century. Apart from its economic, political and social analyses, it is a vivid picture of nineteenth-century England. It is written in economic, historical and political terms which convey, step by step, the development of industrial capitalism. While *Capital* is unrivaled as a work of social theory, it is also an enormously complicated work because of its immense historical coverage and theoretical scope.

As a historical and theoretical study, *Capital* Vol. 1, can be divided into three main sections: (i) the economic analysis of capitalism; (ii) the historical analysis of capitalism; and (iii) the social consequences of capitalism. The first nine chapters constitute the core of the economic analysis and these tend to be difficult. When read in context with the historical chapters on 'cooperation,' 'the working day,' 'division of labour,' and 'primitive accumulation,' the economic theory becomes clearer in terms of the way it fits into the overall plan of the work as a whole. While it goes beyond the scope of this study to cover the entire text of *Capital*, it is possible to cover the two main substantive sections: (i) those related to the economic theory in particular, such as the chapters on commodities, theory of value, process of exchange, labor process and surplus value, and (ii) those which trace the historical origins of capitalism, such as the

94 Marx, *Grundrisse*, pp. 100–5.

chapters on the working day, the division of labor, machinery and large-scale industry, wages, and primitive accumulation.

Capital, Vol. 1, Part A: Economic and Social Elements of Capitalism

Commodities: Use Value and Exchange Value

Marx began his analysis of capitalism by looking at the commodity. A commodity, according to Marx, is a thing whose qualities are capable of satisfying human needs.[95] Examples of commodities are bread, shoes, gasoline, heating oil, etc. In addition to this, a commodity can be looked at from two different points of view: its use value and its exchange value. Since the distinction between 'use' and 'exchange' is central to Marx's theory of capitalism, let us look more closely at the meaning of the terms.

First and foremost, the use value of a commodity may be defined as the particular quality a commodity has to satisfy human need. The use value of a commodity has several characteristics. First, it refers to the specific social functions a commodity performs in meeting human needs, and so, understood in this sense, use value is the ability of a commodity to render a particular service to an individual. For example, a coat provides warmth, bread diminishes hunger and gasoline facilitates transportation. A second characteristic of the use value of a commodity is its ability to fill only one particular need or function. For instance, the ability of a coat to render warmth cannot be rendered by another commodity such as bread or coal. Understood in this sense, each commodity fills only one particular need, a need which is not transferable to another commodity. This capacity of a commodity to meet only one need was explained by Marx when he talked about the relationship between the physical characteristics of the commodity and the specific function it serves. For instance, bread and coal are commodities whose use values are tied up with the physical properties of the commodities themselves.[96] A third characteristic of use value therefore is that it 'serves directly as a means of existence,' as something that sustains life.[97] Marx thought that because use values perform specific human needs and sustain life, their meaning is always concrete and particular since it serves a direct human purpose.

Marx next turned his attention to the concept of exchange value. While the discussion of exchange is more obscure and difficult to grasp, a first step in understanding Marx's meaning is to note that exchange value only arises in developed economies, and therefore is found only in capitalism. Earlier it was pointed out that one of the key characteristics of capitalism is that commodities are bought and sold, and thus enter into a system of

---

95 Marx, *Capital*, Vol. 1, p. 125.
96 Ibid., p. 126.
97 Marx, *Contribution to the Critique*, p. 28.

exchange. It is important, therefore, to note that the system of exchange is historical and does not develop until capitalist society develops. The clearest example of this is the absence of exchange in feudal societies. In a feudal society production is predominantly for use, since what is produced is immediately consumed to satisfy human needs and sustain life.[98] Thus, what is produced in feudal society only has use value.

Now that the question of exchange can be linked to capitalistic economies we can look more closely at the issue of exchange value itself. Simply stated, exchange value refers to the ability of specific quantities of one commodity, such as one ton of rice, to be expressed in the value of a specific quantity of another commodity, say a quarter of a ton of coffee. This expression takes the form: the value of a quarter ton of coffee is equivalent to one ton of rice, and vice versa. For one ton of rice to have the equivalent value of a quarter of a ton of coffee, the value of the rice must be expressed in the form of the value of the coffee. What looks to be a trade off of use values is in reality a new form of value – one Marx called 'value in exchange.' Exchange value, then, is not one commodity exchanging for another, or one commodity being traded for another, but it is rather quantities of one commodity being *expressed* in terms of the value of quantities of another commodity – any commodity.

While this may be difficult to follow, the meaning of exchange value is fundamental to understanding capitalist social relations and Marx's entire theory of value. What was of interest to Marx here, is the capacity of quantities of one commodity to have their values *expressed* in the form of quantities of another commodity: one ton of rice has the exchange value of a quarter ton of coffee. What riveted Marx's attention was that, as soon as this comparison is made, a 'common element' is found between the two different commodities making their values commensurable in exchange.[99] Two things happen: first, all commodities become comparable in terms of their value in exchange and use value drops out of the equation. Second, in capitalism exchange value becomes dominant to an unprecedented degree, so much so that it shapes all other social relations.

As soon as this takes place, Marx believed a new relation of value emerges which has never been seen before: value in exchange or exchange value. There are three reasons why Marx thought exchange value was so central. First, in reality commodities are not comparable as exchange values, since each commodity serves a unique human function and satisfies a different human need. Second, Marx thought that 'value in exchange' is historical and found only in capitalist society and not in other modes of production. Third, since in exchange, use value disappears because commodities are mutually replaceable with one another, all value in capitalist society is expressed abstractly in terms of a quantitative relation between

---

98 J.M. Barbalet, *Marx's Construction of Social Theory*, London: Routledge, 1983, pp. 89–90.

99 Marx, *Capital*, Vol. 1, p. 127.

one commodity and another.[100] The importance of this will become apparent in a moment.

To illustrate the problem, Marx compared two different commodities: corn and iron. He explained that, whatever their exchange relation may be, both of these commodities have the capacity to be represented by an equation in which a given quantity of one commodity is equated in value with a given quantity of another – two tons of corn with one ton of iron. The crucial importance of this observation is that as soon as the value of one commodity is equated with the value of another, a common ground is established between two essentially different use values: corn and iron.[101] This common ground, Marx believed, does not exist in reality, since each commodity has a unique use value.

The Commensurability of Use with Exchange

After discussing the distinction between use and exchange, Marx turned his attention to looking at the origins of exchange value and its historical derivatives. Marx believed, first, that exchange value arises as a result of a social process having to do with changes in the system of social relations occurring in the transition from feudalism to capitalism. Since in a feudal society there is no system of exchange, and value is not determined by exchange but by use, how then does exchange value arise?

As a capitalist society becomes established, the means of production become the exclusive property of one class, which has the effect of making production private. Subsequently a market forms and what is produced enters into the medium of exchange created by the market. As commodities become subject to buying and selling, Marx stated, exchange value emerges. This can only occur, however, when a comparable basis is found between two commodities so that their values can be expressed in relation to each other. Marx referred to this process as establishing a 'commensurable magnitude' between two commodities.[102] For example, if one ton of rice is to have an exchange value equivalent to a quarter of a ton of coffee, a commensurable quantity of each commodity is arrived at which determines their value in exchange. This takes place, Marx thought, when a quantitative measure is used to arrive at value in the act of exchange.[103] Thus, when commodities are compared in terms of exchange, their values are determined by identifying comparable quantities of each commodity which make them commensurable in the act of exchange. More to the point, 'commensurable magnitude' refers to a process in capitalist society whereby a quantitative measure is established between different quantities of two commodities. If one ton of rice is to have the

100 Marx meant that use drops out only within the context of exchange and within the medium of the market. See ibid., pp. 126–8.

101 Ibid., pp. 127–8.

102 Ibid., p. 141.

103 Ibid., p. 129.

equivalent exchange value of a quarter ton of coffee, Marx is saying that specific quantities of each commodity have to be arrived at to make rice and coffee commensurable in the act of exchange. This exchange value is now expressed by stating that one ton of rice has the same value as a quarter ton of coffee, and vice versa. When commodities enter into exchange with one another, 'one use value is worth just as much as another so long as it is represented in appropriate quantity.'[104]

How, then, is exchange value arrived at? Basically Marx outlined five distinct steps. First, the exchange value between two commodities is arrived at when one kind of use value (rice) is represented by another (coffee).[105] Second, a given quantity of one commodity (one ton of rice) comes to represent the exchange value of a given quantity of another commodity (a quarter ton of coffee). For this to occur, the use value itself has to be immaterial to the act of exchange since, in exchange, commodities are 'mere clumps' represented only by the common magnitudes of weights and measures. Third, a universal ground is established between all commodities in exchange and this ground is represented by quantitative measures only. This, said Marx, reduces all use values to an identical element which they share in common.[106] Fourth, as far as Marx was concerned, this common element cannot be based on the size, shape or intrinsic utility of the commodity since this relates to its use value. Rather, exchange value must itself be based on something else and he reasoned that this 'something else' constitutes the common ground which is found in their quantitative relation to each other.[107] Fifth, 'when commodities are in the relation of exchange, their exchange value manifests itself as something totally independent of their use value.'[108]

Consequences of Exchange on Social Relations

In his discussion of exchange value, Marx went on to look at the effects of exchange on the system of social relations and isolated three separate consequences. First, whenever commodity exchange takes place it is abstracted from use because only the common element of quantity determines exchange. Marx believed that in reality, however, commodities are not comparable in terms of quantity because each commodity serves a unique function and satisfies a particular human need. The importance of this criticism centers on the fact that in order for commodities to be commensurable in exchange, all the useful distinctions between different

104 Ibid., p. 127.
105 Ibid., p. 126.
106 Ibid., p. 127.
107 Ibid., p. 141.
108 Ibid., p. 128. An example of 'exchange being independent of use value' is found in Alfred Sohn-Rethel's *Intellectual and Manual Labour*, London: Macmillan, 1978, where he states: 'there in the shop windows, things stand still. They are under the spell of one activity only; to change owners. They stand there waiting to be sold. While they are there for exchange they are not there for use.' p. 25.

kinds of commodity must be eliminated. A second consequence of exchange is that it eliminates the qualitative distinctions between the different kinds of human labor which produce commodities. Marx thought that all labor was heterogeneous or distinct and that this distinctiveness is expressed by the different skills and abilities of labor – skills and abilities which allow different use values to be produced. This individual quality of labor can be illustrated by comparing two different types of commodities: shoes and coats. The labor which makes shoes and coats is qualitatively different since each has different kinds of skills and abilities, and this is reflected in the different use values of shoes and coats. In capitalist social relations, however, the shoemaker and coatmaker are paid a wage according to the labor time required to produce the shoes and the coats, and the value of the commodities is set according to the price paid to labor. Shoes and coats are thus compared, using a quantitative measure of labor time as a way of arriving at the value of their labor. Marx believed that it is precisely the 'act of equating' the labor of the shoemaker with the labor of the coatmaker that reduces both of their different kinds of labor to characteristics they have in common.[109]

What Marx wanted us to consider here is that the labor which produces the shoes and coats is qualitatively different, so much so that they do not lend themselves to comparison. Their difference exists on two accounts: first as use values – shoes and coats serve two distinct social functions and satisfy two different human needs. Second, since shoes and coats are produced by different kinds of labor and different qualitative skills, neither are comparable and share no common ground. This can be shown by the fact that the labor which produces shoes and coats is the product of the activity of different individuals and, therefore, the result of individually different kinds of labor manifested again in the different use values of shoes and coats.

A third effect of exchange value is its impact on social relations. The criticism which Marx made here is pivotal. He stated that the dominance of exchange becomes so great in capitalist society that it shapes all other social relations, so much so that it acts as the sole determinant of value. Under these circumstances, Marx believed that social relations between persons take the form of economic transactions in which all relationships are reduced to exchange and become subject to buying and selling. This is only possible in a society where all value is determined by the ability of things to enter into the medium of exchange – the market. Marx thought that this was a major reversal of earlier systems of social relations in which human beings were valuable in themselves, independent of the medium of exchange.[110]

109 Marx, *Capital*, Vol. 1, p. 129.
110 Ibid., pp. 133–6.

Labor Theory of Value and the Dual Character of Labor

Following the discussion of exchange, Marx turned his attention to the question of what makes a commodity valuable and this takes us directly into the labor theory of value. At this juncture, it will be useful to look at Marx's predecessors.

Both Smith and Ricardo had put forward a theory of value which took the position that commodities are valuable because of the labor that goes into them. For the most part, Smith and Ricardo focused their arguments on the idea that labor was the sole source of all value, stating that 'it was the real measure of the exchange value of all commodities.'[111] Ricardo, for his part, refined the theory stating that the measurable quantities of labor time were the essence of value and went on to state that these 'quantities' could be calculated in units of labor time. Thus, where Smith tended to locate value in labor generally, Ricardo focused on specific units of labor time that produce amounts of value. This view is called the labor theory of value and it essentially holds that the value of a commodity is created by labor and that value inheres in a commodity as a thing or substance.

While Marx adopted the rudiments of the labor theory of value from Smith and Ricardo, he took two additional steps beyond their work. First, he disagreed with the claim that labor only imparts exchange value to the commodity and thought that political economy had completely overlooked the question of how 'value is transformed into exchange value.'[112] Second, he rejected the view put forward by Smith that only one kind of labor is embodied in the commodity and insisted that there are two elements that labor puts into the commodity. Marx referred to the two elements as the 'dual character of labour' and it is precisely in this that his revision of the labor theory of value went beyond political economy. He believed that the concept of the 'dual character of labour' was one of his most important discoveries.

Useful Labor Marx began by putting forward two characteristics of labor: useful labor and abstract labor.[113] In order to illustrate the distinction between useful and abstract labor, Marx compared two distinct types of commodities: ten yards of linen and one coat. The coat, he observed, sells for twice what the linen sells for and, therefore, has twice the exchange value of the linen. What, asked Marx, makes the coat have twice the value of the linen? This, according to Marx, is a mystery that no political economist has ever solved. He began by pointing out that both the linen and the coat have a use value in that they satisfy distinct human needs and that both the linen and the coat require a certain kind of productive activity to bring this utility into existence.[114] This productive

---

111 Adam Smith, *Wealth of Nations*, p. 44.
112 Marx, *Capital*, Vol. 1, p. 132.
113 Ibid., p. 132.
114 Ibid., p. 132.

activity is determined by a distinct human aim, using a particular means and aiming for a particular result.[115] This he calls 'useful labour' and it may be defined as the capacity of human labor to bring about utility in a commodity and produce simple use values.

Then, stated Marx, it is important to note that the capacity of labor to produce these use values in commodities is, in fact, qualitatively different in each of the different kinds of labor, as is evident in the skills and craft that it takes to produce linen and coats, evident again by the specialized trades existing for weaving and tailoring. It is absolutely essential to understand that 'useful labour' is qualitatively distinct since if it were not, linen and coats could not meet in the market as commodities with different exchange values; they could not, in short, confront each other as commodities. Marx reasoned that since all commodities contain useful labor, use value cannot exist in commodities unless 'the useful labour contained in them is qualitatively different.'[116] What is important to note here is that useful labor, not labor generally, creates use value.

Next Marx looked at how individual acts of useful labor are transformed into commodities. The short answer to this problem is that useful labor is transformed into commodities only in a society in which the products of labor take the form of the commodity. While this may seem obvious, the observation is epochal because Marx has stated that only in capitalist society do the products of useful labor take the form of commodities. In order to illustrate the point, he compared useful labor in different societies. In feudal society, for instance, the products produced by labor never take the form of commodities since there was no system of exchange. Again, neither did the products produced in tribal society assume the form of commodities because their labor was the product of cooperation rather than isolated acts of labor. Looked at from a historical point of view, useful labor has been going on for thousands of years since it is nothing more than the simple creation of utility.[117] Human beings have produced 'coats for thousands of years under the compulsion of the need for clothing' without the coats becoming a commodity or their producers becoming tailors.[118] Labor in its useful form is thus a condition of human existence since it serves a specific material purpose – to sustain life. Labor in its useful form is, therefore, independent of society and is thus a simple condition of human life.

To summarize: while the products of useful labor have always been objects of utility, they have not always been commodities. This indicates that the products of useful labor made under different historical circumstances and different productive arrangements, did not assume the form of commodities. Only in capitalist societies, stated Marx, do the products of

115 Ibid., p. 132.
116 Ibid., p. 133.
117 Ibid., p. 134.
118 Ibid., p. 134.

labor assume the form of commodities and thereby become subject to exchange.

Abstract Labor   Next, Marx turned his attention to abstract labor. The question at hand is, what makes the value of the coat twice that of the linen? To this point we have two distinct types of useful labor (weaving and tailoring), two distinct trades (the weaver and the tailor), and two kinds of value (the value of the linen and the value of the coat). Marx went on to reason that if we set aside what useful labor is in its ability to produce different utilities, what remains is that weaving and tailoring are both 'expenditures of human energy, products of human brains, muscles, nerves, hands etc.'[119] Seen from this perspective, all useful labor shares in common the fact that it is a physiological expenditure of energy.[120] From the perspective of capital, it is possible to leave aside useful labor in all its qualitative distinctions, and focus on nothing more than the expenditure of energy. This central shift from a qualitative to a quantitative framework yields what Marx called 'abstract labour'. From this point of view, tailoring and weaving are now but the quantitative expressions of what was a qualitative distinction in labor. In order to get from useful to abstract labor, an abstraction is made from all the specific qualities, skills and aims of useful labor, an abstraction that focuses only on what is comparable in all labor – an expenditure of energy.

What makes the value of the coat twice that of the linen can now be looked at with some clarity. Marx believed that in a capitalist system of production the useful labor contained in the coat is measured in quantitative terms, and only in this sense is it the same as the labor contained in the linen. When labor is conceived in this way it is abstract labor, and abstract labor is arrived at only in capitalist society when useful labor is measured in terms of 'a temporal duration of labour time.'[121] Here then is the point: in actuality the linen and the coat have the same use value insofar as they both have useful labor in them. In this sense, the value of the coat and the linen is the same, at least when considered in the light of qualitative criteria. But when measured quantitatively, in terms of the duration of labor time, the coat contains *twice* as much labor time as the linen. While from the standpoint of useful labor the amount of labor contained in the linen and the coat are the same, from the standpoint of capitalist production the coat is worth twice as much as the linen precisely because it has quantitatively more labor time in it.

While this may be difficult to grasp, the point is crucial for understanding how Marx went beyond Smith and Ricardo in his revision of the labor theory of value. From the perspective of capital, all labor is conceived of quantitatively as a physiological expenditure of energy and

119 Ibid., p. 134.
120 Ibid., p. 135.
121 Ibid., p. 136.

this reduces all useful labor to a certain amount of movement, nerve, muscle, etc. Labor conceived of in this general rather than differentiated sense is abstracted from useful labor, and Marx called this 'abstract labour'.[122] He wrote:

> to measure the exchange value of commodities by the labour time they contain, different kinds of labour have to be reduced to uniform, homogeneous, simple labour; in short to labour of uniform quality, whose only difference, therefore, is quantity. This reduction appears to be an abstraction, but an abstraction which is made every day in the social process of production. The conversion of all commodities into labour time is no greater an abstraction, and is ño less real, than the resolution of all organic bodies into air. Labour, thus measured by time, does not seem, indeed, to be the labour of different persons, but on the contrary the different working individuals seem to be mere organs of this labour. In other words, the labour embodied in exchange values could be called human labour in general. This abstraction, human labour in general, exists in the form of average labour which, in a given society, the average person can perform, productive expenditure of a certain amount of human muscles, nerves, brain, etc.[123]

It is this abstract labor which has the characteristic of being equal in an expenditure of energy according to the capitalist, and it is thus abstract labor which forms the exchange value of commodities.

A proof of Marx's reasoning exists in the example of modern industrial production. In a complex society with an advanced division of labor, two coats can be produced in the time it took to produce one in previous societies. From the side of useful labor, this means twice the use value has been created. But, from the perspective of capital the same amount of labor quantitatively conceived has been spent and is paid at the rate of one hour of labor. While this increase in the production of use values (two coats for one) means an increase in material wealth for the capitalist, this wealth is not shared by the worker. No matter how productive, the same labor carried on for a specified amount of time produces value by units of time.

Capital, Vol. 1, Part B: The Theory of Value

The Origin of Value and the Value Form

After the discussion of useful and abstract labor, Marx turned his attention to putting forward a theory of value, focusing on the history and origin of value itself. Essentially, he began with two kinds of facts in hand. The commodity has a dual nature in that it is both an object of utility and a bearer of value in exchange. But, asked Marx, in what form does this value exist? While his response is confusing and even controversial, it is absolutely fundamental to understanding Marx's theory of value. Marx

122 Ibid., p. 137.
123 Marx, *Contribution to the Critique*, pp. 30–1.

began by asserting that the value a commodity has is not part of its nature. Value in this sense is not a substance found in a commodity, for this is impossible. 'Not one atom of matter enters into the objectivity of commodities as values.' If we take the linen or the coat, 'we may twist and turn a simple commodity as we wish, it is impossible to find the substance which represents its value. No chemist has ever found this substance reposing in the commodity as such.'[124]

It is clear that almost all of Marx's theoretical rigor is brought to bear on this single point of analysis; namely, in what form does value exist? In his response to the question he rejected the claim put forward by political economy that the commodity is a bearer of value. Marx maintained that the exchange value of a commodity does not lie in it as a substance, but is rather a product of a social framework and thus lies hidden in what he called the 'value form.'[125] He believed that for the answer to this question we had to look behind the value form itself. According to Marx, the origin of value lies not in the laws of the exchange of commodities but rather in the system of social relations. So, in order to arrive at the secret of value, 'we have to perform a task never attempted by political economy.'[126]

Marx went on to reason that since the value a commodity has is not a substance which lies in it, then value must be an expression of something else! This form of value Marx called the 'relative form of value,' and this is the key to his theory of value.[127] Once this crucial step is understood, the commodity can be taken out of the shadows as a thing possessing value in its own right and seen in reality as a thing in relation to other things.

Relative and Equivalent Forms of Value

Our starting point is the idea that value does not inhere in the commodity itself. Therefore the value of a commodity, according to Marx, is of a relative form. By the term 'relative,' Marx meant that the value of a commodity can only be arrived at in 'relation to' other commodities. In this view, no commodity can have value in isolation, by itself. Rather, the value of any commodity must be expressed relatively – or, to put it another way, in relation to some other commodity. The example used by Marx is the value of linen. He stated, the value of 20 yards of linen cannot be expressed in terms of the linen itself. We can't say '20 yards of linen is worth 20 yards of linen.'[128] For linen to have value, the value must be expressed in relation to some other commodity. Hence, no value as such lies hidden in the commodity as a solitary independent object. But, when

124 Marx, *Capital*, Vol. 1, p. 138.

125 For an expanded discussion of this question see I.I. Rubin, *Essays on Marx's Theory of Value*, Montreal: Black Rose, [1928] 1973, pp. 63–75.

126 Ibid., pp. 63–75.

127 Marx, *Capital*, Vol. 1, pp. 139–40.

128 Ibid., p. 139.

linen is compared with another commodity the picture changes and exchange value emerges as soon as this comparison is made.[129] For this to take place some other commodity such as a coat must confront linen in an equivalent form of value.

The mystery of value can now be resolved. Stated simply, 'value' emerges at the moment when one commodity is compared with another commodity and is brought into relation with it. Marx reasoned that if no commodity has value by itself, then value does not belong to a commodity naturally but is rather a product of social relations which exist within an ongoing framework of society. Hence 'exchange value' emerges only at a historically given epoch, precisely at the moment when, in capitalist production, the value of one commodity is brought into a relation of exchange with another commodity.[130]

To this point the value of a commodity is determined by its relation to some other commodity, and this Marx called 'relative value.' But in order to complete the analysis, we have to get behind the phenomenon of value itself and to do this Marx introduced the term 'equivalent value.' While theoretical debate on the concept of equivalent value is unclear and contentious, it will be sufficient to state only some rudiments of the concept of equivalent value. Marx stated that value occurs when the relative and equivalent forms of value confront each other. Thus the relative and equivalent forms of value constitute 'two poles of the expression of value' and, therefore, in order for value to occur commodities must confront each other in these two forms.[131] Value emerges, according to this view, only when two commodities enter into a comparison with respect to their relative and equivalent forms.[132] For example, as stated previously the value of linen cannot be determined until it is brought into comparison with the value of the coat. Linen does not know its own value until it is reflected in the mirror provided by the value of the coat.[133] The valuing moment, Marx reasoned, occurs when the relative and equivalent forms of value swap meanings so to speak, so that the value comes to rest temporarily in the commodity and, in this case, assumes the form of the coat. 'The whole mystery of value,' wrote Marx, 'lies hidden in this simple form.'[134]

The distinction between relative and equivalent forms of value can be made clear by drawing on Marx's example of linen and coats once again. We can say that the linen has value only in relation to the coat since it is in relation to it that the exchange value of linen emerges. 'The first commodity plays an active role, the second a passive one. The value of the

129 Ibid., p. 139.
130 Ibid., p. 142.
131 Ibid., p. 139.
132 Ibid., p. 148.
133 Alan Carling, 'Forms of Value and the Logic of Capital,' *Science and Society*, 50, 1986, pp. 52–80.
134 Marx, *Capital*, Vol. 1, p. 139.

first commodity is represented as relative value. The second commodity fulfils the function of equivalent, in other words it is in the equivalent form.'[135] The coat serves in the role of equivalent value for two reasons: its state is more 'worked up' than the linen and, second, it is the standard against which the value of linen is established. Marx stated: 'the relative form of value and the equivalent form are two inseparable moments which belong to and mutually condition each other, but at the same time they are mutually exclusive or opposite extremes, i.e., poles of the expression of value.'[136] A good example of this problem is provided by Alan Carling who compares the two forms of value to Lacan's mirror stage of development. He says, the linen 'does not know what it is until it is reflected in the mirror of the coat; until it sees itself as the coat. Like the infant, linen exists only in the eyes of another.'[137] Or as Marx put it: 'the value only comes to look like the coat,' that is, it takes the form of the coat, or the coat form.

Fetishism of Commodities

To this point we have shown that Marx's criticism of capitalism centers on the question of the commodity and the dominance of exchange value over use. Marx's view on this issue raised two fundamental theoretical questions: first, that a commodity only has value in relation to some other commodity, and second, that value is part of a social framework rather than a substance which inheres in a commodity. We now turn to the final extension of Marx's investigation of value which is found in his discussion of commodity fetishism.

Marx began *Capital* by tracing the origin of value down to what he often called its 'inner connections' and by this he meant that it was necessary to look for the social origins of value within society and the system of production. This line of investigation was unique because the underlying claim by Marx was that commodities only have use values and that 'value' itself was not a substance to be found in commodities. This position taken by Marx is key to understanding his theory of value since his assertion was that value is not a substance found in commodities but rather a product of a social framework. If value is not to be found in commodities, then where is it to be found? Stated simply: value, according to Marx, only exists in use or utility, and this form of value is distinct from exchange in that it is directly connected to existence. Exchange value, on the other hand, is distinct and different. Simply put, 'not one atom' of exchange value lies in the commodity and therefore the origin of value itself must lie within the social framework.[138] It is at this point that the concept of the fetish took on meaning for Marx. Simply stated, a fetish is

---

135 Ibid.
136 Ibid., pp. 139–40.
137 Carling, 'Forms of Value,' pp. 52–80.
138 Marx, *Capital*, Vol. 1, p. 138.

the display of unusual devotion toward a material thing or object in the belief that it has extraordinary powers. The concept of commodity fetishism is used by Marx to indicate the process whereby individuals assign value to commodities and believe that they have extraordinary powers. But, why the fetishism of commodities? Commodities have only simple use values, and not one atom of value is to be found in the commodity as a substance.[139] Marx used the term fetishism, then, to describe the tendency in capitalism first, to believe that value is a substance inherent in commodities; and second, to pinpoint the inclination to assign extraordinary powers to commodities.

Marx's theory of value stands in dramatic contrast to the theory of value put forward by Smith and Ricardo. It was Marx's view that they had overlooked the question of value on two specific counts: first, on economic grounds political economists believed that commodities were bearers of value as was evident in their price; and second, on methodological grounds they terminated investigation into the 'nature of commodities' and thus came to the question of value *post festum*.[140] As a result, political economists left aside the actual social process by which value came to reside in commodities. Let us look more closely into Marx's theory of commodity fetishism.

Marx began his discussion by pointing out that while commodities appear to be trivial things, they have a mysterious nature in that they manifest powers which we believe are part of their nature.[141] This mysterious power, however, arises not from the use value of a commodity since, at the level of use, commodities satisfy only human needs and thus there is nothing mysterious about them. But as soon as a system of exchange arises, commodities acquire a mysterious nature. Only in societies whose social relations are at this stage, Marx argued, are individuals compelled to believe that 'value' is a substance which inheres in the commodity and only at this stage does the commodity begin to take on extraordinary powers. While this may be difficult to grasp, the point is central to Marx's theory of value. The mysterious nature of commodities occurs only in societies whose social relations mistakenly compel individuals to believe that the value of a commodity is, in fact, part of its nature.

Marx asserted that when commodities are believed to have value in and of themselves, we mistakenly assign powers to them which they do not have in reality. To understand this process, Marx looked at religion in

139 Marx stated: 'Not one atom of matter enters into the objectivity of commodities as values. We may twist and turn a simple commodity as we wish, it is impossible to find the substance which represents its value. No chemist has ever found this substance reposing in the commodity as such.' ibid., p. 138.

140 Literally, 'after the feast.' Marx used the term to point out that there must have been a process by which value was formed and that, historically, this formation had been overlooked by political economists because they examined only the product of this process.

141 Marx, *Capital*, Vol. 1, p. 163.

tribal societies.[142] In tribal societies, individuals assign magical powers to objects because they believe these powers grow out of the nature of the objects themselves. Marx argued that it is their beliefs, in fact, that lead them to think that powers reside in the object. Marx stated that, by themselves, objects have no powers, and he thought that the hidden source of this power was, in fact, the individual's active relation to the object. This relation is shaped by none other than the system of social relations in which these beliefs are imbedded. Marx thought that the same process takes place in capitalist societies, where individuals confer extraordinary powers and capacities on commodities – a process he called commodity fetishism. How, then, do commodities obtain these powers and how do we come to believe that their value is part of their nature?

The first thing that Marx looked at was the system of exchange. In capitalism, commodities are produced for exchange and so capitalism is a society whose system of commodity production is based on exchange. Marx believed that it is only at this stage in the history of social development that, as articles of exchange, 'the products of labour acquire a socially uniform objectivity as values.'[143] From this perspective, commodity fetishism is historical in that it arises only in societies whose commodities enter into the medium of exchange. Marx then pointed out that the objectivity that commodities have in exchange is different from the 'objectivity [they have] as articles of use.'[144] The defining moment, for Marx, was that commodities appear to be bearers of value only when production is for exchange rather than in the service of use. Having been produced for exchange, commodities appear to enter into social relations with one another and their value appears to be part of their nature.

To make this point clear, it will be useful to make a distinction – which Marx made often enough – between feudal and capitalist societies. In feudal societies the relation of the individual to the society was predominantly governed by use values, since production was primarily for immediate use.[145] Here, the serf is directly connected to the means of production and labor is for purposes of creating use value which serves immediate economic purposes. The important fact about feudal society is that production is not separate from consumption since everything produced is used for the maintenance of life. Thus, what is produced does not assume the form of a commodity because it does not enter into the medium of exchange. To reiterate Marx's point: what is produced in feudal society never assumes a form different from its reality as use value. Hence their social relations do not take the form of exchange and there is no fetishism of commodities.

---

142 Ibid., p. 165.
143 Ibid., p. 166.
144 Ibid., p. 166.
145 Barbalet, *Marx's Construction of Social Theory*, pp. 89–90.

Contrast this with capitalist society. Here, the producers' direct relation to the land has been dissolved and, as workers, they are compelled to sell their labor in exchange for a wage. Under these circumstances, what is produced by labor is not consumed directly, since it must enter into the medium of exchange. In this case, and only in this case, do the products of labor assume the form of commodities.[146]

To get to the bottom of the problem of fetishism we need to take a few more steps. So far, we have shown that in a feudal society the products of labor do not acquire a form different from their reality as use values and their direct function of fulfilling human need. The question, then, is: in capitalist social relations, how do commodities obtain powers beyond their simple use values? The answer to this question is twofold. First is in the system of exchange created by capitalism. Capitalism is distinct from feudalism since it is only in capitalism that commodity production is based on a system of exchange. In all societies up to the development of capitalism, production was primarily for use and recognized as a social process. Fetishism can thus be described as the stage in the development of commodity production when value is believed to grow from the physical properties of the commodity as it enters into the circuit of exchange. Second is in the transformation of social relations which occurs in capitalism. In all societies up to the development of capitalism, social relations have been between individuals. Only in the stage of commodity fetishism, however, does it appear that social relations are between things (articles of value) rather than between individuals.[147] Fetishism, in this sense, can only be described as the stage in which human beings are dominated by their products and compelled by the powers these products have over them.

A further characteristic of commodity fetishism is the tendency to eliminate what Marx referred to as the 'two-fold social character' of production.[148] Marx believed that production serves two basic and primary purposes: first, it provides use value which serves directly as a means of existence; and second, the production of use value is inherently a social activity in that it plays a role in collective social processes and is fundamental to the extension of social life. This situation existed in feudal society so far as production filled the needs of others, was inherently useful, and part and parcel of collective life. Under these circumstances, everyone is dependent – serfs, lords, laymen and clerics.[149] This dependence characterizes their social relations of production as much as it did other spheres of social life. Precisely because these relations of dependence form the basis of their social frameworks, 'there is no need for labour and

---

146 Marx, *Capital*, vol. 1, p. 166.
147 I.I. Rubin's discussion of fetishism is among the best. See his *Essays on Marx's Theory of Value*, pp. 5–60.
148 Marx, *Capital*, vol. 1, p. 166.
149 Ibid., p. 170.

its products to assume a fantastic form different from their reality.'[150] In fact their social relations take the form of their transactions and appear in the form of services and obligations in kind. Here, 'the natural form of labour is its immediate social form and the form that their labour takes in fact parallels the form of their social relations. Here, social relations between individuals in the performance of their labour appears as their personal relations and is not disguised as social relations between things.'[151] Their labor, according to Marx, is labor in common and what is produced does not confront them as commodities with independent value. The labor which creates these products is in their natural form, social functions, since their socially useful character is manifested in their direct use value to others.

In capitalism, by contrast, social relations take the form of exchange. The relations of dependency which once existed in feudal society are replaced by what Marx called the 'private producer.'[152] In this case, all the characteristics of labor are individual rather than social. Essential to capitalism, therefore, is the isolated individual who performs common social functions only for the purpose of private economic gain. All the activities of buying and selling, of producing and consuming are for private gain and private interest. All the relations connecting the individual producer to the rest of society are in fact mediated by relations of exchange. Thus, all their social relations can be looked upon as taking exactly the same form as the transactions of society, namely ones of exchange.[153] It is Marx's view that only when social relations are dominated by exchange do individuals confront each other as buyers and sellers, producers and consumers and as possessors of commodities. This, asserted Marx, leaves human beings in a narrow, shrunken individuality – the individuality of exchange relations. In capitalism, private producers can only find the socially useful nature of their labor by personally reflecting on the utility of what they produce. The specific social character of their private labors consists, therefore, only in its nature as human labor.[154] Furthermore, what they produce conceals the social nature of their private labors and thus the social relations between individuals appear as relations between material objects. Social relations between individuals become obscure since they assume the form of relations between things; between buyers and sellers, producers and consumers.

It is at this point in the development of commodity capitalism, Marx believed, that the transactions between material things take on the fetish

150 Ibid., p. 170.

151 Ibid., p. 170.

152 Sometimes Marx refers to the private producer as 'private labour,' and in some cases the 'isolated individual.' Whatever the usage, it is key to understanding the system of social relations in capitalism. See ibid., p. 172.

153 Ibid., p. 170. Marx's discussion of the connection between the shape of society and the system of transactions is significant.

154 Ibid., p. 167.

form. Commodities appear to have a life of their own and enter into social relations with one another, and as such appear to have human qualities. Fetishism 'is nothing but the definite social relation between human beings which assumes the fantastic form of the relation between things.'[155] Under these circumstances, what was once human is now thing-like and what was thing-like is now human. As a direct consequence, human social relations become 'thing-like' insofar as individuals confront each other as the possessors of commodities, and insofar as they believe that value resides in the commodity rather than themselves. Things appear to have a human form only so far as they enter into social relations; while human beings appear to have a thing-like form because they are themselves subject to acts of exchange and in this sense lose their human qualities. Since their social relations reflect their transactions, all their social relations are not direct relations between individuals but rather 'material relations between persons and social relations between things.'[156] Fetishism in this sense brings about a 'fantastic reversal.' That is, to the extent that social relations between individuals are governed by the interaction of things, the interaction of things assumes human qualities so far as they have: (i) social relations among one another because they enter into exchange; and (ii) because they are believed to be exclusive determinants of value. Like objects of religious worship, they are 'endowed with a life of their own which enters into relations both with each other and with the human race.'[157]

Marx believed that the social effects of the process of fetishism can be outlined in several ways. First, under commodity fetishism, relations among people take the form of the relation among things. At this stage, social life is mediated by what he calls the exchange of matter. In this 'fantastic relation,' human beings confront one another as economic subjects – as agents of economic categories and as possessors of commodities. As possessors of commodities, human beings are simply carriers of economic processes and, so long as this is the case, it obscures both their human form and the human form of society.

Reification of Economy and Society

After his discussion of fetishism Marx looked at the overall effects of exchange on the system of social relations. He referred to this as the process of 'reification.'[158] He began the discussion of reification by assuming at the outset that human beings make society. In fact; he believed that the individual and society are unitary things, since human beings create society by their labor. Taking into account the fact that human beings make society, reification reverses this process by making it

155 Ibid., p. 165.
156 Ibid., p. 165.
157 Ibid., p. 165.
158 Ibid., pp. 1045–55.

appear as if society gives birth to human beings. To the extent that economic functions make it appear as if society creates human beings rather than the other way around, reification is the experience of society in the form of objects and processes which are independent of human beings and which dominate over them. In the process of reification, stated Marx, the forces of society confront the individual as something objective or ready-made, existing as if it were without their intervention.[159]

Marx believed that reification originates from the fact that economic categories in capitalism are so predominant that they lead to the belief that society and human behavior stem from the categories of production, when, in fact, it is the other way around. While in reality economic categories stem from human labor and are produced by human beings, reification reverses this process by attaching human purposes to economic forces (for example, the 'needs' of capital and the 'drives' of production), and this makes them appear as if they were human. When this takes place economic processes are 'personified' and take on human qualities, consequently reifying human activity by making it thing-like. In this case, individuals become outcomes of capitalist social functions and appear to enter into economic activity as if it were their nature. From this standpoint human beings appear as if 'they arose' from economic processes and 'belonged to them' in the first place.[160] Reification can be conceived of as the historical moment in the process of commodity capitalism when the characteristics of 'thinghood' become the standard of objective reality.

Capital, Vol. 1, Part C: Theory of Surplus Value

To this point we have looked at some of the central arguments in the development of capitalism, focusing on the commodity and the dominance of exchange. This has taken us from the discussion of commodities to the theory of value; to the stage of the fetishism of commodities, abstract labor and reification. The commodity occupied the center of discussion.

The focus of the next section of *Capital* hinges on Marx's discovery of surplus value. In order to adequately understand what Marx meant by surplus value we have to go through four separate steps: (i) to describe the emergence of what Marx called 'free labour' and labor power; (ii) to make the distinction between necessary and surplus labor; (iii) to describe the importance of the working day and its relation to the history of surplus labor; and (iv) to describe the development of the wage form in relation to unpaid labor. In addition to these steps, there are two conceptual problems remaining which will make our discussion more complete. These are the concepts of labor power and the wage form. Let us begin with free labor and labor power.

159 Ibid., pp. 1045–55.
160 Ibid., p. 1055.

Free Labor and the Emergence of Labor Power

The starting place of the theory of surplus value begins with the concept of free labor. Marx's discussion of the development of 'free labour' and 'labour power' is to be found in Chapter 6 of *Capital*.[161] While only a short chapter, the concepts in this section are key to understanding Marx's theoretical position. We can begin by pointing out two fundamental historical facts: first, capitalism has replaced feudalism. As a result, the serfs' relation to the land as source of livelihood has been dissolved, forcing serfs to sell their labor as a commodity. Second, in capitalism the aim was to purchase labor at sufficiently low rates to make a profit. For the capitalists to make a profit, they must be able to find a commodity on the market which has the property of creating more value than it costs to purchase. According to Marx, the only commodity that answers this demand is human labor. Marx went on to say that human labor has two essential attributes which fit this demand: (i) it is found on the market and can be purchased as if it were a commodity; and (ii) it produces more value than the price it is purchased at. The name Marx gave to the commodity which the capitalist buys is 'labour power.' But, why not just labor?

The answer to this question is reasonably straightforward. The term 'labour power' enabled Marx to make a central distinction between 'labour' as a human activity and 'labour power' as a capacity to add use values to commodities – a distinction not made by the political economists. Both Smith and Ricardo believed that it was simply 'labour' that was exchanged and purchased by the capitalist. Marx thought, however, that political economists had erred in their understanding of the term and went on to make a distinction between 'human labour' and 'labour power' in order to show that there existed an intervening category of labor.[162] Human labor, in contrast to labor power, is the actual work and physical activity incorporated in the body of the laborer. Labor power, on the other hand, refers to the capacity of labor to add use values to commodities and is the name Marx gave to the commodity sold to the capitalist at a value less than the value it creates. Here is the point: in purchasing the worker's capacity to labor and add use values to commodities the capitalist is able to profit while at the same time paying less to the worker in wages than the value created by his or her labor. This distinction between 'labour' and 'labour power' allowed Marx to pinpoint the precise mechanism which creates profit in capitalist society since, in order to profit, capitalists must find a commodity on the market which has the property of creating more value than it costs to purchase. What Marx pointed out in his distinction was that what the capitalist actually buys is not 'labour' outright, since if it were, slavery would be reintroduced. Rather, the capitalist buys 'labour

161 Ibid., pp. 270–80.
162 Raya Dunayevskaya, *Marxism and Freedom*, London: Pluto Press, 1971, p. 34.

power'. Labor power has two essential attributes: (i) it is found on the market and purchased as if it were a commodity; and (ii) it produces more value than the price at which it is purchased. In this respect, Marx had taken a leap beyond political economy. That is, in splitting labor into two categories – human labor and labor power – Marx found that the second category, labor power, was what the worker sold to the capitalist.[163]

In order for the capitalist to find labor power on the market as a commodity, two essential conditions must be met. First, the possessor of labor power (the worker) must be in a position to sell his or her labor as a commodity, and second, the laborer must seem to be the 'free proprietor' of his or her own 'labour capacity' in the sense of being able to dispose of it as he or she sees fit.[164] This very precise condition of being 'free' to dispose of one's own labor capacity on the market is called 'free labour' and it is fundamental to capitalism since it makes the buying and selling of labor power possible.

As Marx stated earlier, for capitalism to exist the owner of labor power must be in a position to sell his or her labor to a buyer. Under these circumstances, one would tend to assume that in a free market both seller and buyer meet on an equal basis and that both are governed by the laws of exchange. Both Smith and Ricardo believed this to be true. They took the view that in capitalist societies laborers are free to sell labor power in the market and, because of this, they are the sole proprietors of their own commodity. This position led Ricardo to take the view that so far as workers seek to sell their labor power for a price, they may be thought of as existing on the same economic footing as the capitalist, since both enter into free economic exchange.

Marx disagreed with this on several grounds. First, the laborer is without the means to sell products of his or her labor since, by definition, a laborer is in the condition of being without the means of production. Second, since laborers cannot sell commodities produced by their own labor, they must sell as a commodity the labor power existing in their own bodies.[165] Marx reasoned that when we look again at the drama between buyer and seller, it is obvious that the advantage is conferred to the buyer of labor power since 'the buyer of labour power strides out in front as a capitalist; the possessor of labour power follows as the worker. The one smirks self importantly and is intent on business; the other is timid and holds back, like someone who has brought their own hide to market and now has nothing to expect but a tanning.'[166]

'Free labour' thus constitutes only the 'appearance of freedom' since in all cases the worker is compelled to offer his or her labor for sale and cannot exist without doing so. If we look carefully at the conditions which

163 Ibid., p. 34.
164 Marx, *Capital*, Vol. 1, p. 270.
165 Ibid., p. 272.
166 Ibid., p. 280.

make it appear as if the worker is a 'free' agent who enters into contractual relations to sell his or her labor power, in reality the 'period of time for which he is free to sell his labour power is the period of time for which he is forced to sell it.'[167]

Surplus Labor, Surplus Value and the Maintenance of the Worker

The next step Marx took was that of fitting the concept of necessary and surplus labor into the picture. We can look at this by reviewing the process Marx described as the 'reproduction of the worker.'[168] This refers to the process by which workers must use part of their wages to maintain their actual physical existence as workers. Since labor power exists in the living body of the individual, it makes sense to reason that the physical energy the worker expends must be replaced. As labor power expends itself, it must be replaced each day in order for the laborer to repeat the process. In this regard, the physical needs of workers such as food, shelter and clothing have to be satisfied each day in order for workers to maintain themselves and continue to sell their labor power. Thus, laborers have to be supplied on a daily basis with the necessary food and fuel in order to 'renew their life processes.'[169]

Drawing on the discussion of the maintenance of the worker, Marx made a conceptual distinction which triggers the first key observation regarding surplus value. This consists of essentially two concepts: (i) necessary labor and (ii) surplus labor. Necessary labor refers to the part of the work day it takes for the worker to produce in wages the cost of his or her own maintenance. Marx reasoned that if the workday is 12 hours, it takes approximately 6 hours of labor to produce the cost of maintaining the worker in food, fuel, shelter and clothing. Surplus labor, on the other hand, refers to the part of the working day in which the laborer expends labor power, but creates no value for him or herself.[170] In this part of the workday the laborer adds value to the products worked on, and the value the worker creates during this part of the day belongs to the capitalist alone, not to the laborer.

Marx took this reasoning one step further. He stated that the laborer is paid only for one part of the workday – 6 hours rather than 12 – and that the unpaid part constitutes the 'surplus,' and it is this part which produces the value for the capitalist. In the concept of surplus labor, Marx identified the portion of the working day in which the labor of the worker is over and above the labor workers need to reproduce themselves. Marx called this added labor, 'surplus labour.' In surplus labor 'the workers expend their labour, but this creates no value for them. Instead, they create surplus value which, for the capitalist, has all the charms of something

167 Ibid., p. 415.
168 Ibid., p. 275.
169 Ibid., p. 276.
170 Ibid., p. 325.

created out of nothing. This part of the working day, I call surplus labour time, and to the labour expended during that time, I give the name surplus labour.'[171] Surplus value, therefore, is the value created by surplus labor. Surplus value has four central attributes: (i) it is the value created by the surplus labor of the worker; (ii) it is unpaid and therefore creates value for the capitalist but not the worker; (iii) it presents a deception since it claims to be paid labor; (iv) it is the recognized form of overwork and thus goes to the heart of the exploitation of the worker in that the worker is not paid for the wealth he or she creates by producing surplus labor.

The History of Surplus Labor: the Working Day

The third step in resolving the theory of surplus value is to be found in Marx's discussion of the workday and the history of surplus labor. In Chapter 10 of *Capital*, Marx pointed out that 'surplus labour' is not new and in fact has a historical basis, only reaching its highest stage of development in capitalist societies.[172] This can be made clear if we contrast capitalism with feudal and slave societies. In a feudal society the surplus labor carried out by the serf for the lord 'is demarcated very clearly both in space and time.'[173] In the corvée right, the lord demands free labor service and this is clearly unpaid. In slavery, the unpaid nature of the labor is also clear in that all labor by the slave appears as labor for the master. In these two instances – feudalism and slavery – unpaid labor appears as unpaid. Only in capitalism, however, does unpaid labor appear as paid. Marx stated that the unpaid portion of the worker's labor disguises itself as paid labor and, therefore, the capitalist system of wages and the means of their calculation is deliberately deceptive. In all other systems of production, including feudal and slave societies, unpaid labor is clearly demarcated. Only in capitalism is surplus labor 'extorted from the immediate producer' since it presents itself as paid and thus enters into a deception.[174]

To get to the bottom of this question, Marx believed that surplus labor had its recognized form in all societies and that it had obvious roots in the social inequalities created by the system of ownership and class structure. The recognized form of overwork in feudal society was the corvée system, in Greece and Rome it was slavery, and in capitalism it is wage labor.[175] Capital, Marx wrote 'did not invent surplus labour, since whenever a part of society possesses the monopoly of the means of production, workers, free or unfree, must add to the labour time necessary for their own maintenance an extra quantity of labour time in order to produce the means of subsistence for the owner of the means of production, whether

171 Ibid., p. 325.
172 Ibid., pp. 344–53.
173 Ibid., p. 680.
174 Ibid., p. 325.
175 Ibid., pp. 344–8.

this proprietor be an Athenian, an Etruscan theocrat, a Wallachian boyar, a modern landlord or a capitalist.'[176]

It stands to reason that since surplus labor benefits the owner of the means of production, then the appetite for surplus labor would be unlimited. In order to demonstrate this Marx examined the history of overwork in various societies. A dramatic example, used by Marx, occurs in Roman history when, in the Roman gold mines, workers were compelled to work until they died. In the feudal system, surplus labor appears in the form of a debt obligation in which the serf owes the lord 12 days of labor.[177] Only in capitalist society does this exploitation take the form of surplus value, and its form of overwork is wage labor.

The Wage Form: Unpaid Labor

Finally, the fourth step. In Chapter 19 of *Capital*, Marx examined the history of wages and looked closely into the development of the 'wage form.'[178] Marx believed that the 'wage form' was a deceptive method of compensating the worker, and argued that it makes unpaid labor appear as if it were paid labor. By making surplus labor appear as paid labor, the workers are deceived into believing that, by their labor, they only maintain themselves, when in reality the unpaid portion increases the wealth of the capitalist. As far as Marx was concerned, this was the most powerful expression of appearances distorting reality. This is stated very clearly in the text:

> We see further: the value of 3 shillings, which represents the paid portion of the working day, i.e., 6 hours of labour, appears as the value or price of the whole working day of 12 hours which thus includes 6 hours which have not been paid for. The wage-form thus extinguishes every trace of the division of the working day into necessary labour and surplus labour, into paid labour and unpaid labour. All labour appears as paid labour. Under the [feudal] system it is different. There the labour of the serf is for himself, and his compulsory labour for the lord of the land is demarcated very clearly both in space and time. In slave labour, even the part of the working day in which the slave is only replacing the value of his own means of subsistence, in which he therefore actually works for himself alone, appears as labour for the master. All his labour appears as unpaid labour. In wage labour, on the contrary, every surplus labour or unpaid labour appears as paid. In the one case, the property relation conceals the slave's labour for himself; in the other case the money-relation conceals the uncompensated labour of the wage-labourer. . . .
>
> All the notions of justice held by both the worker and the capitalist, all the mystifications of the capitalist mode of production, all capitalist illusions about freedom, all the apologetic tricks of vulgar economics, have as their basis the form of appearances discussed above, which makes the actual relation invisible, and indeed presents to the eye the precise opposite of that relation.[179]

176 Ibid., pp. 344–5.
177 Ibid., p. 347.
178 Ibid., pp. 675–82.
179 Ibid., p. 680.

Capital, Vol. 1, Part D: The Genesis of Capitalism

Primitive Accumulation

Technically speaking, all the major economic and theoretical steps of *Capital* are more or less complete, and we can now turn our attention to the historical steps. In line with this, Marx turned his attention to the historical events leading to capitalist development, and one of the first issues he looked at was the process called 'primitive accumulation.' This is one of the key concepts Marx put forward in this section, and to understand its origins and genesis, we need to look more closely.

Marx's discussion of primitive accumulation occurs relatively late in his overall treatment of the process of capitalist development, almost near the end of the work. Nevertheless, it is a key concept in Marx's discussion of the history of capitalist social relations. To repeat once again, Marx wanted to expose the internal links underlying capitalist social relations and to do so he had to look at the underlying mechanisms of development. In a very important sense, primitive accumulation is the 'original' event giving rise to capitalism, and Marx called it the economic equivalent of original sin.[180] Simply stated, primitive accumulation is the name Marx gave to the process whereby the means of production become the private property of one class of persons and create the 'pauperization of the direct producer.'

To elucidate, Marx began by drawing on the popular legend which explains the existence of two different groups in society: the rich and the poor.[181] Most people believe, according to Marx, that rich people are industrious, well disciplined and frugal; whereas poor people are lazy, spendthrift and undisciplined. This myth tells how humankind came to be blessed with wealth or condemned to poverty. 'And it came to pass that the first group accumulated wealth and riches, the latter having nothing to sell but their labour.'[182] But, in actual fact, the truth is otherwise. The poverty of the great majority is a tale of 'coercion, expropriation and robbery.'[183]

Earlier, we stated that Marx believed that money and commodities alone do not make capitalism. Capitalism only comes into being, he thought, as a consequence of a network of social relations. Primitive accumulation then is a concept used by Marx to understand the coercive forces at work bringing about capitalist society. So far, Marx has shown that capitalism can best be understood as the coming together of two different kinds of commodity owners; on the one hand, owners of the means of production; and on the other, those whose commodity is their labor. The key to understanding primitive accumulation is the concept

180 Ibid., p. 873.
181 Ibid., p. 873.
182 Ibid., p. 873.
183 Ibid., p. 873.

of 'free labour,' and so we look briefly, once again, at this important term.

For Marx, the 'free labourer' is the focal point of capitalist development in several respects. First, in order to be free the laborer had to be relieved of the means of production and thus separated from it. Second, the appearance of the free laborer constitutes the formation of the laboring classes who, having nothing to sell but their labor power, dispose of it in exchange for a wage. Thus the 'free labourer' can only come into existence upon the dissolution of feudalism and serfdom. Previously, in feudal societies the direct producer was connected to the means of production as a natural right and this right furnished the producer with a livelihood. The concept of 'free labour,' then, constitutes the moment in historical development when the direct producer is divorced from the means of production and emerges as the seller of labor power – free to dispose of his or her commodity as he or she sees fit.[184] For this to occur, Marx reasoned, the old feudal restrictions and guild regulations on individual labor had to be eliminated. At the same time, the legal rights of the worker over how this labor was to be disposed of had to be established.

Primitive accumulation, therefore, describes the historical movement which transforms the direct producer of feudal society into the wage laborer of capitalist society, and this occurs, stated Marx, as soon as the emancipation from serfdom takes effect. The newly-created 'free labourers' – the sole possessors of labor power – can only be free to sell their labor once they have been separated from the means of production, and it is precisely this single moment that Marx sought to explain with the concept of 'primitive accumulation.'

Free labor occurs in the transition from feudalism to capitalism. In this respect, capitalism begins when two very different kinds of commodity owners meet in the market, both of whom are unencumbered by feudal restrictions.[185] The key to understanding primitive accumulation lies in the use of land in a feudal society. In feudal society, all land is under the jurisdiction of the monarch, whose right it is to dispose of lands to the aristocracy in exchange for military service and homage in the form of obligation. In such a system, no one owns land as private property. Instead, a web of obligations link king, lord and peasant, with no one owning land outright. Peasants enjoy rights to use common lands and to produce their livelihoods. In exchange, they are obligated to perform free labor service or provide exchange in kind. The point to be highlighted here is that in a feudal society the means of production form a part of what the serf does and how the serf lives.

By contrast, the free laborer of capitalism is separated from the means of production, and this constitutes the fundamental precondition of capitalist development.

184 Ibid., pp. 874–5.
185 Ibid., pp. 874–5.

As soon as capitalist production stands on its feet, it not only maintains this separation between the worker and the means of production but reproduces it on a constantly extending scale. The process which creates capitalist relations can be nothing other than the process which divorces workers from the ownership over the conditions of their own labour. . . . It is a process which operates two transformations, whereby the social means of subsistence are turned into capital and the immediate producers are turned into wage labourers. [Thus,] primitive accumulation is nothing else than the historical process of divorcing the producer from the means of production. It appears as primitive because it forms the pre-history of capital and the mode of production corresponding to capitalism.[186]

The Stages of Primitive Accumulation

So far, we have seen that primitive accumulation is a term Marx used to pinpoint the process by which the means of production become the sole property of one class. He believed that the process of primitive accumulation takes place in two distinct historical stages or epochs. The first of these stages is marked by the expropriation of the agricultural laborer from the land. This stage began during the last third of the fifteenth century when large populations of agricultural peasants were 'forcibly' thrown from the land by eviction and foreclosure as land became more valuable and was 'enclosed' by landholders. This first stage of the process led to the dissolution of a whole way of life – the disappearance of towns, parishes and the use of common lands as a means of producing a livelihood. Marx argued that this period marked the beginning of the transfer of the means of production into the hands of a dominant class. The second stage of primitive accumulation, formally called by Marx the proletarianization of the feudal peasant class, was marked by the legal transfer of feudal lands into private hands by direct seizure and foreclosure. This took place 'without the slightest observance of legal etiquette.'[187] The transfer of feudal land into private hands took the form of the Bills of Enclosure which expelled the serf from the land. By the middle of the nineteenth century, this had created the industrial worker, the free laborer of capitalism, who had been relieved of his or her relation to the means of production. By the nineteenth century the free laborer – free in the sense of being relieved of a direct connection to the land – had been fully formed, leaving no evidence of having been forcibly created from the agricultural peasant of former times.

Cooperation and the Division of Labor

Next, Marx focused on the development of industrial manufacturing and the creation of the factory as the center of capitalist production and livelihood. He conceived of the impact of industrial manufacture upon the worker as taking place essentially along three broad planes of activity and

186 Ibid., pp. 874–5.
187 Ibid., p. 884.

change. Each of these involves substantial shifts in the way labor was carried out and is discussed under three separate categories: (i) co-operation and large-scale industry; (ii) division of labor and manufacture; (iii) machinery and large-scale industry. Let us begin by looking at cooperation.

The starting place of 'cooperation and large scale industry,' Marx wrote, is the assembly of a large number of workers in the factory. For this to occur, a large number of workers are brought together in one place for purposes of production. This step presupposes the decline of the trade guilds who formerly restricted the unification of crafts and trades under one roof to protect their hold over professions. Capitalist production then proceeds by unifying many workers and many trades under the command of one capitalist. Marx's interest was to focus on 'the combined effect of labour.'[188]

Marx observed three broad effects of combined cooperation. First, he pointed out that the effect of combined labor could not have been produced by the isolated worker and so he reasoned that the combined effect creates a form of cooperation which increases the productive power of the individual. This putting to work of a number of workers thus produces a combined effect and, therefore, a quantitative gain results from a qualitative act. But what exactly is it? Marx believed that the combined cooperation creates a qualitative effect in that it concentrates the means of production in one place.[189] The advantage is to the capitalist, since the total value of labor power is greater than the total sum of wages the capitalist pays to the workers. Marx then pointed out that the cooperation between workers gives rise to what he called a 'system of interconnections' which emerges between the individual laborers.[190] This system is neither the plan of workers as a group nor the plan of one individual worker, but rather is created by the capitalist. In this respect, their interconnections confront them in two ways: (i) the system does not serve the workers as individuals, since their activity is for the most part for the capitalist that brings them together; and (ii) what they do collectively is not the result of their own plans, since their unification into a single body is not something they understand – it 'lies outside of their competence.'[191]

Division of Labor: Simple and Complex Cooperation

Marx moved on to look at the process of the division of labor. He believed that the division of labor and the form of cooperation which it presupposes are found first and foremost in classical manufacture. The division of labor, he stated, developed throughout the period of the nineteenth century with the development and progress of manufacturing

188 Ibid., p. 443.
189 Ibid., p. 447.
190 Ibid., pp. 449–50.
191 Ibid., p. 450.

and industry. According to Marx, the division of labor leads to a 'particular sort of cooperation' which he called 'complex cooperation.'[192] As soon as an extensive division of labor takes place, there is an important change from manufacturing based on simple cooperation to complex cooperation. But what exactly did Marx mean by the terms simple and complex?

According to Marx, complex cooperation occurs when the skills formerly embedded in the worker become functions of the process of the division of labor itself. Previously, guilds had restricted the division of labor in order to preserve the integrity of distinct trades and crafts. But as soon as these trades are combined under one roof, the qualitative skill formerly belonging to the worker becomes the property of the combined division of labor – and this robs workers of their skill. As an example, Marx drew from the carriage trade. He said that formerly this trade involved various handicrafts and skills: coach work, enamel work, carriage work, upholstery and wheelwright work. Before capitalist production, each of these operations were specialized trades regulated by guilds in order to maintain their separation from each other. As soon as the division of labor is established, however, the carriage maker becomes 'exclusively occupied with making carriages.'[193] As a result, individual trades immediately lose their specialized skills and this concentrates their combined activity exclusively in making carriages. Marx wrote: 'at first, the manufacture of carriages appears as a combination of various independent handicrafts and trades. But it gradually began to involve the splitting up of carriage production into various and detailed operations and each single operation crystallized into the exclusive function of a particular worker, the manufacture as a whole being performed by these partial workers in conjunction.'[194]

Marx then went on to make the distinction between simple and complex cooperation more explicit. Simple cooperation may be defined as a situation of production in which one capitalist employs a number of craftsmen who all perform the same work, for example, making carriages. Each craftsman makes the entire commodity from beginning to end and performs the series of operations necessary to produce the entire commodity. Complex cooperation, on the other hand, occurs when each individual performs operations which are disconnected and isolated from one another and carried on side by side. Each operation is assigned a separate craftsman and the commodity is produced by the combined action of the cooperators, but no individual craftsmen produce the commodity themselves. In this case, according to Marx, the commodity has gone from being a product of the individual craftsman to becoming the social product of the union of craftsmen, each of whom performs only one operation. The development of the division of labor presides over the

192 Ibid., pp. 455–8.
193 Ibid., p. 454.
194 Ibid., pp. 455–6.

breakdown of handicraft skills and the 'decomposition of handicrafts into different and partial operations.'[195] Labor as such becomes transformed into a 'life long partial function.'[196]

Theory of Alienation

History of the Concept in Hegel

The term alienation came into general use during the nineteenth and twentieth centuries to describe a state of disruption and change taking place in the system of social relations as a result of the development of modern society. It was first used as a philosophic concept in the last half of the eighteenth century in the work of Georg Hegel, one of the first thinkers to develop the concept. Following Hegel, Feuerbach and Marx were the first to give systematic expression to the theme of alienation, and it is their work which constitutes the starting place for a full-blown theory of alienation.

In 1807, Hegel used the term 'estrangement' in a work called *The Phenomenology of Mind* to outline a framework for the development of human consciousness. In his theory of development, Hegel put forward the idea that human beings essentially strive to realize themselves in history, a process he referred to as 'self-actualization.' Hegel believed, however, that individuals do not realize themselves directly but, in fact, always encounter obstacles which act against them. Hegel called these obstacles 'oppositions,' in which the external world acts to negate the individual by 'shutting out their existence.'[197] Hegel was perhaps the first to understand that human beings can experience their own activity as something external to them, something that is 'not self,' and he described this moment in human experience as alienation. In fact, Hegel was one of the first thinkers to capture the idea that individuals can experience themselves as not fully human, and that human beings can live their lives without ever being completely developed. The idea that the 'self' could be experienced as incomplete or not fully developed was altogether new, and fitted the experience of modernism by giving expression to the fragmentation of human experience associated with modern society.

Feuerbach's Theory of Religious Alienation

A second contribution to a theory of alienation is found in the work of Ludwig Feuerbach, a German philosopher who was a contemporary of Marx. Feuerbach's early writings were extremely critical of religion and in 1830, as a result of his attacks on Christianity, he lost his university post.

195 Ibid., p. 458.
196 Ibid., p. 458.
197 Hegel, *The Phenomenology of Mind.* See, in particular, Section IV on self-consciousness, pp. 218–27.

In 1841, he wrote one of his most controversial works, *The Essence of Christianity*, which received immediate critical attention.

Feuerbach's writings served as a central theoretical focus for Marx in several key respects. First, Feuerbach provided a stunning criticism of Hegel's philosophy by stating that insofar as Hegel believed in a philosophical world which ruled over the real world, his philosophy duplicated theology and in this sense was nothing more than religion. Second, Feuerbach established a link between philosophy and religion by claiming that both constituted human alienation in that they misrepresented reality and humanity. This criticism had an enormous impact on philosophy, since Feuerbach showed that philosophy, in being based on belief rather than reason, was a mythology similar to religion. Third, by moving away from Hegelian idealism, Feuerbach was moving in the direction of materialism, and this served as a basis for Marx to crystallize his thinking on the economic origins of alienation.

In *The Essence of Christianity* Feuerbach had claimed that he had arrived at a new philosophical perspective based on a rejection of Hegel. What was controversial about Feuerbach's work was its claim that idealist philosophy was nothing more than religion disguised as systematic philosophical thought.[198] Feuerbach put forward his argument forcefully. He took the position that Hegel's idealism was identical to theology since both looked for and believed in universal truths which ultimately existed outside the realm of the material world. He claimed that philosophy, in fact, followed a path of development similar to theology since both pursued lines of reasoning which deify ideas and concepts, and ultimately identify worlds outside of the real world and assume that these worlds actually rule over everyday existence.[199] Feuerbach reasoned that idealism was nothing more than a philosophic movement to find God in ideas essentially by placing ontological authority in human reason itself. One of the more radical claims of Feuerbach's work was the view that Hegel's philosophy, in stressing the reality of abstract thinking, was tantamount to alienation because it separated human beings from their physical existence by denying the material realm of experience.

Feuerbach's main argument focused on religion, and his views were nothing less than sensational. He had argued that in making religion, human beings unwittingly project their human essence onto an image and, in making this image into God, they assign qualities to it that are distinctly non-human. They do this to the point that the image meets the criteria of perfection. This image, argued Feuerbach, becomes the birth place of rules and prescriptions which, in turn, are reimposed on the lives of human beings in the form of unwanted regulation and self-denial. Feuerbach maintained that the self-imposition of restraint constituted the height of alienation, because, in making religion, human beings simply experience

---

198 Feuerbach, *The Essence of Christianity*, pp. xiii–xxiv.
199 Ibid., pp. 1–32.

their own essence acting back upon them in the form of alien rules – rules which reproach them for their natures and forcibly narrow their lives to the image of perfection. 'Religion,' he wrote, 'is the disuniting of human beings from themselves.'[200] In Feuerbach's view, religion is non-human or anti-human.

There were immediate philosophical consequences of Feuerbach's criticism of religion. In asserting that physical being was true being, Feuerbach turned Hegel right side up by placing the emphasis on the material origin of religion. In stating that religion had a material base, Feuerbach was one of the first to point out that religion itself was an 'anthropology' to the extent that it showed human material development in terms of the accumulated layers of belief. In this view, belief was no longer in the domain of theology but rather was seen as an anthropology.[201] This extreme departure by Feuerbach from Hegel's idealist impulses was seen by some as an attempt to found religion on materialist premises, and this attracted Marx to Feuerbach's work.

Marx's Rejection of Feuerbach

While Marx thought that Feuerbach had taken a step forward in stressing the material realm over the ideal, he believed that Feuerbach did not go far enough. To grasp the importance of Marx's departure, let us look at Marx's sixth thesis on Feuerbach. He states:

> Feuerbach resolves the religious essence into the human essence. But the human essence is not an abstract [thing], inherent in the single individual. In reality it is the ensemble of social relations. Feuerbach does not go into the criticism of this real essence, and is therefore compelled to abstract from the historical course of events, to fix a religious mental disposition, and to presume an abstract human individual. This essence can therefore be conceived of as an inward mute generality, binding the many individuals naturally. Feuerbach does not see therefore, that the religious mental disposition itself is a social product and that the abstract individual whom he analyses belongs to a particular form of society.[202]

Marx's main criticism of Feuerbach was social and historical. Note the emphasis Marx places on the question of Feuerbach's abstraction of the human essence. For Feuerbach, the human essence was a religious abstraction which had no particular being, neither social nor economic, and as such was nothing but a 'dumb generality.' This was significant because, in looking for the material origins of human religion, Feuerbach did not go far enough. Marx believed that human existence could only be understood in terms of economic production, so in his view Feuerbach reverts to Hegel by assigning a religious and philosophical essence to human existence. Marx's departure from Feuerbach and Hegel, therefore,

200 Ibid., p. 33.
201 For a discussion of the connection between Feuerbach, Hegel and Marx see Rotenstreich, *Basic Problems of Marx's Philosophy*.
202 Marx and Engels, *German Ideology*, p. 198.

was based on his assertion that alienation was to be treated as a real consequence of social and economic development. In stating this, Marx took alienation outside the realm of abstract religious experience and placed it squarely within social and economic experience.

Marx's Theory of Alienation and the 1844 Manuscripts

Marx wrote the *Economic and Philosophic Manuscripts* during the summer of 1844 while he was living in Paris. Only 26 years old at the time, he had already obtained his doctorate and was working on economic problems. The manuscripts did not make their appearance until they were first published in 1932 and were subsequently translated into English in 1950. Initially, they were written as separate segments and each of the themes of the manuscripts form independent studies. Only one of these, entitled 'Estranged Labour', contains Marx's discussion of alienation.[203]

In order completely to understand Marx's theory of alienation, it will be useful to briefly compare it to Hegel's work. For Hegel, as we saw, the concept of estrangement demanded an investigation into abstract philosophical concepts and spiritual forces such as consciousness and reason. Though Hegel believed that the struggle for self-emancipation takes place between self-consciousness and abstract forces in the external world, Marx thought that this struggle was, in fact, acted out on the economic front. As far as Marx was concerned, Hegel had conceived of the struggle between the individual and the external world in terms of abstract forces he called 'oppositions' and 'negations.' But, for Marx, these 'oppositions' and 'negations' were material insofar as they were economic realities materialized in the form of social classes. For Marx, then, the struggle for self-realization is a material struggle played out on the economic front and this shift replaced Hegel's abstract struggle in thought.

Marx developed the theory of alienation to convey two central and dominant ideas. First, he wanted to convey the idea that human beings make society, and at some point society is a natural extension of their nature and their being – it reflects them and they feel at home in it. Second, Marx wanted to convey the idea that, as modern society develops, human beings begin to feel that society is not of their own making and no longer reflects their being or their nature, but instead appears to be alien and thus stands over and against them. The idea that society starts out as an extension of human beings and ends up as something apart and external, is precisely what the theory of alienation attempts to explain.[204]

203 For discussion of the history of the manuscripts, see Rubel and Manale, *Marx Without Myth.*

204 K. Marx, *The Economic and Philosophic Manuscripts of 1844*, New York: International Publishers, [1932] 1964, p. 106. See Bertell Ollman, *Alienation: Marx's Conception of Man in Capitalist Society*, London: Cambridge University Press, 1971 and John O'Neill, 'The Concept of Estrangement in the Early and Late Writings of Karl Marx,' *Philosophy and Phenomenological Research*, 25, 1, 1964, pp. 64–84.

Marx's Theory of Human Nature   To understand completely Marx's theory of alienation, it is important to look at his theory of human nature. In many of his writings, Marx stressed the idea that human beings define themselves in nature and history primarily through their laboring activity. He believed that laboring was so central to humans' existence that it was a part of their being and in this sense formed part of their human essence – part of what defined them as human beings. Laboring, according to Marx, was the primary means by which human beings realized themselves in nature and history. In this respect, he thought that labor defined human beings in at least three specific senses. First, through it individuals exert control over nature and natural obstacles, and therefore feel themselves to be active rather than passive in history. Second, labor is the source of human existence in that it produces the material necessities of food, shelter and clothing. Third, labor is part of human self-definition since through it individuals control their circumstances and actively feel confirmed in their activity and their being.

In addition, Marx went on to reason that laboring performs connective functions by linking human beings to existence in three important ways. First, it connects them to nature insofar as they are reliant on the means of production to fulfill themselves by producing food, shelter and clothing. In this sense they are connected to the means of production in terms of economic subsistence and survival. Second, labor connects them to the means of self-affirmation since it helps them gain control over nature and facilitate well-being and existence. Third, it connects them to the product of their labor to the extent that the product has a use value which is directly used as a means of existence. Alienation, according to Marx, breaks this fundamental connection human beings have to the self-defining aspect of their laboring activity.[205] He went on to identify four distinct types of alienation: (i) alienation from the product of labor; (ii) alienation from productive activity; (iii) alienation from the human species; and (iv) alienation from fellow human beings.

Alienation from the Product   The first type of alienation is product alienation. This takes place, Marx said, when human beings become estranged from the things they produce. But how can workers lose their product? To answer this question, we can briefly look at production in feudal society. In a feudal society, what the laborers produce belongs to them directly, and they consume it to satisfy their immediate economic needs. In this sense, the laborers' product directly satisfies their material needs and this sustains their life and existence. What laborers produce in feudal society not only has immediate use value to them but it affirms their relationship to themselves in their own productive powers.

In capitalist society this situation is completely different. To begin with, production is for exchange and what is produced enters into a medium of

---

205 Marx, *Economic and Philosophic Manuscripts*, p. 110.

exchange called the market; what is produced is not owned by the laborer, since it belongs to the capitalist. In addition, since ownership over the means of production is concentrated in another class, both the object of labor and the labor itself confront the worker externally as a thing not of their own making.[206] In this sense, the life which the worker confers upon the object confronts the worker as something alien and hostile. In this way, product alienation alters the individual's relation to the natural world. In the beginning Marx believed that the worker is connected to nature and can produce nothing without it since 'it is the material upon which labour is manifested.'[207] This bond to nature is expressed in two ways: first, they receive subsistence from it in that it provides a means of livelihood without which human beings cannot live. Second, they receive self-definition from it in that it affirms their powers through production. In capitalist society, by contrast, the workers lose this connection to nature in the sense that the means of production no longer belong to them but are privately owned. Thus the product of labor may be said to stand over and against workers because they never engage the means of production directly since it is mediated by ownership and exchange. As the means of production become the property of one class, they stand over and against the workers and are opposed to them as an alien thing. Marx reasoned that the loss of the workers' relation to the means of production increases their dependence upon it in two ways: first, they receive work from it, and second, they receive the means of physical subsistence, but only indirectly in the form of a wage.[208]

Lastly, product alienation breaks the connection workers form in identifying with the product of their production. In feudal society, what laborers produce affirms the relationship they have to their own productive powers since 'labour is realized in its object or product.'[209] This tells us that the product of labor is always the 'summary of the activity of production' and what is produced constitutes a source of self-identification.[210] As exchange becomes the dominant social relation, product alienation becomes greatest when the workers cannot use the product they produce.

Alienation from Productive Activity The second form of alienation discussed by Marx is alienation from productive activity. In this type of alienation human beings lose control over the capacity of their labor to affirm their being and define their self-existence. Alienation from productive activity is distinct from product alienation and to understand this category as fully as possible we must look at the way Marx used the

206 Ibid., p. 110.
207 Ibid., p. 109.
208 Ibid., p. 111.
209 Ibid., p. 108.
210 Ibid., p. 110.

concept of 'relation.' For Marx, the term is used to describe the connection between the individual and the outer world, and to pinpoint the way in which human beings are essentially connected to existence and to the external world through their labor. Understood in this sense, individuals are connected to existence in two ways: (i) in respect to themselves, and (ii) in respect to others and the social world. Looked at from this point of view, every relation can be viewed from two distinct perspectives: from its relation to itself and from relations external to itself.[211] Marx went on to describe alienation from productive activity in the following way:

> What, then, constitutes the alienation of labour? First, the fact that labour is external to the worker, i.e., it does not belong to his essential being; that in his work, therefore, he does not affirm himself but denies himself, does not feel content but unhappy, does not develop freely his physical and mental energy but mortifies his body and ruins his mind. The worker only feels himself outside his work, and in his work feels outside himself. He is at home when he is not working, and when he is working he is not home. His labour is therefore not voluntary, but coerced; it is forced labour. It is therefore not the satisfaction of a need; it is merely a means to satisfy needs external to it. Its alien character emerges clearly in the fact that as soon as no physical or other compulsion exists, labour is shunned like the plague. External labour, labour in which man alienates himself, is a labour of self-sacrifice, of mortification. Lastly, the external character of labour for the worker appears in the fact that it is not his own, but someone else's, that it does not belong to him, that in it he belongs, not to himself, but to another. As a result, therefore, the worker no longer feels himself to be freely active in any but his animal functions – eating, drinking, procreating, or at most in his dwelling and in dressing up etc.; and in his human functions he no longer feels himself to be anything but an animal. What is animal becomes human and what is human becomes animal. Certainly eating, drinking and procreating, etc., are also genuinely human functions. But abstractly taken, separated from the sphere of all other human activity and turned into sole and ultimate ends, they are animal functions.[212]

In that productive activity acts to 'affirm' the individuals' relation to themselves, to their productive powers and their essential being, alienation breaks the connection to the self-affirming nature of laboring activity in four broad ways. First, labor is external to the worker in that it belongs to the capitalist rather than belonging to the worker's essential being. Because it is external to workers and does not belong to them, it cannot 'affirm' them. The external character of labor means that workers do not own their labor as if it were their property to dispose of as they see fit, but rather it is owned by someone else. This has a double impact: while the labor of the worker belongs to someone else, workers do not belong to themselves and thus do not preside over the buying and selling of their labor. This is labor which has as its end the loss of the worker, since the workers' labor operates on them independently of their will, purpose and desire. Second, alienation from productive activity reverses the individuals' relationship to themselves and their own powers. Workers 'only feel

211 S. Hook, *From Hegel to Marx*, London: Victor Gollancz, 1936, p. 23.
212 Ibid., p. 23.

themselves outside their work, and in their work they feel outside themselves.'[213] Third, the labor of the worker does not hold out the direct satisfaction of his or her needs because what is produced enters into the medium of exchange. This, Marx said, converts the workers' activity into nothing more than a means to satisfy their external needs, so that the sole purpose of life becomes that of fulfilling material needs. This alienates individuals from the capacity of their labor to define their essential being since, in capitalism, labor is performed only to fulfill immediate economic needs. Under these circumstances, the laborer can only understand work as springing from need and thus labors only to satisfy physical necessities. The worker comes to believe that the maintenance of individual existence is thus the single and solitary goal of their life activity. In this formula, the worker therefore lives to acquire the means of living. Fourth, labor that is experienced as external does not 'affirm' the worker but is only the labor of self-sacrifice and this 'mortifies the body and ruins the mind.'[214]

Marx went on to reason that alienation from productive activity reverses the individual's relation to his or her own physical body and to his or her person in several ways. First, while in earlier societies productive activity defined the sphere of free actions in all functions, in capitalism productive activity (labor) is free only in those functions workers share with animals such as eating, sleeping, drinking and procreating, since only these functions are free and unsupervised. In their human laboring functions, however, workers feel themselves to be like animals, since 'what is animal becomes human and what is human becomes animal.'[215] Second, though eating, drinking and procreating are clearly human functions, they become restricted to the domain of animal functions once they have been separated from 'the sphere of human activity and turned into sole and ultimate ends.'[216] Third, because human beings are defined through their productive activity, alienation breaks the link between workers and their self-defining powers. Since productive activity no longer belongs to the workers, the defining relation to themselves and their powers is reversed: 'activity becomes suffering; strength becomes weakness; action becomes emasculation' and in this state the workers can no longer depend on their own activity for their life.[217] Marx believed that alienation of productive activity breaks the most important connection – the active connection human beings have to themselves.

Alienation from Species   The third type of alienation discussed by Marx is alienation from the human species. In species alienation, Marx contended

---

213 Marx, *Economic and Philosophic Manuscripts*, p. 111.
214 Ibid., p. 111.
215 Ibid., p. 111.
216 Ibid., p. 111.
217 Ibid., p. 111.

that human beings are alienated from their own species-being. In order to be clear on Marx's meaning, this category of alienation requires some further explanation. Marx essentially believed that human beings live in an active relation to the natural world and in this sense have certain characteristics which mark them off from other species. He thought that the chief quality separating human beings from the animal world is what he called conscious being – the ability to take oneself into account and be conscious of oneself. By contrast, Marx thought that animals have only physical being, but not conscious being; thus their life activity is qualitatively different from human life activity. Species alienation thus breaks the connection human beings have to their conscious being in two fundamental respects. First, because it turns laboring into a physical act, it revokes what nature has given human beings over animal life, thus converting conscious being into physical being. Second, by converting conscious being into physical being, it makes human labor like the labor of animals. In this form of alienation, human nature is turned against itself in that human beings become creatures of physical activity.

Marx maintained that the individual's relationship to nature differs from that of animals in several respects. First, animals live directly off nature and thus do not have to create use values by production. Human beings, on the other hand, 'prepare nature and make it palatable and digestible' and in this sense must labor upon it to work it up.[218] Second, human beings are a species distinct from animals because they have conscious being, with which they reflect upon themselves, their lives and their own powers. Third, animals produce only to satisfy their direct physical needs, whereas human beings create an objective world by their own social action. In this, they work up inorganic nature by producing social institutions of various kinds – and through these they create social history which survives them as a species. In producing in this way, human beings proclaim themselves to be a species since the object of their labor is the 'objectification' of the human species, 'for they duplicate themselves not only in consciousness, but actually in reality.'[219]

Marx believed that species alienation transforms the individual's relation to his or her species in two particular ways. First, it turns species nature into a means of individual life because it estranges the life of the species from individual life, and in doing this it makes individual life abstract from the life of the species. By the term abstraction, Marx referred to the stage at which the individual's relation to him or herself and the external world becomes unclear and inexplicit. Second, in estranging labor from the species, the individual's relationship to his or her species' uniqueness is reversed, since human laboring no longer acts to affirm conscious life activity but acts only as a means of existence – so that 'life itself appears

218 Ibid., p. 111.
219 Ibid., p. 114.

not as affirmation and power but only as a means.'[220] This is evident in capitalism which, according to Marx, reverses the species advantage by transforming human conscious life into mere physical existence.

Alienation from Fellow Humans The fourth type of alienation discussed by Marx is alienation from fellow human beings and from the human social community. This comes about, he reasoned, when the sole aim of life is competition and all social relations are transformed into economic relationships. There are two important senses in which alienation from fellow human beings occurs. First, so far as capitalism compels individuals to be isolated from one another and to pursue their private interests for personal gain, they enter into competition with each other. While at one time individuals were essentially collective beings, they have become individual beings. Second, the alienation of human beings from their fellow humans occurs as society makes another class the sole beneficiary of the product of their labor.

As human beings are estranged from their product, their productive activity and their own species, so also are they estranged from their relationship to their fellow human beings. In Marx's view, this category of alienation breaks the social relationships which human beings have to each other as part of the human social community.[221] There are two principle ways in which this has occurred. First, so far as individuals are isolated from one another by competition, they are made into individual beings where they were once collective beings. As universal competition becomes the norm, individuals thus find themselves alone in society. Second, alienation from fellow human beings occurs as society makes another class the sole beneficiary of the product of their labor. Marx pointed out that during earlier periods, the product of individual labor was once for the 'gods', and the main aim of production must have been in the service of gods (temples, pyramids, etc).[222] In capitalist societies the products of labor do not belong to the worker but to one class, which is able to realize itself in history since it has become the sole recipient of the products of labor.

Objectification and Alienation In his discussion of alienation, Marx drew a distinction between the end result of alienation and the process of 'objectification.' He stated: 'labour's realization is its objectification.'[223] The process of objectification can be clarified if we look at alienation once more. If alienation can be described as the loss of the ability of laborers to realize themselves, objectification is the realization of labor in that it refers to the capacity of human beings positively to 'duplicate' themselves in the

220 Ibid., p. 114.
221 Ibid., p. 114.
222 Ibid., p. 115.
223 Ibid., p. 108.

world they create.[224] This duplication in society through labor is the realization of human aims. It is through this that human beings can 'contemplate' themselves 'in the world they have created.'[225] By thus producing things, an individual necessarily becomes an object for others within the structure of social relations. In this sense, the value of labor resides in the subjects' ability to produce use values for others and, in this respect, confirm themselves. What is important is that the social connection is between individuals – between human beings – not things or commodities. For Marx, then, objectification is necessary if individuals are to humanize nature, to transform it into an expression having human qualities. In this respect, objectification is not synonymous with alienation in that it is a positive realization of laboring activity. By making the distinction between alienation and objectification, Marx had grasped the historical character of labor and argued that the end of alienation will emancipate the species by rehumanizing labor. For Marx, the true 'object of labour is the objectification of the workers' species life.' Hence, in 'tearing away the object of their production,' alienated labor 'tears human beings from their species life.'[226]

Marx's Political Writings

History of Marx's View of the State

Marx became interested in political theory after moving to Dresden in 1842. During his stay there, he began studying the conditions of the political revolutions in France and England, and this led him in the direction of political philosophy. As a result, he began reading the works of political thinkers such as Rousseau, Tocqueville, Machiavelli and Hegel and, as a consequence, developed an interest in democracy and state functions.[227] In an early writing entitled *Critique of Hegel's Philosophy of Right* published in 1843, Marx undertook a critical revision of Hegel's political philosophy, and this led to one of Marx's first systematic discussions of the state.[228] Later, in a work entitled 'On the Jewish Question' published in the same year, Marx looked at the relationship between civil society and the development of the modern state.[229] Eight years later, in 1851, Marx undertook a historical study of the state in a work called *The Eighteenth Brumaire of Louis Bonaparte*, focusing on the 1848 rebellion in France and the rise of Louis Bonaparte. Finally, in *The*

224 Ibid., p. 114.
225 Ibid., p. 114.
226 Ibid., p. 114.
227 Rubel and Manale, *Marx Without Myth*, pp. 28–31.
228 Marx, *Critique of Hegel's Philosophy of Right*, J. O'Malley (ed.), Cambridge: Cambridge University Press, 1970.
229 R.C. Tucker, *The Marx-Engels Reader*, (2nd edn), New York: Norton, pp. 26–52.

Civil War in France, written in 1871, Marx focused on the development of the French political state.[230]

Though Marx's political writings do not form a single line of argument or develop a coherent theory of the political state, they do constitute a set of fundamental principles which frame discussion about the formation of the state and the nature of state activities. Consistent with this view, there are at least four central propositions which form the basis of Marx's theory of the state. The first of these is the assertion that the state has a material origin and is, therefore, not independent of the economic structure of society. In this regard, Marx thought that the state arose out of the productive relations of society and therefore had its origins in economic activity. Second, Marx asserted that the modern state develops only under certain historical conditions arising in the productive forces of society, and under these circumstances is historical and social in nature. Third, Marx asserted that the state reflects the prevailing class structure of society and thus acts as an instrument of the dominant classes. In this regard, Marx believed the political function of the state derives from the underlying economic base and productive relations, meaning that the interests of the state always coincide with the interests of the dominant classes. Fourth is the assertion by Marx that the appearance of the state in society is historically dependent upon the development of what he called 'civil society.'

Hegel's View of the State

Like so much of Marx's early writing, his theory of the state can best be understood by looking at Hegel's discussion of the political institutions of society. Hegel had written an important work on the historical development of the state, entitled the *Philosophy of Right*, published in 1821.[231] The view Hegel took up formed almost a complete philosophical sketch of the political structure of society, and he founded these views on an idealist conception of the origins, functions and activities of the state.

Hegel's perspective can best be set out in a series of five assumptions. First and foremost, Hegel assumed that the state was the embodiment of what he called 'right action.' By the term 'right,' Hegel meant the whole sphere of rules and ethical norms which guide human action toward what is ethically good in the human spirit. Hegel thought that the expression of 'right action' was nothing more than the manifestation of human 'ethical will' in history. This ethical will, insisted Hegel, reached its highest point of development in the political sphere of society, which concerned itself with ethical functions and rules of conduct that guide human action along the path of what is politically good. In this view, all the conventions of the state could be seen to be nothing more than the manifestations of human

---

230 K. Marx, *The Civil War in France*; Peking: Foreign Languages Press, [1871] 1970.
231 Hegel, *Philosophy of Right*.

'ethical will' embodied in the state itself. This tendency to view the state as a form of ethical will led Hegel to take the position that the state was involved in maintaining ethical relationships between the various spheres of society.

Second, Hegel assumed that while state functions serve the purpose of mediating the various social spheres of society, the political realm of the state was completely separate from the civil realm of the economy and economic exchange, which he tended to refer to in terms of particularistic interests. In this way the state serves what Hegel called 'mediating' functions in maintaining ethical harmony, between the sphere of public interest on the one hand and the sphere of private interest on the other. Third, Hegel had assumed that since the state is an expression of human 'ethical will,' it must represent the common good of society and, through historical and dialectical processes, ensure that the 'universal interest' always prevails over the particular interest of any one individual or group.

Fourth, Hegel thought that the activities of the state were separate from the activities of civil society.[232] The activities of the political sphere of society, according to Hegel, pursued ends reflecting the 'general' interests of the whole community and were thus universal in nature. Actions in the civil sphere, on the other hand, pursued ends which reflected the 'particular' interests and private rights of individuals and groups, and were thus 'particularistic' in nature. In this view, ethical actions reach their highest stage of development in the political sphere of society when office holders exercise the common good in the name of the ethical community and the universal interest. Thus the political sphere, for Hegel, is synonymous with the ethical life. Fifth, Hegel asserted that since the state emerged from human ethical will, it did not have a social or historical character but was rather the manifestation of the 'ethical idea' deified in the political structure of society and, in this sense, was historically eternal.

Marx and the Materialist Origins of the State: Base and Superstructure

By 1843, Marx had undertaken a critical revision of Hegel's theory of the state in two early works entitled *Critique of Hegel's Philosophy of Right* and 'On the Jewish Question.' But it wasn't until *German Ideology* that Marx began to set out some of the historical and materialist principles of state development. Marx began to establish a historical focus on the state by rejecting Hegel's view that the state was an embodiment of ethical ideas. He thought that the central abstraction in Hegel's work made it appear as if political institutions were 'determined by a third party, rather than being self determined.'[233]

Marx countered Hegel's idealist conception of the state in two broad

---

232 Ibid., pp. 155–6.
233 Marx, *Critique of Hegel's Philosophy of Right*, p. 22.

ways. First, while Hegel had tended to deny the social and historical character of the state, Marx was able to show that the state, in fact, had a historical origin by linking its development to economic production and productive relations. In this way, Marx was able to demonstrate the material origins of the political structure of society. Second, in contrast to Hegel, who believed that the state was eternal and existed for all time, Marx showed that the state only came into existence at a certain stage of historical development in the productive forces of society. Thus, Marx was able to demonstrate that the state emerged at certain stages in productive relations rather than being a philosophical abstraction that was eternally given. This consolidation by Marx of the material and historical origin of the state made his theory of political society distinct from previous political thinking, and distinct from Hegel's political philosophy.

The assertion by Marx that the state has a historical origin is explicitly discussed in the 1859 preface to *A Contribution to the Critique of Political Economy*, where he stated:

> In the social production which men carry on they enter into definite relations that are indispensable and independent of their will; these relations of production correspond to a definite stage of the development of their material forces of production. The totality of these relations of production constitutes the economic structure of society, which is the real foundation on top of which arises a legal and political superstructure to which correspond definite forms of social consciousness. It is not the consciousness of men, therefore, that determines their existence, but instead their social existence determines their consciousness. With the change of the economic foundation the entire immense superstructure is more or less rapidly transformed.[234]

In this passage, two important ideas regarding the state are put forward. First is the idea that the relations of production constitute the economic structure of society which, Marx maintained, is the 'real foundation' or economic base of society. Second is the idea that on top of the economic foundations of society arises a legal and political superstructure which corresponds directly to the productive relations. What Marx is saying explicitly here is that the central features of the state grow out of the economic base of society and thus the state is not independent of economic foundations. Within the scope of this reasoning, not only does the economic base give rise to the superstructure of society and its institutional configuration, but, as the productive system changes, so does the political and legal superstructure of the state.

In arriving at a connection between the economic base and the state, Marx was able to show that the state had a material and historical origin. This conceptualization was important to Marx's thinking, in that the state could be seen to be no more than the political expression of the class structure of society and a derivative of the relations of production. This

---

234 K. Marx, *A Contribution to the Critique of Political Economy*, pp. 22–4.

material link between the political and economic structure of society can be shown directly by looking at the main premises of the materialist theory of history. In the act of producing the material means of existence, stated Marx, individuals produce the subsequent shape of society. From this viewpoint, the shape of society always coincides with the way people produce, since the manner in which this production is carried out determines the system of social relations which tend to arise from it, so much so that it creates the division of society into two distinct classes – one of which is dominant because it presides over the means of production; the other subordinate, because it is subject to the will of those who rule over them.[235]

Marx's assertion that the shape of society always coincides with the way individuals produce and the nature of their production derives its force from the simple fact that the first act of individuals is always economic production. From this simple starting place, we can see that the system of social relations always reflects the social relations of production. But, Marx was able to go further than this by showing that the political structure of society takes the shape of the productive relations and that on top of these relations 'arises a legal and political superstructure.'[236] Two conclusions can be drawn from this perspective. First, economic production shapes social relations and hence the political structure of society. Second, economic production gives rise to a legal and political structure which comes to represent the productive relations. Taking Marx's materialist theory into account, the political structure of society, and later the state, always reflects the prevailing class interests and is not independent of them.

The Historical Origins of the Modern State: the Period of State Formation

Marx next turned his attention to the historical formation of the state. This was first outlined in *The Eighteenth Brumaire of Louis Bonaparte*, in which Marx recounted the story of the historical stages leading to the formation of the French political state.[237] These stages can be enumerated in broad outline by looking at the central features of the state which developed from the dissolution of feudal society and the productive forces of the new class interests which were emerging at the time. The process began, according to Marx, with a clearing away of the old localized powers of feudal estates with their separate economic and political jurisdictions. With the break up of separate feudal economies and political jurisdictions, the possibility of a centralized authority was created and there was a transfer of power from landlords to the new political and

---

235 Marx and Engels, *German Ideology*, pp. 4–16.

236 Marx, *A Contribution to the Critique*, pp. 22–4.

237 K. Marx, *The Eighteenth Brumaire of Louis Bonaparte*, Moscow: Progress, [1852] 1977, pp. 50–9.

economic classes. Once this had occurred, the centralized state machinery was in a position to be 'perfected' by the material interests being mobilized by the ruling political and economic classes.[238] These new interests created the need for a state administration and bureaucratic apparatus.

After tracing the development of the state in the *Eighteenth Brumaire*, Marx turned his attention to the political developments in France between the rebellions of 1789 and 1851. The historical context of the rebellion began, Marx pointed out, in 1848 – a period of unprecedented industrial production. At the time, increased industrial activity had led to prosperity for a small commercial class and greater poverty and social distress for workers. Low wages, poor working conditions and unemployment led many to criticize capitalism for its social inequality and restriction of economic advantage to only one class in society. There was widespread rebellion throughout Europe and workers began to protest against their limited social opportunities. In France, this led to an open rebellion by the working class to claim the French Republic on behalf of the worker. There are three distinct periods of state formation which Marx dealt with: first, the February days marking the rebellion by the workers. Second, the period of the constitution of the French Republic, which occurred between May 1848 and May 1849. Third, from May 1849 to December 1851 was the period of the Constitutional Republic. In looking at these periods, Marx explicitly focused on the political play between what he called the particular and general interest – terms which derive from Hegel. The formation of the state arises, Marx wrote, from the new class interests emerging at the time, involving what he called 'the severing' of the 'common interest' from the 'general interest' of society.[239]

Marx traced the steps of state development emerging from the three periods. The first period, the February period, was described by Marx as the prologue to the revolution. During February of 1848, the workers mounted an open rebellion against the authorities and breached the barricades which had been put up by the National Guard. The French troops put up little resistance and many believed that it was a victory for the workers against the monarchy and the commercial classes. The workers, Marx pointed out, had 'proclaimed it to be a social republic.'[240] In the second period, formally called the period of the constitution, the bourgeoisie acted to block the advances of the workers by parliamentary devices and reduced the revolution to a victory by the commercial classes. In the third period, headed by Louis Bonaparte, there was the formation of the Constitutional Republic in which the commercial classes ruled in the name of the people and the demands of the workers were suppressed by the emerging 'general interest.'

Marx's discussion in *Eighteenth Brumaire* focused on how the French

238 Marx, *The Civil War in France*, p. 11.
239 Marx, *Eighteenth Brumaire*, pp. 104–5.
240 Ibid., p. 16.

state was formed as the circle of its rule contracted and a more exclusive interest was maintained against a wider, more general interest. The name Marx gave to this process, was the 'severing of the common interest from the general interest of society.' Two central passages illustrate this key process in Marx's theory of the state.[241] The first of these is from *The Civil War in France*, the second from *Eighteenth Brumaire*.

> The centralized state machinery which, with its ubiquitous and complicated military, bureaucratic, clerical and judiciary organs, encoils the living civil society like a boa constrictor, was first forged in the days of absolute monarchy as a weapon of nascent modern society in its struggle of emancipation from feudalism. The seignorial privileges of the medieval lords and cities and clergy were transformed into the attributes of a unitary state power, displacing the feudal dignitaries by salaried state functionaries, transferring the arms from medieval retainers of the landlords and the corporations of townish citizens to a standing army; substituting for the anarchy of conflicting medieval powers the regulated plan of a state power, with a systematic and hierarchic division of labour. The first French Revolution, with its task to found a national unity, had to break down all local, territorial, townish and provincial independence. It was, therefore, forced to develop, what absolute monarchy had commenced, the centralization and organization of state power, and to expand the circumference and the attributes of the state power, the number of its tools, its independence, and its supernaturalist sway over real society which in fact took the place of the supernaturalist concept of heaven, with its saints. Every minor solitary interest engendered by the relations of social groups was separated from society itself, fixed and made independent of it and opposed to it in the form of state interest, administered by state priests with exactly determined hierarchical functions.[242]

> The legitimate monarchy and the July monarchy added nothing but a great division of labour within bourgeois society creating new groups of interests, and, therefore, new material for state administration. Every common interest was straightway severed from society, counterposed to it as a higher, general interest, snatched from the activity of society's members themselves and made an object of government activity, from the bridge, a schoolhouse and the communal property of a village community to the railways, the national wealth and the national university of France.[243]

Marx showed that, as the new material interests become consolidated, the agents of these interests (whether political, economic or military) 'sever' themselves from the common interest and begin 'counterposing' it to a 'higher general interest.'[244] This 'general interest' wrote Marx, is thus 'snatched from the self-activity of society's members and made an object of state machinery and governmental activity from the bridge, the school house, the judiciary and the church which act as its representatives.'[245]

241 Further discussion of Marx's theory of the state can be found in Hal Draper, *Karl Marx's Theory of Revolution*, New York: Monthly Review Press, 1977.

242 Marx, *The Civil War in France*, Peking: Foreign Languages Press, 1970, pp. 162–3.

243 Marx, *Eighteenth Brumaire*, p. 104.

244 Ibid., pp. 104–5.

245 Ibid., pp. 104–5.

The State and Civil Society in Smith, Hegel and Marx

The next step in tracing the development of the political structure of society is Marx's discussion of the emergence of civil society found in 'On the Jewish Question.' No discussion of Marx's theory of the state would be complete without looking at the relationship between political and civil society. The term 'civil society' first made its appearance in the works of Adam Smith and later in the work of Hegel.[246] Initially, Smith used the term to refer to a sphere, separate from the political, in which competition and self-interest were played out in the market. This confrontation of many individual self-interests engaged in individual acts of buying and selling and in market exchange was, for Smith, what gave civil society its particular character of competition and motivated self-interest. Smith believed, however, that the individual economic acts of self-interest contributed to the common good of society by promoting national wealth and economic well-being.

While Hegel had read Smith, his conception of civil society was completely different. In contrast to Smith, Hegel saw civil society as a separate sphere existing outside the political state. In the *Philosophy of Right*, Hegel had argued that while civil society and the political state were separate spheres, he thought that the political state itself acted to 'mediate the particular interest through the universal interest.'[247] Hegel reasoned that 'individual self-seeking turns into a contribution to the satisfaction of the needs of everyone and, by a dialectical advance, self seeking turns into the mediation of the particular through the universal, with the result that each individual's earning, producing and enjoying, is at the same time producing and earning for the enjoyment of everyone else.'[248] While, for Hegel, civil society is associated with the sphere of self-interest and individual acquisition, it is opposed to political society and is separate from it. Thus, unlike Smith, Hegel thought that the state was above self-interest and overcame the contradiction between the self-interest of the individual and the public obligation of the citizen by upholding the universal interest or common good.

In two early writings, *A Critique of Hegel's Philosophy of Right* and 'On the Jewish Question', Marx rejected as absurd Hegel's assertion that the state 'mediates' the private interest by upholding the common good of society. Instead, Marx took the position that the state was complicit in the split between the political and civil realm and, in fact, actively supported self-interest in its defense of private property. Marx went on to show that, in its defense of private property, the state is the instrument of the dominant classes since it supports the outright ownership of the means of production by only one class in society. Marx thus equated the state with the economically powerful classes who act through state coercion and

---

246 Hegel, *Philosophy of Right*, pp. 129–30.
247 Ibid., pp. 129–30.
248 Ibid., pp. 129–30.

power. From this viewpoint, the state is equated with the capitalist classes, since only these classes are able to use the state as an 'instrument' to realize their own economic ends and interests.

The remaining questions are, how does civil society arise and how has it come to be defended by the state? In order to answer these questions we have to look more closely at Marx's concept of civil society. Marx borrowed the term from Hegel's writing. In the *Philosophy of Right*, Hegel had asserted that the state rises above self-interest by mediating it through the universal interest.[249] Marx fundamentally rejected this view by asserting that it was not possible for the state to rise above 'self-interest,' since the state promoted it through its defense of private property. Marx thought that only when the state renounces property relations can it stand above the particular interest, and only then can the state constitute itself universally.

Subsequently Marx turned his attention to the historical development of civil society. He pointed out that in feudal times, all of society had a political character and there was no formal separation between the civil and political realm. In this sense, all aspects of civil life such as property, occupation and family had been subsumed under the political in the form of lordship, caste and guild.[250] While individuals were commonly part of larger political bodies and the state encompassed the political and the civil realm at the same time, there was no independent private or civil sphere defined by the economy as such. The modern state, therefore, comes into existence only with the institutionalization of the capitalist economy and the effect of this economy on the political structure. The term civil society, then, is intended to point to the precise historical moment when there is the development of an independent economic realm which emerges as a consequence of individuals pursuing private interest through economic gain. With the emergence of civil society, therefore, there is a shift in the center of political gravity from the state to the economy. Historically, this change is thought to have come about as a consequence of the Industrial Revolution, and the term civil society is thus used to designate the split occurring in society between the political and civil spheres that is unique to modern times.

At the center of civil society stands the 'free individual' stripped of all ties to communal bodies, individuals who pursue their private interest for individual gain. These individuals, Marx wrote, are the 'citizen whose political rights and freedoms are simply the rights of the egoistic individual, the individual separated from community, isolated and withdrawn into themselves.'[251] According to Marx, the development of civil society presupposes three distinct but interrelated elements: (i) the satisfaction of

249 Ibid., p. 134.
250 Karl Marx, 'On the Jewish Question,' in Robert C. Tucker, *The Marx–Engels Reader* (2nd edn), New York: W.W. Norton and Company, 1978, p. 44.
251 Ibid., p. 42.

all wants through the pursuit of private economic gain; (ii) the protection of private property; and (iii) the replacement of direct ties with society by abstract political and legal links.

These developments were central to the formation of the modern state in several respects: (i) as the breakup of the old political bodies of estate, caste and guild took place, the individual became an autonomous sphere of social and economic action; (ii) all action became a 'private affair' of the individual rather than part of the wider community; (iii) the separation between society and the state came into existence after the decentralization of the political monarchy; (iv) state affairs became the public affair of the people rather than the private affair of the monarch; (v) political links between members of society were abstractly conceived in the form of laws, rights and freedoms; and (vi) with the advent of economic society and the market, there was a shift in the center of political gravity from the state to the economy and as a result this led to the split between the political and civil spheres.

Marx believed that civil society brought about the breakdown of the individual's relation to society and community by fragmenting the political whole into economic and social parts. At the end of this process, said Marx, is the isolated individual whose private autonomy is a political and social absurdity. In his view, modern civil society sets individuals into conflict in two specific ways: first, so far as it encourages individuals to pursue their private interests, they are thrown into competition with one another since each seeks to maximize their private economic gain. Second, so far as the state confers upon them common political rights, the individual's relation to society appears to be cooperative, when in reality it is coercive. Where Hegel saw civil society and the political state as separate, Marx saw them as one and the same. 'At certain periods,' wrote Marx, 'the political state comes violently to birth in civil society.'[252]

Marx's Dialectical View of History

Marx did not explicitly outline his methodological views of history and society or his theory of dialectical change and development. Frederick Engels, however, did write a work on the dialectic entitled *Anti-Dühring*.[253] For Marx's own view on the dialectic, some fragments are accessible in works such as *Capital* (1867–94) and *The Poverty of Philosophy*, published in 1847. In the latter work, Marx referred to the 'emancipation' of the worker, and in the same passage he repeated the belief that while human beings are essentially free, they are everywhere subordinated to economic conditions in which one social class is subject to another. One of the central points of departure of Marx's work was to show that social classes

252 Ibid., p. 36.
253 Engels, *Anti-Dühring*.

were products of historical social relations. What was and still is important about this observation is that, for the first time, he had shown that social relations were not fixed for all time but could, in fact, be altered. What is key about Marx's thinking along this line, is his drawing into question a process by means of which individuals are gradually freed from conditions which make them economic subjects. What is unique here is the emancipatory nature of his thinking and the belief that social emancipation would mark the transition from class history into human history.[254] It is, therefore, important to trace Marx's thinking on this question. We begin with the famous passage from *The Poverty of Philosophy*:

> Economic conditions had first transformed the mass of people of the country into workers. The combination of capital has created for this mass a common situation, common interests. This mass is thus already a class against capital, but not yet for itself. In the struggle, of which we have noted only a few phases, this mass becomes united, and constitutes itself as a class for itself. The interests it defends become class interests. But it is a question of making a precise study of [the] forms in which the proletarians carry out before our eyes their organization as a class, some are seized by real fear and others display a transcendental disdain. An oppressed class is the vital condition for every society founded on the antagonism of classes. The emancipation of the oppressed class thus implies necessarily the creation of a new society. For the oppressed class to be able to emancipate itself it is necessary that the productive powers already acquired and the existing social relations should no longer be capable of existing side by side. Does this mean that after the fall of the old society there will be a new class domination cultivating in a new political power? No. The condition for the emancipation of the working class is the abolition of every class, just as the condition for the liberation of the third estate, of the bourgeois order, was the abolition of all estates. The working class, in the course of its development, will substitute for the old civil society an association which will exclude classes and their antagonism, and there will be no more political power since political power is precisely the official expression of antagonism in civil society. Indeed, is it at all surprising that a society founded on the opposition of classes should culminate in brutal contradiction, the shock of body against body, as its final dénouement?[255]

The language of development used by Marx in this description – 'class in itself', 'class for itself', 'opposition', 'antagonism', 'contradiction' etc. – is distinctly Hegelian. In order to trace in what way Marx had borrowed from Hegel in putting forward a theory of development, it will be useful briefly to look at the history of the dialectic and then look specifically at Hegel's dialectical thinking.

History of the Term 'Dialectic'

The term 'dialectic' can be traced to early Greek philosophy beginning with the work of Socrates and Aristotle, who essentially used it as a method to get at underlying truths which could not be obtained using

254 Marx, *The Poverty of Philosophy*, p. 170.
255 Ibid., pp. 173–4.

techniques of observation and sense perception. Later, in the eighteenth and nineteenth centuries, dialectics reached its highest stage of development in the work of Hegel who had employed the method in showing the interconnections between categories of existence such as history, spirit, and consciousness. Somewhat later, in the twentieth century, dialectics fell into disuse after British philosophers claimed that it was unreliable as a method due to its speculative nature.

Though Marx never completely outlined his methods or explicitly developed a view of dialectical theory, Engels did elaborate on the principle of the dialectic in a work entitled *Anti-Dühring*, published in 1878. According to Engels, the central principle of dialectical thinking is to be found in the concept of 'relation' or 'interconnection.'[256] According to these concepts, the natural world and the human world appear as a vast set of interrelations in which everything is related in terms of the past, present and future.[257] Under these circumstances, stated Engels, it is possible to visualize these interconnections when we picture ourselves, the world, and others in terms of relational concepts such as humanity, history, the world, experience, existence, etc.:

> When we reflect on the nature or the history of mankind we see the picture of an endless maze of connections and interconnections, in which nothing remains what, where and as it was, but everything moves, changes, comes into being and passes away. This primitive, naive, but intrinsically correct conception of the world is that of ancient Greek philosophy, and was first clearly formulated by Heraclitus: everything is and also is not, for everything is in flux, is constantly changing, constantly coming into being and passing away.[258]

Given this broad outline, it is possible to isolate three interrelated features of the dialectic which make it distinct as a methodological tool. First is its tendency to view all human beings as being linked to the world and to others through a series of interconnected social and historical relations which confer unity and difference at the same time. For example, we are individuals, yet we are also members of nations which unify our political purposes. These commonalities shared by all human beings may be understood in terms of collective concepts sometimes called totalities. These include concepts such as humanity, history, reality, existence, etc. Thus, interconnection refers to the fact that while we are distinct individuals, we are at the same time connected in some fundamental way to these larger totalities. Second is the tendency to believe that the totalities and our links to them form an interconnected web of relations which defines our being and humanity in some fundamental way. Third is the tendency to assume that all history and matter are in a state of constant change, movement and transformation in which things are coming into being, existing and passing away. Under these circumstances, no individual

256 Engels, *Anti-Dühring*, p. 24.
257 Ibid., p. 24.
258 Ibid., p. 24.

thing, no part or segment, is entirely separate from any other, but is always a part of a larger whole or unity to which it is essentially connected.

Hegel's Dialectic

In 1812, Hegel had worked out a theory of dialectics in a work called *The Science of Logic*.[259] In it he propounded a theory of historical development, self-emancipation and change. Hegel's theory began by stating the view that all things are in a continuous state of motion and change and that the general laws of motion are intrinsic to the development of the individual, history and thought. Hegel thus viewed the world, existence and being in terms of processes in which all things were interconnected and related to one another, rather than being separate entities. Viewed in this way, everything is subject to change and development since nothing remains unchanged. The existence of any one thing, Hegel thought, can only be understood 'in relation to' another, and this relational view led to an understanding of the integration of separate things into larger totalities of being which Hegel essentially conceptualized in terms of the categories of history, spirit, consciousness, and reason.[260]

The doctrine that all things are interconnected to larger wholes later became the theoretical basis for the dialectical view of reality and history. According to this perspective, no individual is independent of or separate from others since each is connected to larger historical wholes such as history and humanity which define their relation to the social world. Hegel's concept of 'being in relation to' not only established the interconnectedness of what appeared to be disconnected, it also challenged the view of the world which had asserted that each thing is separate in itself. The concept of a thing existing in itself as well as the belief that there are sharp distinctions between stages of existence, such as being and non-being, freedom and slavery, self-realization and estrangement, were being rethought in the light of a dialectical perspective.

Hegel went on to reason that one of the key features of development was the process he called 'contradiction.' Stated simply, the principle of contradiction refers to the existence of opposites or conflicting elements in reality. Hegel believed that there can be no development without contradiction and that, in fact, contradiction was rooted in reality and history. Contradiction, therefore, refers to the presence of the principles of affirmation and negation co-existing simultaneously. Hegel believed that contradiction is present in the world, in reality and in thought, and is reflected in the existence of opposing elements which brings about the process of change and development. In religion, for instance, contradiction exists in the struggle between two opposing tendencies in human

---

259 G.W.F. Hegel, *The Science of Logic*, Vol. 2, London: Allen & Unwin, [1812] 1929.

260 For discussion of Hegel's dialectic see, J.N. Findlay, *Hegel: A Re-Examination*, London: George Allen & Unwin, 1958.

experience, such as good and evil. In theological reasoning, neither of these exist independently of each other but only in relation to some other principle from which each derives its existence and so on. Hegel's theory of contradictions amounts to nothing more than the belief that existence, being and thought reflect the principle of tension through which there is development and change. In everyday life, the essentially contradictory natures of conflicting elements express themselves in the wider struggle of existence.

In his larger philosophic works, Hegel went on to develop the principle of contradiction into a full-blown theory of development. He believed that there were three main stages in the process: first is the stage he called 'affirmation,' sometimes referred to as the thesis. Hegel used the term affirmation to refer to anything which has being or existence. Understood in this sense, affirmation is the capacity of an existing thing to affirm itself and to be in the world, actively rather than passively. This means that in its being, it 'affirms' itself, and this affirmation is a principle of its own being or existence. Moreover, as it affirms itself, it expresses inherent 'potential' for development and propagation.

The second stage of the dialectic is referred to as the 'negation,' sometimes called antithesis. In Hegel's view, this refers to the principle in the world which acts to limit or resist development. Negation is key to the dialectical process since it refers to any limitation which acts to thwart or restrict the capacity of an existing thing to develop its own being. In this sense, the principle of negation not only stands as the opposite of affirmation but it also implies the stronger connotation of that which shuts out existence along with connoting limit or boundary.[261] Hegel used the term primarily to understand the tendency of a thing or individual to encounter limitations which act to 'negate' development by imposing boundaries. While Hegel believed that all things had their characteristic way of being negated, he thought that negation itself gives rise to further development and ' therefore is an act in the sequence of development.'[262] According to Engels, the negation 'does not mean simply no, or declaring that something does not exist, or destroying it in any way one likes.'[263] Rather, negation can be looked upon as a principle of development in that it sets up the tendency to resist, and such resistance acts as a means to affirmation.

A third principle of the dialectic is the concept of 'negation of the negation' or synthesis.[264] While Hegel had used the term to express what he saw as the completion of a cycle of development, its primary reference

261 Hegel often used the term 'shutting out existence' to describe negation. Simply stated, a negation is an external thing or principle which acts to negate that which exists. Hegel, *Phenomenology of Mind*, p. 510.

262 Engels, *Anti-Dühring*, p. 181.

263 Ibid., p. 180.

264 See Z.A. Jordan, *The Evolution of Dialectical Materialism*, New York: St. Martin's Press, 1967.

is to the capacity of the negation to be reconstituted or fundamentally altered in its nature. Since negation itself stands for limit or boundary, then 'negation of the negation' is simply that principle of development which reconstitutes the limits by bringing an end to, or surpassing, the boundaries or limitations. Hegel went on to reason that both terms expressed laws of development because the negation of the negation altered the state of the individual's limitation and in this sense was transformative. This can be seen in Hegel's favorite example of the master and slave. Hegel believed that slaves are transformed into beings who are for themselves only when they re-appropriate their self-activity through a conscious 'negation of the negation,' in a process Hegel referred to as 'formative activity.'[265] In this formative activity, he reasoned, the slave 'destroys the negative elements which stand over and against the slave as an individual and thereby becomes someone existing on their own account.'[266] What is important here is that Hegel's categories of 'freedom' and 'emancipation' are implicit within development.

This cycle of affirmation, negation, and negation of the negation (thesis, antithesis and synthesis) represents dialectical movement and change. While these concepts have a problematic status since Hegel's original formulation, when looked at in straightforward terms they reveal a theory of existence, development and change.

Marx's Dialectic

Marx took the dialectic in a completely different direction and, in order to outline his contribution, it is important to look again at the distinction Marx made between materialism and idealism. Idealism had asserted that, before anything else, thought had primacy over matter in the development of history. Hegel believed that the 'idea' came before reality and therefore was the fundamental concern of philosophy. Marx, by contrast, believed that the material world preceded the world of ideas and this laid the foundation for a theory of historical development based on human economic needs. The doctrine of materialism, therefore, held that since the material world is first, then the development of mind must be derived from material existence.[267] The problem with Hegel's thinking, as Marx saw it, was that Hegel believed that ideas were ultimate realities, so much so that relations between human beings were seen as consequences of the relations between ideas. So much did Hegel view ideas as dominant forces in history that he believed that ideas rather than individuals were the ultimate causal

---

265 Hegel, *Phenomenology of Mind*, pp. 229–40.

266 G.W.F. Hegel, *Phenomenology of Spirit*, Oxford: Oxford University Press, 1977, p. 118.

267 This was made evident in Marx's statement in the 1859 preface to *A Contribution to the Critique*, where he states: 'It is not the consciousness of men that determines their existence, but their social existence that determines their consciousness,' p. 21.

agents in historical development. This meant that, for Hegel, ideas were always the focal point of historical process and change.

Marx rejected this view and went on to criticize it in a number of ways. First, he thought that Hegel's dialectic was mystical because of its extraordinary emphasis on the idea rather than on historical processes. Second, Marx thought that Hegel's understanding of the principles of motion in the theory of development offered little opportunity to explain detailed historical mechanisms. Third, he claimed that Hegel's system provided no clues on how to establish an empirical basis of development founded upon historical reality.

One of the key assumptions of materialism was its presumption of the existence of motion and change as the key principles of development. Both Marx and Engels believed that motion was the primary existence form of matter. But, in order to distinguish their view from Hegel's, they had to develop the principle of motion more explicitly – and this meant that it had to be explained and classified. In order to do this they had to adopt, at least in part, the laws of development which had been worked out by Hegel. Borrowing primarily from Hegel's *Logic*, Engels took the view that motion was the central principle of historical change and believed it accounted for the changing nature of the society, experience and matter.[268] From this position, Engels argued that motion was the principle determinant of change and, as a theory of change, he believed it explained the conditions under which matter forms links with larger wholes and transforms itself from one state to another. This doctrine, later described as the first law of the dialectic, was referred to as the doctrine of leaps, and it maintained that matter undergoes qualitative change as it moves from one form to another and changes from one substance into another, such as water to ice, liquid to gas, etc.[269]

Marx and Engels believed that the doctrine of the dialectic was a central explanatory principle and therefore regarded it as a formal theory of development. Understood in this way, the dialectic explained two key principles of social and historical change: first, it put forward the view that change was inherent in all matter; and second, it implied that in the process of change and development there is an interconnection between the historical, political and social spheres. On these two assumptions, Marx and Engels were able to put forward a theory of change which explained the process of transformation from one state of being to another and, at the same time, they were able to describe the decisive moment of change itself.

For his part, Engels found support for this view in scientific discoveries of the nineteenth century, especially the evolutionary theories of Charles Darwin.[270] Evolutionary thought had assumed that the stages of

268 Engels, *Anti-Dühring*, pp. 24–5.
269 Ibid., pp. 69–94.
270 Jordan, *Evolution of Dialectical Materialism*, p. 168.

development were in fact connected in a series marked by the movement from complex to more refined structures through the addition of more and more elements or properties. Darwin's thinking had led to the view that the apparent diversity of things was in fact rooted in some underlying principle, the development and ultimate determinants of which give rise to complex existence leading to greater and greater diversity. The impact of Darwin's work on Engels was significant since he believed it provided the scientific basis for a dialectical theory of development.[271] Darwin had shown that the interconnection between species led to a discovery of the underlying principle of development which created structural leaps (different species) related to the accumulation and succession of changes in relation to the environment.

The key assumptions of evolutionary thought are as follows: (i) material reality is made up of various levels and structures whose interconnections can be reduced to essential laws; (ii) an existing stage of development has emerged from a level preceding it; and (iii) the structure of the developing stage or level is tied to the previous one and can be discerned from its interaction with the levels that are related to it.[272] In short, these levels are related to the development of the previous level or stage. Each of the levels, in fact, exists in the empirical world as well as in nature. While Darwin had shown that all nature was interconnected and that the process of development of the species was tied to a sequence of events whose interconnections were law-like in their development and which themselves led to new structures providing evidence for leaps, other discoveries in physics and biology led to the view that the apparent diversity of things was, in fact, related at some other underlying level of reality.

Differences Between Marx and Hegel in the Dialectical View of History

Having stated Hegel's and Marx's views on the dialectic, it is possible to discern at least four key differences between them. First, the difference in their doctrine of development; second, the difference in the principle of contradiction; third, the difference in the stages of development and how the stages are historically expressed; and fourth, the difference existing in their use of the 'doctrine of relations.' First, let us look at the doctrine of development.

Hegel believed that development occurs in the changes taking place in ideas. Marx, on the other hand, took the view that change occurs in material conditions and in concrete historical processes. In contrast to Hegel's dialectic, Marx's doctrine of development is called the materialist dialectic in order to indicate the shift from the dominance of ideas to the dominance of material conditions. Whereas Hegel had believed that the

271 Ibid., p. 168.
272 Ibid., pp. 151–73.

principles of development (contradiction, affirmation, negation, negation of the negation), were represented by ideas acting in history, Marx took the opposing view that the principles of change were in fact manifested in concrete historical development of economic production in society. Marx had thus placed a decisive materialist emphasis on what Hegel had seen as ideas.[273]

Second, on the question of contradictions, Hegel's doctrine stated that any existing thing encounters opposition without which there can be no development in history. Marx, by contrast, believed that Hegel's concept of contradiction was too abstract since it referred to processes and development only in mystical terms. In direct contrast to this, Marx thought that the law of contradiction was manifested historically in the form of the coercive class structure of society, since it was a material expression of the law of contradiction (opposition and negation) expressed at the level of economic relations.

Third is the question of the stages of development. While Hegel believed that the stages of development progressed from inexplicit and undifferentiated stages to more explicit and differentiated levels, he never went beyond the speculative dimension in conceiving of this development. Marx, by contrast, saw the stages of development taking place in societies and thought that their historical progression was related to economic production and the system of social classes. In this sense, Marx's historical configuration of successive societies and class structures made the dialectic historically real.

Fourth is the doctrine of relations. This concept is extremely important in the thinking of both Hegel and Marx, to say nothing of how Marx systematically used the concept as a major analytical tool in *Capital* and other works.[274] While the concept of relation embodies complex philosophical precepts, its basic underlying principle is simple and goes to the heart of dialectical thinking. Simply stated, one of the key assertions of the doctrine of dialectics is the web of interconnectedness between things. The term relation, then, is a philosophic concept used to describe the connection between two disparate wholes or realities which act in respect of each other. Looked at from this point of view, what Marx and Engels had learned from Hegel was that every relation can be viewed from two distinct vantage points: (i) from relations to itself, and (ii) from relations with others and to the world.[275] Both Hegel and Marx spoke of these relations in terms of subject–object relations. Hegel, for his part, believed in the reality of opposites (subject–object, general–particular, unity–difference) and took the view that only when taken together could these opposites be understood. Hegel used the concept of relation, therefore, as a way of indicating that in looking at opposites – such as master and

---

273 On this point see Engels, *Anti-Dühring*, pp. 12–15.
274 Hook, *From Hegel to Marx*, p. 70.
275 Ibid., p. 70.

slave, subject and object – one must comprehend two sides of the relationship, for without both sides there is no unity. Since, in this view, the essence of reality has two sides – a subject and an object, part and whole – all analysis must capture the experience and reality of each side in the relation to form a complete representation of the whole. Taking the principle of development into account, Hegel believed that no process could be understood completely by itself as any development must form relations in the movement from one stage into another. The term relation, therefore, is a way of getting at the intermediate causal connection implied in the movement between stages.

When applied by Marx, the concept of relation became an extraordinary analytical tool. For Marx, each relation had two sides which were fundamentally related and it is only the totality of these relations which form reality. Like Hegel, Marx examined the connection between both sides of the relation since he believed that either side represents a dimension of experience and reality which is necessarily excluded when only one side is examined.[276] This is nowhere more evident than in Marx's criticism of Smith and Ricardo. He believed that they failed to see the fundamental connection between economic categories such as capital, labor, production and consumption. He thought that these central concepts could not, in fact, be used to define independent economic events – such as capital and labor, production and consumption – but in every case made reference to fundamental interconnections and human social relations. His critique of theories which lose sight of these interconnections is therefore fundamental to his procedure.

Engels and the Dialectic

By the time Engels was writing *Anti-Dühring*, he was familiar with three laws of the Hegelian dialectic: (i) the law of the transformation of quantity into quality; (ii) the law of the interpenetration of opposites; and (iii) the law of the negation of the negation.[277] While Engels believed that the laws of the dialectic were scientifically valid, he differed from Hegel insofar as he applied the dialectic to society and history rather than to the realm of ideas. Engels reasoned that, because the doctrine of dialectics applies to the natural and social world, it could be universally applied to history and this made the laws of development empirically valid.

The first law of the dialectic stated that one structure can be transformed into another through cumulative change, leading ultimately to qualitative development. In the natural world this transformation of matter can be found at the level of physical substances, such as when water changes into a solid or when a liquid forms a gas. In the natural world one substance is transformed into the other when qualitative change

276 Ibid., p. 70.
277 Engels, *Anti-Dühring*, pp. 150–201.

takes place, but this occurs only when new properties accumulate to a sufficient extent that it creates the 'leap' into structural change. The second law of the dialectic claims that the nature of existence is full of contradictions. Engels believed that these primarily operate in the material world and exist in the form of class contradictions. Lastly, the third law of dialectic, the negation of the negation, assumed its expression in the material world in the form of the opposition to the economic and political dominance of the ruling classes. Negation arises from its own implicit existence and 'develops out of itself elements which put an end to its existence and transform it into its own opposite.'[278]

Application of the Dialectic to History

So far, two precepts characterize the materialist dialectic: first, the view that there is a tendency for a social form to pass into another due to the economic contradictions inherent within it. Second, the belief that there is a capacity of a given social form to be replaced by a new one in which the preceding social relation forms part of the new society, giving rise to a class struggle from which a new formation emerges. Both Marx and Engels believed that the principle of development, put forward by Hegel, expressed itself directly in the form of historical development. While Hegel had believed that history demonstrated the process of coming into being, passing away, etc., Marx's and Engels' point of departure was to show how this pattern of development operated at the historical level.

According to Marx, historical events tended to confirm the existence of such a pattern. The events of 1789 and 1848 – both of which were revolutionary expressions of change and development – confirmed the tendency of the pre-existing social order to pass from one social form into another and upheld the belief that, as the old order gave way to a new one, old productive forces were gradually replaced by new productive forces. At the same level of historical reality, other events, such as the workers' uprising of 1831 and the agitation by factory workers during the Chartist rebellion of 1842, pinpointed the consistency of the class struggle between two kinds of groups in society: between the sellers and buyers of wage labor; between the proletariat and the bourgeoisie, between the class of property owners and the class of laborers. This pattern of development, Marx thought, made possible the economic interpretation of history in a way not seen before. Engels stated this clearly when he wrote: 'the new facts made imperative a new examination of all past history. Then it was seen that all past history, was the history of class struggle, that these social classes warring with each other are always the products of the relations of production and exchange; in a word, of the economic relations of their epoch.'[279] As Engels stated, a way had been found for a materialist

278 Jordan, *Evolution of Dialectical Materialism*, p. 190.
279 Engels, *Anti-Dühring*, p. 33.

treatment of history in which human consciousness could be explained by economic being.[280] This dialectical view of history is expressed clearly in Engels' comment on Marx's method:

> It was Marx who first discovered the great law of motion of history, the law according to which all historical struggles, whether they proceed in the political, religious, philosophical or some other ideological domain, are in fact only the more or less clear expression of struggles of social classes, and that the existence and thereby the collisions, too, between these classes are in turn conditioned by the degree of development of their economic position, by the mode of their production and of their exchange determined by it. This law, which has the same significance for history as the law of the transformation of energy has for natural science – this law gave him here the key to an understanding of the history of the second French Republic.[281]

Marx reasoned that society and history can be understood as a sequence of economic laws which reflect a distinctive pattern of development. This pattern of development takes the historical form: primitive communism, slavery, feudalism, capitalism, socialism. This development, in fact, shows that the succession of societies and their system of social relations are interconnected and confirm the underlying process of development described by the materialist dialectic, and that its material expression is to be found at the level of economic existence.

Marx and Engels believed that the materialist theory of development was, in fact, realized at the historical and social level in the existence of social classes. More than any other historical principle, social class constituted the theoretical affirmation of the materialist dialectic. This meant that Marx and Engels had developed precisely what Hegel's laws were lacking when they provided an empirical basis to historical development itself.

But, in what way can a social class undergo historical transformation? Marx thought that a social class can surpass its limits when the contradictions existing between the classes become so great that the subordinate class comes to realize that they share common conditions of poverty and exploitation. This increases their conscious awareness of the fact that they share similar external conditions and, in this, they are transformed from being a 'class in itself' into a 'class for itself'. For Marx, this meant that social classes were 'carriers of the transformative principle,' and this constituted the empirical basis of historical social change.[282] If this is true, what causes classes to act?

We know that societies create social contradictions which act as intermediate stages of transformation and development and Marx himself looked at the social mechanisms which produce these conditions. Contradictions were thus principles of social change. In this sense, a social class is a transformative principle historically when it acts as a class for itself and

280 Ibid., p. 33.
281 F. Engels, preface to Marx, *Eighteenth Brumaire*, p. 9.
282 Ibid.

when its social cohesion is effected by contradictions which create common conditions of experience. Marx thought that social classes reflected these common conditions and argued that they are a basis of unity and class cohesion.[283] Each historical stage, Marx thought, begins with a mode of production, the economic organization of which creates specific conditions leading to a class that is socially dominant over another. This class structure of society conforms to the laws of dialectical development to the extent that one class negates the other, the other existing to maintain the economic well-being of the class existing over them. In this process of development, contradiction and opposition, Marx thought, the negation promotes the cohesion of the subordinate class. They form a class whose common conditions of poverty and exploitation constitute a principle of development and change – the negation of the negation. All Marx's examples of the materialist dialectic are historical. In the first case, the French Revolution of 1789, it is the opposition by one class against the dominance of another. As a second example, Marx uses the revolution of the second Bonaparte which occurred in 1848. In both these cases Marx was able to draw clear historical patterns whose formation demonstrated the dialectical principles of change.

---

283 Hook, *From Hegel to Marx*, p. 71.

3

Emile Durkheim

The Historical Context of Emile Durkheim's Work

Emile Durkheim was born on April 15, 1858 in Épinal, a small town in rural France. He grew up in a traditional Jewish family which lived on a modest income. Durkheim's father was an orthodox rabbi who served the Jewish community in the surrounding province while his mother added to the family income by working outside the home.[1] At an early age, Durkheim was a successful student, acquiring the personal discipline which enabled him to focus on academic pursuits early in his life. As an outstanding student, he obtained entrance to the École Normale in Paris in 1879 where he worked on his doctorate. In 1885 he received a fellowship to study at the University of Berlin for a year and, after returning from Germany, obtained a university position at Bordeaux at the age of 29. During his stay at Bordeaux, Durkheim completed several major sociological works, including *The Division of Labor in Society*, *The Rules of Sociological Method* and *Suicide*. In 1902, after obtaining a position at the Sorbonne, Durkheim moved to Paris where he began work on one of his most ambitious studies, *The Elementary Forms of the Religious Life*, published in 1912. At the Sorbonne, Durkheim established himself as a major figure in French social thought. By the time of his death in 1917, at the age of 59, he had produced a large body of scholarly work and founded one of the most coherent sociological perspectives of the nineteenth century. He is best known for founding sociology as a scientific discipline and for defining the boundaries of its subject matter.

Historically, the circumstances shaping Durkheim's sociological interests are rooted in the political climate existing in France between 1870 and 1895. By 1871, France was in a deep political crisis which had led to a decline in its national unity. The ensuing social and political changes taking place in France during this period shaped the intellectual and social climate in which Durkheim worked. By 1880, France had begun to pursue a policy of political consolidation to rebuild its national identity and this led to a stress on two broad social themes. First was the national stress on science and social progress. Discoveries in the natural sciences had increased the prestige of the scientific method, giving rise to what one

---

1 S. Lukes, *Emile Durkheim: His Life and Work*, Stanford: Stanford University Press. 1973.

historian called the 'cult of the sciences' in France.[2] This led many thinkers to take the view that the moral direction of the nation could be best served by promoting scientific development and by studying the problems of society scientifically.[3] This national stress on science and social progress unified the French educational system and brought about changes to social institutions by promoting political reforms. As French nationalism began to grow, new intellectual currents such as positivism developed and this led to the use of science to solve social problems.[4]

The second theme to emerge in France was that of anti-individualism. While this had its roots in the social upheaval of the French Revolution, a political crisis known as the Dreyfus Affair in 1894 threatened to divide France by drawing attention to the individual and by calling national unity into question. The controversy over individualism centered primarily on the autonomy of the individual from society. Many believed that since the revolution, the individual was separate from society and entered into relations with it only out of economic necessity and self-interest. Durkheim believed that this threatened the cohesion of social institutions and obscured the authoritative nature of group life. The social upheaval and lack of national direction arising from the Dreyfus Affair led Durkheim to take a strong anti-individualist stance which is reflected in his tendency to criticize the growing autonomy of the individual.[5] As a result, Durkheim's central investigative focus was based on the view that individual autonomy grows only at the expense of the collective forces of society.

Intellectual Influences on Durkheim's Work

A number of key theoretical influences helped shaped Durkheim's views on society. Of these, at least three influences are significant. First was Comte's perspective on scientific methodology which helped Durkheim found an investigative method to examine society scientifically. Second were the debates related to the problem of individualism, which were common in France after the revolution. Third were the influences derived from the political writings of Thomas Hobbes and Jean-Jacques Rousseau, whose individualist doctrines tended to trace the origins of society to individual human nature. Beginning with Comte, let us look at some of the influences on Durkheim's work.

Though Comte did not obtain the academic stature which Durkheim had, the impact of his writings on Durkheim was significant. Historically,

2 D.G. Charlton, *Secular Religions in France 1815–1870*, London: Oxford University Press, 1963.

3 For a description of the social and historical context in France see D.G. Charlton, *Positivist Thought in France During the Second Empire, 1852–70*, Oxford: Clarendon Press, 1959.

4 Steve Fenton, *Durkheim and Modern Sociology*, Cambridge: Cambridge University Press, 1984, pp. 1–22.

5 Durkheim's anti-individualist stance is most clearly developed in his 'Individualism and the Intellectuals' (trans. S. and J. Lukes), *Political Studies*, 17, [1898] 1969, pp. 14–30.

Comte is best known for developing a philosophical perspective called positivism which had an enormous influence on Durkheim's work as a whole and on the development of the social sciences throughout Europe.[6] Comte had outlined his views on positivism in a work called *Course in Positive Philosophy* which was published in 1830. Mostly developed in response to what he perceived as the anarchy of philosophic speculation that had prevailed since Hegel, Comte defined positivism as a scientific movement which sought to extend the scope of scientific investigation to the study of society. Central to positivism were two points of departure which took it beyond the dominant philosophy of the eighteenth and nineteenth centuries: first, it proclaimed the end of speculative philosophy and the mystical view of nature and history; and second, it established the authority of observation in developing a theory of knowledge.[7]

Generally, there are two interlocking assertions that made Comte's positive philosophy so influential. First, Comte put forward the 'law of three stages' which tended to equate science with historical development. Second, he developed a classification of the sciences by arranging them in terms of a definite order and by hierarchically organizing them in relation to their complexity.[8] Both these steps had an enormous impact on the social sciences which, up to that time, had been governed by speculative thought. Comte's law had asserted that the human mind develops in three distinct and unalterable stages: the theological stage, in which human beings explain causes in nature in terms of the will of anthropomorphic gods; the metaphysical stage, in which causes are explained in terms of abstract concepts and speculative truths; and the positive stage, in which causes are explained in terms of scientific laws relying on observation and fact. While Comte's understanding of scientific development was clear enough, what proved to be so controversial was his straightforward claim that the replacement of the speculative stage by the positive was inevitable and, therefore, a fact of historical progress. In essence, this meant that for many positivism became associated with progress and social reform; suddenly it became a matter of historical urgency that all disciplines develop from the speculative to the positive stage, thereby marking their scientific stature.

In addition to this, Comte developed a system for classifying the sciences and for drawing comparisons between the sciences in terms of rank.[9] He had shown that the most developed sciences were positivistic and that sciences such as mathematics, physics and biology were successful precisely because they were positivistic. This had the effect of drawing positivistic disciplines into comparison with non-positivistic ones such as

6 W. Simon, *European Positivism in the Nineteenth Century*, New York: Cornell University Press, 1963.

7 On this point see Charlton, *Secular Religions in France*.

8 Simon, *European Positivism*, pp. 4–18.

9 Ibid., pp. 4–18.

history, political economy and philosophy. This proved to be devastating for the social sciences because their non-positivistic stance was associated with an outright lack of development. By 1880, there was widespread diffusion of positivistic methods in France and England, and Durkheim, who was the direct heir of Comte's positivism, instituted the study of sociology as a scientific discipline at Bordeaux.[10]

Having looked at the impact of positivism on the social sciences, we can now define some of its central characteristics. First and foremost, positivism may be defined as a scientific outlook on the world, the aim of which was to place all the speculative sciences such as history, philosophy, and political economy on the same footing as the natural sciences. It did this by stressing three central criteria. First, it advocated that the search for ultimate or abstract truths be abandoned in favor of a search for law-like regularities. Second, positivism asserted that all statements about the world should be based on observation and that observation alone be the basis of a theory of knowledge. Third, positivism stressed the search for facts and believed that relationships among facts would lead to the discovery of general laws. From this perspective, positivism was nothing less than the 'extension of the scientific method to the study of society.'[11]

Comte's ultimate stress on the scientific study of society influenced Durkheim in several respects. First, he accepted the positivistic thesis that the study of society be founded on the examination of facts, and that facts must be subject to observation.[12] Second, Durkheim upheld the view that the only valid guide to objective knowledge is the scientific method. Third, he agreed with Comte that sociology as a science of society could be validly constituted only when it was stripped of its metaphysical abstraction and philosophical speculation.[13]

The Problem of Individualism

A second major influence on Durkheim's work was the prevailing views on individualism, prominent in the last quarter of the nineteenth century. In

10 For discussion of Durkheim's historical background, influences and views on the social sciences during the 1880s, see 'Emile Durkheim's Inaugural Lecture at Bordeaux,' (trans. Neville Layne) in *Sociological Inquiry*, 44, 1974, pp. 189–204.

11 Charlton, *Positivist Thought in France*, p. 29.

12 This is made clear in an 1897 statement by Durkheim: 'Sociological method as we practice it rests wholly on the basic principle that social facts must be studied as things, that is, as realities external to the individual. There is no principle for which we have received more criticism, but none is more fundamental. For sociology to be possible, it must above all have an object of its own. On the pretext of giving [sociology] a more solid foundation by establishing it upon the psychological constitution of the individual, it is thus robbed of the only object proper to it. It is not realized that there can be no sociology unless societies exist, and that societies cannot exist if there are only individuals.' *Suicide*, New York: The Free Press, [1897] 1951, pp. 37–8.

13 For Durkheim's discussion of how sociology must free itself from philosophy, see *The Rules of Sociological Method*, New York: The Free Press, [1895] 1938, pp. 141–6.

fact, many of Durkheim's views on society cannot be completely understood without providing some historical background to his thinking about the individual and society. In France, the concept of individualism had become a full-blown problem by the time of the French Revolution.[14] Following the 'Declaration of the Rights of Man', the individual had become the absolute center of society and for many this signified unheard of constitutional and legal reform. At the center of these reforms were individual political rights and for many this not only served to place the individual at the political center of society, it also jeopardized the collective authority of the state. While French society endorsed the concept of the individual at the political level, at another level many believed that the focus on the individual tended to undermine the authority of collective concepts of society and the state.[15] By 1870, many began to concern themselves with the excesses of individualism and it came under attack as thinkers of the period began to adopt an 'anti-individualist' stance in their political and social views.[16] This led to key debates among thinkers who began to take up positions on the relationship between society and the individual, and between collective obligations and individual rights. Durkheim, for one, set out to pursue these questions by showing that 'social life would not be possible unless there were interests that were superior to the interests of individuals.'[17]

In order to make this stance as explicit as possible, Durkheim had to wage theoretical battles and stake out claims regarding the relation between the individual and society. Chief among these was his opposition to utilitarian social theory which had become an influential doctrine by the second half of the nineteenth century. Primarily advocated by John Stuart Mill and Jeremy Bentham, utilitarianism put forward two principal views which placed the individual at the center of social life. First, they asserted that individuals act on their free will and are completely autonomous and self-determined. Second, utilitarians put forward a theory of human motivation which held that individuals have common motives impelling them to realize their self-interest by private economic gain. In this view, individual social action was based on economic interchanges with society, but beyond this the individual owed nothing to society in its own right. To the extent that individuals were autonomous, owed nothing to society, and entered into exchanges with it only on the basis of rational self-interest, the larger context of social rules outside the individual were irrelevant. In

14 See R.R. Palmer, 'Man and Citizen: Applications of Individualism in the French Revolution,' in M.R. Konvitz and A.E. Murphy (eds), *Essays in Political Theory*, New York: Kennikat Press, 1972; K.W. Swart, 'Individualism in the Mid-Nineteenth Century (1826–1860),' *Journal of the History of Ideas*, 23, 1962, pp. 77–90. For Durkheim's contribution to the problem of individualism, see his 'Individualism and the Intellectuals,' pp. 14–30.

15 On these issues see, Swart 'Individualism in the Mid-Nineteenth Century,' and Palmer, 'Man and Citizen.'

16 S. Lukes, *Individualism*, Oxford: Basil Blackwell, 1973, pp. 3–16.

17 Durkheim, 'Individualism and Intellectuals,' p. 20.

this light, utilitarians maintained that the laws of society were nothing more than the actions and passions of individuals acting in the world, and that all social phenomena were to be reduced to the decisions, actions and attitudes of individuals.[18]

In direct opposition to this, Durkheim asserted that the tendency exhibited by utilitarians to reduce society to individuals led them to ignore the larger system of social rules which acted as restraints on individual action. He went on to attack utilitarian doctrine on several distinct fronts. First, in focusing on individual autonomy and self-interest, Durkheim argued that utilitarian theory had completely overlooked the existence of social rules which acted as constraints on individuals.[19] Second, he reasoned that since society is always prior to the individual historically, then society alone must shape individual dispositions and beliefs. Third, since society comes first, individuals are not analytically separable from it and thus society and the individual constitute a total organic whole. In this view, individuals are neither separable from society nor are they to be studied independently of it since they are a part of the total social whole. Fourth, so far as society precedes the individual historically, it would be scientifically defensible to focus on society without taking into account individuals' separate attitudes or dispositions.

Individualist Theories of Hobbes and Rousseau

A third influence on Durkheim's work was the social theories of Thomas Hobbes and Jean-Jacques Rousseau.[20] Durkheim set out to separate his own views of society from the individualist theories put forward by Hobbes and Rousseau, who had generally looked for the origins of society by focusing on individual human nature. In order to see how Durkheim dealt with these theories, let us look at the arguments.

In *Leviathan*, Hobbes began by tracing the origins of society to what he called the 'original state of nature.' This state, Hobbes thought, was characterized by individuals living in a condition in which law and government were absent. What Hobbes tried to do was describe what life would be like if there were no laws or restraints on individuals. Hobbes went on to reason that without law or government to restrain them, individuals would be free to use violent means to satisfy their immediate needs and would continually subdue others to maintain dominance over them. From this starting place, Hobbes deduced two central social and political premises inherent in the formation of society. First, he argued that the absence of law and government would lead to an uninterrupted

---

18 C.B. Macpherson, *The Political Theory of Possessive Individualism*, London: Oxford University Press, 1962, p. 231.

19 Durkheim's criticism of utilitarian social theory can be found in Durkheim, *The Rules of Sociological Method*, p. 4.

20 Durkheim's discussion of Hobbes' and Rousseau's individualist theories can be found in his *Rules of Sociological Method*, pp. 121–4.

struggle for dominance and power in which none could secure peace or safety; and second, he took the view that, in a state of nature, individuals would be subject to violent attacks from others since they would all be free to use physical force to obtain their ends. Hobbes reasoned that the struggle for dominance would lead to war against all and constant fear of violent death.[21]

Hobbes went on to assert that society thus comes into existence only when individuals contract out of nature and into society, so as to secure peace and safety. According to Hobbes, as individuals contract out of nature they form society by placing common rules at the disposal of a leader who is capable of restraining them all. The formation of society is complete, Hobbes argued, when individuals renounce violent means to pursue their own ends in exchange for the peace and safety of common social rules.

While Hobbes' theory of the political state was one of the first to highlight the restraining nature of society, Durkheim disagreed with the emphasis Hobbes had placed on the individual in stating the origins of society. Hobbes had proclaimed that society originates from individuals when they contract out of nature. According to Durkheim, this view accepts the idea that individuals are naturally resistant to society and comply with it only when they are compelled by the force of restraint inherent in law. Taken one step further, if society is only an association serving ends dictated by individuals, then individuals must create society.[22] For society to exist in this framework, the individual has to be persuaded to comply with social rules by an appeal to the interest of self-preservation.

Durkheim disagreed with Hobbes' individualist doctrine on several fronts. First, he pointed out that according to Hobbes, individuals impose restraint on themselves by contracting out of nature and that restraint is nothing more than a by-product of individual will which is added incrementally to social reality. In contrast, Durkheim believed that restraint was imposed externally by society, independent of the individual, and this made constraint the center of Durkheim's view of society. By suggesting that constraint springs from collective life rather than from the individual, Durkheim thought that it could be studied in its own right as an independent social phenomenon.[23]

Another individualistic approach to the study of society is found in Jean-Jacques Rousseau's work. In contrast to Hobbes, who focused on restraint, Rousseau concentrated on the question of the creation of

---

21 Hobbes' wording is: 'In such condition, there is no knowledge, no account of time, no arts, no society; and which is worst of all, continual fear and danger of violent death and the life of man is solitary, poor, nasty, brutish and short.' Thomas Hobbes, *Leviathan*, Middlesex, England: Penguin, [1651] 1968, p. 186.

22 Durkheim, *Rules of Sociological Method*, pp. 121–4.

23 See Durkheim's, *Rules of Sociological Method* and *The Division of Labor in Society*, New York: The Free Press, [1893] 1933.

common social rules in society. Like Hobbes, Rousseau gave priority to human nature in the formation of society. He reasoned that when society is formed, it tends to create private property and self-interest and, as a result, individuals begin to fight and compete in a world in which jealousy and envy prevail. Rousseau focused his attention on society by looking at how a common interest arises to replace individual self-interest. He reasoned that a common interest arises only when human beings subordinate their individual will to what he termed the 'general will' of society.[24] When this takes place, he thought, the conditions of society come into play as the common interest replaces the self-interest of the individual. Rousseau's description of the formation of the 'general will' is significant in two respects. First, he asserted that the general will is formed by individuals pooling their own distinct wills. Second, when this occurs, a transformation takes place in the nature of individual will – to the extent that the individuals involved become subject to the totality formed by their common union. In other words, it is by the common act of individuals that the general will takes its shape and 'receives its unity.'[25] Rousseau went on to argue that the act of pooling individual wills would produce the collective will of society. In these terms, society takes the form of an association whose moral and collective authority is made up of many members; accordingly, Rousseau believed that, in the last instance, society was a reflection of individual will.

While Durkheim's view of society parallels Rousseau's in many respects, he rejected Rousseau's individualist doctrine in a number of ways. First, he thought Rousseau's tendency to ultimately derive society from the individual was mistaken. Rousseau had used a method which started from individual disposition in order to arrive at society and, in this sense, Rousseau's individual was complete organically and morally – and thus owed nothing to society.[26] Durkheim, in contrast, believed that the collective structure of society was separate from the individual and thought it could be studied as a reality in its own right, in this way being independent of the individual. Second, Durkheim reasoned that Rousseau's account of the emergence of society was unsatisfactory because it was overly reliant on philosophical and idealist concepts of individualist natures and, in this sense, it failed to take the scientific step of treating society as an independent reality. Third, Durkheim criticized Rousseau's explanation of the individual's obligation to collective authority. According to Rousseau, society could always be reduced to individual wills, and this called into question the obligatory nature of normative rules which Durkheim saw as

24 Jean-Jacques Rousseau, *The Social Contract and Discourse on the Origin of Inequality*, New York: Simon & Schuster, 1967, pp. 18–19.

25 Ibid., pp. 18–19.

26 Lukes, *Emile Durkheim*, p. 285; Durkheim, *Rules of Sociological Method*, pp. 121–4. He states 'Neither Hobbes or Rousseau seems to have realized how contradictory it is to admit that the individual is himself the author of a machine which has for its essential role his domination and constraint.'

an independent source of investigation since they stemmed from society. We now turn to Durkheim's central sociological works.

The Division of Labor in Society

Central Thesis

The Division of Labor in Society was Durkheim's first major theoretical work.[27] It was written during the 1880s as part of his doctoral requirement and was later published as a complete study in 1893 while Durkheim was at Bordeaux. *The Division of Labor* is first and foremost a study that developed a way of thinking about society which was completely new and, as such, it has several key aims. First, Durkheim wanted to make inquiries into the nature of the links connecting the individual to society and the social bonds which connect individuals to each other. Second, he wanted to examine the specific nature of these social bonds and see in what way they were related to the overall function of social cohesion in society. Third, Durkheim wanted to see if the system of social links changes as society becomes more advanced and subject to changes in the division of labor. Durkheim's central problematic in the *Division of Labor* is: 'why do individuals, while becoming more autonomous, depend more upon society? How can they be at once more individual and solidary?'[28]

Durkheim's explicit focus in *The Division of Labor* is on social solidarity. Initially, Durkheim used the term solidarity in several distinct ways: first, to refer to the system of social bonds which link individuals to society. 'Without these social links,' he wrote, 'individuals would be independent and develop separately, but instead they pool their efforts.'[29] Second, Durkheim used the term solidarity to identify a system of social relations linking individuals to each other and to the society as a whole. Without these 'social links,' he stated, individuals would be separate and unrelated. Third, he used the term to refer to the system of social interchanges which go beyond the brief transactions that occur during economic exchange in society. This system of interchanges forms a vast network of social solidarity which extends to the whole range of social relations and acts to link individuals together in some form of social unity. Fourth, Durkheim uses 'solidarity' to describe the degree of social integration which he thought linked individuals to social groups outside themselves.

---

27 Durkheim, *The Division of Labor.*
28 Ibid., p. 37.
29 Ibid., p. 61.

Characteristics of Mechanical and Organic Solidarity

Next, Durkheim turned his attention to looking at how social solidarity is expressed in different societies. Solidarity, according to Durkheim, can be expressed in two very broad and distinct ways, and the terms he used to designate these are 'mechanical' and 'organic'.

Societies whose solidarity is mechanical are based on common roots of identity and similarity.[30] In these societies, the individual is directly linked to society through various points of attachment which act to bind all the members of the group together equally. The force of these social links is such as to discourage individual autonomy, and the social whole envelops the individual so completely that there is no distinction between the individual conscience and the collective conscience.[31] Collective rules and social practices are predominantly religious in nature and pervade all aspects of social life. The kinship group is the dominant social institution, and domestic (familial and political) activity forms the basis of social cohesion. The division of labor is rudimentary and divided up so that individuals perform tasks for collective purposes. Beliefs are primarily religious in nature and the common conscience is rooted in religious law. Offenses against the common beliefs are punished by repressive sanctions which act to reaffirm the beliefs and social rules by deliberate punishment. The individual's relation to society is such that the individual is an indistinguishable part of the collective whole, and any individual differences are subordinated to the solidarity of the group. Individuality is at its lowest point of development and there is no individual autonomy. Social bonds are ones of obligation rather than contract. A fundamental criterion of mechanical solidarity is its ability to mobilize the entire social mass of society due to the immense leverage the common conscience has over the beliefs and social practices of the group. Because the degree of proliferation of common values and beliefs extends throughout the entire society, the social cohesion of the group is intense and the links binding individuals to society are strong and unified. The greater the unification of common beliefs, the greater is individual similarity and the ties linking the individual to the society form an almost perfect consensus.[32]

Societies of this type are characterized by: (i) a homogeneous population which is small and isolated; (ii) a division of labor based on social cooperation, with little or no specialization; (iii) a system of social institutions in which religion is dominant; (iv) a system of beliefs which is uniformly diffused throughout the society, creating uniformity in attitudes and actions; (v) a low degree of individual autonomy; (vi) a social

---

30 Ibid., pp. 129–32; 116; 147–73; 174–81. For characteristics of organic solidarity, see pp. 181–229.

31 Ibid., p. 152.

32 Ibid., pp. 129–32; 147–54. Durkheim stated: 'The consensus is then as perfect as possible; and their consciences vibrate in unison.'

organization in which the individual's place in society is determined by kinship; (vii) a system of penal law based on repressive sanctions which punish individual transgressions swiftly and violently, serving the function of reaffirming core beliefs and values; (viii) a system of social cohesion which produces a high degree of consistency in values and beliefs, and in individual attitudes and actions; (ix) a state in which individualism is at its lowest point of development; (x) a system of social links between individuals based on custom, obligation and sentiment.[33]

In direct contrast to mechanical solidarity, is the form of solidarity Durkheim refers to as 'organic.' In societies whose solidarity is organic, labor is specialized and individuals are linked more to each other than they are to society as a whole. The nature of these links, Durkheim reasons, stems from the development of the division of labor, where individuals become more reliant on others to perform separate economic functions which they are not able to carry out themselves.[34] This system of social links ties individuals to each other in ways that create greater dependency on specialized economic functions individuals perform for each other. The force of social bonds integrates individuals in their economic and occupational functions, and the ties to society become indirect and operate through the division of labor. Social bonds between individuals are enforced by contracts rather than by the force of prevailing customs or religious beliefs. The individual's place in society is determined by occupation rather than by kinship affiliation. The system of laws is based on restitutive sanctions in which judicial rules redress social wrongs by restoring things to their original state. Individualism is at its highest point of development, and the individual has greater autonomy and becomes the object of legal rights and freedoms. In addition, social bonds are formed on the basis of interdependencies created by increased reliance on each other's occupational functions. Autonomous social organs develop in which political, economic and legal functions become specialized and there is a minimum of shared understandings between members of the group.[35] The collective conscience is less resistant to change, and becomes weaker as its content becomes secular and economic. There is a minimum of shared understandings between members of the group and, instead of individuals resembling each other, their weaker solidarity presupposes individual differences.

The primary characteristic of organic solidarity is the development of a division of labor. The division of labor alters the nature of the social links since these links no longer tie individuals directly to society, but rather establish social relations between individuals based on mutual economic interdependence. The fundamental change is in the nature of the way social links are formed between individuals who are carrying out separate

---

33 For the best substantive discussion of the characteristics of mechanical solidarity, see ibid., pp. 176–81.

34 Ibid., p. 182.

35 Ibid., pp. 183–9.

and specialized functions and between the specialized organs of society which determine the nature of relations which regulate functions in the society as a whole.[36] Durkheim maintains that the division of labor acts to reorganize the basic pattern of social relations as individuals begin to perform specialized economic functions brought about by acute alterations in the division of labor.

Organic solidarity is characterized by an increase in the density of society due to the expansion of population, the growth of cities, and the development of means of transportation and communication. The main characteristics of organic solidarity are: (i) larger populations spread over broader geographic areas; (ii) an increased complexity of division of labor leading to specialized economic functions in which individuals are more reliant on others to perform economic functions which they cannot perform themselves; (iii) a system of social relations in which individuals are linked to each other by contract rather than by sentiment and obligation; (iv) a system in which individuals obtain their place in society by occupation rather than by kinship affiliation; (v) an increased individual autonomy based on a system of laws recognizing rights and freedoms of individuals; (vi) the development of contract law predicated on restitutive sanctions in which judicial rules redress social wrongs by restoring things to their original state.[37]

The Common Conscience

One of the central concepts in *The Division of Labor* is the common conscience, sometimes referred to as the collective conscience. Essentially, Durkheim used the term to refer to a body of beliefs, practices and collective sentiments which are held in common by all members of a society.[38] These beliefs are diffused throughout the society, define social purposes, give meaning to action and generally structure the pattern of social life. Durkheim believed that the common conscience evolves according to its own laws and is not an expression of individual consciousness and, in this sense, is analytically separable from it. It may be thought of as a determinate system of ideas and beliefs which creates social likenesses among all members of society.

In addition to providing a broad definition of the common conscience, Durkheim went on to elaborate a number of elements related to the substance of the common conscience itself. Among these, he thought that the common conscience is a 'determinate system' which acts as the main 'organ' of society.[39] It reaches throughout the entire collective space of

36 Ibid., pp. 183–9.

37 For further discussion of the characteristics of organic solidarity, see ibid., 185–90.

38 Ibid., pp. 79–80. For an extended treatment of Durkheim's concept of the common conscience, see S. Lukes, 'Prolegomena to the Interpretation of Durkheim,' *European Journal of Sociology*, 1971, pp. 183–209.

39 Durkheim, *Division of Labor*, p. 79.

society and is diffused throughout its physical or geographic boundaries. It creates common conditions of existence, functions to connect successive generations to each other, and acts to define individual relations to each other and to society in the form of binding obligations.[40]

Durkheim went on to distinguish four interrelated characteristics of the common conscience: volume, intensity, determinateness and content. First is the volume of the collective conscience. This refers to the pervasiveness of collective beliefs and the degree to which they extend throughout society as a whole. The volume of the common conscience denotes the capacity of the collective beliefs to 'envelop' the individual and to extend their reach throughout society.[41] In addition, the volume of the common conscience refers to the degree of intrusiveness of beliefs and practices into the lives and attitudes of the individuals in society. The greater the volume of the common conscience, the greater is the individual's attachment to prevailing collective beliefs. The extent of the attachment is greatest when society completely 'envelops' the individual.

A second characteristic of the common conscience is its intensity. Durkheim used this term to refer to the degree of leverage collective beliefs exert over individuals. The greater the intensity of the common conscience, the more leverage is exerted by the collective beliefs and social practices. Consequently, the more intense the common conscience, the greater the social cohesion and the more developed is the social uniformity. In addition, the intensity of the common conscience refers to the extent to which the collective rules exert claims on the individual. The more intense the collective beliefs, the greater is the likeness between individuals and the more encompassing is the common conscience.[42]

The third characteristic of the common conscience is its determinateness. This refers to the amount of resistance offered by collective beliefs and how willingly they give way to change, transgression or violation. The more uniform and well-defined the collective beliefs, the greater the consensus and, therefore, the greater the resistance to change in the prevailing social rules. When collective sentiments lack determinateness, they are less resistant to change and to individual transgression.[43] In this case, the more general and vague the rules become, the more they encourage individual discretion. In such circumstances, the common conscience has little determinateness and collective social rules are subject to individual interpretation. Since the determinateness of the collective conscience refers explicitly to the degree of definition of collective social rules, the less resistance these rules have, the greater is the likelihood of individual discretion. By direct contrast, the more defined the collective beliefs, the less inclination there is for individuals to vary in their understanding of common social rules.

40 Ibid., p. 79.
41 Ibid., p. 152.
42 Ibid., p. 152.
43 Ibid., p. 153.

Hence, the greater the determinateness of the common conscience, the more perfect the consensus and 'all consciences vibrate in unison.'

The fourth characteristic of the common conscience identified by Durkheim is content.[44] Though he did not explicitly elaborate on the question of content, some substantive points can be drawn from his discussion. Essentially, the content of the common conscience refers to the dominant characteristic of the society and to its collective disposition. In this sense there are two prevailing forms of content: first is religious content, in which the primary form of collective sentiments originate from religious law and exert a hold over individuals through religious expiation. Second is secular content, which entails a process whereby the collective sentiments are divested of their religious content and 'little by little, political, economic and scientific functions free themselves from religious functions and constitute themselves apart by taking on a more acknowledged character.'[45] In this case, the overall content of society and its social relationships are mediated by practical and economic necessities of life.

Systems of Laws and Social Solidarity: Repressive and Restitutive Sanctions

The next step Durkheim took was to look at social solidarity from the perspective of law and judicial rules. In fact, Durkheim believed that there is a fundamental relation between judicial rules and social solidarity. But what exactly did he mean by this? Simply stated, Durkheim contended that the way a society punishes is a clue to its system of solidarity. He stated that 'since law reproduces the principal forms of social solidarity, we have only to classify the different types of law in order to discover which are the different corresponding types of social solidarity.'[46] Durkheim believed that the best way to establish the relationship between judicial rules and solidarity is to examine the way societies punish offenses against collective sentiments.

Penal Law and Repressive Sanctions Durkheim began his theory of punishment by asserting that there are fundamentally two distinct systems of law: penal and contractual.[47] Penal law can be distinguished from other forms of law by its straightforward intention of imposing harm and suffering upon the offender. It does this in one of two distinct ways: either (i) by reducing the social honor of the offender and thus 'inflicting' some form of 'loss'; or (ii) by depriving the offenders of either their freedom or their life. In a system of penal law punishment is severe, often bringing physical harm to the offender and applying sanctions against offenders which are 'repressive.' It is the essential function of repressive sanctions to

44 Ibid., pp. 167–9.
45 Ibid., p. 169.
46 Ibid., p. 68.
47 Ibid., p. 69.

maintain social cohesion by setting examples which act to preserve the vitality of the collective rules and the common conscience.

In direct contrast to penal law is contract or written law. In this system of judicial rules, the intentions of the social sanctions are not to inflict suffering upon the offender, but only 'to restore things to their previous state,' that is, before the offense took place; to 're-establish what has been disturbed back to its normal state.'[48] In this form of judicial sanction, the aim of the law is not to punish the wrongdoer so much as to cancel out the damaging act by annulling it and by divesting it of its social value. Such a system of law, according to Durkheim, is linked to 'restitutive' rather than repressive sanctions.

In order to understand Durkheim's views on penal and contractual law more fully, it will be useful to examine the characteristics of repressive and restitutive sanctions. At the base of Durkheim's argument is the idea that each form of solidarity can be expressed by different types of judicial rules and a system of laws and punishments corresponding to them.[49] To make this as explicit as possible, we can keep in mind two things when discussing Durkheim's theory of law. First is that the body of social rules, prohibitions and violations set by society are called judicial rules by Durkheim. Judicial rules, moreover, can be of two sorts: those that are unwritten and are part of customary understanding, emanating from religious laws; and those that are written and part of a tradition of legal reasoning. A second thing to bear in mind is that the system of punishment related to offenses against social rules was called sanctions by Durkheim, and these sanctions refer to acts which are considered by society as appropriate in punishing offenses. This gives us two systems of laws and sanctions: penal law, giving rise to repressive sanctions and contract law, leading to restitutive sanctions.

The key observation, for Durkheim, is the connection he made between types of judicial rules and sanctions on the one hand and types of solidarity on the other. Penal law, as we have discussed, corresponds to mechanical solidarity. In practice, the acts which this system of judicial rules prohibits and labels crimes are of two kinds: (i) acts which are particularly violent in nature and manifest an extreme contrast between the act of an offender and the accepted norms of the group; and (ii) those acts which directly offend or attack the common conscience.[50] In the first case, acts offend the common norms and prevailing social rules whereas, in the second, they offend the sacred customs of the group by defiling core beliefs and social practices. In either of these cases, the distinguishing characteristic of penal law is that its repressive force is always proportionate to the damage caused by the offense itself. Thus in repressive sanctions 'the punishment matches the severity of the crime as exactly as possible.'[51] In addition,

48 Ibid., p. 69.
49 Ibid., p. 68.
50 Ibid., p. 106.
51 Ibid., p. 88.

punishment is always severe, swift and based on passionate emotions, the main function of the sanction being to maintain as much social cohesion as possible by reinforcing the sentiments 'and vitality of the common conscience. Severe punishment and repressive sanctions have the effect of reaffirming core sentiments in acting swiftly against the individual. The aim of repressive sanctions is thus total 'public vindication.'[52]

A second characteristic of penal law is its tendency to enlist the collective force of society as a means of carrying out punishment. The spectacle of 'moral outrage' of the group tends to be so severe that it mobilizes the entire force of society and marshals social disapproval on the focal point of the offender. The mobilization of the collective force of society stands as a measure of the degree of outrage which the group expresses toward the offender. This observation extends to early societies in which it was commonplace for punishment to signify the collective outrage of the group. The form which punishment takes in penal law is, therefore, always efficient in its effects and 'neat and precise' in its punishment.[53] It is clear that the intention of penal law is not to provide justice through a measured response to an offense, but to 'strike back' with the greatest possible force.[54] In this respect Durkheim thought that penal law always seeks public vindication and, therefore, acts without fully weighing the circumstances of the crime.

A third characteristic of penal law and repressive sanctions is their origin in religion and religious beliefs. Durkheim maintained that the rules which these wrongdoings offend are so central to the well-being of the group that they are endowed with a sacred authority. Understood in this light, the purpose of repressive sanctions is to 'expiate' the offense and offender from the collective experience – to eliminate them entirely from collective memory. In this view, the main function of penal law and repressive sanctions is to preserve the vitality of the collective rules and regulate offenses against them by ensuring that individuals who would be a menace to the collective unity are discouraged from committing offenses. The protective function provided by laws and social sanctions serves to maintain the unity and social cohesion of the group by preserving and reinforcing the vitality of the common conscience.[55]

Contract Law and Restitutive Sanctions The second system of law Durkheim looked at is called contract law and its sanctions are restitutive in nature. In contrast to penal law and repressive sanctions, the system of contract law arises in societies whose solidarity is organic. By contract law, Durkheim meant the system of modern law in advanced societies. Under this system of judicial rules, sanctions are restitutive rather than

52 Ibid., p. 88.
53 Ibid., p. 79.
54 Ibid., p. 86.
55 Ibid., p. 106.

repressive. But to be completely clear on the distinction between contract law and restitutive sanctions as it relates to solidarity, we must look more closely.

Contract law is a derivative of industrial society. This is evident if we remember that one of the most important characteristics of industrial society is its system of autonomous social institutions. It was on this understanding that Durkheim put forward the idea that the development of specialized social institutions was a consequence of an advanced division of labor which encouraged the emergence of separate and interdependent social organs. Only in this sense did Durkheim believe that the emergence of separate legal institutions with a system of written laws comes to reflect development in the division of labor. But this was not all. Clearly, one major way in which the system of judicial rules comes to reflect changes in the division of labor is through its sanctions and punishments. Hence, restitutive sanctions.

First and foremost, Durkheim thought the system of legal rules found in industrial societies is distinct from penal law in several major ways. First, he thought that industrial society leads to the development of various social organs which become increasingly specialized.[56] Second, these organs function through specialized institutions such as the courts, arbitration councils, tribunals and administrative bodies.[57] Third, Durkheim maintained that the authority of the legal rules is exercised through specific functionaries such as judges, magistrates and lawyers who possess specialized credentials.[58] Fourth, he thought that sanctions and punishments themselves ultimately reflect changes in the division of labor and these he called restitutive sanctions.

One of the central characteristics of restitutive sanctions is their direct concern to establish a criterion of justice by ensuring that the punishment adequately fits the crime. In contrast to repressive sanctions, restitutive sanctions have the aim of restoring things to the way they were before the offense occurred. The intention of restitutive sanctions is not to inflict suffering upon the offender but to undertake to restore and compensate for damage. A second characteristic of restitutive sanctions is the sphere of their social functions. Specifically, they function to regulate relations between particular individuals or parties rather than acting in the name of the collective norms of the group. To this extent, Durkheim maintained that the rules which restitutive sanctions protect do not directly emanate from the common conscience, but bypass it in some fundamental way.[59] The job of contract law is to develop rules which bind individuals to each other by regulating contractual obligations. Durkheim took the view that this system of law does little for social solidarity since it does not regulate

56 Ibid., p. 113.
57 Ibid., p. 113.
58 Ibid., p. 113.
59 Ibid., p. 115.

the bond between the individual and society but rather restricts itself to regulating contractual links between individuals. This is evident when we realize that restitutive sanctions 'are established not between the individual and society, but between restricted special parties in society which they bind.'[60] In addition, because restitutive sanctions are more specialized in the sense that they only reconcile interests between contracting parties, they tend not to arouse collective social sentiments and thus do not contribute directly to the overall cohesion of society.

The characteristics of restitutive sanctions become clear when we look at the nature of written law itself. Written law essentially has two specific functions: (i) to prescribe obligations and expectations by binding contracting parties; and (ii) to define sanctions as they relate to offenses and breaches against contracts. When we look at civil law, for instance, these two tasks are treated separately as independent procedural functions. While this tends to achieve a better fit between the offense and its punishment, the decision making regarding sanctions is always procedural in nature and reflects specialized functions. To the extent that rules and sanctions are separate in written law, the purpose of defining sanctions is precisely that of determining, as practically as possible, the most appropriate sanction. This is in direct contrast to the motives of penal law which is repressive in its sanctions and unconcerned with arriving at a balance between the offense and appropriate punishment.

Another distinction drawn by Durkheim between penal and contract law pertains to the degree sanctions spring from the common conscience or are removed from it. Primarily it is penal law, with its repressive sanctions, which 'corresponds to the direct sentiments of the common conscience' and which directly connects the individual to society. Restitutive sanctions, on the other hand, are removed from the common conscience since the 'rules which are restitutive, are strangers to it.'[61] This distinction is useful since it tells us that contracts create ties 'not between the individual and society, but between individual parties whom they bind.'[62] In industrial societies, contracts have the specific function of acting as the judicial expression of the individual's connection to society and, in this sense, enforce obligations by prescribing expectations rather than by the force of sentiment. The contract, Durkheim pointed out, 'is the juridical expression of cooperation.'[63]

---

60 Ibid., p. 115.
61 Ibid., p. 112.
62 Ibid., pp. 112–15.
63 Ibid., p. 123. 'In great part, the form of the contract primarily expresses cooperation. The contracts of society must put all those associated on the same level, their shares must be identical and their functions the same. Such a case is never presented in a conjugal division of labor. Over against this type, there is the multiplicity of contracts in industrial society which have as their object the adjustment of special, different functions to one another: contracts between buyer and seller, contracts of exchange, contracts between employer and workers, between tenant and landlord, between lender and borrower, between principal and agent etc.,' pp. 124–5.

In this view, society 'can only intervene through the intermediary of special organs charged with representing it.'[64] Thus, every written law has two aims: to prescribe obligations of individuals in their conduct and to define the sanctions which are attached to laws when they are violated or breached.[65]

Transition from Penal Law to Contract Law   After outlining the distinction between repressive and restitutive sanctions, Durkheim turned his attention to identifying the points of transition from penal law to contract law. Predominantly, he believed that contract law develops only in societies in which the division of labor is advanced, and that only through the division of labor could specific changes in the sanctioning mechanism of society take place. Of these, Durkheim maintained that three central changes were significant: first, restitutive sanctions are mediated by specialized social institutions in which the actual sanction no longer stems from the collective conscience itself. In this case it is only a 'feeble expression of its state.'[66] Second, because society intervenes in restitutive sanctions through the intermediaries of specialized agencies (courts and tribunals), the link asserted between the commission of an offense and its actual punishment may grow indistinct and ambiguous.[67] Consequently, society loosens the grip which it has over individuals by direct repressive punishment and, in Durkheim's view, this lowers social cohesion. The exact opposite exists in the case of penal law. Since repressive sanctions stem directly from the common conscience, they function entirely without mediation by courts or tribunals. Punishment, therefore, is swift and regulation of the individual is immediate and direct. Third, Durkheim thought that the shift from repressive to restitutive sanctions creates changes which alter the perception of damage perceived to be caused by the offense. For instance, in cases where sanctions are repressive, damage is perceived to occur to society and the collective unity of the group. Where sanctions are restitutive, however, the primary binding agent is the contract and damage is perceived to be between 'contracting parties' rather than to the society. On the whole, this alters the social understanding of damage from that of a collective concept to an individual one. Damage occurs not to the society as such or to its collective interests, but to restricted individuals.

Segmental and Advanced Societies: The Causes of the Division of Labor

After developing a theory of law, Durkheim turned his attention to describing mechanical and organic solidarity more explicitly. To this end,

64 Ibid., p. 115.
65 Ibid., p. 74.
66 Ibid., p. 74.
67 Ibid., p. 113.

he identified primarily two ways societies link individuals: mechanically and organically. In this respect, the concept of linkage is fundamental to Durkheim's argument in the division of labor. One of the primary means that Durkheim had of illustrating this point can be found in his discussion of 'segmental' and 'advanced' societies.[68] Broadly speaking, Durkheim identified two different societies which correspond to mechanical and organic forms of solidarity. These are segmental societies, which resemble mechanical solidarity; and advanced societies, which correspond to organic solidarity. Because Durkheim's discussion of segmental and advanced societies extends our understanding of the division of labor, it will be useful to look into the structure of these societies in some detail.

Segmental Societies Essentially, Durkheim used the term 'segmental' to describe a type of society which is made up of small groups linked together in a defined social territory. Segmental societies have a structural organization that is like the 'rings of an earthworm.'[69] He used this central image to signify separate segments or rings which are integrated into one body. He maintained that in societies of this type, the groupings making up the whole are of one body which forms separate segments or tribal rings. After describing the main characteristic of segmental societies, Durkheim went on to outline some additional properties of these societies. He thought that: (i) they are made up of small groups or segments separated into tribes; (ii) they have close proximity to each other; (iii) they have a division of labor which patterns their activity so that links of cooperation develop between the segments along domestic and political lines; and (iv) they produce strong social bonds between the segments which are formed by social relations based on common beliefs and social practices that have their roots in religious laws.

Segmental societies take their basic form from the family and political unit. All members are considered as kin, creating affinities which unite them. Societies of this type are made up of several thousand people who share domestic and economic relations, and members from each segment act as the central political authorities.[70] While the structure of the group forms a total social whole whose solidarity ensues from their similarities as a common 'people,' segmental societies are made up of distinct segments or units arranged in a linear fashion over large areas of land.[71] The native tribes of North America are examples of the social structure of segmental societies. While each of the segments is distinguishable from the others and has different features, they resemble one another in fundamental respects. This is in their basic beliefs, their system of social rules, their form of

---

68 This discussion is one of the most detailed and can be profitably read for factual information on mechanical and organic solidarity. See ibid., pp. 174–99.

69 Ibid., p. 175.

70 Ibid., p. 176.

71 Ibid., p. 176.

social sanctions and their legends and mythologies. In addition, their religious systems are their most active social component. In this respect, they are fundamentally alike. 'Religion,' wrote Durkheim, 'pervades the social whole and social life is made up almost exclusively of common beliefs and practices which derive from unanimous adhesion of a very particular intensity.'[72]

In addition to these characteristics, the physical organization of segmental societies can vary considerably. For instance, in some circumstances there can be a contiguous system of clans arranged in a linear fashion, such as the native tribes of North America; or they can be intertwined in a pattern, similar to Australian aboriginal tribes.[73] Because their religious beliefs are the most active element of their society, religion permeates the entire social life of the tribe. This serves to produce a system of social practices that creates common customs and social rules which provide almost total social cohesion. Their solidarity is mechanical because they share underlying traits, have similar beliefs and values, act in unison, and have their social personality defined by their religious beliefs. In addition, the ties linking individuals to society are direct and have no intermediary. In this sense, their social bonds tie the individual directly to society.[74] Individuals are more dependent on the central authorities and the collective personality is invested with unusually strong powers. In segmental societies, individuality is at a minimum since social similarities tend to absorb the individual almost completely within the group. The authority of the social whole stems directly from the common conscience, which is highly developed and performs supreme regulatory functions. The common conscience finds itself operating through the medium of definite institutions such as religion and mythology, and exercises its authority by regulating individuals in a determinate manner.

Characteristics of Advanced Societies   The structure of advanced societies is substantially different to that of segmental societies. The main characteristics of advanced societies bear upon the size of population, the proximity of cities and the development of the division of labor. Generally, in advanced societies there is greater social density among the overall population which tends to be spread out over a larger geographical area. In such circumstances, the total social mass of society is larger in scope and, therefore, more differentiated.[75] This social differentiation is more developed than in segmental societies and requires, in Durkheim's view, a system of interlocking means of integration and social cohesion which is capable of obtaining the unity of a diverse society with a complex division of labor. As the division of labor intensifies, simple social cooperation is

72 Ibid., p. 178.
73 Ibid., p. 177.
74 Ibid., p. 180.
75 Ibid., pp. 181–2.

replaced by individuals performing separate and specialized functions.[76] This alters the nature of the social bonds connecting individuals to each other and to society. This new system of social links emerges from the material links created by the division of labor and, as the division of labor increases, individuals grow simultaneously more autonomous and yet more dependent on society for what they cannot produce individually.[77] Individuals come to share only those links assigned to them by legal rights and freedoms.

Durkheim believed that the structure of advanced societies is arranged along the lines of a system of organs which become specialized to perform various social functions. Thus, in advanced societies, autonomous social organs replace the links existing between similar social segments. Their organization thus differs in several major ways. For one thing, the central social mass is not organized in terms of similar segments but rather is coordinated around parts which are related to one another and formed around a central political organ that exercises a moderating influence on the others.[78] Second, the central social organ is not of the same social material as that found in segmental societies, and therefore it usually arises in relation to the functions it performs. Societies of this type rest on principles of organization which are completely opposite to segmental societies in a variety of ways. As Durkheim states, 'the social material must enter into entirely new combinations in order to organize itself upon completely different foundations.'[79] Generally, advanced societies have large populations, are spread out over large geographical areas and there is a loss of proximity between individuals and social units. This loss of proximity leads to a reorganization of the social mass propelling individuals to perform specialized functions, which in turn alters the nature of their social links. Their social links become patterned by the division of labor and are based on contracts. The connection to society is through occupation, and individualism is at its highest point of development. Third, individuals are generally grouped by occupation rather than by kinship. Occupation, not family ties, marks their place within society. Durkheim reasoned that as advanced societies begin to appear, they utilize the existing social elements of segmental societies, and, as this takes place it causes the segments to rearrange the dominant social principle. One of the first of these changes is that segments become 'permeable' and thereby lose their resistance to change.[80] Fourth, advanced societies transform segments into organs which come about due to the pressure of occupational functions. These changes can be so complete that the new social organs which are created bear little, if any, resemblance to the previous segments.

---

76 Ibid., p. 183.
77 For the characteristics of advanced societies, see ibid., pp. 181–90.
78 Ibid., p. 181.
79 Ibid., p. 183.
80 Ibid., p. 187.

Transition from Segmental to Advanced Societies   After outlining the characteristics of segmental and advanced societies, Durkheim turned his attention to describing the changes taking place in the transition from segmental to advanced societies, changes which are central to the development of the division of labor. He believed there were at least two key changes that can be observed: first, he thought that as segments are transformed into organs, their functions become more and more specialized; and second, as organs develop they produce new aptitudes which tend to efface their former segmental structure.[81] As a result, the social material forms into new combinations and proceeds by organizing itself on completely new foundations. As these changes take place, all resemblances formerly based on common beliefs and social practices begin to disappear. Dissimilarities begin to emerge and the system linking individuals to society based on similarities is replaced by ties which link individuals indirectly through the division of labor. In addition, the new system of links does not directly add to the group's social solidarity, since these ties are largely governed by contracts. As distinct from segmental societies, advanced societies can be identified by: (i) a centralized authority in the form of legal and political organs; (ii) a set of stable and regular social functions which fill social prerequisites; (iii) separate and specialized administrative functions; (iv) a system of judicial organs relying on restitutive sanctions; (v) social and economic relations regulated by contract law; and (vi) separate and autonomous economic functions.[82]

One of the key changes of advanced societies outlined by Durkheim is found in the adjustments taking place in their political organization. In segmental societies, the family is the social basis of political functions; but, as this gradually disappears in advanced societies, it is replaced by a central social institution which performs specialized and distinct functions. Durkheim thought that the development of a central political organ had the effect of setting segments into new relations with one another so that the functions performed between them became coordinated. Under these circumstances, the segments no longer functioned as separate familial aggregates but rather as interrelated territories.[83] As a result, the social similarities between segments began to diminish and this altered the social bonds derived from common conditions. Boundaries separating segments became less resistant to change and, consequently, the social layers became more 'permeable' and began to lose their cohesion.[84] As the new segments began to reorganize, they took the form of an occupational structure which ultimately carried with it the tendency to specialize. Such occupational specialization brought about a new principle of group formation. Formerly, individuals were grouped around units of family and clan. As

81 Ibid., p. 182.
82 Ibid., pp. 188–9.
83 Ibid., p. 187.
84 Ibid., p. 187.

the division of labor advanced, the members in the group began to organize according to occupation. Durkheim believed that, in and of itself, this constitutes a fundamental difference in the principle of social organization since, as social ties once formed links based on common beliefs, they now find these links emerging from the interdependencies of occupational functions and the larger division of labor. In this view, social links derive not from common characteristics but from differences arising from specialized occupational functions. As the new social framework develops, it replaces the organization of the segment and finds its solidarity operating organically.

Main Causes of the Division of Labor

After examining the main differences between mechanical and organic solidarity, Durkheim turned his attention to the causes of the division of labor itself. He believed that one of the primary causes leading to the growth in the division of labor becomes apparent as the boundaries separating segments become more 'permeable.'[85] In order to understand this process, we have to look once again at segmental societies. Durkheim described segmental societies as social groupings separated into distinct tribes integrated on the basis of common beliefs and religious practices.[86] Segments were distinct aggregates made up of several thousand people which constituted significant social groups. Durkheim believed that the division of labor begins when the social, economic and political boundaries dividing segments begin to break down and segments come together. As the segments become more and more 'permeable,' they become less resistant to change and this creates movement between the parts of the social mass.[87] Instead of social life being dispersed over separate segments, it becomes more consolidated and localized, and this tends to increase the moral density of society.

Durkheim went on to identify three primary causes of the division of labor. First is the change which occurs in the geographical proximity of individuals. Populations begin to concentrate themselves in more confined areas instead of being spread over larger territories. This 'presupposes a certain tightening' in the social fabric as its human elements come closer together and more geographically proximate.[88] Second is the 'formation of cities,' which occurs as the social density is increased.[89] This creates an intensification of interaction between individuals leading to an increase in the overall social mass. As the social mass is increased, it tends to accelerate the mixing of segments into consolidated social organs. Third is the increase in social volume. This comes about, Durkheim reasoned, when

---

85 Ibid., pp. 187, 256.
86 For a concise elaboration of segmental societies, see ibid., pp. 174–99.
87 Ibid., pp. 256–82, 174.
88 Ibid., p. 258.
89 Ibid., p. 258.

the growing social mass produces more frequent communications and the need for transportation. This new form of interchange acts to 'suppress gaps' between segments, thus leading to an increase in moral density, intra-social relations, and frequency of contact between individuals.[90]

A Definition of the Division of Labor

So far we have looked at the differences between mechanical and organic solidarity and discussed how the differences between the two grow out of the way society connects individuals to the larger social whole. But we have not looked, in any explicit way, at the changes implied by the division of labor. Two central questions remain: what is the division of labor and exactly how does it act on society?

Simply stated, the division of labor refers to the process of dividing up labor so that different tasks are performed by different people. To illustrate the workings of this process, it will be useful to draw on the distinction Durkheim made between the economic and sociological division of labor. Early in *Division of Labor* Durkheim stated that 'the division of labor appears to us otherwise than it does to the economist.'[91] Used in its economic sense, the division of labor refers to the process of the dividing up of labor into separate and special operations with the express purpose of increasing the rate of production. Used in its socio-logical sense, however, the division of labor refers to the principle of social cohesion which develops in societies whose social links result from the way individuals relate when their occupational functions are separate and specialized. According to Durkheim, the stages in the development of the division of labor are as follows: first, the division of labor grows as the intensification of the struggle for existence increases due to the additional density in population.[92] Second, individuals living in close proximity find that they must live cooperatively and this social cooperation takes the form of the division of labor – providing the most efficient means of material survival to the greatest number of individuals. Third, lines of demarcation emerge between tasks and functions in order that material needs can be met, and as these arise they lead to the specialization of function in which labor is separated to meet the various material needs. Fourth, a system of mutual social relations arises from the form of interdependence produced by the division of labor and this is expressed in rights, contracts, laws and social rules. The relations these legal rights and social rules govern derive from a moral framework which serves as a basis of social cohesion. Fifth, a system of social links ensues from the material links and these links make up the new system of social cohesion based on the functional division of labor. Sixth, moral links emerge from the

---

90 Ibid., pp. 259–60.
91 Ibid., pp. 39–40; 275.
92 Ibid., p. 278.

material links, giving rise to the principle of social cohesion based on the functional division of labor itself.[93]

As the division of labor develops, major social functions within society are broken down into smaller units which have specialized functions. The fact that social functions are divided up into distinct social categories and allotted to individuals who may be separated in time and space goes to the heart of the system of social cohesion. Individuals are functionally interconnected through the division of labor since they are reliant upon others for what they cannot produce on their own. This is key to the new system of social cohesion, since individuals are more dependent upon society while at the same time being more autonomous.[94] The essence of the division of labor, therefore, is that it alters the system of social cohesion by compelling individuals to form social bonds based on their occupational interconnections. In this way, their links to society are based on their performance in specialized economic roles and in contributing to society by their specialized functions.

These developments not only bring about social differentiation of society into component parts, but the connection between each of the parts arises anew.[95] The new social components (economic, legal, political and religious) are separated by specific occupational functions which act to restrict the sphere of individual experience by confining social ties to occupations. Beliefs and values become narrowed in scope and are confined to the particular occupational sphere. Specialization creates different interests among individuals, since they are able to share common interests only with those whose occupational experiences are the same and with those whose values and beliefs are associated with shared occupations. As the division of labor advances, it narrows what individuals do in society down to tasks and roles determined by training and occupational interests. Common beliefs and values are now confined to occupational roles and this reduces the individual's grasp of society as a whole and of its overall collective unity. The individual's link to society is thus diminished and the collective unity is weaker.[96]

In addition to labor being divided into specialized functions, production and consumption narrow as well. Since individuals no longer produce the goods and services which correspond to their needs, they must rely on social links with others who produce what they cannot. In effect, the division of labor dictates that individuals are more reliant on various sectors of society for goods and services which they need to maintain their own existence. These new social links produce spheres of competence and work whose allocation is no longer determined by custom. Social

---

93 For a discussion of how cooperation and the division of labor are a social rather than an economic function, see ibid., pp. 278–9.

94 Ibid., p. 279.

95 Ibid., pp. 278–9.

96 Ibid., pp. 329–31.

experience, in this case, is reduced to the occupational sphere. Individual identities, in turn, are shaped by the various social spheres of the family, education and economy through which they pass as they progress through society. Under these circumstances, individuals begin to pick and choose only those values, beliefs and social attachments relative to their occupational experiences and this reduces their direct link to society. In addition, values and beliefs become more ambiguous since individuals adhere only to those values which are functionally necessary for their occupational links to the division of labor. By definition, individuals pursue different ends, and have different and differentiated goals which present them with a pluralistic set of ethical choices. This results not only in social differentiation, but in a less cohesive social whole and, ultimately, in what Durkheim referred to as the 'cult' of the individual.[97]

In addition, these shifts in the division of labor bring about a change in the function of the common conscience. This can be seen more readily in the changes occurring in the volume and density of the common conscience itself. The larger the geographical space of the social segment and the greater the population, the more difficult it is for the common conscience to exercise control over the extent of the differentiated social units. As the volume of the common conscience is diminished, the extent of its moral reach throughout society is reduced.[98] As a result, weaknesses begin to emerge as the common conscience becomes less able to exert restraints directly since these are now applied by contractual rules established by laws and other litigating organs and agents in society. The more the social density is diffused over wider geographical areas, the greater is the reduction in the volume, intensity, and determinateness of the common conscience – and the more diffuse is the connective tissue binding the individual and society. The social links become indirect and mediated through various social organs, the overall social bonds tying the individual to society change at the point of contact and, as a result, the individual becomes more autonomous.

Individualism and the Division of Labor

Another change which Durkheim attributed to the division of labor is an increase in individual autonomy, a process which he referred to as 'advanced individualism.' Durkheim believed that individualism tends to be more fully developed in industrial societies than in the segmental societies which existed in earlier times. But what exactly does this mean? Generally, Durkheim believed that one of the outcomes of the division of labor was an overall weakening of the links tying individuals to society, leading, in this case, to an increase in individual autonomy. While this may be a difficult assertion to understand, Durkheim was not alone in holding

---

97 This argument is developed in ibid., p. 172.
98 Ibid., pp. 171–3.

the view that the transition from mechanical to organic solidarity increased the autonomy of the individual.

Some of the earliest concerns of French social thought, in fact, had focused on the problem of advancing individualism, which many believed came about as a result of the breakup of the collective authority of society and the state. In *The Division of Labor*, however, Durkheim wanted to go a step further by showing that 'individualism' has a social origin and can therefore be explained sociologically.[99] Durkheim's reasoning took several different directions. First, he believed that the individual is not a conspicuous social unit in societies integrated by mechanical solidarity.[100] Individuality, according to Durkheim, must be at its lowest point of development and this occurs because the 'toll' exerted upon the individual by the common conscience is so great as to absorb all individual purposes into collective purposes. If mechanical solidarity is the stage at which the individual is 'subordinate' to collective forces of society, then organic solidarity must mark the beginning of individual separateness and autonomy. This can take place only when the 'toll' exerted by the common conscience is diminished.

A second direction taken by Durkheim was to look at the 'individual' from the point of view of social development in various societies. He asserted that, in the historical sense, 'individuals' must have first made their appearance in society in the form of the chief of the tribe or clan. Chiefs, he reasoned, must have been the first individuals since their position makes them 'distinct from the social mass.'[101] Chiefs, he maintained, must have been the first to differentiate themselves and step out as individuals who were separate from the undifferentiated social mass. They are separate because their authority puts them beyond others and because the distinctness of their experience and responsibilities confers individuality upon them, making chiefs distinct from others. The 'power of chiefs makes them autonomous and capable of activity beyond the collective norm' and this opens up the possibility of personal initiative, and constitutes the 'first moment when the individual steps forth from the group as someone distinct from its usage.'[102]

It is on the basis of this argument that Durkheim put forward the view that 'individualism' is a direct product of industrial society. This comes about, he suggested, as social cohesion reduces the strength of the social bond between society and the individual. In the earliest societies the individual tended to be totally absorbed in collective life, and links to society were direct and social control repressive. As the force of social links began to weaken the bond between the individual and society,

99 Ibid., pp. 171–3.
100 He stated clearly that individuals *per se* do not appear in mechanical solidarity, since 'individuality is something the society possesses.' Ibid., p. 130.
101 Ibid., p. 195.
102 Ibid., p. 195.

individuals became the recipients of rights and freedoms in which their ties to society were expressed indirectly. As these societies developed, adjustments in social solidarity changed the overall nature of the social mass, and this encouraged the development of individual autonomy in a number of ways. First, individuals were generally freed from the claims which society placed upon them in the form of social allegiances. As a result, beliefs and customs which were not directly part of social life began to develop.[103] Second, as the social density of society grew, individual ideas began to dominate over collective ones. This stretched social life beyond the limits set by previous beliefs and values. Third, as the division of labor accelerated, individuals were placed within a framework of causes which connected them to their own needs and wants rather than to the needs of society. This encouraged individual appetites and created the need for exploration and initiative. Fourth, as population increased, social activity grew more varied and created a more variegated social life. Fifth, changes occurring in the dependence of the individual on society as a whole brought about new activity, giving rise to 'traits of psychic life' that became developed to an extent 'never before seen in human society.'[104] Sixth, as societies developed in their division of labor, they became more condensed and this caused one form of 'psychic life' to disappear and be replaced by another. Initially, individual differences started out by being subordinated to collective forces; but as societies developed, a psychic life of individuals appeared, which in turn transformed the psychic life of society. As a result, society itself became freer and more extensive.

As the social density of the population increases, 'personal bonds become rare and weak' and one loses clear sight of the other, and thus loses interest in them.[105] As this 'mutual indifference grows it results in a loss of collective surveillance and the sphere of free autonomous action of each individual is extended in scope and, in fact, becomes a right.'[106] The common conscience begins to lose its hold over the individual and becomes more vague, ambiguous and indeterminate. Collective social rules lose their clarity and, due to the increasing density of the population, the center of social life changes. Individuals no longer live at the center of social life since it is spread over a larger territory. Under these circumstances, public opinion has less effect on the individual and exerts less constraint. As the collective grasp of society over the individual loosens, there is individual divergence and society is divided into smaller compartments enclosing the individual.[107]

103 Ibid., p. 345.
104 Ibid., p. 346.
105 Ibid., p. 346.
106 Ibid., p. 346.
107 Ibid., p. 300.

Abnormal Developments in the Division of Labor: Anomie and the Forced Division of Labor

In the concluding section of *The Division of Labor*, Durkheim turned his attention to problems occurring in the division of labor that are inconsistent with what he called its 'normal' development. He stated: 'up to now, we have studied the division of labor only as a normal phenomenon, but like all social facts it presents pathological forms which must be analyzed.'[108] In order to have a full understanding of the concept of abnormal forms, it will be useful to look briefly at what Durkheim means by 'social pathology.' The term pathology derives from the biological sciences and is primarily used to indicate the occurrence of disease in an organism. Durkheim believed that the 'social body', like the human body, can become diseased and he referred to this state as a form of social pathology or, more commonly, 'abnormal forms.'[109]

Book Three of *The Division of Labor* focuses on the question of abnormal forms and the discussion begins with Durkheim isolating three distinct categories of abnormal forms which occur in advanced societies. These are: (i) the anomic division of labor; (ii) the forced division of labor; and (iii) the poor coordination of functions resulting from the division of labor itself.[110]

Durkheim's examination of abnormal forms took two important directions: first is its focus on what deregulates individuals from society; and second is the stress on what deregulates social functions among themselves. The first abnormal form Durkheim referred to is one he called the 'anomic' condition of the division of labor. Generally, he believed that the anomic division of labor arises during an industrial crisis when there is widespread commercial failure. This crisis, he suggested, tends to breach the social solidarity existing between specialized functions and creates a decline in social cohesion.[111] There are, essentially, two distinct senses in which the anomic division of labor occurs. First is in the form of erosion that takes place as social solidarity diminishes; and second is in the inability of individuals to understand all of the separate functions of society as a whole. This lack of comprehension over the functions of society occurs, Durkheim believed, when society becomes so large in its scope and size, and so displaced over wider territories, that individuals are unable to visualize its processes and boundaries and cannot comprehend the social whole at a glance.

Industrial and commercial crises are examples of the anomic division of labor of the first type. These occur, wrote Durkheim, when 'social functions are not adjusted to each other.'[112] In such circumstances, the

108 Ibid., p. 353.
109 Ibid., p. 353.
110 Ibid., p. 389.
111 Ibid., p. 354.
112 Ibid., p. 354.

divisions between social functions grow rigid due to the intervention of various social groups. The differing interests between capital and labor are an example of this kind of conflict. Consequently, the social solidarity existing in these groups is no longer mediated by social processes, but by individuals who have more at stake due to their specialized roles. Groups previously mediated by links of social cohesion grow rigid and solidarity is jeopardized. This contrasts with the situation in pre-industrial societies, where lines of social interchange between worker and employer were connected by common social purposes. Individuals worked side by side in the same work environment and in a tighter framework of solidarity. In modern industrial societies, where functions and operations are specialized, individuals no longer feel that their common work unites them.[113] In circumstances where the anomic division of labor is allowed to develop, specialization is usually taken so far that, if taken any further, social disintegration would occur. In addition to this, functions become so specialized that the principle which makes them reciprocal within the division of labor is actually lost by the participants occupying the functions. In such circumstances, a common authority no longer links persons to each other, but only to their private interest. As a result, the social organs 'grow opaque' and lose the ability to maintain social linkages between individuals.

A second form of social pathology is the process Durkheim referred to as the 'forced division of labor.'[114] This occurs when the functions of specialization and the social organs representing them become instruments placed at the disposal of certain social classes and their interests. In addition to class interests representing organs and functions to the exclusion of others, the process of forced division of labor rearranges social functions in such a way that they become unrelated to natural demands of society and begin to represent divisions based on special interest groups, and in this sense the division between functions is forced.[115] As a consequence, the division of labor no longer meets the social needs of cohesion, but rather serves the interests of certain social groups.[116]

Because the division of labor only produces solidarity when its divisions are spontaneous and meet natural demands, the forced division of labor replaces spontaneous functions with forced functions. Durkheim believed that this leads to a loss in the social functions of solidarity since, when restricted social classes manipulate functions in order to satisfy their own interests, it disrupts the process of natural cohesion. In addition, the forced division of labor prevents individuals from occupying their natural place within the social framework as it allocates functions based on birth

---

113 Ibid., p. 368.
114 Ibid., p. 374.
115 Ibid., p. 356.
116 Ibid., p. 374–84.

or class.[117] In Durkheim's view, the development of a social caste is an example of the forced division of labor which has been taken too far – closing avenues of chance and social opportunity for other groups in society.

Similarly, when inequalities due to social segregation are imposed on groups, Durkheim believed that it not only forces the division of labor but also undermines social linkage in a fundamental way, resulting in the third form of social pathology – the poor coordination of functions in society. He maintained that when inequalities are imposed in society they tend to undermine linkage first, by mis-attaching individuals to their functions through force or coercion; and second, by disrupting the connection which acts to link individuals to each other and to functions between themselves. In addition, the forced division of labor engenders conflicts not only by imposing social inequalities, but by creating irregular and unjust forms of exchange. Under normal conditions of exchange, what is exchanged is usually equivalent in value and this functions to maintain equilibrium between exchanging parties. But when one group takes unfair advantage of another without equally imposing restraint on itself, or imposes checks on other groups without checking itself, the system of exchange is no longer balanced.[118] In the forced division of labor, restraint does not come from a centralized authority.

The Rules of Sociological Method

Aim of the Rules

Durkheim wrote *The Rules of Sociological Method* between 1893 and 1894, while he was in Bordeaux. *The Rules of Sociological Method* was Durkheim's second major work and was published in 1895.[119] Largely a methodological study, the primary aim of the *Rules* is to outline the nature of sociological subject matter and to set out the steps of sociological investigation. By and large, the text of the *Rules* covers four broad areas of investigation: (i) it identifies the nature of social subject matter by putting forward a definition of social facts and collective representations; (ii) it outlines the rules to be used in observing social subject matter; (iii) it sets out criteria for making judgments about healthy and unhealthy societies; and (iv) it identifies a system for classifying societies according to their structure and complexity, a process Durkheim referred to as 'social morphology.'

Durkheim had three aims in writing the *Rules*. First, he wanted to establish the existence of social realities outside the individual and to begin the investigation of these realities by scientific methods. Second, he wanted

117 Ibid., p. 375.
118 Ibid., p. 383.
119 Durkheim, *Rules*.

to make sociology independent of philosophy by replacing speculative thought with factual observation.[120] Third, he wanted to set out what he thought was the specific subject matter of sociological investigation.

Having stated some of the central objectives of the *Rules*, it is important to keep in mind the primary focus of the work. This, above all, is to establish the existence of social realities outside the individual. In fact, there are several reasons for thinking that Durkheim believed that he alone had to establish the independent nature of social subject matter. First, by 1890 Durkheim saw himself as the leader of a sociological school with well-established followers, and this led him to believe that methodological guidelines were necessary if sociology was to develop into a science. Second, Durkheim frequently concerned himself with the issue of consistency in sociological work and wanted to set out rules of investigation which would promote a coherent approach to the study of sociological subject matter. Third, Durkheim was concerned with the existing reluctance of some scholars to make adequate distinctions between psychology and sociology, and, more than anything else, this prompted him to take serious steps to outline the difference between the two disciplines and the importance of society as a subject matter in its own right.[121] One of the central problems compelling Durkheim to stress the nature of social subject matter was the individualistic doctrine being put forward at the time by utilitarian social theory. Because no complete understanding of the *Rules* is possible without first examining some of the precepts of utilitarian theory, let us briefly look at the arguments.

By the second half of the nineteenth century, utilitarian social theory had become one of the most influential perspectives of the age, exerting a pervasive hold over social thought. Principally espoused by John Stuart Mill and Jeremy Bentham, there were two assumptions which led to the dominance of utilitarian theory as a form social explanation. First, utilitarian theory put forward a doctrine of action which asserted that individual acts were completely autonomous and self-determined. As a result, utilitarians tended to believe that human intention was the springboard of all action.[122] Second, utilitarians put forward a theory of human motivation which held that all individuals had common motives, impelling them to pursue self-interest and economic gain. On this assumption, individual satisfaction was found in private interchanges with society, but beyond this, the individual owed nothing to society in its own right. To the extent that each individual was autonomous, owed nothing to society, and entered into exchanges with it only on the basis of rational

---

120 Durkheim, like Comte before him, wanted to change sociology from a science of existence to a science of things and thereby establish a factual basis for the existence of social phenomena, thus eliminating any further need to 'speculate into their reason for being.' See Durkheim, *Rules*, p. xxxvii.

121 Ibid., p. li.

122 Elie Halevy, *The Growth of Philosophic Radicalism*, Boston: Beacon Press, 1955.

self-interest, utilitarians had completely overlooked the existence of the larger framework of social rules which acted as a restraint on individuals. It was Durkheim's view that utilitarians had neglected the fact that human societies are associations which tended to create what he called 'groups of cooperators.' Durkheim stated:

> This important truth has been disregarded by utilitarians and is an error rooted in the way they conceive of society. They suppose isolated individuals who, consequently enter into relationships only to cooperate, for they have no other reason to clear the space separating them and to associate. This theory deduces society from the individual. With autonomous individualities, nothing can emerge save what is individual and consequently cooperation itself, which is a social fact submissive to social rules, cannot arise.[123]

The Existence of Social Facts

In considering some of the problems Durkheim had in asserting the existence of social realities outside the individual, we can begin to look more closely at the assertions he made about the existence of social facts. In Chapter One of the *Rules*, Durkheim began by stating: 'it is important to know which facts are commonly called social.'[124] If we look, he wrote, at the things individuals do such as eating, sleeping and reasoning etc., none of these activities may be called social, since these acts only identify a set of individual facts.[125] In addition, if all these facts were to be viewed as social, then 'sociology would have no subject matter exclusively its own, and its domain would be confused with that of biology and psychology.'[126] All these individual acts, he went on, cannot be counted as social facts and, if they were, sociology would have no distinctive subject matter – no social reality, only individual reality. But, according to Durkheim, in every society there exists a group of phenomena which may be studied independently of these individual facts. He stated:

> When I fulfill my obligations as a brother or citizen, I perform duties which are defined externally to myself and my acts, in law and in custom . . . I feel their reality objectively, for I did not create them. [We find these] beliefs and practices . . . ready made at birth; their existence is prior to our own and implies an existence outside of ourselves. Here, then, are ways of acting, thinking and feeling that present the noteworthy property of existing outside the individual consciousness.[127]

Durkheim reasoned that this group of phenomena, differentiated from all others and 'defined externally in law and custom,' have two distinct properties which qualify them as social facts as distinct from individual

---

123 Durkheim, *The Division of Labor*, pp. 278–9.
124 Durkheim, *Rules*, p. 1.
125 Ibid., p. 1.
126 Ibid., p. 1.
127 Ibid., pp. 1–2. Slightly modified.

facts. First, they present the noteworthy property of existing outside the individual; and second, their existence is prior to the individual and as such they are more historically continuous than individual existence and, therefore, precede individuals in the historical sense. Here, wrote Durkheim, 'are a class of externally independent rules or customs which are clearly withdrawn from individual discretion.' These, he went on, 'constitute a new variety of phenomena, and it is to them exclusively that the term "social" ought to be applied.'[128]

This claim by Durkheim, that 'social facts' can be withdrawn from individual discretion, was pivotal in setting out the study of society and it challenged utilitarian thinking on at least two separate and distinct fronts. First, in stating that society preceded the individual historically, it shifted the focus from individual motives to the laws of society. Second, in asserting that society exerts constraints on individuals, it showed that individual action in fact derives from society, thus placing the individual within the framework of larger social rules. When the term constraint is used in this way, stated Durkheim, 'we risk shocking the partisans of absolute individualism who profess the complete autonomy of the individual.' Those who take this view believe mistakenly that the individual's 'dignity is diminished whenever they are made to feel that they are not completely self-determinant.'[129]

Collective Representations

Next, Durkheim turned his attention to classifying things which are socially given, and the general name he gave to this group of social phenomena is 'collective representations.'[130] Simply stated, collective representations may be defined as any subject matter into which the ideas of society have been condensed so that they come to 'represent' collective values and beliefs. Examples of collective representations into which social subject matter is concentrated are religious doctrines, legal rules, myths, legends, proverbs, customs and traditions. Durkheim maintained that collective representations reflect social subject matter in four distinct ways: (i) they reflect a reality different from that of the individual; (ii) they have characteristics of their own which are autonomous from individuals; (iii) they can be investigated in their own right without being subsumed into psychological or biological laws; and (iv) they arise from group life. What collective representations convey, according to Durkheim, is the 'way the group conceives of itself.'[131]

In addition to these characteristics, collective representations are distinguished by the fact that they exercise a coercive influence upon the individual that is due not to individual disposition but to the 'prestige with

128 Ibid., p. 3.
129 Ibid., p. 4.
130 Ibid., pp. xli–lviii.
131 Ibid., p. xlix.

which these representations are invested.' He went on to point out that 'they dominate us and impose beliefs and practices upon us, and these practices act on us from without.'[132] Fundamentally, the essential characteristic of 'collective representations' is their ability to exercise social constraint and this, Durkheim reasoned, marks the reality of collective ways of thinking and acting which cannot be evaded.

The Characteristics of Social Facts

Having established the reality of social facts, their prior historical existence in relation to the individual and the nature of their collective representations, Durkheim turned his attention to outlining the characteristics of social facts themselves. Let us look at what he had to say about social facts:

> A social fact is every way of acting, fixed or not, capable of exercising on the individual an external constraint; or again, every way of acting which is general throughout a given society, while at the same time existing in its own right independent of its individual manifestations.[133]

> Thus apart from the individual acts to which they give rise, collective habits find expression in definite forms: legal rules, moral obligations, popular proverbs, social conventions, etc. As these forms have a permanent existence and do not change with the diverse application made of them, they constitute a fixed object, a constant standard within the observer's reach, exclusive of subjective impressions and purely personal observations.[134]

Three distinct characteristics of social facts stand out from others: (i) they are 'general throughout society' and 'diffused within the group'; (ii) they are 'external to individuals' and exist independently of their will; and (iii), 'they exercise external constraint over individuals which is recognized by the power of external coercion, by the existence of some sanction or by the resistance offered against individual efforts to violate them.'[135] This category of facts, wrote Durkheim, 'consists of ways of acting, thinking and feeling, external to the individual and endowed with the power of coercion by reason of which they exert control.'[136] 'These ways of thinking,' he went on, 'could not be confused with biological phenomena, and thus constitute a new variety of phenomena to which the term "social" ought to be applied.'[137]

132 Ibid., p. iv.
133 Ibid., p. 13.
134 Ibid., p. 45.
135 Ibid., pp. 2, 10, 13.
136 Ibid., p. 3.
137 Ibid., p. 3.

Observations of Social Facts

After setting out the characteristics of social facts, Durkheim shifted his attention to outlining the rules for the observation of social facts and put forward five general rules. The first of these is that social facts are to be considered as things.[138] To understand this somewhat controversial assertion we have to recall that, for Durkheim, what separates the scientific investigation of social phenomena from the speculative doctrines of past social thought is the direct focus on 'social realities' as opposed to 'ideas.' In stating that social facts are 'things,' Durkheim was asserting that for social phenomena to be the subject of scientific investigation they must be 'things' rather than 'ideas.' The crucial difference between 'ideas' and 'things' is that 'ideas have no reality,' whereas things have physical substance and are subject to observation.[139] Thus, to treat legal rules, customs and moral regulations in this way means that they can be treated as objects or realities in the natural scientific sense. Second, Durkheim maintained that for the adequate observation of social facts, social phenomena must be considered as distinct in themselves and separate from 'consciously formed impressions' in the mind.[140] This requires that social facts be considered apart from any conscious or individual representations in the mind of the observer. In Durkheim's view, social facts are not synonymous with mental images or constructs, but rather are distinct phenomena in their own right having a social rather than an individual nature. Third, social facts, according to Durkheim, must never be looked upon as if they are products of individual will, but rather should be looked at as capable of shaping actions by external coercion.[141] The fourth rule of observation states that in order to consider social facts as they are, we are merely adjusting our way of observing things in order to conform to their nature.[142] Fifth, Durkheim believed that social facts must be viewed as having independent existence. All social facts, he maintained, must be treated independently of individuals, and thus be considered as part of a world whose regularity and patterning exists independently of psychological characteristics.[143]

Problems in Observing Social Facts

After defining the characteristics of social fact and outlining the rules for observing them, Durkheim turned his attention to problems encountered in the observation of social facts. The importance of this discussion rests on one of the key aims of the *Rules*: to establish the existence of social

138 Ibid., p. 14.
139 Ibid., p. 23.
140 Ibid., p. 28.
141 Ibid., p. 29.
142 Ibid., p. 29.
143 Ibid., p. 45.

facts independent of abstract philosophical speculation. For this to be possible, the primary criterion of social facts is that they be treated as 'things' subject to observation. Durkheim, however, encountered a number of problems in achieving this aim. First, in claiming that social facts such as moral rules, customs and conventions are capable of exerting constraint and external coercion, Durkheim was powerless to grasp these 'forces' conceptually or make their 'causal nature' subject to direct observation. Second, any causal connection between the putative powers of social facts and their actual effects on the conduct of individuals had to be assumed. In this light, the causal capacity inherent in social facts to exercise constraint had to be forces inferred in society's rules. This meant that the causal powers of facts were only 'indirectly' expressed in the various customs, social rules and legal regulations of society.[144]

The next step which Durkheim took was to separate social facts from a priori impressions which may be in the mind. In taking this step, Durkheim's aim was to consider social facts as independent regularities 'distinct from our consciously formed representations of them.'[145] He maintained that when this procedure is followed, certain facts will become present which will be consistent with and show regularity in relation to the techniques of observation. Furthermore, elements of consistency and regularity are more likely to be found than impressionistic representations of their objectivity. In addition, this step ensures that the objectivity of social facts is real rather than illusory. In describing social facts as a certain kind of subject matter, he went on to state that procedures are needed to indicate their objective reality more firmly. If followed, this method promises to secure a greater likelihood of arriving at laws of society than is possible with economics or psychology. Durkheim then outlined a number of steps to be taken. These can be broken down in three distinct procedures, as follows: first is the procedure of eradicating all preconceptions when observing social facts. This serves the function of maintaining objectivity and eradicating any presuppositions inherent in the mind. Second is the importance of the definition of things to be investigated. This serves the function of defining the subject matter to be known. Third is the procedure of ensuring that the subject matter studied is always made up of a group of phenomena that are defined by their external characteristics.[146]

Distinction between Normal and Pathological

The next step Durkheim took in setting out the subject matter of sociology, was to prescribe a set of criteria for making judgments about healthy and unhealthy societies. He began by pointing out that just as

144 Ibid., p. 45.
145 Ibid., p. 28.
146 Ibid., pp. 27–36.

disease can threaten the life of a living organism, so it can threaten the life of society. In this case, Durkheim wanted to know whether it is possible to find a criterion which would allow sociologists to distinguish between 'health and morbidity' in various social phenomena.[147]

Essentially, the term morbidity is used by Durkheim to refer to anything which impairs the functioning of society by inducing diseased states.[148] In fact, he reasoned that since all the sciences are able to distinguish between normal and pathological, then it must be possible to look at social institutions and moral standards in society and make judgments about their health or morbidity. 'If we can find,' wrote Durkheim, 'an objective criterion inherent in the facts themselves which enables us to distinguish scientifically between health and morbidity in the various orders of social phenomena, science will be in a position to throw light on practical problems' related to the functioning of society.[149]

Since 'health and disease' are states of all living organisms, there must be comparative links with societies. He went on to reason that a social fact can be judged as normal for a given society only if it is looked at in relation to the stage of that society's development. In a healthy state all phenomena, including social ones, assume two distinct forms: (i) a 'normal' state, by which the social conditions are most widely distributed and occur in other societies under general conditions; and (ii) a 'morbid or pathological' state, which occurs when social phenomena depart from what is widespread or normative.[150] Durkehim went on to suggest a procedure for making distinctions between healthy and unhealthy states in society: first, establish whether or not a fact is generally disposed throughout the society. Second, examine the conditions which lead to the generality of this phenomenon. Third, see whether or not the fact in question has become more or less intense by determining the degree of its change. Fourth, compare the original facts with the present state of affairs and if the condition exists in relation to the original, the situation should be judged to be normal.[151] If, on the other hand, a fact relating to an early period of social history has operated as an essential part of a prevailing social framework, then we should conclude that its disappearance is pathological.

Crime as a Normal Phenomenon

To illustrate the effectiveness of these criteria, Durkheim drew upon the example of crime and criminal activity in society. He began by stating that a phenomenon is to be considered morbid or unhealthy, only if it does not

---

147 Ibid., p. 49.
148 Ibid., p. 49. He stated that 'for societies as for individuals, health is good and desirable; disease, on the contrary, is bad and to be avoided.'
149 Ibid., p. 49.
150 Ibid., pp. 55–6.
151 For a general discussion of these procedures, see ibid., pp. 59–64.

maintain its proper relationship to the dominant social institutions.[152] This proviso is important because Durkheim was saying that if a condition serves a function in relation to the larger social framework, then it is not to be judged as pathological. He pointed out that while many tend to assume crime is pathological in nature, the opposite is true, and the common conclusion that crime is 'unhealthy' is unwarranted and does not fit the facts. He demonstrated this by first asking how general crime is.[153] Crime, he stated, is present, not in the majority of societies but in *all* societies. Therefore, no society is exempt from the problem of crime. Second, as societies progress from simple to complex, the number of crimes in proportion to the population tends to decline. Hence, though still normal, crime tends to lose its character as normal the more complex society becomes. Third, statistical records enable us to follow crime rates historically and their tendency is to increase in relation to the development of city life. Fourth, no phenomenon more readily demonstrates the condition of normality better than crime since crime is such a common condition of collective life. Thus, in Durkheim's view, crime is 'normal.'[154] But how can such a conclusion be drawn?

In classifying crime as normal, Durkheim was not confirming anything about the criminal nature of individuals, but only stating that crime is a factor in 'social health' and therefore an integral part of healthy societies. But how could he claim this to be the case? Durkheim explained by examining the sociological role played by crime in society. He stated that historically no society is exempted from crime; in fact a society exempt from crime would be a society of 'saints.' Second, insofar as criminal acts offend the collective sentiments, in societies where criminal acts are no longer committed, these sentiments will become blurred.[155] The conclusion that can be drawn in this case is that where crimes are not committed core social values and sentiments will become obscured. Durkheim's reasoning here is key. He was saying that since the commission of a crime leads to punishment, the act of punishment re-establishes the values and sentiments which the crime offends. Thus, crime serves the social function of protecting and reaffirming collective sentiments and, in this sense, is healthy rather than pathological.

Social Morphology and the Classification of Social Types

After having discussed the nature of social facts, Durkheim turned his attention to classifying societies by the nature and type of their organization. Here, Durkheim was concerned with setting out the study of the 'structures' of societies as a valid subject matter of the sociological

152 Ibid., pp. 63–4.
153 Ibid., p. 65.
154 Crime is normal, according to Durkheim, because 'a society exempt from it is utterly impossible.' See ibid., p. 67.
155 Ibid., p. 67.

sciences. He began by stating that if there are only individuals, then societies would be nothing more than the sum total of their populations. If this were the case, then we should set out to inventory all the characteristics of individuals. If we are to study society, asserted Durkheim, a criterion must be found which extends beyond the individual to the distinct characteristics of societies.[156]

The very first thing we should look for, according to Durkheim, is the 'social elements' of these societies. Using the concept of 'elements,' Durkheim put forward the idea that societies are organized in relation to social elements in two basic ways. First, by the nature and number of elements which are to be found in societies; and second, by the extent to which the elements form combinations leading to more complex elements. The name Durkheim gave to the study of these elements is 'social morphology.'[157] Stated simply, social morphology refers to the study of the form and structure of societies and how these structures may be classified according to their various social attributes. Durkheim believed that social morphology is the first principle of social classification since it examines the most elementary forms of society. In order to completely understand what Durkheim meant by morphology, we must look more closely.

There are, according to Durkheim, two broad morphological classifications: first, there are societies whose organization is simple. These societies have few parts and the relationship between the parts leads to an uncomplicated structure. Second, there are societies whose organization is complex. These societies have multiple parts which form more complex structures leading to a more variegated social life. Durkheim maintained that the procedures for classifying societies should begin with the step of understanding the morphology of simple societies. Once this is accomplished, sociologists can examine the principle of internal change in the elements of these societies and the conditions leading to societies whose development is more complex. In beginning with simple societies and progressing to complex ones, said Durkheim, we are able to understand the principle of morphological change.

To begin developing this system of classification, Durkheim looked at the characteristics of simple societies. These have two basic structural attributes: they form a whole whose functions are not dependent on other parts; and they have no regulating center. The first example of a society of this type, Durkheim suggested, is a society he called a 'horde.'[158] A 'horde' is the most elementary social form and is characterized by the fact that it 'contains a single segment.'[159] What riveted Durkheim's attention to the organization of the horde is the fact that there are no special groups within

156 Ibid., pp. 79–80.
157 Ibid., p. 81.
158 Ibid., pp. 82–3.
159 Ibid., p. 82.

its structure, unlike other simple societies. 'The horde is a social aggregate which does not include any other more elementary aggregates or group but is directly composed of individuals.'[160] From this, we can conclude that the 'horde' is the most basic social form, the simplest of societies and the sociological correlate of the biological world of protoplasm.[161]

The next morphological type referred to by Durkheim is called a 'clan.' Clans may be formed by the combination of various hordes or groups whose union forms a more complex group structure. In contrast to the horde, clans are aggregates which have formed segments, and though they were once hordes morphologically, their parts have reorganized and their morphology has changed.

Another type of classification Durkheim referred to is 'polysegmentals.' These societies are made up of the combination of many groups which form a total social structure. Examples of these types include the Iroquois nation, whose social elements are formed around aggregates of confederated groups which form a common tribe. The same is true for the early organization of tribes whose structure later gave rise to the Roman city states.[162] After these come polysegmental societies, which are doubly compounded. These social groups, according to Durkheim, are the outcome of the juxtaposition of polysegmented societies such as the city states of Greece and aggregated tribes.

Rules for the Explanation of Social Facts

In Chapter Five of the *Rules*, Durkheim turned his attention to the explanation of social facts. Most sociologists, he stated, think they have explained social facts when they have provided examples of the functions which they serve and the needs these functions fulfill. But to show the function which facts serve is not the same as showing how social facts have originated.[163] Durkheim was careful at the outset to make a distinction between 'functions' and 'causes' so that, in explaining social facts, they are not confused.

The first distinction to be made is that functions and causes must be separate. Briefly, 'functions' are distinct from causes so far as they serve to explain the utility or purpose which a social fact serves. Causes, on the other hand, explain how facts have 'originated.'[164] Another reason for making the distinction between functions and causes is that since functions tend to cite the purposes of social facts, it is easy to resort to explanations which take individual needs as reasons for the origin of social facts themselves. Far from relying on individuals, Durkheim was looking for explanations of social facts that will confirm their independent existence,

160 Ibid., p. 83.
161 Ibid., p. 83.
162 Ibid., p. 84.
163 Ibid., p. 90.
164 Ibid., p. 90.

and the distinction he made between causes and functions serves this purpose. Since social facts themselves are forces which are superior to the individual and have an independent existence, the cause of a social fact must sought by going back along the chain of tradition and custom to grasp the tangible causes of social facts.[165] Durkheim did not want to revert here to teleological explanations which appeal to the intrinsic purposes of things to explain causes. Rather, he believed that the first step in explaining social facts is to state their causes and origins. In this exercise, he made it clear that there are three kinds of explanations which should be avoided: (i) seeking causes in ultimate purposes which would hold that social phenomena serve some ultimate end in and of themselves; (ii) equating causes with the functions associated with particular facts; and (iii) most importantly, seeking causes in individuals.

These steps led Durkheim to put forward an explanatory rule for elucidating social facts. He stated: 'the determining cause of a social fact should be sought among the social facts preceding it and not among the states of the individual consciousness.'[166] It is easy to see that the first rule is preventive, since it seeks to avoid explanation of social fact by looking to human individual causes. To take this route would ultimately reduce sociological assertions to psychological laws rather than to the laws of society, and were such a view of collective life to be adopted, society would only 'emanate' from human nature.[167] In this view, psychology will always have the last word.

Therefore, the injunction to look for the cause of social facts among other social facts prevents explanations from being based on speculative grounds, on ultimate purposes (teleological explanations), or on individual grounds. The importance of the first rule, therefore, is that it confines the search for causes of social facts to within the framework of society rather than to causes which are psychological, individual, or teleological in their subject matter. 'Since we have shown,' wrote Durkheim, 'that all obligation lies outside the individual, the principle of social life presents the same character and is explained by the same principle.'[168]

In addition to looking for the causes of social facts, a primary task of sociological investigation is to discover the distinct features of the social milieu being investigated. Two distinct kinds of facts fulfill this condition: first, those relating to the size of the society as they concern its structure and organization; and second, those facts related to the proximity of individuals to each other. The term Durkheim used to describe this latter characteristic is 'dynamic density.' This determines the degree of 'concentration of aggregates' and the conditions under which concentrations of individuals can – or will – lead to certain kinds of economic, social or

165 Ibid., p. 95.
166 Ibid., p. 110.
167 Ibid., p. 98.
168 Ibid., p. 105.

political activity in society. Measurements of 'dynamic density' may determine how intense social life is and what the 'horizon of thought and action of the individual' may be.[169] The concept of social milieu helps establish relations of causality among families of social facts and prevents recourse to explanation based on human individual causes.

Durkheim's Study of Suicide

Historical Background

Durkheim began working on the problem of suicide in 1888 while he was in Bordeaux. His interest in the problem was aroused while he was working on an article related to suicide and the birth rate.[170] Shortly after completing this work, he offered a series of public lectures on this topic between 1889–90. Seven years later, in 1897, his third major sociological work, entitled *Suicide*, was published.

In broad historical terms, there are several reasons why Durkheim took up the theme of suicide when he did. First, suicide was a growing social problem in Europe by 1850 and many felt that it was associated with the development of industrial society. ˙Industrialization had advanced individualism, accelerated social fragmentation, and weakened the social bonds tying the individual to society.[171] Second, industrial society had made the economy dominant over other social institutions and this served to place individual self-interest and economic gain over the collective forces of society. As individual autonomy and political freedoms increased, the individual became the center of society and this served to call into question the nature of collective social purposes. Third, the political crisis of the Dreyfus Affair in 1894 was a serious blow to national unity and drew attention to how much egoistic forces and social dissolution had replaced the collective authority of society. This led Durkheim to believe that the theme of social dissolution could be examined sociologically by looking at the mechanisms in society which link individuals to social purposes outside themselves. Fourth, evidence made available by comparative mortality data linked suicide to social factors such as industrial change, occupation, family life and religion, and this served to focus attention on society and social institutions rather than on psychological factors.

The statistical data collected by Durkheim contained records of suicidal deaths that were categorized according to age, religion, sex, occupation and marital status. Overall, the records of 26 000 suicides were studied by Durkheim. Marcel Mauss, Durkheim's nephew, helped assemble the maps

169 Ibid., pp. 113–14.
170 Lukes, *Emile Durkheim*, p. 191.
171 S. Fenton, *Durkheim and Modern Sociology*, Cambridge: Cambridge University Press, 1984, pp. 8–47.

contained in the work and aided in compiling the statistical tables on suicidal deaths relating to age and marital status.[172]

A Social Theory of Suicide

Durkheim's attempt to formulate a social theory of suicide led him to look for the cause of suicide within the framework of society rather than in the psychological states of individuals. This shift in perspective from a psychological to a sociological analysis of suicide was disconcerting for many, and perhaps the best way to understand the shift is to look at the problem of suicide prior to Durkheim's work. At the time Durkheim began his study, suicide was largely viewed as a nervous disorder and its causes were believed to derive from individual psychological states. Many thought that suicide was the result of a weak disposition and a psychological response to the burdens of life. Durkheim called these views into question by essentially shifting the focus from individual motives to social causes in at least two distinct ways. First, by stating that social causes of suicide precede individual causes, Durkheim eliminated the need to look at the various forms suicide assumed in individuals. Second, in focusing his attention on the various social environments to which the individual was connected, Durkheim eliminated the necessity of looking at individual disposition or personality. He put this clearly when he stated that, 'the causes of death are outside rather than within us, and are effective only if we venture into their sphere of activity.'[173] The suicidal act, 'which at first seems to express only the personal temperament of the individual, is really the supplement and prolongation of a social condition which they express externally.'[174] The shift from psychological to social factors is stated in the following way:

> When suicide is considered as an individual action affecting the individual only, it must seemingly depend exclusively on individual factors, thus belonging to psychology alone. Is not the suicide's resolve explained by his temperament, character, antecedents and private history? If, instead of seeing in them separate occurrences, unrelated and to be separately studied, the suicides are taken as a whole, it appears that this total is not simply a sum of independent units, but is a new fact *sui generis*, with its own unity, individuality and consequently its own nature – a nature, furthermore, more dominantly social.[175]

The Social Suicide Rate

No complete understanding of Durkheim's theory of suicide is possible without looking at the concept of the 'social suicide rate.'[176] Durkheim

172 Durkheim, *Suicide*, p. 39; Anthony Giddens, 'A Typology of Suicide,' *European Journal of Sociology*, 7, 1966, 276–95.
173 Durkheim, *Suicide*, p. 43.
174 Ibid., p. 299.
175 Ibid., p. 46.
176 Ibid., p. 51.

arrived at the concept of the social suicide rate by a careful examination of mortality data which had been obtained from public records of societies such as France, Prussia, England, Denmark and Austria. These records contained information about cause of death, age, marital background, religion and the total number of deaths by suicide of the country from which they were gathered. The 'social suicide rate,' therefore, is a term used by Durkheim to refer to the number of suicidal deaths in a given society and the extent to which the 'rates' themselves could be looked upon as establishing a pattern of suicide for a given society. But what does this mean in relation to individual suicide? As stated earlier, the theories of suicide prevalent at the time looked at individual motives and psychological causes. Suicide, many believed, was the desperate act of an individual who did not care to live or who could not face life's burdens. From this perspective, suicide was seen as an individual act dependent on factors which could only be explained psychologically.

Durkheim, however, took a completely different approach. Rather than looking at individual motives or psychological states, he began by looking at the 'social suicide rate' from individual countries. What he wanted to find out, was whether the suicides committed in a given society could be taken together as a whole and studied collectively. Durkheim's central question, therefore, was can the rates be studied independently of individual suicide? In order to establish a theoretical footing, he began by looking at the number of suicidal deaths contained in public records of countries such as France, Germany, England and Denmark. The suicide rates for these countries had been collected between 1841 and 1872 and they contained a substantial amount of information relating to social factors such as marital status, religion, occupation and military service.

After studying the rates, Durkheim made some central observations. First, he noticed that the rates varied from society to society. For example, they were higher in France in comparison to Germany; lower in Denmark in comparison to England; and so on. Second, he observed that between 1841 and 1872, the number of suicidal deaths in each of the countries did not change dramatically and were considered to be stable. For example, between 1841–42 the number of suicidal deaths in France was 2814 and 2866 respectively; whereas in Germany for the same years they were 290 and 318.[177] The stability of the rates within a particular society was crucial. It meant that each society not only produced a 'quota of suicidal deaths,' but that certain social forces were operating to produce what Durkheim saw as the 'yearly precision of rates.'[178] This turned out to be decisive because, when considered collectively, the rates pointed in the direction of underlying social causes. This led Durkheim to reason that the predisposing cause of suicide lay not within the psychological motives of

177 Ibid., p. 47.
178 Ibid., p. 51.

the individual, but within the social framework of the society. Third, the observed stability of the rates meant that each society was a distinct social environment with different social characteristics, different religions, different patterns of family life, different military obligations and, thus, different suicide characteristics. Under these circumstances, each produced rates of suicidal deaths distinct from the other. Fourth, when compared to the mortality rate, Durkheim noticed that the suicide rate demonstrated far greater consistency than did the general mortality rate, which fluctuated randomly.

As a result, Durkheim drew three fundamental conclusions which turned on the question of the stability of the rates. First, he believed that the stability of the rates showed that, while individual motives for suicide vary from case to case, the regularity exhibited by the social suicide rates was consistently stable. Second, though the rates varied between societies, the stability of the rates within a particular society meant that each society produces a 'quota of suicidal deaths.'[179] Third, Durkheim took the position that the suicide rate must represent a 'factual order' that is separate from individual disposition and therefore presents a regularity which can be studied in its own right.[180] Given that the 'social suicide rate' is independent of individual suicide and has a stability of its own, it should be the subject of a special study, the purpose of which would be to discover the social causes leading to a definite number of people taking their own lives in a particular society.

Taking the suicide rate into consideration, the difference between the psychological and sociological study of suicide lies in the sociologist's focus on the social suicide rate. This contrasts with the 'psychologist who', wrote Durkheim, 'looks at individual cases isolated from one another and establishes that the victim is either nervous, bankrupt, or alcoholic. Then he explains the act by reference to one or another psychological states finding, thereby, a motive. But this motive does not cause people to kill themselves in each society in a definite period of time, and thus the productive causes of this phenomenon naturally escapes the observer of individuals. To discover it, one must raise their point of view above the individual suicide and perceive what gives them unity.'[181]

Suicide and Social Integration

One of the central concepts used by Durkheim in the study of suicide is social integration. Though he did not explicitly define the term, it plays a predominant role in the study and is, therefore, key to understanding the connection between individual suicide and society. Initially, Durkheim had

179 Ibid., p. 51.
180 Ibid., p. 51. Durkheim wrote 'the suicide rate is therefore a factual order, unified and definite as is shown by both its permanence and its variability.' The question, then, is can it be studied in its own right?
181 Ibid., p. 323–4.

used the term social integration in the *Division of Labor* to stress the nature of social links which attach individuals to social groups outside themselves.[182] In this sense, social integration can be defined as the extent to which individuals are linked to and feel allegiance for social groups to which they are attached. From this early definition, it is clear that Durkheim believed that individuals do not exist by themselves autonomously and are, therefore, not separate from society.[183] Durkheim went on to maintain that social integration serves several key functions. First, it connects individuals to society by ensuring a high degree of attachment to commonly-held values and beliefs and thus forms bonds between the individual and the group. Second, social integration acts as a check against individualism by imposing restraints on needs and wants and by focusing interests outside the self. Third, social integration serves connective functions so far as it propels individuals out into the wider society by creating links to larger social groups and by promoting the perception that they are part of a larger social whole. Durkheim went on to state that the three groups possessing the quality of social integration in society are the religious group, the family group, and the political or national group.[184]

Suicide, the Integrative Pole: Egoistic and Altruistic Suicide

Durkheim's theory of suicide is divided into two explanatory parts. In the first, Durkheim explained suicide by drawing on the concept of social integration, referring to the strength of the social bonds between the individual and society. Here, egoistic and altruistic suicide form opposite poles of social integration. In the second part of the theory, Durkheim explained suicide by drawing on the concept of social regulation. Social regulation, in contrast to integration, refers to the restraints imposed by society on individual needs and wants. Here, anomic and fatalistic suicide form opposite poles of social regulation.

Durkheim began with the integrative pole and egoistic suicide. The term 'egoism' originates from the nineteenth century and was widely used by Durkheim and others at the time to indicate the breakdown of social ties. Egoism can be described as the process by which individuals detach themselves from society by turning their activity inward and by retreating into themselves.[185] Egoism is characterized by excessive self-reflection on personal matters and a withdrawal from the outside world. In this state, the 'springs of action' are relaxed and individuals turn toward themselves and away from society.[186] Egoism occurs, according to Durkheim, because the tie binding 'the individual to others is slackened and not sufficiently

182 Only a general discussion of social integration can be found in Durkheim's *Suicide*. See pp. 208–16.
  183 Ibid., pp. 208–9.
  184 Ibid., p. 209.
  185 Ibid., p. 279.
  186 Ibid., p. 279.

integrated at the points where the individual is in contact with society.'
Egoism results from too much individuation and from the 'weakening of
the social fabric.'[187] When the social bonds have broken down, individual
ends are more important than the common ends of society and the
individual's personality dominates over the collective personality. In such
circumstances, 'the individual ego asserts itself in the face of the social ego
and at its expense.'[188] Under these circumstances, egoism constitutes a
threat to society, to aggregate social maintenance, and to collective
authority.

Religious Integration and Egoistic Suicide   The first point at which the
individual is in contact with society is the religious group. Religion,
according to Durkheim, serves the function of social integration by linking
individuals to persons and things outside themselves. Specifically, it integrates individuals into various spheres of social life by placing restrictions
on individual autonomy and self-reflection. Taking this integration into
account, one of the first things Durkheim discovered in the suicide rates
was that Protestant countries had much higher numbers of suicidal deaths
than Roman Catholic countries. In fact, the statistical data showed that
the suicide rates were dramatically higher in Protestant countries, with the
difference between Protestant and Catholic suicides varying from a
minimum of 20 to 30 percent to a maximum of 300 percent.[189] But what
social factors would lead to these differences? Durkheim noted that both
religions condemn suicide with equal intensity and that each attaches
religious sanctions prohibiting it. Still, Protestants kill themselves more
than Catholics by as much as 300 percent in some countries. Durkheim
reasoned that the most significant difference between Protestantism and
Catholicism is their religious doctrine and teaching, and therefore the only
way to explain the difference in suicide rates is to examine the hold which
the doctrines have over their lives.[190]

   To begin with, Durkheim observed, Protestantism and Catholicism
differ fundamentally in the degree of authority that beliefs have over the
individual. Catholics tend to accept religious demands more readily than
do Protestants. They rarely question religious doctrine and never openly
criticize the demands which religious beliefs put upon them. Similarly, in
Catholic teaching, customs are fixed and unchanging and this places
expectations on individuals which link them more closely to the church.
Moreover, among Catholics, the system of traditional sacraments such as
confession and communion are intact, and the role played by ritual in the
church and in religious life remains unchanged. Catholics, therefore,
accept their doctrine without question or criticism.

187 Ibid., pp. 279–81.
188 Ibid., pp. 279–81.
189 Ibid., pp. 154–5.
190 Ibid., p. 153.

With Protestants, the situation is completely different. For one thing, Protestants encourage change at all levels of religious life and adopt a critical attitude toward formal doctrine. This freedom Protestants have to criticize religious beliefs, according to Durkheim, is unprecedented and the result is the undermining of religious discipline. Under such circumstances, Protestant doctrine diverges from Catholic teaching in several respects. First, Protestants are free to supervise their own religious observances and have greater freedom in interpreting beliefs. Since this makes them responsible for maintaining their own faith, they have become immune to influences which the doctrine exerts over their lives. Second, Protestants claim the right critically to evaluate religious doctrine and this has led to self-reflection and self-consciousness. The greater the self-reflection, the greater is the withdrawal from the religious community. Third, Protestants assert their autonomy from the hold that religious beliefs have over their lives to a greater degree than Catholics, making it more difficult for the believer to accept the world as it is. Fourth, Protestants disrupt the pattern of habit which forms around belief more than Catholics, and this makes their activity less subject to the constraints which religion imposes on their lives.[191]

What stands out about Protestant teaching and religious doctrine is the degree of religious autonomy and individualism it creates in contrast to other religions. As this autonomy increases, individuals withdraw from religious society and reject the demands which religious beliefs impose upon them. Here, the most important characteristic of Protestant doctrine is the development of what Durkheim called 'free inquiry.' This, he asserted, leads to the acceptance of a critical attitude toward religious beliefs and goes to the heart of Protestant teaching.[192] Essentially, the term 'free inquiry' was used by Durkheim to refer to the proclivity of Protestants to 'overthrow traditional beliefs' and critically to evaluate religious dogma by making it subject to criticism and reflection.[193] As religious beliefs are subject to critical scrutiny, said Durkheim, they lose their authority over the individual – and the less binding is religious dogma on matters of faith. 'Free inquiry' can therefore be defined as the overthrow of traditional beliefs inherent in religious doctrine.[194] In contrast to Catholics who traditionally accept their doctrine on faith, Protestants develop 'free inquiry,' and this erodes the social integration they have to religious society. This critical attitude, according to Durkheim, undermines religious integration and leads to a higher rate of suicide among Protestants when compared to Catholics. But, if this is true, what is the connection between the breakdown of religious integration and suicide?

One of the central functions of religion is that it creates social

---

191 Ibid., pp. 158–9.
192 Ibid., p. 159.
193 Ibid., p. 159.
194 Ibid., p. 158.

integration by linking individuals to persons and things outside themselves, and by creating a bond between the community of believers and the spiritual world. This integration develops by linking individuals to a common doctrine whose bonds are as strong as the doctrine is strong. The stronger the system of beliefs, the greater is the bond between the individual and the religious community. When these bonds begin to erode, however, the less cohesive and unified is the religious group. As a result, traditional practices lose their ability to maintain discipline and the hold which beliefs exert over the individual becomes weak. As faith in traditional practices is withdrawn from external doctrine, individual reflection becomes more pronounced and individuals are obliged to supervise their own religious activity.[195] This withdrawal to self-supervision accelerates egoism and the withdrawal from everything external.

As religious life becomes more dependent on self-definition and plays less of a role in the activity of the individual, the bonds connecting individuals to things that are greater than themselves become fewer and fewer, and the individual's attachment to the community of believers diminishes. This process of withdrawal from external ideas is evident in the Protestants' abandonment of religious confession. In that confession serves the function of drawing the individual into the center of religious life by creating a link between private thought and public faith, it places a claim on the individual to practice greater morality and, therefore, greater faith. But as Protestants become more individualized, confession is gradually replaced by self-reflection, encouraging freedom from dogma. The same is true for religious ritual. Protestants reduce to a minimum the role ritual plays in religious life, thereby minimizing the obligation which ritual exerts over the individual.[196]

Where Protestants embrace change and encourage freedom in religious thinking, Catholics remain bound to traditional beliefs and reject change as unacceptable. The overthrow by Protestants of traditional belief is significant in two related respects. First, Protestantism loosened the tie linking the believer to religious doctrine by encouraging a critical attitude toward beliefs. Second, as free inquiry is substituted for doctrine, it increases individuals' autonomy by reducing the hold which doctrine has over their lives. As soon as religious beliefs are brought into question, individuals become more reliant on their own judgment and this serves to break the bonds which beliefs create.[197] When beliefs 'have lost their hold' over the individual and when tradition has lost its ability to set boundaries and define daily life, the more individuals turn inward and become egoistic. As a consequence, they tend to bolster their own autonomy and this leads to greater self-sufficiency, egoism and self-reliance.[198]

195 Ibid., pp. 160–1.
196 Ibid., pp. 158–9.
197 Ibid., p. 159.
198 Ibid., pp. 159, 162.

As free inquiry reduces social integration and increases egoism, it brings about a loss of religious discipline. This, in turn, creates what Durkheim referred to as a reduction in the 'general immunity' from suicide which religious integration confers. This immunity, he believed, is evident in the case of Catholic suicide rates which are demonstrably lower due to the bonds existing between the individual and religious teaching.

To support the contention that there is a relation between free inquiry and egoistic suicide, Durkheim looked at the suicide rate among other religious groups. For example, he pointed out that the suicide rate among Jews is low despite the fact that learning and free inquiry play a key role in Jewish life. In fact, Jewish religious life is associated with an intense focus on learning and in some cases even a critical attitude. Yet, the suicide rates for Jews are lower than for Protestants. What accounts for this difference, according to Durkheim, is the degree of religious solidarity. Jewish religious beliefs exert a strong hold over the individual and regulate every aspect of daily life. This cohesion within the religious community is so well developed that integration between the individual and religious society is always high. In addition, religious solidarity among Jews is greater due to the intolerance shown toward Jews by the outside community.[199]

To provide further evidence that free inquiry breaks down religious integration and leads to egoistic suicide, Durkheim compared Protestant suicide rates in Germany with other Protestant countries such as England. He pointed out that suicide in Protestant localities in England is less developed, even though the English actually encourage individual autonomy and free inquiry.[200] Durkheim explained this contradiction between Protestants in Europe and Protestants in England by noting that, in the case of England, the loss of integration brought about by the increase of religious autonomy is offset by the fact that many religious obligations have become instituted into secular law. In England, Durkheim stated, a number of obligatory beliefs and religious practices have been legislated into civil law and thus have become part of everyday life.[201] This affects religious individualism in two distinct ways. First, it restricts daily activity and compels religious observance through secular vehicles which act to cut down on the autonomy created by religious individualism. Second, because England has a greater number of clergy in relation to the population of church goers, priests function as transmitters of tradition and doctrine and thus encourage the culture of self-restraint. This brings forward religious sentiment and increases integrative bonds.

In this case, England serves to verify rather than weaken the theory that religious individualism tends to dilute common beliefs. In fact, as religious individualism increases, the religious community itself grows weaker since Protestantism is constituted differently than Catholicism. The case of

199 Ibid., p. 160.
200 Ibid., pp. 160–1.
201 Ibid., pp. 160–1.

England confirms the theory since Protestants in England 'do not produce the same results' in terms of suicides and this is because their 'religious society is more strongly integrated and to this extent resembles the Catholic church.'[202]

To ensure that the conclusions drawn in relation to free inquiry and religious integration were correct, Durkheim looked at the general population to see if there is a relation between learning and egoistic suicide. In order to answer this question, he looked at the suicide rates among the educated classes and the 'liberal professions.'[203] These, he observed, include a class of persons whose occupations cultivate a 'taste for knowledge' and intellectual activity which tends to accelerate egoism. For example, in France between 1826 and 1880, the liberal professions were highest in the suicide rates. Similarly in Prussia, public officials were among the most educated, and showed an advanced suicide rate compared with the non-educated classes and occupations. This led Durkheim to believe that learning tends to reduce social cohesion and leads to the calling into question of the obligatory character of religious beliefs. While Durkheim was not putting forward the idea that learning increases suicide, or that people kill themselves because they learn, he was saying that the role played by learning in suicide is that it reduces overall cohesion, erodes religious beliefs, and diminishes the authority which beliefs have over individuals.

Family Integration and Egoistic Suicide   The second point of attachment between the individual and society is the family group and domestic environment.[204] Durkheim reasoned that if the social integration of the religious community reduces egoistic suicide, then attachments to the family and the domestic environment would tend to have a similar effect.

Durkheim began by looking at the commonly-held view about marriage and suicide. Many, he stated, tend to believe that suicide increases as the conditions of existence become more difficult, and since family life increases burdens and responsibilities, it must also increase the risk of suicide. Common sense thus holds that marriage increases difficulty and, therefore, increases suicide. Both these views are false, according to Durkheim, and cannot be substantiated by the evidence. In fact, the suicide rates show that when adjusted for age, unmarried persons take their own lives more frequently than do persons who are married.[205] Hence, marriage reduces suicide rates by about half. For example, in

202 Ibid., p. 161.
203 Ibid., p. 165.
204 Ibid., pp. 171–202.
205 Initially, when looking at the number of suicides among unmarried in relation to married persons, Durkheim found that married persons took their own lives more often than did the non-married. This 'disturbing result' was resolved when Durkheim found that children under sixteen were represented in the unmarried population. He reasoned that if adjusted for age, the appropriate result would be evident. For this detailed argument, see ibid., pp. 171–7.

France between 1889 and 1891, of those between the ages of 30–40, there were 627 suicides for those who were unmarried in comparison with 226 who were married.[206] Similarly, of those between the ages of 40–50, there were 975 suicides who were unmarried in comparison to 340 who were married. Stated differently, not being married increases suicide by about 1.6 percent in the population.[207] But what social factors would account for the variation in the rates between married and unmarried individuals?

Durkheim believed that the answer to this question can be found by looking at the nature of the family group and domestic environment. He asserted that there are features of the domestic environment which counteract egoism and reduce suicide and these are found within the family structure itself. According to Durkheim, the family is made up of two distinct groups or aggregates which together constitute the domestic environment. First there is the conjugal group, which is made up of husband and wife; and second, there is the family group which is made up of the conjugal group including children.[208] He maintained that each of these groups within the family constitutes different types of social bonds which contribute to integration in distinctly different ways. Chief among these are the primary ties of the conjugal group whose links are romantic in origin and whose roots are based in bonds of affinity. In and of itself, the conjugal group forms alliances based on generational similarities and forms bonds which are based on friendship and shared experiences. Conjugal links not only supersede the family group itself, but tend to have priority over the family group. Conjugal links thus 'unite two members of the same generation' and form social bonds based on similarity and intimacy.[209] Second is the larger family group, whose bonds are distinct from those of the conjugal group. In this case, bonds stem from blood ties whose links connect members of one generation with members of another. The difference between the conjugal and family group, according to Durkheim, is that the conjugal group is older and organized on the basis of ties of intimacy, whereas the family group is organized at a later date.

Durkheim maintained that marriage constitutes membership in both these communities, conjugal and familial, and both comprise the domestic environment. The remaining question is, how does the domestic environment reduce egoism and protect against suicide? First and foremost, family life reduces egoism by ensuring that greater concentrations of commitment are focused within the family rather than on the individual, and this, in itself, acts to suppress the tendency to withdraw to the self.[210] Family society, like religious society, therefore acts to protect against suicide to the extent that it creates duties and obligations outside the self and, in

206 Ibid., p. 178.
207 Ibid., p. 173.
208 Ibid., p. 173.
209 Ibid., p. 185.
210 Ibid., p. 180.

doing so, attaches the individual to life and counteracts the development of egoism. The family performs this function because it creates two distinct kinds of integrative demands on individuals. One places demands and obligations on the individual which arise from duties of the conjugal group. These may include roles and expectations which arise between spouses. The other exerts demands and expectations on the individual which stem from duties related to the family group, which may arise from roles individuals perform as functionaries and as parental authorities within the family group itself.[211]

While the conjugal group and the family group contribute to social integration and link the individual to the group as a whole, they do so in an entirely different manner. To demonstrate the differences between conjugal and family bonds, Durkheim looked for an indication of which group is stronger. The strength of the conjugal bond, he said, can be observed if we look at families without children and see whether their members are more likely to take their own lives than those families with children.[212] If we compare married men with unmarried men of the same age, we find that married men take their own lives a third less than unmarried men. This changes dramatically when children are involved, since the rates show that the immunity to suicide doubles. This indicates that the integration of the family groups is greater than that of the conjugal group, and this is confirmed by the fact that suicide is less in families where there are children. Durkheim went on to reason that one of the conclusions which can be drawn from the suicide rates is that suicide is neither due to life's burdens nor to an increase in the responsibilities which comes with family life. In fact, the opposite is true since suicide tends to diminish with marriage and the family, and therefore tends to diminish when burdens increase.[213]

Durkheim went on to argue that if suicide varies according to whether individuals are members of families, then it must also vary in relation to the size of family. He pointed out that the larger the family, the greater the sentiments and historical memories and, therefore, the greater the cohesion. This is reflected in the lower suicide rates for larger families. Small families, by contrast, develop less common sentiments and collective memories that lead to social cohesion and, thus, their shared experience is not as intense. In addition, because the members are fewer, their contact is more intermittent and there are times when this contact may be 'suspended' altogether.[214] Thus, the larger the family, the greater the social integration, and the greater is the degree of protection against suicide.

But how does this protective element function? Like the religious group, the family group can be considered to be a society. As such, individuals

211 Ibid., p. 198.
212 Ibid., p. 186.
213 Ibid., p. 201.
214 Ibid., p. 202.

are attached to it to a greater or lesser extent. In the family environment, individuals have responsibilities and obligations lying outside themselves and these act to reduce the inclination to focus exclusively on oneself alone. These obligations, in turn, function to create attachments which act to increase the individual's integration into the family group. Hence, the greater the obligations and social responsibilities beyond the self, the greater is the bond to social life – and thus the greater the immunity to suicide.

Political Integration and Egoistic Suicide   The third point of attachment between the individual and society is the 'political or national group.'[215] This is a more obscure category than either religion or the family and is less well developed by Durkheim than the other forms of attachment. Political society, according to Durkheim, refers to the type of social bonds which occur between the individual and society at large and encompasses the type of links which develop between individuals and their national group. Durkheim reasoned that to the extent that these social links exist, it is possible to look at the extent to which they are manifested in the suicide rates during times of social crisis and political upheaval.

Durkheim began by drawing on historical cases of political unrest and suicide. For example, in Rome an epidemic of suicide erupted as the city states began to break down and become politically decadent.[216] A similar phenomenon occurred in the Ottoman Empire where mass suicides were associated with political decline. Then again, there were suicides in France during the political turbulence of the revolution. Many, therefore, hold the view that political upheaval and social crisis increase the number of suicides. But the facts, according to Durkheim, tend to contradict this view. They show that during the revolutions in France, the number of suicides actually fell at the time the revolution took place, in some cases by 10 percent. Similarly, during the political crisis in Europe in 1848, suicides decreased. Again, in Bavaria and Prussia the suicide rate declined during the crisis of 1849.[217] In addition, large-scale wars tend to produce the same effect, bringing a dramatic decline in the suicide rate. During the Revolution of Louis Bonaparte in 1851, suicide rates fell by 8 percent even though it was a turbulent period in French political history.[218] In another context, the political struggles in France between 1848 and 1849 brought a decrease in the rates as well. Similarly, during the turmoil of 1848–49 in European countries other than France, the rates declined. How can this decline in the suicide rates be explained?

These facts can only be understood, said Durkheim, by one interpretation. Instead of breaking social ties, severe social disruption

215 Ibid., pp. 202–8.
216 Ibid., p. 203.
217 Ibid., p. 204.
218 Ibid., p. 204.

brought about by a political crisis increases the intensity of 'collective sentiments and stimulates patriotism.'[219] In fact, political crisis acts to stimulate partisan spirit and strong feelings of nationalism, and this focuses individual interests toward a single end. It forces individuals to draw together under common interests, leading them to 'think less of themselves and more of common causes.' This, in effect, increases social integration between the individual and the group and 'causes a stronger integration of society.'[220]

In addition to stirring up national sentiment, political crisis creates what Durkheim called a 'moral effect,' which propagates throughout society and, along with arousing public feelings, places moral demands on individuals and increases their patriotic spirit. Often this 'moral effect' is restricted to the urban population who tend to be more involved and impassioned than the population in rural areas. This collective stimulation of sentiments during political upheaval ignites national feeling and this has the effect of strengthening social integration in society. As this social integration becomes strong, 'the individual thinks less of themselves and more of common social purposes.'[221]

Explanation of Egoism and Egoistic Suicide We can now look more closely at the causes of egoism and egoistic suicide. Simply stated, egoistic suicide results from the absence of social integration and a weakening of the bonds which attach individuals to groups outside themselves. It occurs when the links binding the individual to the wider society grow weak and individual goals replace the common goals and purposes of society. In such circumstances individuals rely more on themselves and withdraw their allegiance from collective life. Durkheim gives the name egoism to this state because it identifies a condition in society in which the individual ego prevails over the social ego.[222]

The religious, familial and political groups have a moderating effect on egoistic suicide because they share the common property of being strongly integrated and thus constitute links to society. The weaker the bonds attaching the individual to these groups, the less they depend upon them and the more they depend on themselves.[223] In this view, egoism is the result of the weakening of the bonds which tie the individual to society. But, if this is the case, what is the cause of egoism? Simply stated, 'egoism' is the result of prolonged and unchecked individualism which, in turn, is a consequence of industrial society. In industrial society, Durkheim explained, the 'collective force' attaching the individual to social groups weakens and as this force diminishes, it leads to an increase in the suicide

219 Ibid., p. 208.
220 Ibid., p. 208.
221 Ibid., p. 208.
222 Ibid., p. 209.
223 Ibid., p. 209.

rates — 'the bond that unites the individual to life and prevents them from feeling personal troubles so deeply' begins to slacken and grows weak.[224]

Durkheim believed that individuals, by nature, cannot live without attachment to some object which transcends them. Egoism thus attacks social bonds in at least two fundamental ways. First, by eroding the common bonds linking the individual to society, egoism makes private life a dominant aim and this acts to defeat collective purposes. Egoism is, in this sense, a state in which society is completely lacking in the individual.[225] Second, egoism promotes withdrawal from everything external and, when this occurs, 'society allows the individual to escape' its hold.[226] As a consequence, when individuals become detached from society they encounter less resistance to suicide. In egoistic suicide, therefore, the bond attaching individuals to life relaxes because the bond attaching them to society is slack.[227]

Altruistic Suicide and Social Integration Next, Durkheim turned his attention to altruistic suicide, the polar opposite of egoistic suicide. He began his discussion by citing the suicides of primitive societies. There are, he stated, suicides in some societies where, rather than die of old age, individuals kill themselves to maintain their dignity. In other societies, there are customs which dictate that dying a natural death leads to a life after death that is intolerable and full of suffering. In still other societies, they believe that old men must throw themselves off a mountain when tired of life. In almost all these situations, those who take their life are honored and their families spared humiliation; individuals who fail to take their own life are denied the honor of the funeral and a life of dishonor and pain is presumed to await them.[228] In all these instances 'the weight of society is brought to bear on the individual to destroy themselves.'[229] This type of suicide, in contrast to the type described earlier, is called altruistic suicide. It differs from egoistic suicide in that it results from too much social integration rather than too little. In order to understand what Durkheim meant by this assertion, we must look more closely.

Durkheim first made his observations about altruistic suicide by looking at tribal societies. He observed that the social customs in these societies placed a high degree of social honor on individuals who take their own lives in the name of social purposes greater than themselves. In this category, Durkheim lists three specific types of suicides: (i) the suicide of older men threatened with severe illness; (ii) the suicide of women on the death bed of their husbands; and (iii) the suicide of followers on the death

224 Ibid., p. 210.
225 Ibid., pp. 210–16.
226 Ibid., p. 217.
227 Ibid., p. 219.
228 Ibid., p. 218.
229 Ibid., p. 219.

of their chiefs.[230] Under these circumstances, people take their own lives not because they take the personal right to do so, but because a social duty is imposed upon them by society.[231] So strong is this duty that, when individuals avoid their obligation, they stand to be socially disgraced or religiously sanctioned. Yet, when these duties are carried out, society confers a social honor upon them that is thought to extend to the after-life.

Durkheim thought that the cause of altruistic suicide in tribal societies is to be found in their excessive degree of social integration. This occurs, he reasoned, because the nature of group life in small-scale societies is such that the individual is over-absorbed into the web of society. In tribal societies, social life is focused on the group and all activity radiates from the center of tribal experience. Under these circumstances, the individual ego is overwhelmed by the social ego and is not permitted its own individual expression. In addition, because individuals live in such close proximity to one another, their social customs and beliefs tend to be unified. As a result, collective supervision and surveillance extend throughout society, leading to similarity in beliefs and social observances. Under such circumstances, the individual has no private life that is immune from collective surveillance. As a result, individuals are available to social claims upon their allegiance – allegiance that might otherwise be directed to developing individual tastes. Under these circumstances, the individual has little independence from group life, and individual existence, by itself, has little meaning. In cases where society is able to produce such 'massive cohesion,' it almost always relies on social practices which elicit a high degree of attachment and, accordingly, individualism is under-developed.[232]

Altruistic suicide is therefore at the opposite pole of social integration to egoistic suicide. In egoistic suicide, there is an excess of individualism and autonomy, whereas in altruistic suicide little or no individuation takes place. In egoistic suicide, the bonds between the individual and society grow weak and this takes its toll on individual life; in altruistic suicide, by contrast, the bonds between the individual and society are developed to such an extent that the individual acquires an aptitude for the renunciation of life.[233] Thus, where 'egoistic suicide arises because society allows the individual to escape it, altruistic suicide occurs because society holds the individual in too strict a tutelage.'[234] 'Having given the name egoism to the state of the ego living its own life and obeying itself alone, that of altruism adequately expresses the opposite state, where the ego is not its own property and where the goal of conduct is exterior to the self in one of the groups in which it participates.'[235]

230 Ibid., p. 219.
231 Ibid., p. 219.
232 Ibid., p. 221.
233 Ibid., p. 221.
234 Ibid., p. 221.
235 Ibid., p. 221.

Durkheim maintained that altruistic suicide takes several different forms and went on to outline three distinct types. While he believed that all altruistic suicide is described by the obligation laid upon the individual from outside social forces, he contended that the nature of this obligation expresses itself in three distinct ways: (i) obligatory altruistic suicide; (ii) optional altruistic suicide; and (iii) acute altruistic or mystical suicide. Each differs in the degree of explicitness of the obligation placed upon individuals to take their own life.[236]

(i) In the first category, obligatory altruistic suicide, society imposes an explicit duty on individuals to take their own life, but this duty may lack specific coercive pressure from the community. Obligatory suicide in some societies takes the form of a customary requirement which may be part of the beliefs of the community, or it may take the form of a less explicit expectation which is understood to be part of customary rules. To encourage suicide in instances where an individual is ill or aging, the community may attach social prestige to it – leaving those who resist to experience some stigma or religious sanction. In such circumstances, individual life is assigned very little value over group life and Durkheim made the point that, due to the social expectation put upon them, individuals are often willing to give up their lives at the 'least pretext.'[237]

(ii) A second type referred to by Durkheim is optional altruistic suicide. In this category, the demand placed on the individual by the community is less explicitly clarified or 'less expressly required' than in circumstances where suicide is strictly obligatory.[238] In some instances, the two types may be indistinguishable in terms of the degree of duty felt or the extent of explicitness inherent in the demand. In either case, death may be held out as an expectation, where the duty to take one's own life is clear or where there is honor assigned to the renunciation of life. In such circumstances, 'not clinging to life is seen as a virtue' and for those who renounce life, society attaches honors which produces the effect of actually lowering the importance of the life of the individual over the group interest.[239]

(iii) A third type Durkheim referred to is called 'acute altruistic suicide.' In this case, the individual renounces life for the actual felt 'joy of sacrifice.'[240] In Hindu society, for instance, suicide takes on the form of religious fervor and is looked upon with enthusiasm. In some instances, members of a religious sect will climb to the top of a cliff which has sulfur flames below it. Durkheim maintained that these individuals call out to their gods and wait for a flame to appear. As they utter the words which give their life as a sacrifice, the appearance of the flame is believed to be a sign.[241] In these circumstances, Durkheim maintained individuals actually

236 Ibid., pp. 222–3.
237 Ibid., pp. 222–3.
238 Ibid., p. 223.
239 Ibid., p. 222.
240 Ibid., p. 223.
241 Ibid., pp. 224–5.

seek to 'strip themselves of their personal being in order to be engulfed in something' which they regard as a higher order or as a truer form of existence. In this case, the believers violently 'strive to blend' themselves with an order which is believed to be greater than themselves.[242] Durkheim reasoned that to act in this way, the individual literally must have no life of his or her own, since only after death does the individual believe that his or her true being has been realized. Durkheim stated that to kill themselves so readily, they must not place too much value in their own life since 'altruism is acute.'[243]

Altruistic suicide results from an excess of social integration and is at the polar extreme of egoistic suicide. In egoistic suicide, individualism has advanced to a point where the aims of the individual are above the common purposes of society, resulting in the breakdown of social integration. In the case of altruistic suicide, by contrast, individualism hardly develops since the authority of the group is valued over individual existence. The cause of altruistic suicide is excessive social integration that leads to a lack of development of individualism.

Military vs Civilian Suicides To support the contention that altruistic suicide is the result of excessive social integration, Durkheim turned his attention to comparing military with civilian suicide. He pointed out that, by far, suicide in the military exceeds suicidal death in the civilian population. For example, in countries such as Austria and the United States, the suicide rate is six to ten times higher among the military. Durkheim finds these high rates surprising since military morale is thought to have a mitigating effect on suicide. What are the causes of a high suicide rate among the military?

Durkheim began by looking at popular opinion. Some believe that because many soldiers never marry, the high rate of suicide must relate to bachelorhood. Others, in contrast, take the view that military service itself is the cause since the hardship and discipline of military life create a lack of freedom leading to more suicidal deaths than in the civilian population. Still others maintain that suicide is higher in the military because of the isolation of military life. Durkheim reasoned that none of these views are true. He pointed out that the effects of being unmarried on the soldier compared to the civilian should not be as great, since the soldier is 'anything but isolated.' In fact the soldier, in comparison with the civilian, is a member of a strongly unified group whose bonds are 'partially calculated to replace the family.'[244]

Durkheim maintained that these views are supported by comparative data. For example, with respect to the hardships of military life, he pointed out that military discipline is less rigorous for officers than for

242 Ibid., pp. 224–5.
243 Ibid., pp., 224–5. Durkheim refers to this as the 'euphoria of self obliteration.'
244 Ibid., p. 229.

non-career soldiers, yet officers in France and Italy are twice as likely to kill themselves as non-professional soldiers. Similarly, in comparison with the civilian population over a ten year period, suicide rates in the military tripled 'while for unmarried civilians during the same period it only rose by 20 percent.'[245] In addition, in the Prussian military there were 560 privates who took their own lives in contrast to 1140 who were officers.[246] Military suicide, therefore, is not only different from civilian suicide, it is in 'inverse proportion to the determining causes of civilian suicide.'[247] To what can these differences be attributed?

The military, asserted Durkheim, creates more suicides because first and foremost it is a society which is separate from the wider society. In this sense, it constitutes a sphere of thought and action distinct from the social group which surrounds it. He went on to maintain that this can only mean that the causes of military suicide are, in fact, different from the causes leading to suicide in the general population. In the civilian population, the prevailing cause of suicide stems from excessive individualism – a common characteristic of European society. Military suicide, by contrast, arises because of the very opposite condition of individualism and this cause, according to Durkheim, is 'feeble individuation.'[248] In fact, the traditions of military life, according to Durkheim, resemble those of lower societies and, in the context of the military, traditionalism is thus the chief opponent of individualism. Durkheim went on to suggest that military morality is an anthropological 'survival of primitive morality' and, in demanding too much allegiance from individuals, it leaves them little for the development of individual interests and private inclination.[249] He pointed out that this is reflected in the predisposition of soldiers who take their own life 'at the least disappointment, for the most futile reasons; for a refusal of leave, a reprimand, an unjust punishment, a delay in promotion, a question of honor, a flush of momentary jealousy.'[250]

Suicide, the Regulative Pole: Anomic and Fatalistic Suicide

In the first part of Durkheim's theory of suicide, egoism and altruism formed the two polar extremes of social integration. At one end of the continuum is excessive individualism (egoism), at the other, under-developed individualism or excessive aggregation (altruism). The second part of Durkheim's theory relates to the regulatory function of society and this has two polar extremes represented by anomic and fatalistic suicide. In order to understand what Durkheim meant by the regulatory function of society, however, we must define the term 'anomie.'

Stated simply, anomie can be defined as the decline in the regulatory

245 Ibid., p. 232.
246 Ibid., p. 233.
247 Ibid., p. 236.
248 Ibid., p. 236.
249 Ibid., p. 238.
250 Ibid., p. 239.

powers of society. But how could these functions actually decline? Generally, Durkheim thought that the regulatory functions of society served the purpose of setting limits on social needs and wants. To be clear on this point, Durkheim made the distinction between two different kinds of regulatory functions – between bodily needs and social needs. He thought that bodily needs and wants were self-regulating. In this context, the body's limit on needs and appetites is governed by biological limitations which cannot, as a rule, operate outside set boundaries.[251] In the case of social needs and wants, the situation is otherwise. He pointed out that social wants – such as the appetite for wealth, prestige and power – are essentially unlimited. Only society can set limitations on these social needs and only society can operate to set limits on individual wants. Historically, this function was performed by society through specific social institutions that operated to set moral restraints on individual appetites by linking social wants to the available means for attaining these wants. After the development of industrial society, however, there was a general slackening of restraint as the economy became the dominant social institution and limitation of desire became incompatible with economic life.

Durkheim's discussion of anomic suicide begins by looking at the suicide rates during times of economic crisis, such as a financial recession and periods of economic decline. For instance, between 1845 and 1869 there were repeated economic crises in Europe, creating a dramatic decline in the business cycle and a rise in the number of bankruptcies.[252] During these crises, there was a rapid rise in the suicide rate and this increased as economic troubles worsened. As the crisis disappeared, the rates declined, but when the crisis returned it was followed by a rise in the rates once again. Durkheim reasoned that if we accept these facts at face value, we are led to assume that people take their own lives as life becomes more difficult, especially during times of economic disaster.

According to this view, the cause of the fluctuation in the suicide rate is due to the fluctuation in wealth. Durkheim, however, disputed this explanation on two different fronts. First, he believed that it conforms too readily with popular opinion about suicide and, in this sense, lacks science. Second, he stated that if this proposition were true, the suicide rates would decline as economic prosperity increased; but the suicide rates for other periods show that this decline never takes place. In fact, neither poverty, bankruptcy nor a sudden decline in the business cycle causes suicide and, therefore, the rise in the rates cannot be directly linked to economic disaster. We must, therefore, go further.

Durkheim went on to make a key assertion. He stated that if in an economic crisis there is an increase in suicide rates, it is not because of the

---

251 Durkheim's discussion of the distinction between bodily needs and social wants in relation to anomie is excellent and can be found in ibid., pp. 246–54.
252 Ibid., p. 242.

hardship associated with economic misfortune, since in times of prosperity the same rise in the rates occurs.[253] He reasoned that since the change in the rates takes place with equal intensity during times of economic collapse and prosperity, then suicide rates must be linked to some other phenomenon related to periodic adjustments in what he called the 'social equilibrium.'[254] In fact, Durkheim believed that whenever an abrupt shift in social stability occurs, it alters the mechanism which places restraint on individual desires and social wants. He therefore reasoned that the category of anomic suicide must be related to the shift in the regulatory mechanisms of society which occurs precisely during periods of economic hardship or prosperity. This focus on the 'social equilibrium' allowed Durkheim to isolate the cause of suicide in the mechanisms of society which regulate social equilibrium rather than in causes which seem to attach suicide to fluctuations in the business cycle. Given this reasoning, the category of anomic suicide relates directly to the regulatory mechanisms of society, since anomie refers to that state of affairs which results when there is an overall decline in the regulatory functions of society.

Anomie, then, may be defined as the state which results from the weakening of the powers of society that regulate social equilibrium. In order to see how this process comes about, we must look at how Durkheim understood the connection between society and social regulation. Durkheim directly stressed the importance of the regulatory functions of society, and believed that a system of social regulation serves to set limits to individual desires by placing restraints on wants and by performing the important purpose of balancing individual wants with the means for obtaining them.[255] When social wants exceed the possible means for attaining them, Durkheim thought this led to disappointment and feelings of individual failure and despair. In fact, Durkheim maintained that during the course of everyday life, there are constant internal demands on individuals which can lead to conscious wants and material desires. It is, therefore, the direct function of society to set restraints on individuals so that desires do not become conscious material wants. In this respect, human social wants contrast sharply with the animal world. In nature, the needs of animals are adjusted to bodily wants and thus are naturally regulated. With human beings, the case is otherwise. Since individual social wants are not related to the system of bodily needs or desires and can arise in the imagination, Durkheim believed that explicit limitations on social wants must be set by society. In fact, since nothing in human nature acts to 'sets limits' on social desires, then society alone must act as a means of material restraint and external regulation.[256]

Durkheim maintained that human beings, in fact, have a greater feeling

253 Ibid., p. 242.
254 Ibid., p. 246.
255 Ibid., p. 246. 'Needs,' wrote Durkheim, must be 'sufficiently proportioned to means.'
256 Ibid., p. 247.

of well-being when their needs are proportioned to their wants, and when the means they have to satisfy these wants meet their own capacities. In a state of anomie, the regulatory limits usually imposed by society are absent and limits are not well defined. Disappointment with life and feelings of failure are quick to arise and readily blamed on the individual since externally defined limits are lacking.[257] When the majority of social wants cannot be attained, Durkheim believed that it first leads to disappointment then, eventually, to chronic morbidity, and finally to defeat. When the forces of society fail to set limitations on wants, individuals continually exceed the means at their disposal, and their desires – by definition – become frustrated and out of reach. This can only happen, Durkheim maintained, when individuals constantly aspire to reach ends or goals that are beyond their capacity to obtain. It is important to keep in mind that motives leading individuals to strive for goals which they cannot realistically obtain are due to the failure of the powers of society to set limits and regulate social wants. In fact, to pursue goals which are unattainable ensures repeated disappointment, and when goals are set which have no end or conclusion, individuals become despondent.

Durkheim believed that this circumstance is especially compounded in industrial society. In traditional societies, religious institutions set limits on social wants by providing a framework of meaningful constraints on appetites and individual desires. In modern societies, by contrast, the limitations imposed by religion have been replaced by a 'spirit of free pursuit' and this tends to raise the horizon of desirable goals beyond reach.[258] In addition, the system of restraint existing in society largely disappeared as a consequence of modern economic competition. As economy replaced religion as the dominant social institution, all restraint was suspended since economy taught that all desires were attainable with sufficient effort and hard work. Under these circumstances, restraint and limitation became incompatible with the pursuit of private gain. As the economy removed natural limits, all desires became material wants and this led to an increasing scale of want and desire. The more individual wants increase, the greater the need to obtain the means to satisfy them. With this stress on commercial success, all goals seem attainable and natural limits to wants are removed.

Traditional societies, in contrast, once performed the function of setting a framework of restraints on social wants and this created a regulatory link between wants and the socially attainable means for fulfilling them. Durkheim thought that 'the regulative force in society must play the same role for moral needs as the body plays for physical needs.'[259] Since, according to Durkheim, human social wants 'are not automatically restrained by physiological mechanisms,' they can only be restricted and

257 Ibid., p. 247.
258 Ibid., pp. 247–9.
259 Ibid., p. 248.

channeled by the moral force of society – thus restraint must come from a source outside the individual.[260]

Durkheim took the position that dramatic changes in the suicide rates are a reflection of moral disturbances in the regulatory mechanism of modern society. He thought that so far as it is society's job to set outside limits, when these limits are absent or fail to be set, individuals feel unlimited want. This loss of social regimen can only set off a general decrease in the state of well-being. Durkheim maintained that a social framework exists which precisely regulates the degree of ease of living which each social class feels to a different extent.[261] This framework varies with the shifting moral ideas of society and the collective authority inherent in the moral ideas of the time. These socially imposed limitations on individual desires bring about what Durkheim called 'average contentment' and this creates feelings of well-being and even happiness.[262] When these limits are set by society, individuals desire only what they can legitimately obtain. But as soon as these restraints are lifted, as changes occur in the moral framework of society, anomie ensues. There is no society in which this social regulation does not exist and it can only be imposed by collective authority. When disrupted by social crises, society is unable to exercise its regulatory function and thus cannot act as a source of restraint on individual wants. Hence, a state of deregulation ensues and this acts to increase rather than decrease social wants, making individuals less disciplined.

Causes of Anomie and the Role Played by the Economy   Durkheim believed that one of the direct causes of anomie is the industrial and economic changes of the nineteenth century. 'For a whole century,' he stated, 'economic progress had mainly consisted in freeing industrial relations from all regulation.'[263] Economic progress, he pointed out, can only advance at the expense of social regulation and moral discipline. This happens because the dominance of economic life acts to displace the regulatory functions of other social institutions. Religion is a case in point. Historically, the explicit function of religion is to exert moral influence by teaching tolerance in the face of hardship and contentment with one's position in life. In addition, religion provides a framework of restraint by explaining social differences between classes and promising that compensation will occur in the next world.[264] In this respect, religion serves the function of placing life in perspective and teaching that worldly economic success is not the primary goal of life and that material needs are to be subordinated to intangible goals. This tended to regulate economic life by

260 Ibid., pp. 248–9.
261 Ibid., pp. 248–9.
262 Ibid., p. 245.
263 Ibid., p. 254.
264 Ibid., p. 255.

setting into balance the relation between social goals and individual capabilities.

But with the development of advanced economies, technologies and world markets, individuals were capable of extending their grasp over natural limitations. As production, income and the division of labor began to develop more freely, the social threshold set by earlier periods became redirected. As a result, needs and wants – and even entire perspectives – are raised to a 'feverish pitch.'[265] The replacement of religion by economy subordinated society to economic and industrial ends. The intense economic focus of society freed desires from previous moral limits and replaced moral restraints with utilitarian sanctions inherent in law and social rules. Eventually, the extension and activity of markets acted to extend and expand desire. Thus, stated Durkheim, 'irrespective of any regulatory force our capacity for social wants became insatiable and a bottomless abyss; the more one has, the more one wants, since satisfactions received only stimulate' further wants.[266] In an economically expanding society, ambition is widened to include world markets rather than the restricted locales of former times. This stress on economic activity increases individual desires to such an extent that discomfort and restraint become less tolerable than they were in societies in which restraint was the norm. When the primary focus in society is economic, there is increased risk of and greater possibility for crisis. Thus, it is the economically related functions, according to Durkheim, which create the largest category of suicide when compared to other spheres of society where the 'old regulatory forces' rather than the new commercial spirit still prevail in practice.[267]

History of the Term Anomie   Durkheim first used the concept of anomie in *Division of Labor* in 1893, but it was not until 1897 that he began to use the term in a more narrow sense to describe the overall deterioration of moral restraint in society. Since he believed that the primary function of society was to set limits to social wants by providing a moral framework of restraint, then anomie refers to the state which results in society when there is a decline of the social regulatory mechanisms. In that the regulative force of society plays the same role for moral needs as does the body for physical needs, the higher suicide rate of industrial society is an indication of pervasive anomie.[268] But what is the cause of this deregulation?

Durkheim believed that the causes of deregulation can be traced to two basic sources: (i) the development of industrial society; and (ii) the dominance of the economy over other institutions.[269] In the first instance,

---

265 Ibid., p. 256.
266 Ibid., pp. 247–8.
267 Ibid., p. 257.
268 Ibid., p. 248.
269 See ibid., pp. 254–8. The weight Durkheim gives to the connection between anomie and economic progress is unmistakable.

economic progress removes limits and frees social activity from regulation in three discernible ways. First, the dominance of religion is replaced by the economy. This removes the traditional mechanisms for justifying one's place in the social order, and the loss of this understanding leads to a decrease in social contentment. Religious beliefs thus lose their efficacy over economic functions. Second, industrial capitalism removes regulation in economic matters, making economic life dominant over state and religious functions. Third, as needs and social wants become unregulated and social limits are removed, 'one's present existence seems valueless by comparison with the dreams of fevered imaginations.'[270] In Durkheim's view, society sets desires at a level that only a few could achieve.

Looked at in this way, anomie can be defined as the state which results from the decline in the regulatory force of society brought about by unchecked economic progress. There are two distinctly different forms of regulation that Durkheim referred to: first, the capacity of society to impose material limits and social restraints on wants; and second, the ability to impose restraints that act on individual perception. It is this perception about the relative state of society which confers feelings of well-being and directly affects the individual's relationship to society with respect to meaning.

To this point, Durkheim put forward three concepts making up a social theory of suicide: egoism, altruism, and anomie. The first two concepts, egoism and altruism, explain suicide by looking at the framework of social attachments to society which Durkheim called social integration, and we have looked at the continuum of integration from egoism to altruism. The concept of anomic suicide, on the other hand, belongs to a framework which explains suicide by looking at the changes in the regulatory mechanism of society. Egoistic suicide occurs because the individual is not well attached to society, thus lacking social integration; altruistic suicide takes place because the individual is over-attached to society, to the point that individualism is non-existent. While the first type is due to over-developed individualism, the second is due to a lack of development at the level of the individual.[271] Anomic suicide, in contrast, occurs because of the reduction of the regulatory mechanisms of society. In such circumstances, the limitations set by society are virtually absent or extensively weakened.

Fatalistic Suicide Fatalistic suicide, the last category of Durkheim's theory, represents the opposite pole of suicide resulting from adjustments in the regulatory mechanisms of society. In the same way that altruism serves to pinpoint suicide which occurs because of an excess of social integration, fatalism signifies a form of suicide which Durkheim believed occurs because of an excess of social regulation. Durkheim stated that whereas anomie refers to the absence of regulation, fatalistic suicide occurs

270 Ibid., p. 245.
271 Ibid., p. 221.

because of an excessive degree of regulation and an overly developed regime.[272] As an example of fatalistic suicide, Durkheim cited the suicide of slaves who, seeing no alternative to enslavement under the master, take their own lives.

The Elementary Forms of the Religious Life

The Historical Context of the Work

The Elementary Forms of the Religious Life, Durkheim's fourth major sociological work, was written between 1902 and 1911 while Durkheim was in Paris. By the time it was published in 1912, Durkheim was 54 years old and had become established as one of the leading thinkers of French social thought. Though Durkheim began working on the problem of religion as early 1902, there were several reasons leading him to choose religion as a central subject of sociological research. First, religion had been a leading theme in Durkheim's sociological journal, the *Année Sociologique*. Many issues focused on anthropological questions which were dominant at the time. Second, as early as 1890, anthropologists and ethnographers had come to view religion and religious institutions as the central subject matter of the social and cultural sciences. Studies such as Spencer's and Gillen's *The Native Tribes of Central Australia*, published in 1899, were among the first to carry out ethnographic studies of social and religious institutions not studied previously. In addition, Benjamin Howitt's *Native Tribes of South Eastern Australia* undertook a direct study of Australian tribes using observation and ethnographic techniques. These studies were among the first to look systematically into the religious practices of early societies in central Australia. Third, Durkheim's nephew, Marcel Mauss, was pursuing anthropological interests at the time and many of his articles were featured in the *Année*, giving it a distinctly anthropological focus. By 1895, Durkheim was convinced that religion would be a fitting subject for sociological study since it seemed to be at the heart of the institutional framework of society.[273]

Elementary Forms is a major sociological work in several key respects. First, in its scope and conception, it is the most comprehensive of Durkheim's writings – ranging from its focus on religion to an original discussion of the social foundations of knowledge. Scholastically, it is one of his most mature works, demonstrating a broad conceptual and theoretical grasp of religious practices and social life. Stylistically, it is incisive in its reasoning, demonstrating clarity in its central argument and

---

272 Ibid., p. 276. Durkheim's discussion of fatalism is very brief. His interest in introducing the concept of fatalistic suicide, even in such an abbreviated form, is for purposes of conceptual symmetry. The idea is that each of the pairs of suicide types (egoistic–altruistic; anomic–fatalistic) demonstrate the polar opposites of both integration and regulation in a symmetrical manner.

273 Lukes, *Emile Durkheim*, p. 237.

thoroughness in its method of exposition.[274] And historically, it is one of the first studies in which Durkheim debated his theoretical contemporaries. In this respect, the book has a distinct anthropological emphasis, primarily because its central subject matter focuses on the social and religious structure of totemism.

Fundamental Aims of the Work

The Elementary Forms of the Religious Life has five central aims. The first is to study primitive religion and explain its basic structure. This, Durkheim believed, would lead to an understanding of religion and the religious nature of society. A second aim, according to Durkheim, is to arrive at an understanding of contemporary religions by going back to the most primitive. He believed that only by going back to the earliest religious institutions can we understand the nature of religious life. A third aim of the study is to undertake an examination of religion from the perspective of positive science. This contrasts with earlier studies of religion which assert that religion has its basis in a spirit world. When viewed from the perspective of positive science, Durkheim believed, we are able to make what is observable about religion subject to scientific investigation rather than just speculate on a spirit world. This, he thought, leads to the discovery of the most basic elements underlying religious life, and these he called its 'elementary forms.' It is the study of these 'forms' which will facilitate the discovery of what is fundamental to religious life in all societies and, eventually, to finding the basis on which all religious life depends. A fourth aim of the study is to look at the relationship between religious ideas and the organization of bodies of knowledge and systems of classification.[275] Religion, Durkheim believed, must have been the first way of knowing the natural and social world and, as such, must have functioned as a body of knowledge explaining the universe to the human mind. Finally, the fifth aim is to demonstrate that, when reduced to its basic elements, religion is nothing more than the expression of society consecrated.[276]

Durkheim's Search for a 'Positive' Definition of Religion

Durkheim began the discussion by stating that to study religion in a systematic way a definition must be arrived at that would be applicable to all religious life, since without one we cannot study the system of practices that all religious phenomena possess. It is important that a definition of religion be arrived at which eliminates preconceived ideas about religious

---

274 The textual structure of the argument, however, adds to the difficulty of developing a reasonable grasp of the central premise of *The Elementary Forms of the Religious Life*, London: Allen & Unwin, [1912] 1915.

275 Ibid., p. 8.

276 Ibid., p. 9.

experience, since these often have no validity. Examples of these definitions already exist in popular opinion and many of these have not been
arrived at methodically. One author, for instance, views religion as the
expression of supernatural forces, involving ideas which surpass the limits
of the physical world.[277] This definition implies that knowledge of religion
always 'surpasses' the natural world and is a mysterious experience in
itself. But, asked Durkheim, how can we explain a mystery? Another
author stated that religion is born from the feeling of the 'infinite' which is
derived from the ultimate mystery believed to be behind existence.[278] In
this case, the definition of religion is synonymous with the mystical, which
is expressed in the powers mystical forces have. But, Durkheim countered,
we cannot capture the characteristics of religion from that which is unseen.
Still others hold that religion is to be explained in terms of the concept of
divinity, in which strong bonds are thought to exist between individuals
and a powerful deity.[279] This definition, however, compels us to see
religion as synonymous with a supreme being whose powers are greater
than those of ordinary beings. But not all religions have as their basis a
supreme being greater in power than the believer. In fact, Buddhism and
Brahmanism recognize no central god or deity.[280]

If we take these views as our starting place, said Durkheim, we will have
as many theories of religion as there are religious beliefs, since each of the
views arrive at different conclusions as to what precisely the elementary
forms of religion are. These definitions can be discounted, therefore,
because they are based on preconceived ideas often originating from
religious doctrine itself, and from the belief that religion is unseen and
invisible.

After setting these definitions aside, Durkheim stated that in order to
put forward a definition of religion, the first step is to identify the
underlying elements of religious life and to look for the common features
to be found in all religions.[281] For these elements to be identified we must
examine the constituent parts of religion before we can describe the system
produced by their unity. Any adequate definition of religion, therefore,
must take into account the specific elements of religious life before it can
describe those features common to the whole. Durkheim's search for a
definition of religion takes two important directions. First is its positivistic
direction. By 'positive' Durkheim meant the ability to describe religion in
terms which are subject to observation, as opposed to speculative thinking.
Second is its investigative direction. This direction pursues religion by
reducing it to elementary parts, looking for what is common to all
religions.

277 Ibid., p. 24.
278 Ibid., p. 25.
279 Ibid., pp. 29–31.
280 Ibid., pp. 34–5.
281 Ibid., p. 36.

Durkheim then went on to outline a definition which has two central parts or elementary forms. First, he said that all religions can be defined in terms of a system of beliefs and rites.[282] Beliefs refer to a set of ideas and attitudes held in relation to sacred things, whereas rites are defined as a system of action which is developed toward religious things or objects. Second is that all religions can be defined in terms of their tendency to divide the world into two regions, the sacred and the profane. This division of the world 'into two domains, the one containing all that is sacred, the other all that is profane, is the most distinctive trait of religious life.'[283]

Sacred and Profane

Since no proper understanding of Durkheim's theory of religion is possible without elaborating on the distinction between the sacred and the profane, we turn to a brief discussion of these important concepts. To begin with, all religions can be defined by their tendency to divide the world into the sacred and the profane. The division between these two realms forms one of the central principles of a social theory of religion and, in fact, it is the most distinctive element of religious life.[284] Durkheim believed that the sacred and profane form the basis of religious life in several respects. First, he asserted that the sacred embodies not only gods, spirits and natural things, but it also embraces beliefs as well. A belief, practice or rite can have a sacred character and what makes it sacred is its tendency to be viewed by others as a 'consecrated' thing. Second, words and expressions, and even combinations of words can be sacred. These can be uttered only by consecrated persons and involve gestures and movements that only certain people can perform.[285] In addition, a system of rites, beliefs and social practices emerges from sacred things and radiates around them.

In direct contrast to the sacred is the profane. The profane, according to Durkheim, is something subordinated in dignity to the sacred and therefore is seen as radically opposite to the sacred. In this respect, the profane is the principle which has the capacity to contaminate the sacred, and to this extent the sacred and profane are linked together. In all religions, rules exist which regulate the separation between the two and precautions must always be taken when they come into contact. Durkheim went on to outline six characteristics of the sacred and profane. First, the sacred is always separated from all other objects and therefore constitutes things set apart. Second, a system of rites and social practices arises which

---

282 Ibid., p. 36. The term 'elementary forms' is misleading. Stated simply, the term refers to the fundamental features (composite elements) underlying religions and religious phenomena. The two elementary forms of religion put forward by Durkheim are: (i) a system of beliefs and rites which specifies attitudes taken up toward the world; and (ii) the division of things into the sacred and profane.

283 Ibid., pp. 37–47.

284 Ibid., pp. 37–42.

285 Ibid., p. 37.

sets out how the sacred is to be approached and how members of the group are to conduct themselves in the presence of the sacred object.[286] Third, sacred things are things protected by interdictions which have the force of prohibitions or taboos acting to protect and isolate the sacred. Fourth, sacred things are segregated from profane things and are thought to be superior in dignity. Fifth, the sacred and profane represent a unifying principle which separates the natural from the spiritual world and in this way provides society with a model of opposites such as good and evil, clean and dirty, holy and defiled, and so on.[287] Sixth, passage from the profane to the sacred must be accompanied by rites which are thought to 'transform' one state into the other through rituals of initiation or rebirth.[288]

After putting forward three elementary forms of religious life – beliefs, rites, and the division between the sacred and the profane – Durkheim defined religion by stating that it 'is a unified system of beliefs and practices relative to sacred things, that is to say, things set apart and forbidden – beliefs and practices which unite into one single moral community all those who adhere to them.'[289] We now turn to Durkheim's discussion of totemism which forms the central part of the study.

The Search for the Most Elementary Religion

Having outlined a definition of religion based on the elementary forms, Durkheim turned his attention to searching for what he called the most elementary religion. He began by reviewing some of the early claims regarding which religions are the most rudimentary. In his discussion, he looked at two prevailing views: first, those put forward by Edward Tylor who had claimed that 'animism' was the most elementary religion; and second, a view asserted by Max Müller who had argued that 'naturism' was the most basic of all religions. In order to understand some of the steps Durkheim took in this regard, let us briefly examine the views of Tylor and Müller.

Edward Tylor's major work, *Primitive Culture*, was published in 1871 and was one of the first studies to put forward a theory explaining the origin of religion. The name he gave to this religion was 'primitive animism.'[290] As propounded by Tylor, animism is the belief that human beings occupy two states of existence: a waking state in the everyday world and a sleeping state in a dream world. Tylor went on to suggest that in the sleeping state, the spirit of the individual is freed from the body and can wander uninhibited by physical constraints. According to Tylor, among

---

286 Ibid., p. 41.
287 Ibid., p. 40.
288 Ibid., pp. 39–41.
289 'The division of the world into two domains, the one containing all that is sacred, the other all that is profane, is the distinctive trait of religious thought.' Ibid., p. 47.
290 Ibid., pp. 49–70.

tribal societies this leads to the belief that the dream world is occupied by all the spirits who have ever lived. Tylor reasoned that, when looked at from the perspective of everyday reality, primitive people must believe that the spirit world in fact animates their action. When, for example, individuals possess extraordinary energy, or become sick, or are overtaken by rage, it is because a spirit animates them. Tylor thought that once primitive religion had worked out a view of the forces of good and evil, there was not anything in the natural and social world that could not be explained by these forces. Tylor proposed that the entire religious apparatus of prayer, offerings, sacrifice and worship originates from the idea that actions in the everyday world are animated by souls and spirits. In Tylor's view, animism is the first religion to attribute causes to the 'spirit' world.

Next, Durkheim looked at the views of Max Müller who wrote about religion in a work called *Comparative Mythology*. Müller had asserted that the origin of religion was based on what he called 'sensuous experience.'[291] Using this concept Müller deduced that nature's powers were capable of causing such profound terror that an impact was felt on the unconscious mind of human beings. These forces, he thought, create an overwhelming sensation which surrounds us and dominates us. Müller took the view that religion begins the moment these forces are personified in human-like agents. This act of personification, Müller argued, creates gods who are believed to have the powers which nature has and human beings do not. These forces are so powerful that human beings become dependent upon them, so much so that they found a religion upon them.

Durkheim rejected Tylor's and Müller's arguments on several fronts. First, he stated that in Tylor's view religion appears as a spirit world that is vague and indeterminate rather than as a system of actions and practices found in reality. Tylor's 'spirits' and 'souls' are not subject to observation, have no objective foundation and are, therefore, not amenable to scientific study.[292] Second, as far as Tylor and Müller are concerned human beings create the seed for religion. This, according to Durkheim, is only to adopt an individualistic view in which religion itself is seen to originate either from individual beings or from nature. But this is not possible since neither the individual nor nature are sacred by themselves.[293] Third, Durkheim thought that since neither human beings nor nature are sacred on their own, they must get their sacredness from some other source and this can only be society. Other than individual nature, therefore, there must be a reality from which religion comes and there should be another more elementary form from which religions derive. Human beings, stated Durkheim, have a religious nature not because of the spirit world or the natural world, but because they live in society.

291 Ibid., pp. 71–84.
292 Ibid., pp. 48–55.
293 Ibid., pp. 81–2.

Durkheim went on to reason that there must be a religion more fundamental than animistic and naturistic ones. This religion, he asserted, is totemism since it is more elementary than the others we have examined. There are several reasons supporting this claim. First, there are many societies which practice totemism in North America and in Australia. Second, the beliefs and practices of totemic religions are relatively homogeneous in different societies, and this more readily leads to finding a common principle underlying the practices and beliefs which unify them. Third, the anthropological and ethnographical evidence is more complete on totemism than it is on other religions; in fact, work on totemic religions is the most developed. Among early work, for instance, MacLennan was one of the first to study the religious phenomenon of totemism in ancient societies. After him, Lewis Morgan studied the characteristics of totemism among North American Indian tribes and was among the first to look at religion in terms of a system of beliefs and social practices. Then, in a series of ethnographic studies documenting the characteristics of totem religions, there was the work by the American Bureau of Ethnology.[294] In addition, an important work by Spencer and Gillen which provided observations of totem religions among Australian tribes was among the first to undertake a systematic study of totemism.

For these reasons, Durkheim believed that Australian totemism exemplifies the most elementary religion and that the underlying system of beliefs best exemplifies the nature of religious life. Australian totemism, he pointed out, is the 'most primitive and simple religion that is possible to find,' and Durkheim believed its 'form' is ideal, among all other religions, for sociological investigation.[295]

The Nature of Totemism and Totemic Belief

Having selected totemism as the elementary religion, Durkheim looked more deeply into the nature of totemic beliefs and into the structure of totemism itself. His discussion of totemism began in a simple but fundamental chain of observations.[296] First, he pointed out that all members of the totem group refer to themselves by a tribal name, even though they are not blood relations. This binds them together as if they were blood relations, and identifies them as if they were family members, even though they are not. Second, the totem name they use designates them as a social group. Third, the totem compels them to recognize duties and obligations toward each other which are on the level of blood obligations, including reciprocal aid, vengeance, mourning, and the obligation not to marry among themselves.[297] The totem thus binds them together collectively as if they were a family united by blood. Fourth,

294 Ibid., p. 89.
295 Ibid., p. 95.
296 Ibid., p. 102.
297 Ibid., p. 102.

totem beliefs involve a system of prohibitions and taboos which keep the totem apart from profane things and distinct as a sacred thing. Fifth, totemism is above all a tribal religion so far as it represents the tribe as a whole descending from a mythical being whose beliefs and practices are sufficiently strong to have survived over time. A sixth characteristic of totemism is its tendency to extend outward from the affairs of the group to include a system of ideas representing the universe and human existence, specifically ideas representing causal forces.

The totem may thus be described as an institution which leads to three distinct kinds of religious activity: first is a system of beliefs and rites which unifies and binds the social group together around a sacred object. Second is a system of interdictions that sets out what individual obligations are toward this sacred object. Third, totemism is a system of rites for worshipping the sacred object.

Under these circumstances, a totem may be either an animal, a vegetable, or, in some cases, an inanimate object. The totem, in addition, is the name for an object from which beliefs and rites flow, and in this sense it is also what Durkheim called an 'emblem' which represents the group. This emblem designates the name of the group and stands for the group as its 'badge' or insignia.[298] Durkheim pointed out that the totem emblem is not unlike the coat of arms we see in advanced societies in that it serves the function of assigning to each person who bears it a proof of their identity as a member of the group of which they are a part. In addition, the emblem takes a form, called the 'churinga.' The churinga, according to Durkheim, is the physical embodiment of the totem and is typically a piece of wood or a polished stone on which there is a design representing the totem of the particular group.[299] There are several important characteristics of the totem emblem or churinga which should be pointed out. First, it is implicated in virtually everything individuals do – from its function in religious ceremony, the powers it has over sickness, the ability to bestow courage, and the capability it has to empower members of the clan against their enemies. Second, it is believed to have extraordinary sacredness, so much so that it must be kept at a distance from the profane and the uninitiated cannot approach it. Third, the sacredness of the totem derives from the ability of the totem emblem to represent the group. This capacity of the totem to represent the group extends to its customs, traditions and social practices and to the individuals themselves who are also sacred. Durkheim believed that the religious nature of the totem and the sacred role it plays in group life arise directly from the function it performs in its 'representation' of the group. The totem, according to Durkheim, represents the group in three important respects. First, it represents the collective beliefs and social practices of the group to the individuals who make it up. Second, it

298 Ibid., p. 113.
299 Ibid., p. 119.

represents the collective to itself historically in its legends and myths. Third, it represents the collective to itself in the form of a total social reality.[300]

The Clan, the Totem and the Universe: the Fundamental Organizing Principle

To this point Durkheim has shown that totem religions give rise to a set of beliefs which hold that: (i) the totem is sacred; and (ii) the emblem representing the clan, the name of the clan and its members is also sacred. At the heart of this view lies the central totemic principle that, as the totem makes the group sacred, the group in turn projects its own divinity onto the natural world and the universe; from this arises the tendency to substitute the divisions and classifications of the totem for the classifications and divisions of nature. In this respect, totemism is a complete system of religious ideas relating to the world since it provides a total comprehension of the world and the universe in relation to itself.

While this may seem complex, the principle by which the group projects its own sacredness onto nature is fundamental to understanding Durkheim's thesis. Simply stated, Durkheim contended that as the totem is classified and divided into sacred and profane, the divisions are projected onto nature. From this arises the tendency to divide the natural world into classes, groups, and categories – and thus to classify nature itself. In this view, all the things in the natural world, including the sun, the moon, stars, earth, plants, etc., are understood to belong to different classes and groups.[301]

Durkheim went on to reason that the principle of religious organization is thus the model of group organization, which in turn is the first model for classifying things in the world. From the central idea that a connection exists between religious beliefs and the organization of individuals into groups, Durkheim deduced that all understanding of the natural and social world derives from a religious system of ideas. Religion, according to this view, must have been the first system to explain the natural world by class and category, and this must have extended to the social world. Why else would the Haida of North America classify the things of nature exactly like the divisions within their group, and why would these divisions parallel the system of totemic beliefs? Durkheim stated:

> These facts throw light on the way in which the idea of kind or class was formed in humanity. In fact, these systematic classifications are the first we meet with in history, and we have just seen they are modeled upon the social organization, or rather that they have taken the forms of society as their framework. It is the phratries which have served as classes and the clans as species. It is because men were organized that they have been able to organize things, for in classifying these latter, they limited themselves to giving them places in the groups they formed themselves. The unity of these first logical systems merely reproduces the

300 Ibid., p. 119.
301 Ibid., pp. 142–4.

unity of the society. This confirms the earlier idea that the fundamental forms of thought may be the product of social factors.[302]

Totemism and the Concept of Religious Force

We have seen that the totem is sacred, that rules are set out regarding how it is to be worshipped and approached, and that interdictions arise to separate the totem from the profane. In addition to this we know that the totem occupies a considerable place in the social life of the group and that a religion grows from it. After outlining these considerations, Durkheim turned his attention to two sorts of issue. The first is to find out why the totem has the extraordinary power of being separated and set apart in the social world of totem tribes; and the second is why there emerges a system of rites specifying how the totem is to be worshipped. Both these issues go to the heart of the question of how the totem comes to be represented as a powerful force.

This takes us to the concept of religious force which is key to Durkheim's overall theory of religion. He described this force in the following way:

> When we say that these principles are forces, we do not [use] the word in a metaphorical sense; they act just like veritable forces. In one sense, they are even material forces which mechanically engender physical effects. Does an individual come into contact with them without having taken proper precautions? He receives a shock which might be compared to the effect of an electric discharge. In addition to this physical aspect, they also have a moral character. [The individual] acts in a certain way toward the totemic beings not only because the forces resident in them are physically redoubtable, but because he feels morally obliged to act [as if] he is obeying an imperative, that he is fulfilling a duty.[303]

The term 'religious force' may be defined as something lying outside the individual and whose moral authority is capable of obtaining compliance to religious beliefs by bestowing the totem with extraordinary powers of respect and authority. According to Durkheim, the 'religious force' has the following characteristics: (i) it provides the underlying basis of religious experience to the extent that its powers compel individuals to render pious duties toward it; (ii) it creates moral obligations which cannot be canceled by individual wills, making individuals obey obligations as if they were moral imperatives imposed upon them externally; (iii) it remains continuous over time while individuals are constantly being replaced; (iv) it is protected by a system of interdicts or prohibitions; (v) it is at the foundation of the principle of the sacred; (vi) it is the prototype of the theory of causality in that it serves the function of explaining the origins of the universe; and lastly (vii) it takes the form of society.[304]

---

302 Ibid., pp. 144–5.

303 Ibid., p. 190.

304 Durkheim uses the terms 'interdict' and 'interdiction' to separate out a special class of rules which have the force of religious prohibitions or taboos, ibid., p. 300.

The Nature of Positive and Negative Interdicts

To show how the 'religious force' is manifested, Durkheim examined the social practices called interdicts.[305] Interdicts denote a special class of rules which have the force of prohibitions in relation to religious activity, usually in respect to the rules involved in very sacred acts such as approaching a totem or handling it in some way. In relation to religious activity, interdicts indicate that a moral requirement is placed on individuals and that lack of compliance with the interdict causes serious danger.

Durkheim identified two distinct kinds of interdicts, ones he called 'positive interdicts', others 'negative interdicts.'[306] Both positive and negative interdicts form themselves into two distinct classes of rites which are performed toward the totem: one governing the rites and duties associated with approaching the totem and maintaining it; the other specifying what cannot be done while approaching the totem. Positive interdicts, according to Durkheim, set requirements which bring individuals into contact with the sacred. The purpose of these rites is to secure bonds between the members of the group and to reinforce or reaffirm the social and sacred efficacy of the totem. Positive rites and interdicts concern themselves with how individuals approach the totem, whether in silence, under conditions of fast, whether by day or night, and even specify what ornamentation is required and considered to be appropriate. Positive interdicts, therefore, ensure that individuals approach the totem with the highest possible feeling of 'religious gravity.'[307] In some instances, positive interdicts may involve members of the clan in sacrificial performances. Among one group, for instance, a rock representing ancestors is considered highly sacred and, in order to perform their rituals, all male members of the group must let streams of their blood drain onto the rock until it is entirely covered.[308] In cases of this sort, the interdict requires male members to mix something of their own body with the sacred object, thus making the rite 'more efficacious.'[309] Positive interdicts range from celebration to sacrifice, and from initiation to obligatory performance. Their specific function is to increase the bond between the individual and the totem, and between the group and the totemic beliefs.

In circumstances where negative rites and interdicts apply, the case is completely different. Negative rites may be classified into three major categories: (i) prohibitions pertaining to the natural world; (ii) prohibitions applying to the world of human perception; and (iii) prohibitions related to human contact with the totem. Generally, negative interdicts signify the dangers inherent in human contact with the totem, particularly those

---

305 Durkheim's full discussion of 'interdicts' can be found in ibid., pp. 299–325.
306 Ibid., pp. 299 ff.
307 Ibid., p. 328.
308 Ibid., p. 330.
309 Ibid., p. 330.

involving touch, sight, and verbal expression. Making verbal utterances in the presence of the totem constitutes a contamination just as serious as interdicts prohibiting eye contact. Some restrictive rites and interdicts forbid contact with prohibited foods and organic material, while other categories of interdicts impose sexual taboos on individuals months prior to being in the presence of the totem. The main function of negative interdicts is to maintain separation from classes of things which pose dangers to the totem.

Violations of interdicts result in diminishing the power of the sacred. Conversely, positive rites invariably produce feelings of renewal in which the novice is transformed by undergoing initiation or sacrifice. Clearly, feelings aroused during the performances of rites would not only transform individual perceptions, but would also arouse group sentiments – reinforcing the connection to the totem by reaffirming its power over them. The function of interdictive rites is thus to reinforce the beliefs associated with the totem and the degree of leverage these beliefs exert over the attitudes of individuals. This constitutes a first elementary form so far as their religious practices function to arouse important emotions in individuals that, in increasing their attachment to the totem, increase their connections to society.

So far, we have seen that the totem principle derives its power from the religious forces which underlie it. But from what source of power does the religious force itself stem? The answer to this question was taken up by Durkheim in Book Three where he looked at the system of negative interdicts and their capacity to set prohibitions in relation to the totem. Negative interdicts, first and foremost, concern themselves with maintaining the separation of the totem by ensuring that its objects are kept apart from profane things. Since the system of prohibitions functions to keep sacred things separate by 'forbidding certain ways of acting toward them,' then interdictions which contain religious forces perform these functions.[310] The next question is, from what source does this power come and why does it have the force of an 'electric shock'?

In order to answer this question, Durkheim turned his attention to the connection between society and religion, and the view he put forward is of central importance to the study. He stated that if, in fact, religious beliefs and practices establish a bond between the individual and society by arousing strong emotions in them and by raising common passions and animating their beliefs, then society must actively stand behind religious activity. Moreover, since the powers conferred upon the totem act on individuals as if these powers were physical forces, then the extraordinary force of the totem must be reducible to the powers of society.[311] Since, in addition, the totemic principle and the religious force are linked, they must also be reducible to the powers of society. Both principles, in fact, share a

310 Ibid., pp. 299–300.
311 Ibid., pp. 206–30.

common underlying theme which places their powers outside the object in which they are thought to reside. Religious forces, in this sense, must be nothing less than the sentiments of the group mobilized in a common space, and these sentiments are projected outwards and objectified – that is, they are fixed on some object which thus becomes sacred.[312]

According to Durkheim, the power of these prohibitions can be traced first to the religious force, then to the power of interdicts and then to society itself. Their origin, therefore, is nothing less than the collective force of society. Understood in this light, it is easy to see why 'religious forces spread out and diffuse themselves outside the beings in which they reside. In fact, they are only collective forces hypostasized, that is to say, moral forces which are made up of the ideas and sentiments which are awakened in us by the spectacle of society, and not of sensations coming from the physical world.'[313] The feeling of the religious which the sacred produces in them and whose reality has a special emotion, is nothing but the 'spectacle of society' experienced through the residue of group sentiments, and thus does not stem from the nature of the physical world.[314] In this sense, religious phenomena and the power of religious forces are 'nothing other than collective states objectified, which is to say they are nothing other than society seen under one of its aspects.'[315]

Religion and the Social Origins of the Categories of Thought: Durkheim's Theory of Knowledge

Next, Durkheim turned his attention to devising a theory of knowledge which stems from religious activity. Durkheim began by tracing the causal origin of religion first to the practices of totemism, then to religious forces *per se*, next to the force of religious interdictions and, finally, to the sentiments aroused in collective life and thus to society itself. As the argument progresses, Durkheim moved in the direction of relating religion to the origins of conceptual and explanatory thought.[316] But to what extent is this connection possible? The general tendency of religious beliefs, he argued, is to classify the natural and social world into distinct categories and this is ultimately social insofar as it has its origins in group life. Durkheim reasoned that since the first categories for explaining the universe are religious in origin, then intellectual categories must be products of social activity and, therefore, have their origins in society. But how are we to understand this argument?

The best way to understand Durkheim's views is to look at how others have understood the origin of thought. Until the publication of Durkheim's work, many scholars believed that human beings were distinct

312 Ibid., p. 229.
313 Ibid., p. 322.
314 Ibid., p. 322.
315 Ibid., p. 412.
316 Ibid., pp. 8–14.

in their ability to create scientific knowledge. Many took the view that human beings alone possess rational thought and only they are capable of classifying the physical world into categories amenable to understanding. The idea that human beings alone possess reason and rational thought was put forward by Immanuel Kant, an influential philosopher who looked into the question of how human beings come to understand the external world in a work called *Critique of Pure Reason*.[317] Kant, in fact, believed that human beings were unique because they alone were able to understand the physical world. He stated that in order to do this, they had to have something like a structure in their minds which enabled them to recognize broad categories in the physical world, such as space and time. Kant called these the 'a priori categories of apprehension' and reasoned that they allowed human beings to apprehend the physical world as such. Durkheim, however, disagreed with Kant and argued that our complex system of classification and knowledge stems from the fact that we live in social groups. Durkheim claimed that group categories therefore precede the formation of intellectual categories.

The relationship between society and knowledge is thus premised on two fundamental assumptions. (i) Among the ideas that individuals have, religion must have been the first fundamental system of ideas to explain and classify the external world. (ii) Among the classes of ideas which individuals have held, the first conceptions about the universe are derived from religion. Durkheim stated:

> We have shown what light these facts throw upon the way in which the idea of kind or class was formed in humanity. In fact, these systematic classifications are the first we meet with in history, and we have just seen that they are modeled upon the social organization, or rather they have taken the forms of society as their framework. It is the phratries which have served as classes, and the clans as species. It is because men were organized that they have been able to organize things, for in classifying these latter, they limited themselves to giving them places in the groups they formed themselves. And if these different classes of things are not merely put next to each other, but are arranged according to a unified plan, it is because the social groups with which they commingle themselves are unified and through their union, form an organic whole, the tribe. The unity of these first logical systems merely reproduces the unity of society.[318]

Durkheim maintained that the essential categories of thought are products of society and do not spring from individual minds. This position is controversial since it challenged the philosophical claims in relation to reason and human classification. Durkheim's discussion of knowledge therefore takes two important directions. First, it claims that intellectual categories leading to complex systems of thought, such as science, logic

---

317 I.Kant, *Critique of Pure Reason*, New York: St. Martin's Press, 1965. Kant referred to these structures as a priori categories. Kant's discussion of the relevance of the categories for apprehending the external world is outlined in a succinct treatment in his introduction to the *Critique*, pp. 13–37.

318 Durkheim, *Elementary Forms*, pp. 144–5.

and philosophy, derive their classificatory frameworks not from the minds of human beings but from the fact that human beings tend to live in groups and thereby group their ideas. Second, it takes the view that intellectual categories are originally derivatives of group categories, which is contrary to Kant's contention that internal mental categories are primary in the apprehension of the external world. Durkheim drew on three central examples to illustrate this relationship: the categories of space, time and cause. He reasoned that all these concepts not only appear to be universal across all societies, but also find their origin in categories based on how groups divide themselves into clans, phratries and social classes.

Durkheim's Evidence: Space   In order to provide evidence of the relationship between group life and system of classification, Durkheim looked at the concepts of space, time and cause. Beginning with the concept of space, he pointed out that the first framework for understanding the world and classifying other things is the model of spatial relationships.[319] Understanding the concept of direction, for example, depends upon spatial relationships and upon this depends the understanding of the outside world. Durkheim believed that the concept of space is not a general abstraction but rather has its origins in relation to the social group from which the individual perception of space develops. He stated that we can only understand spatial relations by first conceptualizing a 'center' from which everything else 'is disposed in relation to me,' and this focal point is the original space from which all other spaces radiate.[320] Since the concept of space is itself based on an original 'fixed point' the next step is to discover what point or place represents this in the social organization. Durkheim reasoned that the space in which the group defines its existence becomes the first model of a given spatial point. This, he believed, must be the village or camp which represents the fixed territory of the group. Without this, there can be no further conceptualization of north or south, right or left, up or down, inside or outside. It is impossible to conceptualize the world spatially, therefore, unless there is some common standard in terms of which spatial relations can be judged. Durkheim reasoned that this common standard is the social organization of the camp which provides a model for the mental organization of space, thus creating the original point of spatial direction. This can be illustrated by reference to Australian societies which tend to conceptualize space in the form of a circle and, when asked to draw a circle, they draw the exact physical shape of the camp. Durkheim pointed out that the concept of spatial relations actually mirrors the social geography of the camp. He stated:

> Since all the men of a single civilization represent space in the same way, it is clearly necessary that these methods of representation are social in origin. Their

319 Ibid., pp. 11, 441.
320 Ibid., pp. 440–1.

social form is made manifest when we look at the practices of early societies which conceive of space in the form of an immense circle, but they do so because the camp has a circular form; and this spatial circle is divided up exactly like the tribal circle. Thus, the social organization is the model of the mental organization of the idea. The distinction between right and left which, far from being inherent in the nature of man in general, is very probably the product of representations which are religious and therefore collective.[321]

Though the perception of spatial relations is individual, the concept of space has its origins in group life and becomes the basis for all later systems of classification. Durkheim's social theory of knowledge is premised on the assumption that, since human beings live in groups, the social organization of their groups becomes the model for the mental organization of their ideas. The first categories of understanding are thus social in origin since they are utilized to make judgments about the divisions, groups and classes in the world existing around the individual. This system of division serves as a basis for the system of classification in the external world and the system of classification in thought. To the extent that individuals are grouped, and think of themselves in the form of groups, they also group their ideas and systems for understanding the external world.

Durkheim's Evidence: Time as a Social Category   Next, Durkheim looked at the category of time and temporal understanding. He argued that, far from being a universal or abstract idea, the concept of time finds its origins in the rhythmic nature of social life and in the overall tendency of societies to mark occasions such as feasts, rituals, harvests, and even events of nature according to a schedule stemming from collective social practices rather than individual ones. Just as the concept of space originates from the physical territory occupied by society, the idea of time emerges from the tendency of group life to develop rhythmic activities which punctuate social experience.[322]

The concept of time thus has its origins in group life. While this seems obscure, the point Durkheim was making is straightforward. All groups, he said, organize their social experience on the celebration of rituals and rites which establish periodic cycles by moving from work to ritual. These episodic practices form themselves into yearly rhythms, and the essential constituents of these social rites and practices are evident in the cycle of feasts which return regularly at determined periods.[323] In this view, we are able to understand where the tendency to mark off one period of time from another arises. First, the rhythm which religious life follows expresses itself in the rhythm of social life, and results from it. Second, we see from this that 'society is able to revivify itself and its collective practices only by

---

321 Ibid., pp. 11–12.
322 Ibid., pp. 10–11, 440, 441.
323 Ibid., p. 349.

assembling.'[324] Third, since the exigencies of life do not allow the collective to remain in congregation indefinitely, it scatters to assemble anew when it again feels the need, thus giving rise to a temporal cycle.[325] Fourth, the perception of time thus corresponds to the cycle of assembly between feasts, ceremonies, and collective rites.

In these terms, the concept of time is not itself something that uniquely emerges from the human mind, but rather arises from the rhythmic nature of social life and the tendency of societies to divide experience into temporal bits marked off by ritual. Though every individual is conscious of living in a present which is distinct from the past, Durkheim maintained that the concept of time is not personalized but involves a category shared by all members of society. It is not that we naturally arrange our time in days, weeks, years, months or minutes, but that time in general is arranged by the group, whose tendency is to unitize time in terms of categories such as years, weeks and days.

Durkheim's Evidence: the Religious Origin of the Concept of Cause   Next Durkheim turned his attention to the concept of cause and causal explanation. He stated that the concept of cause as understood by science and philosophy must have had its origins in the first conception of religious forces. To the extent that the religious force is the first expression of the concept of cause, philosophy and science are but rational derivatives of what was primarily a religious category.[326] The concept of cause, asserted Durkheim, begins in religion and then comes to rest in science and philosophy. But in what way is religion related to the concept of cause? First, all religions begin by offering explanations of the universe and by putting forward causal explanations of the apparent power or force of nature occurring in the change of seasons, the regularities of tides, phases of the moon and the orderliness of the universe. Among the ideas that individuals have, therefore, religion must have been the first classificatory scheme – the first system for classifying the natural world and the universe. Second, it follows that among the classes of ideas which individuals have held, the first conceptions about the origin of the universe are also derived from religion. Religious forces are the original expression of the concept of force in science since they represent the first historical expression of causality.[327]

If the idea of cause is derived from society, what specifically is its origin? Durkheim stated that it could not have come from individuals alone, since individuals are only a part in relation to a whole and, because of their perceptual limitations, they can never really surpass their individuality. Durkheim maintained that society itself must have been of primary

---

324 Ibid., p. 349.
325 Ibid., p. 349.
326 Ibid., pp. 367–8.
327 Ibid., p. 368.

importance, since it envelops all other concepts and categories. Hence, society must have been the first category of causation. Durkheim pointed out:

> We can show once more how the sociological theory of the idea of causality, and of the categories in general, set aside the classical doctrines on the question. Together with apriorism, it maintains the prejudicial and necessary character of the causal relation. There can be no doubt that, by himself, the individual observes the regular succession of phenomena and thus acquires a certain feeling of regularity. But this feeling is not the category of causality. The former is individual and subjective. The second is the work of the group, and is given to us ready made. It is a framework in which our empirical ascertainments arrange themselves and which enable us to think of them, that is to say, see them from a point of view which makes it possible for us to understand one another in regard to them. It is the error of empiricism to regard the causal bond as merely an intellectual construction of speculative thought. . . .
>
> Religious forces are the original expression of the concept of force in science since they represent the first historical expression of causality. First it has its expression through religion, then philosophy, coming to rest in the scientific conception of the causes of nature.[328]

Not only has society founded these categories, according to Durkheim, but their contents represent different aspects of society's social being. In the first case, it is the rhythm of social life which is at the basis of the category of time; in another, it is the territory occupied by the group which furnishes the material basis for the category of space; and, in yet another, it is the collective force which is the prototype of the concept of causality.[329] In each case the categories are used to do the same things, namely to classify objects into knowable entities so that they may be understood and utilized. This act of classification ought not to be regarded as a purely rational category, but should instead be examined as a social phenomenon. In Durkheim's view, scientific activity is but a secondary extension of the social act of classification, and as such it is not exempt from socially accepted norms of organization.

Categories of Religious Rites and their Social Functions

Next, Durkheim turned his attention to looking at the effect which religious rites have on the individual and society. Earlier we pointed out that all religions make the distinction between a system of beliefs and a system of rites. In addition, we stated that beliefs were distinct from rites so far as they specify ideas and attitudes which are held in regard to religious objects. Rites, on the other hand, involve two specific characteristics: first, they encompass categories of actions taken toward objects; and second, they involve the important capacity of laying down interdictions, that is, limitations or restrictions on what is permissible with regard to the sacred. Since Durkheim's theory of religion cannot be

328 Ibid., p. 368.
329 Ibid., pp. 440, 368, 11.

completely understood without looking once again at the role played by interdictions, it is worthwhile to look briefly into this question before discussing the system of rites.

Durkheim stated that religions are primarily concerned with three kinds of activities: (i) maintaining separation between sacred and profane things; (ii) laying down a system of beliefs for the faithful; and (iii) setting up a system of rules which forbids certain ways of acting. The concept of interdiction, then, is used by Durkheim to refer to any system of rules which carries the weight of official prohibition. These may take the form of rules which restrain individuals from acting in certain ways, or they may involve rules relating to when individuals should be isolated, or rules which withdraw privileges. There is no religion where interdictions do not exist and where they do not perform important functions.[330]

Religious interdicts are therefore the most forceful class of rules with respect to religious rites. Two broad systems of interdicts are important: (i) those which proscribe things or objects which are incompatible; and (ii) those which require separation between the sacred and the profane. Durkheim stated that 'the interdictions against eating sacred animals or vegetables are especially strict for those serving as totems. Such acts appear so sacrilegious that the prohibitions cover even adults.'[331]

Having looked briefly at the role of interdictions, we turn our attention to the system of rites. Durkheim identified four distinct categories of religious rites: (i) sacrificial rites which are related to initiation and sacrifice; (ii) imitative rites, permitting imitation of the totem animal for purposes of reproduction; (iii) commemorative rites, which relate to how the group represents itself; and (iv) piacular rites, which are rites performed to represent loss or suffering.

Sacrificial Rites   The first group of rites are related to sacrificial practices. These are a class of rites which specify and regulate the obligations individuals have toward objects of the group which either serve the clan as a totem or are designated as fundamental to life. These include objects related to survival, such as essential foods and the powers related to regeneration. Sacrificial rites involve ceremonies in which the productive powers of the natural world are celebrated. The Arunta of Australia, for instance, perform rites called Intichiuma. These take place during a particular time of the year when vegetation and plant growth is extremely plentiful and luxurious. The power of regeneration which is assigned to the plant is the object of the rite which proceeds as follows. On a specified day, the male members of the group gather and 'they advance in profound silence without arms or ornaments. Their attitude and their pace is marked with a religious gravity.'[332] The young men are 'obligated to mix something

330 Ibid., p. 300 ff.
331 Ibid., p. 303.
332 Ibid., pp. 328, 330, 331.

of their bodies with the totem in order to make the rite more efficacious.'[333] This can be done because the members are related to the totem in a way that allows them to exchange the principle of life embedded in it. The same principle of life they see in the totem is the principle of life in them, and so it is natural that they use their blood to assure the reproduction of the life principle of the totem. They believe that in revivifying the totem they ultimately reanimate the 'embryos of a new generation' and thus help to perpetuate the group. As Durkheim pointed out, by the 'very fact of gathering' they 'create a kind of concentrated excitement' in which they feel a form of 'ecstasy they would never feel alone as individuals.'[334] In addition, all the separate actions of the ceremony are governed by a system of interdicts which highlights the religious intensity of the ceremonies. In the case of the Intichiuma, the primary interdict applies to a period of time when it is forbidden to eat the animal or plant signifying the totem. They believe that any violation of the interdict would necessarily 'neutralize' the efficacy of the rite. Only after these rites are completed are the interdicts lifted. Durkheim maintained that the entire system of rites 'represents in its most elementary form all the essential principles of the developed religious institutions which have become the foundational basis in the practice of sacrifice and renewal.'[335]

On the basis of this reasoning, Durkheim drew a controversial conclusion. He reasoned that the origins of all sacrificial institutions must have involved a system of rites founded upon renewing the bonds between the members of the collectivity rather than the bonds between the group and their gods. The ceremony of regeneration practiced in the Intichiuma reaffirms this assertion since the ritual not only provides the totem with the life it needs to renew itself, but also furnishes to the individuals the force they need to exist and feel well-being.

> By the very fact of uniting, they are mutually comforted; they find a remedy because they seek it together. The common faith becomes re-animated quite naturally in the heart of this reconstituted group; it is born again because it again finds those very conditions in which it was born in the first place. After it has been restored, it easily triumphs over all the private doubts which have arisen in individual minds. The image of the sacred things regains power enough to resist the internal and external causes which tended to weaken it. In spite of their apparent failure, the individuals can no longer believe that the gods will die, because they feel them in them.[336]

During the celebration of the rites of sacrifice, the system of interdicts accompanying the ritual performs several key social functions. These are evident in the interruptions which are set up between everyday life and religious activity by the high degree of social intensity which is required during the period of celebration. The system of rites related to sacrifice

333 Ibid., pp. 330–4.
334 Ibid., p. 331.
335 Ibid., pp. 331–3.
336 Ibid., p. 346.

performs two important roles in this respect: (i) they sanctify the individuals who take part in them; and (ii) they re-enact and revivify the collective practices and social sentiments of the group.

Imitative Rites and the Principle of Causality   The second category of rites discussed by Durkheim is imitative rites. While the primary function of these rites is to consolidate rituals, they differ from sacrificial rites to the extent that their purpose is to 'imitate' the various movements and habits of animals whose reproductive powers are desired.[337] The actions of these rites entail ceremonies in which individuals decorate themselves in a ritual manner by imitating the figurative forms and actions of animals or insects. The Arunta, for example, perform rituals in which individuals represent insects that play a role in the clan's mythology. As soon as these decor- ations are put on, the actors begin to represent the movement of the insects. They lie down on the ground, bury their face in the earth, and chant in a manner which reproduces the stages of development through which the insect passes. A group who performs one action will be followed by others whose actions reproduce other gestures and likenesses of the insect. Some participants in the rites decorate themselves with designs representing the bush or shrub in which the insect feeds and others may reproduce the 'track' or mark which the insect leaves as it moves from one place to another.

Durkheim believed that imitative rites form a category of their own and that the principle which motivates them is based on two distinct criteria. First, anything touching the object is within the sphere of its influence and, thus, anything affecting the parts affects the whole.[338] In this case, the direction of the influence is exercised over individuals in proximity to others. For example, influences propagate to kin and neighbors, then to relatives, etc. Under these circumstances, it is believed that qualities are transmitted by contagion. The second principle underlying imitative rites is the one which dictates that imitative actions adopt the being of the object imitated. Thus, in rites of imitation, the members of the tribe assume that the condition and qualities of the object being imitated are transferred to the members of the group and, along with this, something new is created. By imitating the animal's being they create the belief that the animal will be reproduced.[339]

This can only be possible, Durkheim reasoned, if their beliefs about reproduction extend into a theory of causality which itself is based on the model of sacred forces.[340] It is this that has direct implication for a theory of knowledge. Since contagion is a view about how properties are trans- mitted from one object to another, Durkheim believed that it must be the

337 Ibid., p. 351.
338 Ibid., p. 356.
339 Ibid., p. 357.
340 Ibid., pp. 361–2.

elementary principle by which we understand how one property inherent in a thing is extended to another. This, he asserted, must be the primitive statement of the law of causality. Since the principle of causation implies mechanisms by which properties are transferred from one thing to another, it contains a primitive theory of regeneration and this, in and of itself, is religious. Thus causal relations must have implied efficacy as a precondition of an effect, especially if they involve the reproductive powers.

The event preceding the effect is called a 'cause' only because the latter event – the effect – affirms the necessary connection between the two movements. Ultimately, it is the mind which assumes the connection by making a judgment a priori.[341] As Durkheim stated: 'Society imposes it, along with its practices, which are derived from it and in this the ritual precept is doubled by a logical precept which is only an intellectual aspect of the former.'[342]

Representative Rites A third category of rites identified by Durkheim is representative rites. These are a type of rite which is related to how society represents itself to the group. To demonstrate the efficacy of representative rites, Durkheim described the ceremony of the Warramunga, a native group who believe that they descend from a single ancestor who propagated their existence over the earth by placing living germs from the body of the ancestor in the physical region of the tribe. After several incarnations, the ancestor comes to earth and settles down as a member of the tribe. Durkheim pointed out that in mythological tales of this type, there is no obligation placed on the members of the tribe and no rituals of imitation leading to reproduction. Instead, these rites 'consist solely in recollecting the past and making it present by means of representation.'[343] Because these rites are distinct from the others, they belong to a category of their own. Their function is to represent the group by putting into practice 'the mythical history of the ancestors from the moment they emerge and they commemorate their actions and works faithfully in a ceremony.'[344] Durkheim observed that since the myth of the Warramunga states that the totem was embedded in each of the locations where the ancestor traveled, the rite represents these actions in the exact same order and represents the events by means of a design which 'may appear on the body of the actors.'[345] These dramas are, in effect, rites enacted because of their efficacy. Since, in this case, everything is a representation of the original myths and legends of the group, the rite functions to 'render the mythical past of the clan present to mind.'[346] The rites thus serve to

341 Ibid., p. 366.
342 Ibid., p. 368.
343 Ibid., p. 370.
344 Ibid., p. 372.
345 Ibid., p. 372.
346 Ibid., p. 375.

sustain the vitality of the beliefs and to keep them from being forgotten. In acting in this way, 'they renew the sentiments which society has of itself and its unity. At the same time, the group is strengthened in its social nature.'[347] These ceremonies have a commemorative effect which serves to activate the dominant beliefs and sentiments of the collective. Because the ceremonies draw on a means of representation which is unique, Durkheim maintained that they should be considered as a class of rites distinct from others, and that their exclusive function is to reaffirm ideas and sentiments by making past events present once again. On these terms, the objects of the rites are to 'act on the mind' by penetrating the consciousness of the members and to represent the past by making its meaning continuous with the present.[348]

In contrast to the sacrificial and imitative systems of rites, the exclusive function of representative rites is that of creating an environment in which individuals 'share in the feeling of comfort which the worshipper draws from the rites performed; for recreation is but one of the forms of moral remaking which is the principle object of positive rites.'[349] Durkheim reasoned that all festivals and feasts must have originated from the practice of representative rites. Even the secular enactment of these festivals takes on the religious elements of ceremony which affect individuals by increasing their awareness of membership in the group, and this serves to mobilize their collective movement and create commitment. This in turn creates excitement and with it comes a kind of religious intensity.

Piacular Rites   The fourth category of rites identified by Durkheim is called piacular rites. This class of rites is reserved for assigning ritual and religious importance to everything that involves misfortune, loss and death. Whereas the other systems of rites all celebrate positive events in group life, piacular rites affirm the religious significance and seriousness of misfortune and distress. The term 'piacular' derives originally from the Latin referring to events which call for relief from suffering or misfortune through atonement and expiation. Ceremonies where the dead are mourned or where a bad harvest threatens the survival of the group occasion rituals involving piacular rites. These often involve several interdicts related to fasting, isolation, weeping and, in some cases, impose obligations to slash or tear clothing and flesh. In most cases, these ceremonies mark the beginning of periods of rites which may last as long as several months. The rites enacted during this period have the distinct function of renewing the group to its prior state of unity preceding the misfortune and may involve all sorts of collective activity such as weeping, lamenting, kissing and wailing.

347 Ibid., p. 375.
348 Ibid., p. 377.
349 Ibid., p. 377.

Piacular rites, according to Durkheim, have a distinct pattern which repeats itself in all societies. 'Everywhere we find this same silence interrupted by groans; the same obligation of cutting the hair and beard or of covering one's head with clay; and finally there is the same frenzy for beating oneself, lacerating oneself and burning oneself.'[350] In these circumstances, rites may be enacted to fight off drought or periods of excessive rainfall. This system of rites shows that 'when a society is going through circumstances which sadden, perplex or irritate it, it exercises a pressure over its members, by imposing upon them the duty of weeping, groaning, and inflicting wounds upon themselves.'[351]

The Social Nature of Ceremony and the Representation of the Group

Durkheim believed that periodic cycles of assembly marked by social ritual put into action the mythical history of the group. Only during these rituals does the group act under conditions of collective unity, and this rivets them to a common social purpose and re-enacts their core beliefs. Their myths function to state their reasons for being and for existence, and they repeat these together in one place. 'The movements which they enact, the whirling, twisting, chanting rhythmically and violently they do because their ancestors did the same thing. These actions are committed to their individual memory which is but an expression of their collective memory which is acted out by ritual in the spot where their ancestors first envisaged the sacred place and the story of the tribe.'[352]

350 Ibid., p. 392.
351 Ibid., p. 412.
352 Ibid., pp. 381–2.

4

Max Weber

The Historical Context of Max Weber's Work

Max Weber was born on April 21, 1864 in Erfurt, a small city located in the south eastern part of Germany. His father was a well known lawyer and politician who played a minor role in his upbringing. Weber's mother, a far more dominant figure in his life, encouraged and supported him throughout his career. At school Weber was an outstanding student and after finishing his secondary education he went to Berlin where he obtained a university degree in law and eventually a doctorate in political economy. After deciding to devote himself to scholarly interests, he received his first academic position in 1893 when he was 29 years old. In 1896, he was appointed to a professorship in economics at the University of Freiburg, and then to a more important position at the University of Heidelberg, where he taught political economy and economics. Only 32 years old at the time, he was considered very young to obtain a professorship at a major German university. However, a severe personal crisis the following year forced Weber to suspend his teaching activities and eventually resign his position at Heidelberg.[1] Between 1897 and 1903, Weber stopped all intellectual work and traveled throughout Europe while he waited for his nervous disorder to dissipate. In 1903, at the age of 39, Weber returned to academic work, but only slowly, starting research on two large essays – one concerned with the relationship between capitalism and religion, the other a methodological essay.

While Weber did not resume teaching duties for some time, he began to return to regular intellectual work in 1904. In 1905, he published the second part of one of his best known works, *The Protestant Ethic and the Spirit of Capitalism*, and in 1909 he accepted the editorship of a sociological publication. By this time, a large circle of friends, including Georg Simmel, Robert Michels and others, met regularly at the Weber household to discuss the issues of the day.[2] By 1909, Weber began writing *Economy and Society*, his most ambitious theoretical and historical work. From 1916–1917, he carried out research on the history of religions which was one of the most abiding themes in his writings. His last academic work was a series of lectures that he gave at the University of Freiburg in 1919–20, entitled *General Economic History*, which was Weber's most sustained

---

1 Marianne Weber, *Max Weber: A Biography*, New York: John Wiley & Sons, 1975.
2 Ibid., p. 65.

treatment of the history of capitalist development. In addition to his academic career, Weber participated in German political life and often gave public addresses on issues such as politics and science which were well received and eventually became famous in their own right.[3] In these talks Weber tried to reconcile what he thought were conflicting value problems related to the role of the expert, such as the politician and scientist. Weber died in June 1920.

Weber's writings as a whole are best known for their historical grasp of modern Western societies and their economic, political, legal and religious development. The scope of Weber's work is broad and wide-ranging, and his contribution to theoretical questions such as social class, the nature of political legitimacy, the development of modern law and the study of world religions, is extensive. In addition, his work has a distinct modernist emphasis, focusing on such issues as the rise of modern society, the formation of bureaucracy, the development of the modern political state, and comparative world economies.[4]

An important aspect of Weber's overall work is his approach to social theory. By and large, Weber was a modernist in his approach. He brought together various traditions of social thought and formed a unique theoretical perspective based on history, economics, philosophy, law, and comparative historical analysis. Weber's intellectual influences derived from two broad schools of social thought. First was the influence of the German historical school of Carl Menger, Gustav Schmoller, Karl Knies and Heinrich Rickert.[5] As a result of his links to historical economics, Weber became involved in a methodological controversy which forced him to take a position critical to historical economics and the methods of the natural sciences. This brought him into contact with Heinrich Rickert, whose participation in the debate led to a central distinction between the subject matter of the social and natural sciences, as we shall see later.[6] Weber's involvement in the controversy shaped his work for the rest of his career, and the issues he pursued in the debate eventually led to the development of a theory of social action.[7] A second influence on Weber's theoretical perspective was the Marxist school of economics. At the time Weber was working, Marx's writings were pervasive and there were many schools of thought which formed a reaction to Marx's economic thinking.

3 Weber's work on contemporary social issues can be found in his 'Politics as a Vocation' and 'Science as a Vocation,' in H.H. Gerth and C. Wright Mills (eds), *From Max Weber: Essays in Sociology*, New York: Oxford University Press, 1967.

4 For a current treatment of Weber's work, see Keith Tribe (ed.) *Reading Weber*, London: Routledge, 1989.

5 Thomas Burger, *Max Weber's Theory of Concept Formation: History, Laws and Ideal Types*, Durham: Duke University Press, 1976; and Susan Hekman, *Weber, the Ideal Type, and Contemporary Social Theory*, Notre Dame, Indiana: University of Notre Dame Press, 1983.

6 For an overall historical view of Weber and Weber's work see, Reinhard Bendix, *Max Weber: An Intellectual Portrait*, New York: Doubleday, 1960.

7 Stuart Hughes, *Consciousness and Society: The Reorientation of European Social Thought 1890–1930*, New York: Vintage Books, 1958.

Weber opposed Marx's thinking on several fronts and this led him to formulate a completely different view of the role played by history and economy in social development.

Weber's Theoretical Perspective and Fundamental Themes in his Work

Weber's most important works were written between 1903 and 1920, and include such writings as *The Protestant Ethic and the Spirit of Capitalism*, *The Critique of Stammler*, *The Sociology of Religion* and *Economy and Society*. By and large, most of his writings were produced between periods of poor health, and thus his work suffered from frequent interruptions. His health affected the way Weber approached his master work, *Economy and Society*, and as a result a great deal of it was written in sketches which Weber intended to elaborate at some later date, but never did. Only a few of his writings are full length investigations, *The Protestant Ethic* being the centerpiece of his major investigative works. Some of these shortcomings meant that Weber's writings have generally not been seen as a unified body organized as a complete thematic whole. Consequently, some commentators have taken the view that Weber's contribution can only be considered as a fragmented collection lacking in thematic organization, while others have stated that Weber's work is too obscure or incomplete to be dealt with in a systematic manner.[8]

Despite these limitations, there are themes in his work which lead to a central body of social theory.[9] Weber's theoretical contribution can be captured by looking at a number of themes which form the focal point of his sociological work. Generally these themes occur along lines of repeated issues in his writings which can be characterized as follows. First is his interest in civilization processes and the focus on how Western society arose when and where it did. Second is his focus on the key role played by rationalization in the development of Western society. Weber was alone in believing that Western society reflected the process of rationalization in its systems of law, science, politics, commerce and religion. Third is his concern with comparative studies of capitalism.

8 For a discussion of the question of the 'thematic organization' in Weber's work, see Stephen Kalberg, 'The Search for Thematic Orientations in a Fragmented Oeuvre: The Discussion of Max Weber in Recent German Sociological Literature,' *Sociololgy*, 13, 1979, 127–39. Also, Benjamin Nelson's, 'Max Weber's Author's Introduction: A Master Clue to his Main Aims,' *Sociological Inquiry*, 44, 1974, 269–77; and Reinhard Bendix, 'Max Weber's Sociology Today,' *International Social Science Journal*, 17, 1965, 9–22. These authors state that the thematic organization of Weber's work provides an overall unity.

9 For a different perspective on the thematic continuity of Weber's writings, see Gerth and Mills (eds), *From Max Weber*, p. 24.

Debate with Marx

As has been pointed out, Weber was influenced by Marx, especially in his economic writings. Whether Weber applied Marx's historical methods or whether he exclusively criticized Marx is still very much in question, but it is clear that Weber fundamentally disagreed with Marx on a number of key theoretic issues.[10] For all practical purposes, these disagreements converge on at least two distinct fronts: first, on the nature and purpose of social theory; and second, on the understanding of history and social development.

To begin with, Weber rejected Marx's assertion that the central task of social theory was to change society. Marx believed that all philosophy and social theory had only observed rather than changed society and history. As a result, he took the view that theoretical work could only be verified by its ability to promote change and eliminate the inequalities created by the class system. Marx, therefore, believed that theory must be linked to social and political action. Weber, in contrast, disagreed with this view in several ways. First, he thought that the ultimate task of social theory was to search for valid historical truths and to gather historical facts about society. He saw social theory as a search for historical patterns and relationships, and believed that knowledge of society could only be discovered by a comparison of different historical periods. Second, Weber disagreed with the way Marx had used theoretical concepts. He believed that Marx used concepts as critical instruments whose purpose was to point up the inequalities in society. This placed Marx in the position of criticizing society in addition to expounding the underlying origins of social inequality. Weber, however, was much less direct in his criticism of society and believed that concepts in the social sciences should be neutral and not based on value judgments. In this respect, Weber felt that Marx's use of concepts such as 'inequality' and 'exploitation' was value loaded and inconsistent with the search for historical truth.

View of History and Social Causation

In addition to differing on views about the nature of social theory, Weber and Marx differed on their understanding of history and historical causes.[11] To begin with, Weber rejected the idea that all social life could be explained by recourse to economic laws. While he agreed with Marx that the economic sphere was a central component of social life, he thought that economic considerations alone could not explain the development of

10 For specific comments by Weber about Marx's historical methods, see *The Protestant Ethic and the Spirit of Capitalism*, New York: Scribner's Press, [1904–5], 1958, pp. 55–6, 61. In addition, Weber frequently refers to Marx in *Economy and Society*, Volumes 1 & 2, G. Roth and C. Wittich (eds), Berkeley: University of California Press, 1978, as 'that talented author,' p. 926.

11 For a useful discussion of Weber's concept of cause, see Susan Hekman, 'Weber's Concept of Causality and the Modern Critique,' *Sociological Inquiry*, 49, 1979, 67–76.

modern societies and that other non-economic factors had to be taken into account. Marx, as we know, believed that history could be understood in terms of underlying laws of economic development, and he thought these laws shaped the material conditions of society. Some take the view that Marx advocated a kind of economic determinism in his approach to history and social causation. Economic determinism refers to the doctrine which holds that historical circumstances are determined by a sequence of economic events connected to the act of production. It includes the belief that history can be understood in terms of laws of economic development, and that the economic foundations of society act as historical determinants which place the economy at the center of the development of society. Weber, in contrast, wanted to show that social phenomena could, in fact, be studied outside the realm of economic forces and he took the view that there were other determinants of social life derived from the political, religious and legal spheres of society. Weber believed that these social spheres were fundamental to an understanding of historical and social development.

The assumption by Weber of the interconnected nature of 'social spheres' is one of the most important theoretical insights in his work. There are, according to Weber, four major social spheres which make up society: the political, legal, economic, and religious. Weber believed that no one sphere was dominant in society, since they tend to overlap in relation to each other. He maintained that the various social spheres acted in different ways to bring about social change and historical development, and therefore acted as causal factors on the rest of society. Marx, in contrast, believed that all aspects of society – including politics, law and religion – were expressions of underlying economic forces and only these were analytically important. Weber, on the other hand, did not see economic forces as the sole determinants of history and society, and wanted to show that other causal factors were important in social development. This is especially clear in Weber's study of capitalism in which he expressed the view that capitalism was shaped by the economic and religious spheres of society.

On a second front, Weber disagreed with Marx's claim that all social functions could, in the last instance, be reduced to economic laws and thus he fundamentally criticized Marx's materialist view of history.[12] In this regard, Marx had claimed that historical process goes on in accordance with laws of development and that the drama of history is played out by economic laws which lead to the division of society into classes. Marx thus reduced social life to economy, stating that political, legal and religious institutions exist on top of the underlying economic base. Weber contrastingly thought that many of the important changes taking place in society occurred in spheres other than the economic realm of society.[13]

---

12 For Weber's criticism of Marx's materialist theory, see Weber, *The Protestant Ethic,* pp. 55–61.

13 Kalberg, 'The Search for Thematic Orientations in a Fragmented Oeuvre,' pp. 127–39.

The Theme of Rationalization in Weber's Work

One of the most important themes in Weber's work is the concept of rationalization. The term occurs repeatedly in his writings, and many of his theoretical investigations are devoted to understanding the process of rationalization by looking at why modern societies took the form that they did. This stress by Weber on the process of rationalization placed him in opposition to Marx. While Marx had claimed that material factors were dominant in history, Weber felt that a far more general principle was key to understanding the pattern of historical development. He referred to this as the process of rationalization.[14] For Weber, all the spheres of society – economic, legal, political and religious – were subject to the process of rationalization and it was this, in his view, that led to the rise of modern Western society. Since no complete understanding of Weber's work is possible without focusing on this concept, let us look more closely.

Weber used the term rationalization in several contexts. The earliest and perhaps most systematic treatment is found in *The Protestant Ethic*.[15] Later, the term appeared in a variety of contexts, including his studies of the world religions, *Economy and Society* and in his study of law.[16] The most extensive treatment of the term is found in 'The Social Psychology of the World Religions' in which he stated:

> We have to remind ourselves in advance that 'rationalism' may mean very different things. It means one thing if we think of the kind of rationalization that the systematic thinker performs on the image of the world: increasing theoretical mastery of reality by means of increasingly precise and abstract concepts. Rationalization means another thing if we think of the methodological attainment of a definitely given and practical end by means of an increasingly precise calculation of adequate means. These types of rationalism are very different, in spite of the fact that ultimately they belong inseparably together. Similar types may be distinguished even within the intellectual comprehension of reality; for instance, the differences between English physics and Continental physics has been traced back to such a type difference within the comprehension of reality. The rationalization of life conduct with which we have to deal here can assume usually varied forms. The supreme ideal of the Renaissance was 'rational' in the sense of a belief in a valid canon, and the view of life of the Renaissance was rational in the sense of rejecting traditionalistic bonds and of having faith in the power of human reason. Rational may also mean a 'systematic arrangement.' In general all kinds of practical ethics that are systematically and unambiguously oriented to fixed goals of salvation are 'rational,' partly in the same sense as

14 See Weber's discussion in Gerth and Mills (eds), *From Max Weber: Essays in Sociology*, pp. 293–4.

15 Weber, *The Protestant Ethic*, pp. 13–31.

16 The most complete discussion of Weber's concept of rationalizaton can be found in Donald N. Levine, 'Rationality and Freedom: Weber and Beyond,' *Sociological Inquiry*, 51, 1981, 5–25; and Stephen Kalberg, 'Max Weber's Types of Rationality: Cornerstones for the Analysis of Rationalization Processes in his History,' *American Journal of Sociology*, 85, 1980, 1145–79.

formal method is rational, and partly in the sense that they distinguish between 'valid' norms and what is empirically given.[17]

Broadly speaking, the term rationalization refers to several fundamental principles which link it to central ideas in Weber's overall approach to historical development.[18] These include themes such as: (i) the principle of development inherent in the process of civilization and Western society; (ii) the stress on the rational containment of everyday life; (iii) the widespread use of calculation as a strategy of social action; (iv) the freeing of social action from all magical thought; (v) the emphasis on a practical orientation to empirical reality; and (vi) the widespread use of technical and procedural reasoning as a way of controlling practical outcomes and mastering everyday life.[19]

Rationalization Defined Weber essentially used the term rationalization to describe the process by which nature, society and individual action are increasingly mastered by an orientation to planning, technical procedure and rational action. He believed that, more than other societies, modern Western societies reflect the tendency of rationalization in their system of law, politics, science and commercial life. Weber thought that all the spheres of society, including the economic, political and legal spheres underwent the process of rationalization, and it was this, he believed, which led to the rise of modern societies. In the economic sphere, for instance, rationalization involved the organization of commercial practices by means of technical rules calculated to produce profits by the use of rational accounting methods. In the sphere of the state, rationalization hastened the decline of monarchies by creating forms of leadership and governance based on principles of legal legitimacy and the universal application of law. In the sphere of law, rationalization altered the principle of legal judgments by creating a system of decision making based on case precedent, universal legal principles, and deductive reasoning.

Weber's concept of rationalization, therefore, refers to two broad trends in historical development. First is the tendency of social and historical processes to become more and more reliant on calculation and technical knowledge in order to obtain control over the natural and social world. Second is the proclivity of human action to free itself from its dependence upon magical thinking as a means of understanding the world, relying instead on what is immediately given in empirical reality. Rationalization depends on two types of activities: (i) strategies of social action; and

17 'The Social Pyschology of the World Religions,' in Gerth and Mills (eds), *From Max Weber*, pp. 293–4.

18 Friedrich H. Tenbruck, 'The Problem of Thematic Unity in the Works of Max Weber,' *The British Journal of Sociology*, 31, 1980, 316–51. For Weber's own discussion of rationalization, see his discussion in the introduction to *The Protestant Ethic*, pp. 13–31; and in Gerth and Mills (eds), *From Max Weber*, pp. 293–5.

19 Weber, *The Protestant Ethic*, pp. 13–20.

(ii) adjustments of the means and ends of action in the attainment of goals.[20]

To illustrate how Weber used the concept, let us turn to an example he drew on in illustrating economic rationalization. He stated that in economic activity we can make the distinction between two related forms of acquisition: forceful and capitalist. In forceful acquisition wealth is obtained by means of military force either inside or outside the law. Acquisition by this means is neither efficient nor 'oriented to obtaining profits from exchange.'[21] In acquisition by capitalistic means, however, profit is pursued rationally by utilizing peaceful means of exchange rather than forceful ones. As a consequence 'action is adjusted to calculations in terms of capital.'[22] This rational pursuit of profit leads to a more general concern with the efficacy of commercial activity. This eventually leads to new procedures such as the concern for striking a 'balance,' in comparison with the earlier technique of calculation by means of estimates.

Weber pointed out that the procedure of striking a balance is born from the earlier practice of obtaining an estimate, since both share the same category of action. The difference between the two is that the latter is rationalized on the basis of calculative activity. 'The important fact is the rational calculation of capital in terms of money is made by modern book-keeping methods.'[23] What distinguishes these activities from the previous practice of obtaining estimates is that, in rational capitalism, 'everything is done in terms of balances. At the beginning of the enterprise an initial balance is taken, before every individual decision a calculation is made to ascertain its profitableness, and at the end a final balance to ascertain how much profit has been made. To the extent that the transactions are rational, calculation underlies every single action' and this contrasts with the pure guesswork of traditional acquisition 'where circumstances do not demand strict accuracy.'[24]

Calculation Most often found in Weber's discussion of *Economy and Society*, the term calculation plays a prominent role in the theme of rationalization. Weber used the term to convey the point at which economic values penetrate the sphere of social life generally.[25] He believed that the introduction of money in the sphere of commerce brought about a form of calculation in human activities which was far more precise than any traditional method of social action and measurement. Weber used the term, explicitly, to describe the way money rationality, with its stress on counting and quantitative reasoning, is the prime 'propagator' of calculation as a

20 Both strategies of social action and adjustment of means and ends reappear throughout Weber's writings. See Weber, *Economy and Society*, pp. 3–30.

21 Weber, *The Protestant Ethic*, pp. 18–19.

22 Ibid., pp. 18–19.

23 Ibid., pp. 18–19.

24 Ibid., pp. 18–19.

25 Weber, *Economy and Society*, pp. 81–107.

framework for ordering the world.[26] He believed that a counting rationality eliminates all but quantitative considerations and as a consequence extends money rationality into the scope of thought and human action.

In addition, Weber used the concept to describe the general process by which the system of money calculation penetrates other spheres of human action and social life. This comes about only at a certain stage in historical development, particularly when monetary calculation begins to dominate over other forms of social action. At this stage, the process of assigning money values to economic activities increases control over practical outcomes in the material world and becomes a general orientation to reality. Because of the immense control it confers to everyday life, calculative reasoning extended its scope to other realms in society. According to Weber, the practice of calculation begins with economic and monetary mechanisms and becomes fully established only when goods and services come to be manipulated by a standard of evaluation and accounting which is strictly outside the immediate sphere of function or utility. Only when goods are 'systematically compared' with a view to opportunities related to evaluation based on the possibility of gain and return does calculation develop. Weber believed calculation is evident at two levels of social action. First at the level of everyday activity, in which quantitative reasoning and calculation control practical outcomes in the material world; and second, at the level of thought, in which individuals weigh up alternatives prior to action by evaluating means and ends in order to increase the chance of success.[27]

The Distinction between Rationality and Rationalization   Another theme in Weber's work is the concept of rationality, which is distinct from the process of rationalization. Weber referred to the term 'rationality' repeatedly throughout his writings on economy, law, religion and social action. For example, he referred to 'economic rationality,' 'instrumental rationality,' 'value rationality,' 'formal and substantive rationality.'[28] While the forms of rationality are diverse, it is possible to focus on four broad types: formal, substantive, practical and theoretical. It is important, in this context, to differentiate rationality from the overall process of rationalization. Rationalization, it was stated, refers to the overall historical process by which reality is increasingly mastered by calculation, scientific knowledge and rational action. Rationality, by contrast, is a term Weber used to refer to the capacity of social action to be subject to calculation in the means and ends of action. While this may seem difficult to grasp, Weber was saying that in modern society action can vary depending on the 'orientation' of the actor and the social situation of action. For example, in carrying out professional duties, scientists and lawyers may be subject to

26 Ibid., p. 107.
27 Ibid., p. 107.
28 Ibid., pp. 63–90.

very different forms of rationality. It is Weber's point that, in situations of action, the means individuals use to obtain their ends vary or change. In and of itself, this can produce variation in rationality and rational action, and leads, according to Weber, to a strict means–ends calculation.

Simply stated, rationality may be defined as a standard of action whose substance lies in its weighing up of means and ends prior to action. In one context, rationality can refer to the 'increasing theoretical mastery of reality by means of increasingly precise concepts.' At another level, it refers to 'the methodological attainment of a definitely given and practical end by means of an increasingly precise calculation of adequate means.' In still another sense, it can refer to a shift in 'the comprehension of reality.' Weber also used it to signify the 'absence of all metaphysics and almost all residues of religious anchorage in the sense of the absence and rejection of all non-utilitarian yardsticks.' Further, it can refer to the adherence of a 'valid canon in which the view of life is rational in the sense of rejecting traditionalist bonds and of having faith in the power of reason.' 'It may also mean a systematic arrangement' in the sense of 'following methods which are rational' in order to manipulate reality. Lastly, it can refer to 'all kinds of practical ethics that are systematically oriented to fixed goals in the sense that they distinguish between valid norms and what is empirically given.'[29]

As we stated earlier, there are four types of rationality which Weber discussed in his work: (i) formal; (ii) substantive; (iii) practical; and (iv) theoretical or technical. (i) First is the concept of formal rationality. Weber used this term to designate the amount of quantitative calculation and accounting procedure that goes into an action or decision.[30] While he used the term to refer to a system of reasoning, rationality may be thought of as formal when there is a view to expressing a situation, solving problems or conceptualizing actions by a straightforward application of numerical, calculable standards.[31] In this sense, formal rationality refers to the amount of quantitative calculation and accounting procedure that goes into a decision to ensure consistency of outcome and efficiency in attaining goals. To the extent that formal rationality imposes order on the world through a system of measurement and calculation, it adheres to the norms of economic accounting, proficiency and practical efficacy. It expresses itself by imposing order on reality in strict numerical, calculable terms. Formal rationality thus creates an orientation to action stressing strict adherence to 'cost effective' measures and formal consideration of means and ends.

(ii) Another form of rationality discussed by Weber is substantive rationality. Weber used this term to refer to the degree to which action is

29 Gerth and Mills (eds), *From Max Weber*, pp. 293–4; and Weber, *The Protestant Ethic*, pp. 24–31.
30 Weber, *Economy and Society*, p. 85.
31 Ibid., p. 85.

shaped by an orientation to values regardless of the nature of the ends or outcome of action.[32] In contrast to formal rationality, substantive rationality is not bound to purely formal criteria of decision making or by an orientation to obtain goals by calculable standards, but by criteria of ultimate values which may be shaped by ethical norms or egalitarian standards as these are measured against a scale of values. Where formal rationality involves a practical orientation of action regarding outcomes, substantive rationality involves an orientation to values. In contrast to formal rationality, therefore, substantive rationality is at home in a number of different 'value scales' and, thereby, always involves considerations of social justice, ethical standards and a concern for social equity.[33] Whereas formal rationality bases its orientation to decision making with regard to norms of efficiency and practical costs, substantive rationality is based on the qualitative content of judgments which may be bound by ethical or aesthetic criteria. Weber believed that formal and substantive rationality are opposed, and that ultimately substantive rationality views formal rationality as inimical to its own purpose.[34]

(iii) A third form of rationality discussed by Weber is practical rationality. This refers to a way of looking at the world in which the meaning of an act is believed to lie in its function or utility. In this sense, the meaning and ultimate validity of action is thought to lie exclusively within the 'technical order.'[35] Within the framework of practical rationality, all the means of procuring desired ends are viewed as 'techniques' or strategies rather than as systems of values which are adhered to on the basis of ethical standards or a criterion of action.[36] Practical rationality postulates no outside mystical causes affecting the outcome of actions but rather sees reality in terms of what is empirically given. Within this framework, action is undertaken for the sake of the technical order, and outcomes are weighed against the expenditure of effort in terms of practical benefits and economic rewards. Within these terms, practical rationality aims at precise and efficient application of rules according to procedural categories and abstract regulation of ends in relation to means. Since the meaning of an act lies within the technical order, practical rationality resists any active orientation to abstraction or to any departure from the confines of the practical attitude of daily life or to an appeal to a transcendental order. As such, practical rationality signals an end to all 'metaphysics' in daily life and is based on a rejection of a religious or philosophical interpretation of either means or ends.[37] Since practical rationality presupposes a straightforward orientation to what is empirically given, it abandons 'all

---

32 Ibid., pp. 85–6.
33 Ibid., pp. 85–6.
34 Ibid., pp. 85–6.
35 Ibid., pp. 65–6.
36 Ibid., p. 65.
37 Gerth and Mills (eds), *From Max Weber*, p. 293.

anchorage' in religious ideas and in metaphysics, and implies a 'rejection of all non-utilitarian yardsticks.'[38]

(iv) A fourth type of rationality is theoretical rationality. In contrast to practical rationality, which imposes order on the world by a straight-forward orientation to what is empirically given in reality and by precise calculation of means as a way of obtaining specific ends, theoretical rationality imposes order on reality by conceptual reasoning. Order is imposed on reality by conceptual mastery of the whole in terms of unified concepts or by patterns brought to light through the reasoning process. Theoretical rationality acts by producing an 'image of the world' by means of abstract concepts and conceptualization.[39] The aim of theoretical rationality is to penetrate the limits of daily routine and practical ration-ality by attempting to understand worldly processes with the aid of abstract concepts that view the world from the perspective of a unity which may or may not be meaningful in terms of some value standard. This leads to a departure from the concrete world to the world of abstraction with the express aim of representing the whole in terms of some system of ultimate meaning whose purpose is fundamentally prac-tical. Theoretical rationality, therefore, undertakes an orientation to reality in the realm of theory.

The Theme of Capitalism in Weber's Work

General Economic History

One of the most predominant themes in Weber's work as a whole is his study of capitalism. Weber, in fact, wrote two theories of capitalism: the first, more well known, is his religious interpretation of capitalism in *The Protestant Ethic*; the second, not as well known, was written in 1919 and given as a series of lectures at the University of Munich entitled 'Outlines of Universal Economic History.' This latter work was later published as *General Economic History* in 1922, and the text of the lectures represents one of the most systematic views of capitalism ever produced by Weber.[40]

In relation to Marx's work on capitalism, there are several points of comparison. First, Marx essentially restricted his analysis of capitalism to Western societies, primarily England. Weber, on the other hand, compared Western capitalism with Eastern economies and drew on the economic conditions of a number of countries including Germany, Russia, China, England and France. Second, Weber disagreed with Marx's stress on the economic causes of capitalism. Marx put forward the view that capitalism

38 Ibid., p. 293.

39 Kalberg, 'Max Weber's Types of Rationality,' pp. 1145–79; and Levine, 'Rationality and Freedom,' pp. 5–25.

40 Weber, *General Economic History*, New York: Collier Books, [1922] 1961. For a view of the historical placement of this work and its significance see Randall Collins, 'Weber's Last Theory of Capitalism: A Systematization,' *American Sociological Review*, 45, 1980, 925–42.

could only be understood by looking at the underlying productive forces which shaped the system of social relations and led to the division of society into capitalist and working classes. For Marx, economic factors alone were the most important determinants of capitalist development. Weber, in contrast, looked at capitalism as a system of social action and based his analysis on a number of interconnections he saw between capitalist development and the influences of various spheres of society such as religion, law, and political institutions.

Economic Background Like Marx, Weber began his discussion of capitalism by looking at economic evolution. Focusing on comparative and historical techniques, Weber began in the eighth century AD and traced the economic development of early agrarian societies by looking at Germany, Russia, China, India, England and France. After some discussion of property relations and the formation of social groups, he traced the development of land systems, showing differences which emerge in household economies, village organization and the development of towns.[41]

Looking for distinct characteristics of Western societies over those of Eastern societies, Weber turned his attention to the economic conditions of feudal economies. He believed that feudal economies emerge only in the West and these, he thought, rested on three decisive characteristics. First, on the power which proprietors had over land holdings. Second, on the development of a dependent serf population who performed productive labor. And third, on the appropriation by an aristocracy of political and legal rights resting on usurpation and enserfment.[42] What stands out about feudal economies, according to Weber, is the degree of judicial authority concentrated in land holdings. In fact, he believed that the degree of political authority of the landholder was unprecedented and this led to enormous powers over serfs and peasants.

Attached to the ownership of land was a system of political and judicial privileges which led to unprecedented social prerogatives of the aristocracy over peasants. Lords had unlimited political powers and serfs were subject to the legal jurisdiction of the lord. Feudal dues and taxes were imposed on serfs by tradition and these increased the wealth of landholders. Peasants had little economic incentive to produce more than was necessary for their own economic maintenance and for payments of obligatory dues and taxes. The rights of peasants were set by customary understanding rather than by written law, and generally the law was applied within the jurisdiction of the manor. Weber went on to compare the characteristics of feudal economies in Germany, Russia, England and France with those in China and India. After comparing the main features of manorial economies in these societies, Weber stated that the origins of the Western

41 Weber, *General Economic History*, pp. 21–53.
42 Ibid., pp. 54–71.

manorial system can be traced to three primary sources: (i) economic utility; (ii) military and political considerations; and (iii) social distinctions supporting prerogatives of a traditional aristocracy.[43.]

Next, Weber turned his attention to looking at the conditions leading to the decline of feudal economies. While his discussion largely parallels that of Marx, Weber pointed out that the process of decline begins as landlords assume the rights of ownership over peasant holdings. Like Marx, Weber sees capitalist development beginning as soon as landholders push peasants off the land and begin to convert small holdings into sheep pastures. This, he thought, leads to the formation of links between the agrarian economy of the country and the industry of the town, especially in woolen manufacturing. 'Thus begins,' wrote Weber, 'the transformation of the common pastures into sheep walks – and the enclosure movement by landlords who regard themselves as the owners of common lands.'[44] As the dissolution of the feudal economy takes place, it frees peasants from their roles as agricultural producers and detaches them from the legal bonds tying them to their lords. As feudal land is freed from the system of rights and obligations, there is a breakdown in traditional political authority. This, Weber pointed out, hastened the decline of the political restrictions on land existing since feudal times and marks the transition from a rural economy to an economy of the town.

As a result of these developments, the manorial system began to dissolve in two distinct ways. First, from within the manor the system of social classes began to deteriorate as peasants left the land. Second, from outside the manor the development of markets and the growth of agricultural products jeopardized the viability of the manorial economy.[45] The pace of these changes varied from society to society. In England, the pace was slow since peasant lands were appropriated by legal procedures which created a gradual transition of lands from peasants to capitalist. In France, by contrast, the Revolution brought an immediate end to the feudal economy and a rapid change in the availability and development of land. In Russia, on the other hand, feudal restrictions on peasants were so harsh that Russian economies were slow to change. The widest discrepancy in terms of the pace of economic development, however, was between England and France.

In addition to looking at the economic changes leading to capitalism, Weber gave the widest latitude to the role played by the various social spheres and the influence these spheres had on historical change. Of central importance is the role played by the legal and political spheres. He believed that the dissolution of the feudal economy eventually made way for a modern system of law, which led the way to abolishing feudal ties. Weber took the view that the abolition of feudal regulations led, in fact, to

43 Ibid., pp. 63–80.
44 Ibid., p. 76.
45 Ibid., p. 82.

the development of the concept of the 'citizen' which first made its appearance in France and then in England. As soon as the concept of the 'citizen' became a legal and political reality, it led to the collapse of the aristocracy and an aristocratic way of life.[46]

The Role of the Guilds in Capitalist Development   Next, Weber turned his attention to the role played by trade guilds in capitalist development. Up until the latter half of the nineteenth century, the professional guilds exercised almost complete authority over occupations and this meant that work was impossible to obtain without guild supervision. Guilds had been established as early as the ninth century AD and were primarily used to regulate trades and crafts by controlling entry into them. One of the primary functions of the guilds was 'the internal regulation of work and the monopolization of income against outsiders.'[47] Under these circumstances, guilds had almost complete authority because they were able to preserve the livelihoods of artisans.

Only as a consequence of the breakdown of the guild system did capitalism begin to show signs of development in England and Germany. In England, for instance, the textile trade became the main focus of capitalist industry and development, and by the early nineteenth century woolen goods had become the central focus of production. As the demand for these goods increased and the restrictive policies of the guilds were dissolved, the organization of the factory system geared itself to mass production based on specialization and the division of labor.[48] Production accelerated and markets were created in the manufacturing of 'luxury requirements' such as soap, glass, silk, sugar, pottery and chinaware. Demand for these 'consumptive requirements' grew as the modern household began to establish itself, and this led to specialized demand in luxury goods and ultimately to the democratization of luxury.[49]

Non-economic Factors in Capitalist Development: Rationality, Law, Citizenship and the State   One of the key attributes of Weber's theory of capitalism is the role he allotted to non-economic factors in capitalist development. In this, Weber was completely unique and differed from Marx significantly. Marx believed that capitalism could only be understood from the perspective of underlying productive forces which led to the private ownership by one class of the means of production. In the last instance, according to Marx, economic production shapes society and social relations. Weber, however, doubted this and believed that other spheres of society were independent of economic influences, and in many cases these spheres shaped capitalist development in their own right.

46 Ibid., p. 233 ff.
47 Ibid., p. 110.
48 Ibid., p. 183.
49 Ibid., p. 107.

Weber referred to these sets of influences as the 'non-economic factors' of capitalism, and he thought there were at least four that are central and important. These are: (i) the emergence of a system of rationality; (ii) the development of a system of law and forms of citizenship; (iii) the rise of the state; and (iv) the growth of the 'gain spirit' and a system of ethics.

The first non-economic factor Weber looked at was the emergence of a system of rationality which first takes hold in commerce and commercial activity.[50] According to Weber, rational commerce is a form of economic activity, the principal elements of which are based on the development of what he called 'quantitative reckoning' and the dominance of quantitative thinking in economic life.[51] Weber maintained that quantitative reckoning emerges only when there is a need for 'exactness' in commercial activities. He pointed out that in earlier periods, commerce proceeded so slowly and informally that 'exactness' in calculation was not necessary. But as soon as the exchange of goods became more common, and the quantity of materials and goods exchanged became more substantial, 'exact computation became necessary.'[52] As competitive markets were created there was a greater fluctuation in prices, and this, Weber reasoned, led to the necessity of bookkeeping and the need to render exact accounts of transactions and trade. Furthermore, as the use of paper money became more widespread, the need for methods of exactness in commercial dealings could only be satisfied by rational means. This gave rise to the commercial ledger which acted to regularize bookkeeping and provide a universal set of standardized commercial techniques for rendering a balance. As a result, the technical means of controlling commerce became more exact, and this led to the acceleration of a quantitative tendency in economic matters and in other spheres of society, such as legal and political institutions.

Weber maintained that as soon as commercial activities became dependent on 'exact reckoning,' the irrational limitations on trading which had existed in feudal economies were immediately lifted. This set into motion the buying and selling of commodities and labor that we see in fully-developed capitalism. For Weber, a key condition of this development was the dependence upon 'rational accounting as the norm of all large industrial undertakings.' Without it, capitalism would have been impossible, since it fundamentally reduced the management of commerce to calculable rules which led, in turn, to what Weber called 'calculable law.'[53]

A second non-economic factor related to capitalist development is 'calculable law.' For commercial enterprises to 'operate rationally,' wrote

---

50 Ibid., p. 170.
51 Ibid., p. 170.
52 Ibid., p. 170.
53 Ibid., p. 228.

Weber, 'they must be able to depend on calculable adjudication and administration,' and for this to occur there must be a conjunction between the spheres of economy and the spheres of law.[54] Weber believed that as the union of economic and legal spheres took place, it emancipated commercial activity from the restraint of inherited tradition, and enabled industry and production to become rational. 'Without the stimulation of law,' wrote Weber, 'the development of capitalism would not have been possible.'[55] In fact, it was only with the emergence of rational law that a system of ethics governing commercial interchanges became possible and from this arose the legal concept of the citizen. According to Weber, the concept of the citizen emerges only in the West because the system of rational law ensured the free pursuit of individual gain.[56] In Weber's view, the concept of the citizen is a precondition to capitalist development, since it places such stress on the political and legal spheres of society. But in what way is this true?

Weber thought that there were several features which were unique to the idea of the citizen as it relates to capitalist development. First, in the economic sense the rise of citizenship signified a class of persons having specific social and economic interests separate from those of the state. Second, in the political sense citizenship implied membership in a state economic community where the individual was a holder of certain political and legal rights resting on the free pursuit of private gain. Third, in the social sense citizenship signified a group of persons whose standard of life, rights of property, accumulation, and profession conferred social prestige and privilege.[57] Weber believed that the combination of economic, political and legal aspects of the citizen had never appeared before and was unique to Western capitalism. While the concept may be traced to earlier societies, such as the Greek city states, its political, economic and legal expression is primarily modern in origin.

Another development related to the concept of the citizen is the emergence of the modern city, with its municipal organization and bureaucracy. Weber pointed out that while the city creates struggles between various factions and political office seekers, it leads to a municipal environment which gives rise to art, science, mathematics and, ultimately, civil life itself. Weber thought that the city was a rational institution whose development can be traced to the decline of magic in all spheres of social life. This stress by Weber on the role played by the decline of magic in social life is completely unique. He believed that the city is a Western institution which arises from the concentration of inhabitants confined to a particular geographical space formed for reasons of common defense.[58] This led to

---

54 Ibid., p. 228.
55 Ibid., p. 231.
56 Ibid., p. 231.
57 Ibid., p. 233 ff.
58 Ibid., p. 238.

the organization of economically autonomous groups whose competence consisted in their ability to bear arms and equip themselves. But as far as Weber was concerned, a precondition to a rational approach to city planning and defense is the erosion of magic, which only begins in Western societies. Magic, Weber reasoned, tends to create monopolies by a priestly class who control spiritual and commercial resources. The rise of a prophecy religion, however, brought about an end to magic because it situated the miraculous outside the collective camp rather than within it. 'Prophecy,' Weber wrote, 'destroyed magic because while magical procedure remained real, it was viewed as devilish rather than divine.'[59] In this view, it was the decline of magic which led the way to a town economy and a political life stressing markets, opportunity, labor, economic objectives and bureaucracy. All of this served to elevate capitalism to an economic system formed around a rational state and city life.

A third non-economic influence in capitalist development is the rise of the rational state. Weber thought that the rational state is defined by a set of social institutions based in law and officialdom which emerges only in modern society. This was not possible in feudal economies like those of Germany and England because there, the dominant classes had too much power over commercial and industrial functions. Along with blocking the development of a centralized political authority, feudalism meant that economies and markets were under the control of aristocratic classes which functioned as autonomous officials. A state of aristocratic officials, Weber pointed out, is distinct from the modern state in several ways. First, 'in reality everything is based on magical theory' relating to beliefs about how the official classes 'keep things in order.'[60] Second, in feudal economies power between peasants and the commercial élite is always unequal and unbalanced. In direct contrast to this is the 'rational state in which modern capitalism can flourish.'[61] In this way, the political and economic organization of the modern state rests on 'expert officialdom and rational law' and decisions are based not on magical considerations but on formal rules and procedures.[62]

In conjunction with these developments, a 'systematic legal doctrine' begins to emerge from independent legal scholars who are responsible only to their positions rather than a class of nobles. This leads directly to the rationalization of procedure based on independent legal rules. The development of an independent system of law puts the social classes on a different economic and political footing and creates equality by universalizing due process. Formal law, unlike its historical antecedents, is therefore calculable and predictable. 'Capitalism,' Weber pointed out, 'could not operate on the basis of magic and so what is required is law

59 Ibid., p. 238.
60 Ibid., pp. 250–1.
61 Ibid., pp. 250–1.
62 Ibid., p. 250.

which can be counted upon, like a machine from which religious and magical considerations must be excluded.'[63]

The rise of the 'gain spirit' and a system of ethics, the fourth 'non-economic factor' of capitalism referred to by Weber, is more complex and demands a separate discussion, which follows.

Rational Capitalism and the Growth of the 'Gain Spirit'   A fourth non-economic consideration of capitalist development which Weber looked at is the relationship between the economic and religious spheres. Weber began by making a distinction between Eastern and Western societies. He believed that geographical distinctions can be made between the historical conditions leading to the development of Western capitalism and those leading to Eastern capitalism. To illustrate, he pointed out that Eastern societies developed entirely different forms of commerce to those of societies in the West. Eastern economies are mostly inland and their system of trade imposes restriction of profit on the capitalist classes. In Western societies, in contrast, the conditions leading to capitalist development are more favorable, and this gave rise to more intense commercial activity, based on international markets and a form of commercial development which was unprecedented historically. While the major factors leading to capitalist development in the West were rational accounting, technology and law, these alone did not account for the full development of Western capitalism. In fact, Weber maintained that an additional element must have been present in the West which failed to develop in the East. This element, he believed, is the 'gain spirit' which is based on a rationalization of the conduct of everyday life in general and a rationalistic economic ethic in particular.[64] By 'gain spirit,' Weber meant a system of conduct based on ethical norms which govern commercial activity and which serve to bring the economic and religious spheres into a relationship with each other.[65]

In itself, Weber reasoned, the 'gain spirit' leads to a tradition of ethics and norms of conduct that create a system of action giving rise to commercial activities. In order to understand this assertion, we must highlight a fundamental difference between Marx's and Weber's understanding of capitalism. For Marx, capitalist development was inevitable because the economic laws of development were implicit in history. For Weber, by contrast, it was not a question of the inevitability of capitalism, but rather how it was possible given the restrictions and forces working against it.

According to Weber, there are several steps involved in the development of a system of action related to the growth of capitalism and an economic ethic. First, is the overcoming of traditionalism which tends to hold back the rational development of trade and commerce. This is evident in

63 Ibid., p. 252.
64 Ibid., p. 260–1.
65 The conjunction of these two spheres is more fully explored in Weber, *The Protestant Ethic*.

societies where incentives for economic gain are not in themselves sufficient to overcome traditional obstacles to trade and commerce. Second, in
order for capitalism to develop, two obstacles have to be overcome: the
system of internal impediments which preserves religious beliefs restraining
the pursuit of gain for its own sake; and the elimination of the fear of
trade which has its roots in the idea that any radical change in the
'conduct of life' is inherently evil and therefore unacceptable.[66] Third is the
imposition of a system of restraints on the forces leading to what Weber
called the 'unrestricted play of the gain spirit in economic relations.'[67] At
one level, unrestricted gain tends to place individuals in competition with
one another, but it also acts externally on society to erode the system of
ethical restrictions that stem from religious beliefs. Weber thought that the
two systems of ethics – one internal, the other external – are completely
distinct and operate in different ways. The dominance of one over the
other, Weber noted, involves introducing calculation into the sphere of
traditional beliefs and ethical norms, acting to displace or rationalize the
old religious beliefs and ethical doctrines. As soon as this development
takes place, two things happen: 'naive piety' is brought to an end, and the
ability of traditional ethics to restrain economic development based on the
gain spirit is diminished.[68] Weber believed that it is precisely this kind of
development which took place in the West but not the East.

The historical restrictions on gain seeking, Weber maintained, could
only occur in societies where religion is dominant. In India, for instance,
economic restrictions apply to certain religious castes and members of
these castes are prohibited from practicing commercial activity. Other
classes have specific restrictions placed on mercantile accomplishments,
and in others, legal rules limit the extent of interest which can be gained in
commercial transactions. Weber's focus on the relationship between
religious beliefs and commerce, and between the economic and religious
spheres, lends authority to his view that a theory of capitalism must take
into account the connection between the economic and religious dimensions as well as make distinctions between the development of capitalism
in the East and the West. In Weber's view, a theory of capitalism must be
historical and comparative, since capitalism did not develop in the East
due to the hostility of religious beliefs toward commercial life.

In order to illustrate the differences in capitalist development between
the East and West, Weber introduced the distinction between 'pariah' and
'rational' capitalism. Pariah capitalism, according to Weber, is ritualistic,
restrictive and based on magical beliefs, whereas rational capitalism is
based on a rejection of magic and faith. In the case of pariah capitalism,
the first commercial agents were priests who tended to monopolize
markets. Here, the prevalence of magic was the most obvious 'obstruction

66 Weber, *General Economic History*, p. 261.
67 Ibid., p. 261.
68 Ibid., p. 262.

to the rationalization of economic life.'[69] But, as religion became less ritualistic and based on external prophecy, magic began to break down and was replaced by rational action. For Weber, the shift from pariah to rational capitalism takes place only when there is a development of prophecy religion. Prophecy, reasoned Weber, places power upon God rather than on an individual's activity. When this occurs religious power and piety become otherworldly and lead to the destruction of magic since magic has no recourse to found a doctrine as does religion. Prophecy religion leads to rational procedure because it compels those claiming miracles to furnish authentic credentials and requires individuals to work within the sphere of the prophecy. This requirement breaks down magic and traditionalism, leading to science, law and rational procedure.[70]

Weber went on to point out that a prophecy religion releases the world from magic and creates the basis for science, technology and capitalism. He believed that these developments were lacking in China and India. For instance, in China, when certain groups attempted to change existing roads in order to improve commerce by introducing a rational means of transportation, many feared supernatural evils and this presented obstacles to the rational pursuit of gain.[71] One of the distinctive achievements of Christianity, therefore, was the formation of a system of religious ideas which made the individual the solitary recipient of prophecy – and thus of ethical responsibility. This meant that in daily life individual conduct had been shaped by the sphere of religious ethical pursuits. In itself this development gave rise to a social and economic way of life replete with obligatory ethical responsibility. Under these circumstances, religious ideas become capitalistically directed and the devotion to labor and thrift become the ethical spirit guiding capitalism.

Class, Status and Party

Weber's theory of social class was written between 1911 and 1920 and appears in the second volume of *Economy and Society*. As early as 1910, Weber had observed that one of the key components of late capitalist society was that social classes were on a different economic footing than they had been previously during the early stages of capitalist development. In fact, Weber set out to show that since Marx's early observations on the history of the class struggle, substantial changes had taken place in the structure of society. Since no complete understanding of Weber's theory of class is possible without first looking at Marx's claims, let us briefly look at what Marx had to say about the class structure in the middle of the nineteenth century:

69 Ibid., p. 265.
70 Ibid., pp. 265–7.
71 Ibid., pp. 265–7.

The history of all hitherto existing society is the history of class struggles. Freeman and slave, patrician and plebeian, lord and serf, capitalist and wage labourer stood in constant opposition to one another, carried on an uninterrupted fight that each time ended either in a revolutionary reconstitution of society or in the common ruin of the contending classes. The modern bourgeois society that has sprouted from the ruins of feudal society has not done away with class antagonisms. It has but established new classes, new conditions of oppression, new forms of struggle in the place of old ones. Our epoch, the epoch of the bourgeoisie, has simplified class antagonisms: Society as a whole is more and more splitting up into two great hostile camps, into two great classes directly facing each other: Bourgeoisie and Proletariat.[72]

Taking as a starting point Marx's assertion that the class struggle is an 'uninterrupted fight,' Weber's theory of social class makes three significant advances beyond Marx. First, Weber made his observations about social class 60 years after Marx's central critique of capitalism and class conflict, and this puts him in a position of observing key changes taking place in the class structure of society since Marx. Second, Weber believed that there was a fundamental division of society into distinct and separate social spheres. For Weber, this meant that the economic sphere was not the sole determinant of the class structure of society, and this led Weber to reject Marx's claim that class conflict was the inevitable outcome of economic forces in society. Third, Weber claimed that there had been fundamental changes in what Marx had called the 'antagonistic' nature of social classes, and these changes could be outlined in the light of three central adjustments taking place in society: class, status and party.

Weber's Theory of Social Class: Class and the Market Situation　Weber put forward his theory of social class by looking at three distinct categories: (i) class in relation to market situation; (ii) class in relation to different types of social action flowing from class interests; and (iii) the formation of social classes in relation to historical types of class struggle. Let us look at Weber's first classification relating to the market.

To begin with, Weber defined the concept of class in relation to the market. He stated that 'a class is a number of people having in common a specific causal component of life chances. This component is represented by economic interests in the possession of goods and opportunities for income under conditions of the market.'[73] Two things stand out about Weber's definition of class. First is the concept of 'life chances.' This may be defined as the possibilities arising from the use of goods and services in the market, and the opportunities these chances present for income. If we follow Weber on this point, class situation is determined by life chances which may arise when individuals sell skills and services on the market.

A second thing that stands out about Weber's definition of class is the emphasis he places on class situation and the market. Essentially, the term

---

72 Marx and Engels, *The Communist Manifesto*, F.L. Bender (ed.) New York: Norton, 1988, p. 55.
73 Weber, *Economy and Society*, p. 927.

'market' for Weber refers to the sphere in society in which economic goods and services are produced and exchanged. The market, in this sense, is distinctly separate from the political and legal spheres of society and imposes conditions on the realization of economic interests and incomes. In taking the step of restricting class to the market situation, Weber modified the historic stress Marx had placed on social classes when he stated that 'property and the lack of property' are major determinants of the class situation.

Where Weber went beyond Marx was in putting forward two categories of social class. In the first category, class situation is determined by the ownership of usable property which creates returns on investments and incomes in the form of rents.[74] These classes have prerogatives and life chances afforded to them by the outright ownership of property. Second is the category of class situation which is determined by the kinds of skills and services which can be put up for sale in the market and is not dependent on the ownership of property. By skills and services, Weber was referring to the credentials and certificates which people obtain through education which act to increase life chances by the opportunities they create for selling labor on the market. This category of class situation is determined by the market for services and may include 'technicians, civil servants and various levels of white-collar workers.'[75] While these classes lack the specific life chances of property, they are able to obtain incomes in the form of salaries as a result of selling their skills and training on the market.[76]

These two class situations – one determined by property, the other by the opportunities arising from incomes – formally define the class situation of modern society. In the first category, class situation is determined by outright ownership of usable property such as 'dwellings, workshops, agricultural lands.'[77] This situation may include disposition over the instruments of production, products of labor, 'transferable monopolies,' etc.[78] In itself this situation creates life chances because the distribution of property has been concentrated in the hands of a group who compete for valued goods and services. In addition, these classes may have control over the transfer of properties from holdings to capitalist ventures, and this puts them in the position of monopolizing opportunities for 'profitable deals' which tends to increase their overall power and life chances in the market. This defines the class situation of the propertied.[79]

In the second category, class situation is defined by the kinds of services which a person can offer in exchange for salaries and wages and describes the situation of the non-propertied. Their life chances are determined by

74 Ibid., p. 928.
75 Ibid., p. 305.
76 Ibid., p. 305.
77 Ibid., p. 305.
78 Ibid., p. 305.
79 Ibid., p. 928.

the kinds of services that they can offer in exchange for income. Under these circumstances, life chances will depend on market conditions since the kinds of chances existing in the market will determine whether or not skills derived from certificates and credentials may be sold under present market conditions.

This shift described by Weber in the life chances of the non-propertied alters 'the effect of the naked possession' of the means of production on the non-propertied classes. Weber pointed out that historically, the 'naked possession' of property must have been 'only a forerunner of the class formation' of early societies.[80] In earlier times, the class situation of the propertied would have emerged as decisive for the life chances of the non-propertied, whereas in the class situation of modern times, possession of property is not conclusive for life chances. Class situation, in this sense, is determined by the market which thus has the effect of placing the outright 'naked' ownership of property into the background.

Action Flowing from Class Interests   Next, Weber turned his attention to issues of social class related to the types of social action which Marx thought would arise directly from 'class interests.'[81] Marx had proposed that individuals are carriers of class interests by virtue of overriding economic forces which assign these interests to them as a function of their class position. He went on to claim that, at a certain point in historical development, these class interests would spring into action against the class structure and ultimately change society. Marx assumed that class interests are assigned by structural determinants in society derived from the social relations of production, not from individual motives or intentions.

Weber disagreed with this view and criticized Marx for conceiving of 'interests' as historically given. He argued that the concept of class interest in this sense is 'ambiguous' as soon as one attempts to look beyond the simple 'factual direction of interests' emerging in the average class situation.[82] The factual direction of interests, according to Weber, cannot be determined with any clarity, since the direction individuals pursue in their actions is likely to vary according to their occupation and the size of the group affected by the class situation.[83] In this sense, the mass social movements based on the cohesion of class interests envisaged by Marx are impossible.

According to Weber, the action by a class against the class structure can occur in only one of two ways: (i) by 'irrational protest' and mass uprising; or (ii) by rational association leading to the formation of trade unions. Class situations of the first type occur in ancient societies where differences

80 Ibid., p. 928.
81 Ibid., pp. 928–30.
82 Ibid., p. 929.
83 Ibid., p. 929.

in life chances are 'transparent' during times when wealth is made by one class who monopolize the means of production.[84] In this category, reactions against a class structure were direct outcomes of mass action against a propertied class. Weber believed that this type of situation applied to the classes of antiquity but not to the modern class situation. He went on to state that in the situation of the modern worker, reaction against a class structure takes the form of rational associations leading to the formation of trade unions. Weber thus rejected Marx's assertion that class interests are assigned to individuals by their structural location in society. He pointed out that in the modern class situation, interests vary among individuals who have different motives and inclinations, in which 'average class interests' cannot be determined. Hence, for Weber, there are no class interests *per se*, only average interests of individuals in similar economic situations.

Under these circumstances, Weber sees class interests not as an objective attribute of an individual's relation to the means of production, but as 'average interests' of different individuals sharing similar market situations and life chances. Insofar as this confers different motives to individuals which vary according to class situation, it differs explicitly from Marx. While for Marx, class relationships were explained by reference to the concept of economic forces functioning outside the awareness of individuals who act within them, Weber sees social action in terms of individual motives which arise from their class situation. As such, the potential for mass behavior of a class due to common experience is diminished to the extent that grievances of individual workers are less likely to lead to mass action. Weber reasoned that social action, in contrast to mass behavior, is more likely in modern times since the class situation to which workers are linked is not the 'naked' class condition existing in earlier times.

Whereas in previous periods peasants could not defend themselves against landlords, the class situation in modern times is more diversified and affords opportunities for individuals to react against a given class structure through acts of intermittent protest that lead to 'rational associations.'[85] The class situation of the first type occurs during the period of 'naked' ownership of property in which aristocracies monopolize products, industry, trading and food stuffs. Class situations of the second type, however, occur during the development of modern society whose class situation is supplemented by legal, political and social enfranchisement.

Historical Types of Class Struggle A third element of Weber's treatment of social class is his discussion of historical types of class struggle. This goes directly to the question of whether classes constitute groups who react

84 Ibid., p. 929.
85 Ibid., p. 929.

with identical interests against the class structure. Marx had asserted that classes are groups whose interests are defined by common conditions of exploitation and poverty. He believed that, because workers share common conditions, they had the social cohesion of groups whose struggle led to outright class conflict. By contrast, Weber thought that 'to treat classes as conceptually equivalent to groups' was a historical 'distortion' on Marx's part.[86] Weber reasoned that classes form into groups only when the interests of workers are defined by a distinct economic opponent, a condition which would have existed between workers and capitalists during the early period of industrial transition.[87] Thus, for classes to be groups, according to Weber, there has to be an 'immediate economic opponent,' and this situation no longer exists or holds true.[88]

Another reason for Weber to assert that classes are not groups was his belief that people have separate motives leading them to compete as autonomous individuals. Having been differentiated from their class, individuals compete alone in the market and to this extent share only what Weber called 'contemporaneous remnants' of their former group structure.[89] Under these circumstances, classes lose their homogeneity as groups to the extent that they compete as individuals in various class situations rather than as a unified group.

In addition to this, Marx had asserted that the antagonism of social classes would become more pronounced in capitalist societies as the contradictions between the classes increased. Inevitably, this would lead to further conflict, class struggle, and eventually social change. Weber denied this on several different fronts. To begin with, Weber thought that class antagonism leading to historical struggles arose only where 'naked' ownership of property existed, as in the classes of antiquity. But, wrote Weber, 'the great shift which has been going on continuously in the past and up to our time' is that the site of class antagonism has 'progressively shifted' from classes of antiquity to classes of modern times. Weber thus saw the struggles of labor in terms of a historical progression; from those defined first by the labor bondage of the serf, through the struggles of wages which took place on unequal grounds, to the rational settlement of modern wage disputes mediated by trade unions on the labor market.[90]

While the class struggles of antiquity focused on by Marx were carried out by peasants directly against a land-owning aristocracy and involved a fight over the means of production, Weber reasoned that these struggles had their origins in property differences which lasted through antiquity and the Middle Ages. These disputes were directly over the means of

---

86 Ibid., p. 930. Weber directly attacks Marx's historical precision.
87 Ibid., p. 931.
88 Ibid., p. 305.
89 Ibid., pp. 929–30.
90 Ibid., pp. 930–1.

survival and were struggles of the propertyless against the propertied. The basis of this antagonism, according to Weber, has been offset in modern times by increasing use of wage disputes and mediated settlements of the modern class situation. In earlier times the propertyless classes of antiquity protested against 'monopolies, pre-emption and the withholding of goods,' whereas in modern times they determine the price of labor through legally mandated disputes over wages.[91] The transition to the modern class situation, said Weber, is characterized by disagreements over access to the market, while in earlier times these fights were between the peasants and landholding classes of the feudal period. In the modern situation, 'class antagonism' between employer and worker is redressed through the modern market, since it functions to adjudicate wage disputes. It is not the worker, therefore, who suffers directly from wage disputes, but the class of 'manufacturers and business executives.'[92] Under these circumstances, the model of the class struggle of antiquity carried on by indebted peasants who are rendered impoverished by a wealthy landholding class no longer applies.

The transition to the modern class situation alters the nature of class conflict in two distinct and fundamental ways. First, there has been a shift from direct confrontations between property owners and workers to mediated wage disputes on the market.[93] This has diminished the direct antagonism between classes. Second, conflicts between classes are resolved through legal means, in which class antagonism is mitigated by recourse to law and to the legal rights of the worker to form associations. This takes place, according to Weber, as the market ensures resolution of conflicts by legal reconciliation, and as modern political parties grow which begin to absorb elements of class antagonism within the political sphere, thus displacing the class struggle from the economic realm into the political arena.

Weber's Concept of the Status Group: the Separation of Status from Class

The second form of adjustment identified by Weber is the development of the 'status group' in modern society. While Weber's discussion of the status group tends to be obscure, it is possible to outline several themes that are relevant to the role of the status group in his theory of class and stratification. To begin with, it is important to recall that Weber saw society in terms of various social spheres which he thought functioned autonomously. The political and legal spheres, for instance, developed different dimensions of social action and rationality, and were distinct in terms of the separate functions they performed. One of the things Weber thought important was to demonstrate how certain social spheres exclude

91 Ibid., p. 931.
92 Ibid., p. 931.
93 Ibid., p. 931.

other realms of activity, and he thought that it would be important to outline types of social activity that are distinct from the class situation determined by the market. The status group, for Weber, is such a sphere of activity.

To begin with, Weber defined a status situation as 'every component of life fate that is determined by a positive or negative social estimation of honor.'[94] In order completely to understand Weber's meaning here, it is important that we look at the distinction he made between class and status. As we saw earlier, Weber defined class situation with respect to the market. In contrast to class situation, however, the status situation is defined by its 'strict separation' from the economic order and the sphere of the market and, in this sense, is functionally separate from class.[95] Where class is restricted to the sphere of the market and characterized by acquisition, status is outside the market and characterized by consumption.

While it may be difficult to separate class from status in conventional understanding, Weber insisted on the distinction and believed that it is key to understanding the role played by the status group in modern society. Perhaps the best way to understand the distinction Weber makes between class and status is to view them as separate dimensions of the stratification system. Where class is defined by the market situation and characterized by economic behavior related to the acquisition of incomes and opportunities, status operates outside the market order and is defined by patterns of consumption, lifestyle and habits of taste.[96] Class and status thus occupy different social spheres and engage different levels of the stratification system. Classes, according to Weber, are stratified in relation to the pursuit of opportunities and incomes. This restricts class activities to 'acquisition.'[97]

A status situation, on the other hand, refers to activities involving individuals acting as members of groups who share lifestyle, habits of taste and the pursuit of social esteem. This restricts status to activities related to patterns of 'consumption.'[98] Thus, where classes are involved in economic behavior related to income and occupation, status groups claim to distribute social honor by pursuing patterns of consumption and lifestyle. To illustrate, Weber drew on the example of exclusive neighborhoods within a city, where only those residents of certain streets who are considered to be part of a social circle are 'visited and invited.'[99] This submission to patterns of consumption, lifestyle and taste qualifies an individual to be treated as a member of a status group and puts forward a claim to status honor.

Where the market bears the stamp of the class situation and the 'naked

94 Ibid., p. 932.
95 Ibid., p. 937.
96 Ibid., p. 937.
97 Ibid., p. 937.
98 Ibid., p. 937.
99 Ibid., p. 933.

power of property,' patterns of consumption show the effects of the status situation. To the extent that status is separate from class, status 'abhors' the market and pretensions of wealth which bear the stamp of acquisition. In this sense, the status order is precisely the reverse of distinctions conferred by the market. Weber went on to state that the 'status order would be threatened to its roots if mere economic acquisition could bestow the same honor' as the status group claims for itself.[100] In this sense, the status order reacts against the pretensions of sheer economic acquisition, and the development of status over the pretensions of wealth constitutes the second form of adjustment in society.

Characteristics of Status Groups Next, Weber went on to outline four distinct characteristics of status groups and their function within society. Status groups, he stated: (i) evaluate social worth and bestow honor; (ii) segregate themselves from other status groups; (iii) uphold patterns of consumption and canons of taste; and (iv) monopolize status privileges. Let us look more closely at some of these activities.

One of the central characteristics of status groups is their capacity to bestow social honor. In contrast to class situation, Weber designated a status situation as determined by 'a positive or negative evaluation of honor.'[101] Status honor is typically expressed in the specific styles of life and patterns of taste which may act as an imposition on others who seek to enter the circle defined by the group. When individuals put forward a claim to qualify on the basis of their adoption of specific styles of dress, or on the basis of submission to specific social badges, they are considered to belong only on the basis of a positive evaluation and acceptance of their social worth. As a result of positive evaluation of social worth, persons are compelled to uphold the canons of style and habits of taste which are deemed appropriate by the group, otherwise they risk negative evaluation. In connection with this expectation are 'restrictions' on social intercourse such as those related to 'marriage within the status circle,' forming what Weber called 'complete endogamous closure.' Once these characteristics are satisfied and it is obvious to everyone that it is not an 'irrelevant imitation of another style of life but a product of consensual actions, status development is underway.'[102]

Insofar as members of the status group share the same component of 'life fate,' two kinds of distinction are central in understanding the evaluative function of the status group. First are the criteria applied to those inside the group, and second, are the criteria applied to those situated outside the group. In the first case, criteria applied to those inside the group include the system of evaluations employed by members to positively or negatively rank the activities of others in terms of their social

100 Ibid., p. 936.
101 Ibid., p. 936.
102 Ibid., p. 936.

worth and status honor. These evaluations apply according to how well or how badly members pursue the habits of taste considered appropriate by the status group. In the second case, criteria applied to others outside the group perform the function of maintaining closed boundaries against all except those whose conventions and education meet the evaluative criteria of the group.

Weber went on to outline three criteria related to the evaluative activity of status groups: (i) status groups make evaluations on the basis of shared qualities and values which are held in common and used as criteria for appraising others; (ii) status honor compels individuals to uphold specific expectations of lifestyle held in high esteem, and award this esteem to others only as honorific preferences; (iii) honorific preferences are normally opposed to pretensions of sheer property.[103] In this case, because Weber saw the pretensions of property as irrelevant to the status sphere he separated prestige from wealth, and, by implication, wealth from status honor.[104]

Another characteristic of the status group is the practices it uses to set itself apart from other groups, and Weber referred to this as social segregation. He thought that the status group sets itself apart from other groups first by its lifestyle and second by its social badges. He pointed out that where status groups have evolved practices of closing ranks to the fullest, they become closed castes.[105] A caste may be defined as a status group whose boundaries have become rigid and backed up by legal or religious sanctions. Where this has taken place, status distinctions which previously were supported by conventions of lifestyle and habits of taste alone find themselves being supported by law and religious sanctions. Under these circumstances, all social interactions between members of different castes are regulated by rules which may carry some type of social stigma or means of detecting ritualistic impurities in persons outside the group. The status structure thus concerns itself with regulatory constraints which in fact control contact between different status groups. Impurities obtained by unregulated contact must be religiously expiated.[106] The dominance of status practices in caste communities often leads to legal and religiously entitled segregation.

As soon as status communities have been organized into separate status groups, their segregation may be driven by habits of taste, customary differences or even by mutual repulsion. This allows each group to see itself, in relation to the others, as most worthy of honor and social esteem. After some time, these hierarchies become 'functional' in relation to the organization of society as a whole since they alone are able to perform specialized functions and, by virtue of this, may be recruited to provide

---

103 For this discussion, see ibid., p. 932.
104 Ibid., pp. 305–6.
105 Ibid., pp. 933–4.
106 Ibid., pp. 933–4.

trained warriors, priests, artisans or leaders.[107] In this sense, the modern military functions as a status group from which certain kinds of specialist would be employed and recruited.

In his discussion of segregation of the status group, Weber made two broad distinctions: (i) between 'positively' valued status groups; and (ii) status groups which are 'negatively' valued. In the first case, status groups are positively valued when it is thought that traits of 'beauty or excellence' are in fact inherent in their being.[108] In the second case, a status group is negatively valued when they see their value as lying beyond this world, or when their religious beliefs in regard to claims of explicit difference from others are based on 'providential' ideas regarding the destiny of a pariah people.[109]

A third characteristic of the status group is the privileges associated with it. Weber asserted that status groups tend to create 'monopolization of material and ideal goods.'[110] The creation of material and ideal monopolies refers to restrictions placed on special items of dress, certain social rituals and the possession of insignia or preferential titles. Material monopolies such as these provide the most explicit claims to social separateness and exclusivity. In some cases, these status privileges become protected by laws or special offices and titles. Certain entitlements may also become objects of monopolization such as aristocratic titles, authoritative rights and, in some cases, even certain trades. When this monopolization is positively expressed, the status group may be empowered to manage scarce goods or titles. However, when it is negatively expressed, the status group may be prohibited from owning or managing such socially coveted resources. In some cases, positively valued status groups become the sole purveyors of social conventions and traditions, for example, the British royal family. Other conventions which may operate to signify the separateness of status groups include the exemption from the performance of physical labor. In certain families this disqualification may become part of their accrued status honor.

Status Groups and the Formation of Communities   Another characteristic of status groups which makes them distinct from the economic activities of social classes is their capacity to form communities with shared common interests. We saw earlier that classes were not considered to be communities with common interests and this meant that they were not groups as such. Status groups, in contrast, do form communities with common interests and purposes. They do this in two specific respects: (i) status groups, in contrast to classes, constitute communities who share common characteristics. These are based on shared conditions and a common

---

107 Ibid., pp. 933–4.
108 Ibid., pp. 933–4.
109 Ibid., pp. 933–4.
110 Ibid., p. 935.

perspective that derives from similar experience of lifestyle and habits of taste. This, Weber thought, stands in contrast to the situation of social classes in which individuals compete alone in the market for life chances. To the extent that the status situation involves a system of values which are divorced from the market, status groups involve individuals acting as members of a group who share specific styles of life, levels of social prestige and social habits which provide them with shared meaning. (ii) Status groups share a common set of criteria of evaluation; under these circumstances status groups are identified not by positions which they assume in economic ranking but rather by the criteria of evaluation they share as members of a group.[111]

Political Parties The development of political parties is the third dimension of social adjustment that takes place in conjunction with class and status. So far, we have seen that social classes are restricted to the sphere of the market order and status groups to the sphere of the status order. Political parties, therefore, are restricted to the realm of power and the political order.

In contrast to the class and status situations which operate in the sphere of the market and status order respectively, the action of parties is oriented toward two kinds of activities: first, the acquisition of power; and second, the influencing of the actions of others for political purposes.[112] In Weber's view, the primary purpose of political parties is to secure power and maintain separation from the economic and status spheres. Weber stated that the most important criterion of the party is its voluntary solicitation and adherence to the rules of the group within the party. All association by persons of the party must be carried out in accord with rules of association which are prescribed by the political and legal spheres. Along with this is the tendency of political parties to take the electorate into account since their neglect would tend to upset chances of future election.[113] A key function of the modern political party, according to Weber, is the mitigation of the class structure, which takes place as the party system absorbs elements of the class struggle within the party itself. This occurs, Weber reasoned, as the stratification of political parties tends to conform to the representation of social classes.

The Protestant Ethic and the Spirit of Capitalism

Weber wrote *The Protestant Ethic and the Spirit of Capitalism* between 1902 and 1903, and it was subsequently published as two separate essays in 1904 and 1905. Weber had started writing *The Protestant Ethic* after

111 Ibid., pp. 936–7.
112 Ibid., p. 938.
113 Ibid., p. 287.

completing a study of methodological issues in the social sciences. At the time, he was returning to academic work after an absence of almost four years. While formally part of Weber's overall study of religion, *The Protestant Ethic* stands alone as an independent work and it represents two distinct themes in Weber's theoretical writing as a whole. First is the theme of religion and religious ideas; and second is the theme of capitalism and capitalist development. In conjunction with Marx's *Capital*, *The Protestant Ethic* constitutes one of the two great theories of capitalism. Both works focus on the historical and causal forces shaping capitalist society.[114] Where Weber differs from Marx, however, is in his interpretation of capitalism and the stress he placed on the interrelationship between the economic and religious spheres of society.

Aims of Weber's Study

Weber had two central aims in writing *The Protestant Ethic*. First, he wanted to show how beliefs influence action by establishing a connection between patterns of belief and the system of social action.[115] In this respect, he wanted to know whether our beliefs are likely to affect our actions. Second, Weber wanted to show that there was a connection between religion and commercial activity, and that capitalism was largely shaped by religious forces. This claim by Weber, that religion and commerce are connected was controversial for several reasons. First, no one had looked at the relationship between economy and religion, since many believed that there was no underlying connection between the two. Second, economic reasoning had put forward the view that commercial activity, particularly capitalism, was based on logic and therefore not governed by faith or by belief. Third, the focus of commercial life was seen to be nothing more than the direct manipulation of the material world for purposes of profit and exchange. Fourth, the world of exchange stood in sharp contrast to the world of religious faith and belief. Weber's point of departure from these views, however, was in his reformulation of economic activity.

Weber's Central Thesis

Weber began by making two fundamental observations. First, he noticed that many of the commercial centers throughout Europe, including France, Germany, England, Scotland and Switzerland etc., had demonstrated intense commercial activity at the same time that Protestantism

---

114 For a discussion of some of the controversy raised by Weber's interpetation, see Kurt Samuelsson's *Religion and Economic Action: A Critique of Max Weber*, New York: Harper & Row, 1957, who finds no 'plausible connection between religion and commercial activity'; and Robert W. Green (ed.), *Protestantism and Capitalism: The Weber Thesis and its Critics*, Boston: Heath & Co., 1959.

115 Weber, *The Protestant Ethic*, p. 95.

was taking hold in Western Europe.[116] Second, Weber noted that Western capitalism is motivated by two kinds of contradictory activities: on the one hand, a devotion to amassing wealth beyond the personal needs of the individual and, on the other, the avoidance of the use of wealth for purposes of personal pleasure or enjoyment. When we look at capitalism, asserted Weber, we see not only production and exchange, money making and profit, but an ascetic attitude toward life. These two characteristics – the devotion to amassing wealth and an ascetic attitude toward pleasurable activity – led Weber to argue that if asceticism had found its way into commercial activity then a religious ethic must underlie capitalism.

In order completely to understand Weber's argument, we have to look briefly at the concept of asceticism. In its most explicit sense, asceticism refers to rigorous self-denial. Historically the term originates from religious piety expressed through self-denial and renunciation of worldly pleasure. As a religious doctrine, asceticism holds that one can achieve a higher state by self-discipline and self-denial. Asceticism, then, may be defined as a conscious denial of worldly pleasure with the aim of reaching a valued goal and a higher moral state. Weber used the concept of asceticism to pinpoint a way of living in the world in which the individual engages in self-denial for purposes of obtaining future rewards. Weber believed that in modern capitalism self-denial has become a category of social action, since only in societies where capitalism flourishes is self-denial linked to achievement.

The 'Spirit' of Capitalism

To provide evidence of this pattern, Weber turned his attention to identifying what he called the 'spirit' of capitalism. He began by noting that, when compared to other systems of money making, Western capitalism is alone in developing a central philosophy or spirit. Weber reasoned that the spirit of capitalism can be identified by three overriding imperatives or demands: first, the devotion to amassing wealth and profit beyond the personal needs of the individual; second, the commitment to unrelieved toil and work coupled with self-denial; and third, the avoidance of the use of wealth for purposes of personal enjoyment. It is this 'spirit', according to Weber, that forms the special nature of Western capitalism.[117]

To show how the 'spirit' manifests itself in economic activity, Weber turned his attention to the works of Benjamin Franklin whom, he believed,

116 Weber stated: 'A glance at the occupational statistics of any country of mixed religious composition brings to light with remarkable frequency a situation which has several times provoked discussion in the Catholic press, namely, the fact that business leaders and owners of capital and commercially trained personnel of modern enterprises, are overwhelmingly Protestant.' *The Protestant Ethic*, p. 35.

117 Ibid., pp. 27–8. As far as Weber is concerned, there were many capitalisms: adventurous capitalism, speculative capitalism, usurious capitalism and modern industrial capitalism (ascetic capitalism). By drawing our attention to the 'spirit,' Weber was saying that the forces shaping ascetic capitalism in the West are unique.

represents the characteristics of the 'spirit' in its 'classical purity.' Franklin was a successsful entrepreneur who wrote a self-help guide in 1736 called *Necessary Hints to those that would be Rich* and in 1748 followed it with another work called *Advice to a Young Tradesman*. Franklin put forward a set of maxims about how to be successful. Let us look at some of Franklin's views:

> Remember, that time is money. He that can earn ten shillings a day by his labour and goes abroad, or sits idle, one half of the day, though he spends but sixpence during his idleness, ought not to reckon that the only expense; he has really spent, or rather thrown away, five shillings besides.

> Remember, that money is of the prolific, generating nature. Money can beget money, and its offspring can beget more, and so on. Five shillings turned is six, turned again is seven, and three pence, and so on, till it becomes a hundred pounds. The more there is of it, the more it produces every turning, so that the profits rise quicker and quicker. He that murders a crown, destroys all that it might have produced, even scores of pounds.

> Remember this saying, the good paymaster is lord of another man's purse. He that is known to pay punctually and exactly to the time he promises, may at any time, on any occasion, raise all the money his friends can spare. This is sometimes of great use. After industry and frugality, nothing contributes more to the raising of a young man in the world than punctuality and justice in his dealings; therefore never keep borrowed money an hour beyond the time you promised.

> The most trifling actions that affect a man's credit are to be regarded. The sound of your hammer at five in the morning, or eight at night, heard by a creditor, makes him easy six months longer; but if he sees you at a billiard-table, or hears your voice at a tavern, when you should be at work, he sends for his money the next day. It shows, besides, that you are mindful of what you owe; it makes you appear a careful as well as an honest man, and that still increases your credit.[118]

What struck Weber about Franklin's language was not its practical outlook towards making money, nor its insistence that honest individuals pay their creditors promptly, but rather that the demand to promptness, prudence, honesty, and saving appear within the context of a proclaimed duty to earn more and more capital. 'Truly, what is preached here,' wrote Weber, 'is not simply a means of making one's way in the world' on a practical basis, but rather 'a peculiar ethic.' He went on to state that the 'infraction of these rules is treated not as foolishness but as forgetfulness of duty.'[119] In Weber's view, Franklin's words go beyond the mere suggestion of prudent business advice. Rather, they refer to a specific ethos or 'spirit,' and they 'take on the character of ethically colored maxims for shaping the conduct of life.'[120] Weber went on to point out that while Franklin's recommendations (be punctual, save money, be frugal, work hard, etc.) appear to have practical outcomes, they contain what Weber

118 Ibid., pp. 49–50.
119 Ibid., p. 51.
120 Ibid., p. 52.

refered to as a 'surplus of virtue.'[121] In fact, Weber stated that Franklin himself believed that the recommendations had virtues which were divine in origin and 'which were intended to lead the individual to the path of righteousness.' This shows, stated Weber, that 'something more than mere utility is involved.'[122]

Weber maintained that the central spirit of capitalism had the effect of putting forward the expectation of the performance of work as a moral duty, and in doing so it made the non-performance of work an 'infraction' of such duty.[123] This elevation of work to a moral duty was historically new and had not been seen in other traditional forms of capitalism. The 'spirit' of capitalism, therefore, may be defined as the introduction of a 'religious' ethic into everyday activity – one that had not been seen in previous systems of money making.

Distinctiveness of the 'Spirit' in Modern Capitalism: Traditional vs Modern Capitalism

Thur far, Weber has shown that the 'spirit' of capitalism is unique in two related respects: first, it developed only in modern Western capitalism and is lacking in other societies where capitalism has existed. Second, it indicated that the appearance of ethical demands in economic activity implied the presence of religious doctrine. In order to support the claim that the 'spirit' develops only in modern capitalism, Weber drew a comparison between what he called 'traditional' and 'modern' capitalism.[124] In modern capitalism, said Weber, employers use the practice of pricing jobs according to different rates and they do this in order to obtain as much from the worker as possible. In cases where high profits prevailed over heavy losses or where employers sought to speed up production, piece rates in modern capitalism added incentives for workers to earn more by increasing the intensity of their work. This benefited employers and workers at the same time since it maximized profits and wages. But, in traditional capitalism, raising piece rates had the effect of creating less rather than more incentive to work. According to Weber, 'the worker reacted to the increase by decreasing the amount of work.'[125] In traditional capitalism, therefore, 'the opportunity to earn more was less attractive than that of working less' since the traditional worker 'did not ask how much can they earn in a day if they do as much as possible? Instead, they asked: how much must I work in order to earn the wages which I earned before and which take care of my traditional needs?'[126]

121 Ibid., p. 52.
122 Ibid., p. 52.
123 Ibid., p. 51. Weber stated it this way: 'Truly what is here preached is not simply a means of making one's way in the world, but a peculiar ethic. The infraction of its rules is treated not as foolishness but as forgetfulness of duty.'
124 Ibid., pp. 59–60.
125 Ibid., pp. 59–60.
126 Ibid., pp. 59–60.

While traditionalism had existed previously in China, India and, briefly, in the Europe of the Middle Ages, in all these cases 'the particular spirit was lacking.'[127]

Calvinism and Capitalism

Next, Weber turned his attention to looking at the origins of religious ideas and the role played by John Calvin in the formation of the capitalist spirit. John Calvin was a Protestant reformer whose work came to prominence in the sixteenth century. Calvin had studied theology and religion in France in the early half of the sixteenth century and had there developed an interest in an ecclesiastical career. In 1534, Calvin took a critical stance toward Catholic theology for its failure to stress the rejection of worldly pleasures and for its permissive doctrine of salvation. Rooted in Catholic thought was the idea that the path to salvation was clearly marked in the cycle of atonement, confession and forgiveness. Calvin thought that Catholic teaching was too tolerant and he put forward a salvation theology that was much more restrictive. Shortly thereafter, Calvin joined the Protestant reform movement in France and began to devise a Protestant theology.[128] After careful study of the Bible, he believed that he had discovered a series of restrictive regulations related to worldly activity and, as a result, began to stress a strict interpretation of the Bible. After settling in Geneva, Calvin taught and wrote on theological matters until his work began to have an impact in Western Europe, especially on the development of Protestant doctrine. Eventually, Calvin's ideas began to spread more widely throughout Europe, and influenced Protestant religious teaching by laying stress on the restrictive rules regarding personal freedoms and the Protestant attitude toward the world. The Protestant reforms introduced by Calvin signaled a serious shift in religious ideas and brought on a wave of reform which was unparalleled in its anti-humanist response.[129]

After working with Calvin's theological writings, Weber focused on what he thought was the center of Calvinist religious reform. This involved a body of ideas known as the doctrine of predestination, which was based on four essential decrees. The first preached that before the world began God had divided all humanity into two classes of persons: the saved and the damned. To those who had been elected to be saved, God gave everlasting life, salvation and eternal grace. To those who were condemned, however, God withheld salvation and gave everlasting death and dishonor.[130] Second was the decree which preached that no believer should or could know their fate until it was revealed to them upon death. Since

---

127 Ibid., pp. 52–3.
128 See Gordon Marshall, *Presbyteries and Profits: Calvinism and the Development of Capitalism in Scotland, 1560–1707*, Oxford: Clarendon Press, 1980.
129 Ernst Troeltsch, *The Social Teaching of the Christian Churches*, London: Allen & Unwin, 1956.
130 Ibid., p. 100.

'the elect differ externally in no way from the damned,' Calvin had claimed that no physical signs or marks distinguished the elect from the damned.[131] Third was the decree which stated that nothing could be done to relieve, forgive or reverse the decrees; no priest, no prayer, no sacrament and no worldly forgiveness by confession or communion.[132] Fourth, Calvin claimed that God had abandoned all but the elect since, in Calvin's view, Christ had endured suffering only for the elect.[133]

In order to contain the anxiety resulting from the decrees, Calvin imposed two basic obligations on believers. First, he stated that believers had an absolute duty to assume they were among the elect, thus eliminating any need for second guessing about whether they were saved or damned. Second, believers were obliged to stave off personal doubt about salvation since any personal misgiving was seen as a loss of faith in God. In addition to this, Calvin introduced two uncompromising restrictions forbidding any reversal or exemption from the doctrine of predestination: (i) however one's fate was decided by God, there would be no hope of appeal and no possibility of change through traditional prayer, supplication or sacraments. (ii) God was transcendent and could not be called upon or approached, and thus was out of reach. All of Calvin's injunctions stood in dramatic contrast to Catholic theology. In the Catholic Church, believers are able to redeem themselves of sin and to undo past error and transgression through penance and prayer.

Weber went on to outline two broad effects of the doctrine. On the one hand, he reasoned that it created a 'feeling of unprecedented inner loneliness' in Protestants and took away 'the most important thing in their life – the hope of eternal salvation.'[134] As a result, he maintained, the Protestant believer had been put into a state of internal anxiety so that the first and most pressing question became: 'am I one of the elect?'[135] Since no direct answer was obtainable, it had the effect of placing the individual on his or her own in religious matters. Second, Weber pointed out that in denying Protestants the opportunity to beseech God through prayer or sacrament, Calvin's doctrine created a crisis of faith, and the question for Protestants became: 'how can I interpret my relationship to God?'[136] Since there was no direct answer to the question, Weber maintained that the feeling of abandonment and the withdrawal of religious support created a new form of self-reflection in Protestants. For one thing, Protestants had to invent a way of being with themselves which would create peace of mind and, at the same time, proclaim worthiness in the face of a severe

131 Weber, *The Protestant Ethic*, p. 110.
132 Ibid., p. 104.
133 Ibid., pp. 104–6.
134 Ibid., pp. 104–6.
135 Ibid., p. 110.
136 Wolfgang Schluchter, 'Weber's Sociology of Rationalism and Typology of Religous Rejection of the World,' in S. Whimster and S. Lash (eds), *Max Weber, Rationality and Modernity*. London: Allen & Unwin, 1987, pp. 92–115.

religious doctrine. Second, Weber thought that anxiety over salvation produced such insecurity that it led to the absence of solidarity, not only with and among other Protestants, but with the external world itself – and this created the need to compensate in the form of internal calculation and cunning against the world. Feelings of separateness and isolation, Weber argued, were manifested in a lack of trust of others and in an attitude of the individual against the world. This eventually led to the development of the principle *sola fide*, which means faith in solitude or 'faith alone.'[137]

As Protestants adjusted to the decrees, they became more individualized and this altered their relationship to the everyday world and to the social community in several ways. First, by eliminating the link to the world provided by sacraments and confession, the decrees warned against trust in friendship and aid in the world.[138] Second, in proclaiming that God was out of reach, Protestants had no one to turn to to demonstrate their faith since all contact with God and priests was withdrawn. In addition, feelings of isolation and abandonment were intensified by the requirements of worldly asceticism, since asceticism required that the world be renounced with inner resistance. This tended to close off most avenues of action, with one exception – the obligation to combat self-doubt with hard work. In fact, Protestants were exhorted to accept as a duty and a calling the certainty of their possible election and 'the daily struggle of life.'[139]

Weber reasoned that Protestants, having only one avenue of action to combat anxiety and loneliness, threw themselves into worldly work. In this way, worldly work became a spring to action. In one way, work functioned to relieve self-doubt and self-denial in daily life. But, in another way it had the unanticipated effect of conferring the feeling of grace since rigorous self-denial in work put Protestants in touch with their morality and purified their presence in the world. The strenuous activity of drawing oneself together and the exercise of collecting one's wits in the face of external anxiety, helped stave off the feeling of damnation and, at the same time, created the belief that one 'earns' a state of grace on a daily basis through inner conviction, conscious laboring and self-control.

The relationship between austere self-control and the attitude of resistance against worldly pleasure tended to increase the Protestant's belief in the 'economic' nature of 'peace of mind' and in the relationship between 'earnings' and mental well-being. This gave the concept of 'pulling oneself together' and of 'confronting oneself with self control' a positive valuation since it 'earned' periodic relief from damnation and brought the Protestant closer to the feeling of grace. The Protestant defense of asceticism, hard work and separateness earned the believer a dispensation from damnation and a temporary feeling of being closer to God. The daily struggle of self-control and self-denial had the effect of creating 'contempt' for others who

137 Weber, *The Protestant Ethic*, p. 80.
138 Schluchter, 'Weber's Sociology of Rationalism,' p. 106.
139 Ibid., p. 111.

lacked the outward signs of internal discipline, leading to an intolerance toward the weaknesses of others. As Weber pointed out, this 'penetrated social relations with sharp brutality,' since Protestants could neither trust in the world nor in others.[140] This tended to result in an inner conviction of 'if I am damned, so are you,' or – more colloquially – 'damn you!'

The Link between Salvation and Work and between Religious Teaching and the Commercial Spirit

Weber went on to assert that there were two broad links between Protestant teaching and commercial activity: first, between the question of salvation and worldly work; and second, between religious articles of faith and the development of the commercial spirit. In the first case, Weber thought there was a link between the withdrawal of salvation and the emergence of self-denial. He believed, in fact, that the elimination of attainable salvation was at the root of Protestant self-denial and asceticism. He demonstrated this by drawing a comparison with Catholicism. In the Catholic Church, the path to salvation is clearly marked in the cycle of atonement and confession; the possibility of attaining salvation by renewal of belief is always held out to the believer. Rooted in Catholic thought and salvation is the concept of forgiveness of human weakness, and this is reflected in the 'cycle of sin, repentance and atonement followed by renewed sin.'[141] In Catholicism one can earn salvation through good works, whereas this is not possible in Protestantism. Weber reasoned that this created two related responses in the Protestant believer: first, there developed the idea that intense worldly asceticism was to be pursued as an end in itself, since it tended to separate Protestants from others and at the same time provided a worldly substitute for grace. Second, toil and hard work became associated with a method for eliminating doubt about whether one was a member of the elect.

In connecting the emergence of self-denial with the loss of salvation, Weber believed he had found a link between the ideas of predestination and asceticism. Asceticism taught that a state of self-discipline was attainable through strict self-denial and that, through this, the individual would attain a higher state. Since Protestant commercial activity was permeated with self-denying actions of prudence, frugality and thrift, Weber felt he had found a link between Protestant religious teaching and the work ethic. Further, since a puritanical attitude toward work coupled with self-denial increased the likelihood of amassing wealth, the attainment of wealth became a sign that one had been successful in worldly activity. The Protestant equation became one of believing that success in commercial activity through hard work and self-denial must be a way the believer can interpret his or her relation to God and thus feel closer to

140 Weber, *The Protestant Ethic*, p. 122.
141 Ibid., p. 117.

salvation. Wealth, therefore, became the basis for interpreting one's relationship to God.

In addition to this, Weber believed he had found the link between the Protestant commercial spirit and Protestant articles of secular religious faith. What was so unique about Protestantism, according to Weber, was that whereas all other forms of religious devotion were accompanied by a rejection of everyday life, Protestantism had introduced a thoroughgoing regulation of everyday life, especially in worldly work. In this distinction lay the difference between monastic asceticism and Protestant commercial asceticism. While monastic asceticism requires believers to isolate themselves from the world at large and reject the world as a form of temptation, Protestant asceticism encouraged believers to practice self-denial in the world. This led to an unprecedented asceticism in worldly acts which had previously been restricted to spiritual activity. Accordingly, Weber was able to identify two historical types of asceticism: otherworldly asceticism and innerworldly asceticism.[142] Both reject the world, but for different reasons. Otherworldly asceticism renounces the world because it presents temptation. Here, salvation is sought after by a path to the otherworldly through religious devotion and self-denial. Otherworldly asceticism requires formal withdrawal from the world, 'from social and psychological ties with the family, from the possession of worldly goods, and from political, economic, artistic, and erotic activities; in short, from all creaturely interests.'[143] Innerworldly asceticism, on the other hand, requires believers to focus their activities in the world, on the understanding that the world is the individual's 'responsibility and that they have the obligation to transform it in accordance with an ascetic ideal.'[144] In this view, confronting oneself with self-control is the basic way of being in the world. The innerworldly ascetics thus see the world in terms of a test – devised by God of their ability to resist temptation, in which each individual becomes an 'elect instrument of God' to perform good works on earth in a life of toil based on self-denial.

Innerworldly asceticism encouraged Protestants to practice self-denial in the world and to separate themselves from others in their own minds. Using this strategy of self-control to thwart salvation anxiety, Protestant believers could economize their energies in two related respects. First, they could conduct their lives so as to devote their energies to the rational order of work and the rational control of themselves. This would lead to a prudent scheduling of the work day and a judicious expenditure of time. Second, in their thoughts they could conduct their lives so as to devote their energies to God in the form of self-denial and to prove themselves worthy in the hope that it draws God's attention. Based on this reasoning, the believer assumes that personal worth springs from self-denial and

142 Ibid., pp. 541–4.
143 Ibid., p. 542.
144 Ibid., p. 542.

that self-denial brings redemption. This hope, combined with worldly asceticism and the focusing of one's energies toward work, creates the inner asceticism necessary for capitalist activity.

Weber thought he had established a third link. This was between the meaning of 'good works' and the feeling of righteousness. To do worldly work, Protestants had to summon up immense self-control and muster the conviction that work in any case would be to one's credit.[145] This brought about a complete transformation in the Catholic doctrine of 'salvation by works.'[146] In Catholic theology, 'salvation by works' was accepted if one lived an ethical life, at least on the whole. 'Good works' were calculated at the end of one's life rather than being seen as a succession of individual acts throughout one's entire life. In the Catholic view, as long as good works outweighed sins, salvation was generally believed to be assured. In contrast, Protestant doctrine required 'not single good works, but a life of good works combined into a unified system.' Weber maintained that the Protestant doctrine of salvation by works eliminated the more humanistic 'cycle of Catholic sin, repentance and atonement followed by more sin.'[147]

Weber maintained that this led Protestants to elevate to systematic pursuit a method of conduct designed to achieve an uninterrupted chain of good works. But this view meant only those who supervised their lives with continuous conscious alertness and internal vigilance could achieve such works. This, stated Weber, led to the development of a new kind of asceticism different from monastic withdrawal from the world. Instead of being directed to otherworldly pursuits, Protestant asceticism brought action under constant rational planning, self-control, and careful evaluation of consequences. Based as it was on the constant vigilance against worldly pleasure and enjoyment, Protestant asceticism had the consequence of bringing about a separation of the individual from two different levels of experience: first, it separated the individual from the world ethically since Protestants felt compelled to surpass worldly morality by pervading everyday life with self-control and discipline; and second, it separated the individual from the social community at large since social relations were 'penetrated with sharp brutality.'[148]

Asceticism, Capitalism and the Transformation of the 'Calling'

Next, Weber turned his attention to looking at the question of the 'calling' and its relation to capitalism. The concept of the 'calling' can be traced back to Catholic doctrine of the Middle Ages and essentially refers to being called to a 'life task' of serving God in a vocation by performing ethical acts of devotion. By the seventeenth century, the concept of the

145 Weber alludes to the idea of faith as being the theological precursor to the commerical concept of credit. See Weber, *The Protestant Ethic*, p. 115.

146 Ibid., p. 116.

147 Ibid., p. 117.

148 Ibid., p. 122.

'calling' had taken on a major role in reformation theology due to the influence of Luther. In Catholic theology after Luther, the concept of the 'calling' denoted service to God in the form of religious duties which were above those of the everyday secular world. Later, the term took on the exclusive meaning of renouncing the temporal world for monastic life. This was based on the idea that the temporal world of experience was valueless in relation to the spiritual world.

Weber pointed out that as soon as the concept of the 'calling' appears within Protestant theology, it takes on a new meaning. In contrast to Catholic theology, Protestants interpreted the 'calling' to signify service to worldly, rather than otherworldly duties. This, of course, had the effect of investing the temporal world with value. Weber highlighted the fact that, while Luther was the first to develop the significance of the concept of the 'calling' for church life, it was with Calvin that the concept began to undergo transformation. This occurred, Weber reasoned, as soon as the concept of 'activity in the world' became subject to Protestant scrutiny. In early church history, activity in the world was viewed as degrading and secular. But, because it was considered necessary to life, the church tended to view it as morally neutral. The theological point of departure came with the introduction of the Protestant doctrine of *sola fide*.[149] *Sola fide*, which essentially means practicing one's faith alone or in solitude, stood in sharp contrast to the Catholic concept of *consilia evangelica* whose equivalent is 'the church council.' The difference between the two concepts of faith and church life was dramatic. On the one hand, the Catholic attitude of *consilia evangelica* was that religious faith took place collectively and was communal in nature so far as it was related to others in the social and religious context of the church. On the other hand, the Protestant attitude was one of religious individualism and personal conscience, or *sola fide*. With the introduction of *sola fide*, the renunciation of everyday life for monastic withdrawal not only lost its significance as a vehicle of faith and moral purpose among Protestants, its personal justification as an act before God was diminished as well.[150] While Catholic thought defined faith as a withdrawal from the everyday world by emphasizing the other-worldly, Protestantism gave it a thoroughgoing worldly character.

Weber pointed out that the consequences of *sola fide* were clear. For the first time there was 'moral justification for worldly activity.'[151] This shift cannot be overestimated. Combined with worldly activity, Protestant asceticism provided an intense moral focus to transforming the world through labor and self-discipline. Combined with this, the Protestant concept of the 'calling' took on a second transformation in which there was a connection between worldly activity, asceticism, and a religious justification to action. In Weber's view, this represented the first systematic

---

149 Ibid., pp. 80–1.
150 Ibid., pp. 80–1.
151 Ibid., p. 80.

attempt to separate the two ethical domains – worldly and otherworldly – and to claim that one could be 'called' to worldly economical pursuits. Weber reasoned that the introduction of the 'calling' into everyday life and into commerce was completely novel. No religion had united the world of the spirit with the world of everyday life in this manner and, as a result, work became equivalent to virtue. In Weber's view, this 'gave everyday worldly activity a religious significance, and created the conception of a 'calling' to commercial activities.'[152]

Another related issue regarding the religious concept of 'calling' is the process whereby occupational pursuits – such as business and commercial activity – become transformed into an 'internal calling' which carries with it the strength of an inner conviction that one has been 'called to business.' The concept of the 'calling' thus indicates a transmission of ideas taking place between ethical and religious impulses in the outer world of daily life and impulses in the inner world of the conscience. The function of being 'called' to the commercial life must have been the psychological equivalent of being operated on by ethical and religious precepts in the form of an inner 'calling' which would serve as a substitute for righteousness and grace. In fact, the fulfillment of one's worldly duty became, in Weber's view, the only way Protestants could understand their actions as acceptable to God. The 'calling' of the individual was to fulfill his or her duty to God through the moral conduct of toil. In this scheme, toil became equivalent to a virtue. This brought dutiful pursuits and worldly activity center stage, and was the link between asceticism in economic activity as a worldly profession. Good Protestants who wanted to supervise their own state of grace in the world through self-control and self-regulation, were 'called' to commercial activity since work was seen as a secular method of attaining virtue and salvation. From this point of view, there could be no relaxation, no relief from toil because labor is an exercise in ascetic virtue, and rational behavior in a calling is taken as a sign of grace. For the Protestant, 'the most urgent task [became] the destruction of spontaneous, impulsive enjoyment.'[153]

Weber's Methodology and Theory of Knowledge in the Social Sciences

Between 1902 and 1903, Weber wrote a series of essays which were central to shaping his views about the nature and purpose of the social sciences. These writings are generally referred to as Weber's methodological works, and they deal specifically with issues regarding the nature of methodology and investigation in the social sciences. Two works stand out as being of central importance in the formation of Weber's methodological views. First is a work entitled *Roscher and Knies: The Logical Problems of*

152 Ibid., p. 80.
153 Ibid., p. 119.

Historical Economics written between 1902 and 1903, and second a work called 'Objectivity in Social Science and Social Policy,' written between 1903 and 1904.[154] In order to look more closely at these writings, we must review some of the issues and questions raised during the period leading up to Weber's involvement in the debates, issues that shaped his methodological thinking. The key issue at stake, according to Weber, was the development of the social sciences. This, Weber thought, would not be possible unless there was a distinction made between the methods of the social and the natural sciences. In order to understand completely some of the reasoning behind Weber's concern about the natural and social sciences, we have to look at the developments in philosophy and science taking place in Germany between 1880 and 1920.

Historical and Philosophic Background of Weber's Methodology

Between 1880 and 1900 there was spectacular growth in the natural sciences in Europe. Steady progress in experimental discoveries and technical advances led to an almost unrivaled dominance of the methodology of the natural sciences. Branches of knowledge such as physics, biology and chemistry had taken enormous strides forward, increasing their prestige in the scholarly community. As a result, the natural sciences had become pre-eminent in discovering certain truths about the natural world, and this led to the unparalleled authority of the investigative methods associated with the natural sciences. As these advances took place, the historical and philosophical sciences began to decline. The authority which philosophy had once held, in refereeing debates between science and theory and in explaining the nature of reality, began to slip and to lose its power. As a result, an open clash developed between the natural sciences and philosophical sciences, and this drew attention to the distinction between the methodologies of the natural and social sciences. Many began to criticize the non-scientific nature of the historical and social sciences such as economics, sociology and political economy, seeing them as largely speculative and intuitive in nature. By 1885, a general crisis had emerged in the legitimacy of historical sciences, and as a result many philosophers began to re-examine the relationship between science and philosophy.

By 1890, a movement based on a return to the work of Immanuel Kant emerged to resolve the problem. Referred to as Neo-Kantianism, the movement was based on a re-examination of the relationship between science and philosophy, and this called into question the foundations of scientific knowledge.[155] The term Neo-Kantian, then, is used to refer to a diverse group of scholars who participated in a philosophical movement in

154 Max Weber, *Roscher and Knies: The Logical Problems of Historical Economics* (trans. Guy Oakes), New York: The Free Press, 1975; M. Weber, 'Objectivity in Social Science and Social Policy,' in E.A. Shils and H. Finch (eds), *Max Weber: The Methodology of the Social Sciences*, New York: The Free Press, 1949, pp. 50–112.

155 Lewis White Beck, 'Neo-Kantianism,' *The Encyclopedia of Philosophy*, Vol. 5, pp. 468–73.

Germany in 'order to secure the legitimacy of the social and historical sciences. Many of the participants in the debates, such as Herman Helmholtz, F.A. Lange and Kuno Fischer, believed that a return to Kant would provide a solution to the problem facing the social and historical sciences.

Two of the central thinkers of the Neo-Kantian movement, Wilhelm Windelband and Heinrich Rickert, believed that two issues had to be pursued to resolve the problem: (i) the need to search for a theory of knowledge; and (ii) the necessity of defining the differences in subject matter between the natural and historical sciences. One of the first solutions to the dilemma of the natural and social sciences is to be found in the work of Wilhelm Windelband.[156]

Wilhelm Windelband's Criticism of the Natural Sciences

Wilhelm Windelband (1848–1915) was a German philosopher and historian. He taught philosophy at Freiburg and was a student of Kuno Fischer, a leading figure in the Neo-Kantian movement. Windelband is best known for applying Kantian philosophy to the historical sciences in a work which focused on philosophy and history entitled *A History of Philosophy*. In 1877, Windelband went to Freiburg where he began work on a writing which looked into the connection between philosophy and culture. At the time, many believed the historical description of society was impossible because history was neither a scientific discipline nor a science of laws. Windelband set himself the task of outlining a philosophic framework in terms of which historical investigation could be scientific and, in this, he attempted to liberate the concept of method from the natural sciences.

Windelband turned to Kant's writings to establish a philosophical justification for the historical sciences. The issue, for Windelband, was whether or not historical investigation could make a valid claim to objective knowledge. In reading Kant's works Windelband found that, while Kant had explicitly laid out the steps for the natural sciences to secure valid knowledge, he had excluded the historical and ethical dimensions of human action from the sphere of legitimate knowledge. According to Windelband, this act of exclusion had left out the realm of human historical and ethical motives which Windelband believed should be the subject of social and historical investigation.[157]

Windelband reasoned that it would be of central importance to devise a theory of knowledge that would be able to make valid claims about the existence of society and history, and thus withstand criticism from the natural sciences. Windelband had several issues to confront, however. First, by 1870 Hegel's idealist theory of history had been criticized and

---

156 See Hughes, *Consciousness and Society*.

157 T.E. Willey, *Back to Kant: The Revival of Kantianism in German Social and Historical Thought, 1860–1914*, Detroit: Wayne State University Press, 1978, pp. 26–8.

even discredited for its distinctly speculative theoretical stance. In addition, Hegel's method implied a split between the abstract sphere of the 'spirit' in history and the concrete factual world of historical circumstance. Windelband knew that, in separating the sphere of the spirit from the world of concrete reality, idealist philosophy had abandoned any hope of explaining perceptible historical facts. This meant that the formulation of any causal laws of history would be impossible. In rejecting Hegel's historical methods as speculative and intuitive, Windelband returned to Kant to find a scientific justification for the historical sciences. But, in reading Kant, Windelband came up against Kant's exclusion of history and human ethical pursuits from the sphere of valid knowledge – pursuits which Kant had relegated to the realm of belief. Windelband argued that Kant had erred in excluding the ethical world and the world of human intention from the domain of factual knowledge, reasoning that if Kant's exclusion of human ethical action were valid, only the natural sciences would be the bearers of legitimate knowledge.

Windelband went on to reason that the natural and social sciences were separate and distinct, and varied in ways which could easily be simplified. From this simplification, he set out to produce a synthesis between Kant's world of knowledge and the world of belief. In 1894 Windelband gave an address at the University of Strasbourg where, for the first time, he outlined a viable methodological distinction between the methodology of the natural and the historical sciences. Some commentators view the speech as so pivotal for the *Methodenstreit* debate that it amounted to 'a declaration of war against positivism.'[158] Windelband took the position that the natural and social sciences are, in fact, two forms of knowledge which attempt to describe two different levels of reality. In the first of these, there is knowledge of facts and of the observable world in which causes and laws can be found in concrete reality. This level of reality is the realm of the natural sciences. In the second, reasoned Windelband, there is knowledge of values and ethics, and this implies knowledge of an ethical realm consisting of the products of human culture – including the pursuits of actors and the judgments which they make in relation to the social world in which they live and act. This level of reality is the domain of the historical and social sciences. Windelband went on to reason that in the first sphere judgments are in relation to facts and observation. In the second sphere, however, judgments are related to theory, which alone is capable of grasping those objects which are not directly subject to observation – such as human values, motive, purpose, morality etc.[159] History, argued Windelband, has its proper subject matter in the values of universal validity which are the organizing principles of culture and civilization. In claiming this, Windelband made the leap from the natural sciences by looking at social and historical values, not in terms of facts but

158 Hughes, *Consciousness and Society*, p. 47.
159 Ibid., p. 47.

as norms of conduct.[160] While the natural sciences investigate concrete facts about the physical world which are unchanging, the historical sciences investigate norms or standards of conduct which may change from society to society depending on what ends are valued and pursued by historical actors.

Next, Windelband focused his attention on the question of method. He thought that the scientific disciplines are distinct from the social and historical sciences not because of their different subject matters but because of their different methodologies. Essentially, he reasoned that there are two kinds of methodological approaches that are distinct from each other. First is that of the natural sciences, which aims at the production of general laws and explains events by observation and by deductive methods – showing that empirical reality conforms to the assumptions which theory makes about the structure of the physical world. In this case, theory looks for confirmation in reality and thus believes that reality conforms to it. This, stated Windelband, leads to what he called the generalizing tendency in the sciences, where the search for commonalities in the concrete world tends to overlook what is individual and unique about particular events.[161] Second is the methodology of the historical and social sciences, the aim of which is to focus on individual events in order to determine their formative characteristics by deriving a picture of what took place. In this case, the historical sciences must adopt methods which are inductive – that is, methods based on observation and information gathered about the event, after which concepts and theories are formed to explain it. Windelband thought that the natural sciences are thus 'nomothetic' or law-giving in their methods and orientations, and this, he thought, makes them generalizing in the way they treat reality.[162] The historical sciences, by contrast, are 'ideographic' in their orientation; that is, they assemble information about events in order to arrive at a picture of the whole. The nomothetic sciences aim at constructing general laws and explain individual events by identifying events as examples of laws; whereas the ideographic sciences look at the individual event to arrive at a general pattern. Windelband went on to argue that any given object could, in fact, be studied by either of these approaches and he took the position that a truer picture of the world could be obtained by using both kinds of method. 'Law and individual event,' he argued, 'remain together as the ultimate incommensurable limit of our representation of the world.'[163] This was equivalent to stating that both general and individual criteria constitute acceptable procedures for the social sciences.

Two essential directions emerged from the Neo-Kantian tradition of investigation: first, it presented a challenge to the authority of observation

160 Willey, *Back to Kant*, pp. 26–8.
161 Ibid., p. 154.
162 Beck, 'Neo-Kantianism,' p. 470.
163 Ibid., p. 470.

in scientific investigation by showing that human perception of the world involved judgment rather than mere sensation. In this view, knowledge was not the product of a straightforward observational encounter with the natural world, but was rather preceded by judgment. Second, it rejected the postulate that human action could be reduced to mechanistic motives of utility by asserting that judgment and value are predicates of human social acts.[164]

Heinrich Rickert and the Debate between the Natural and Social Sciences

A second major contribution to the dispute between the natural and social sciences was the work of Heinrich Rickert, a student of Windelband and a contemporary of Max Weber. Rickert was born in Danzig in 1863, and taught at Freiburg, where he developed a friendship with Weber. By 1896, Rickert replaced Windelband at Heidelberg, and it is here that Rickert made some of his most important contributions. He is best known for devising a method for making valid judgments about society and history. But, where Windelband had focused on the question of the different methodologies of the sciences, Rickert concentrated on both subject matter and method. Rickert believed that the natural and social sciences differed on at least four separate fronts: (i) in their theory of knowledge; (ii) on their generalizing and individualizing tendency; (iii) in their concept formation; and (iv) in their attitudes toward values as a viable subject matter of the social sciences.

(i) Rickert's central work on the theory of knowledge and methodology, *The Limits of Concept Formation in the Natural Sciences*, was published in 1896. In this work, Rickert put forward a theory of knowledge for the social and historical sciences that was valid on both logical and methodological grounds. Rickert focused on devising a theory of knowledge for the social and historical sciences, concentrating on the question of subject matter.

He began by looking at how the natural sciences understood their relationship to empirical reality. By and large, he thought that the natural sciences took the view that knowledge was the result of a straightforward observational encounter with the natural world. From this perspective, knowledge was seen to be the accumulation of facts drawn from the physical world. But Rickert disagreed with this view in several respects. First, he thought that the natural sciences had an erroneous understanding of the procedures used to make sense of the empirical world. While it was widely held that the natural sciences obtained knowledge from the empirical world by forming opinions and drawing factual conclusions after observing nature, Rickert took the view that observation was a form of judgment and this placed judgment before knowing. In substance, Rickert

164 Willey, *Back to Kant*, 1978.

assumed that the act of judgment is, in fact, prior to the act of knowing. This step was central because Rickert could claim that physical reality had substance only through the act of human judgment. This, of, course, had the effect of diminishing the authority of observation in the acquisition of facts since, according to Rickert, observation is human judgment operating in the visible world. In this sense, observation was no longer the experience of the object as such, but simply the operation of human judgment. By making judgment prior to knowing, knowing itself became a kind of valuing – and this gave knowledge and judgment a basis in the empirical world. Rickert's formula was: first we judge and then we know.[165] From this perspective, then, Rickert put forward a theory of knowledge which held that objects exist in the external world only through human processes of judging and valuing. This led to the view that facts themselves were things represented by judgment and thus involved interpretation of some kind.

Rickert went on to reason that the characteristics of history and reality were thus made up of human valuing and judging. He asserted that since the elements of reality comprising human judgment cannot ever be grasped by the generalizing, law-giving perspective of the natural sciences, a new method had to be devised to capture the products of human acts. From this position, Rickert argued that history rather than physics was the true science of reality.[166]

(ii) Next, Rickert went on to look for a justification of historical and social subject matter. Here, he began to focus on the distinction between the natural and social sciences regarding method and methodological approach to subject matter. He took the view that whereas the natural sciences dealt with types of subject matter whose events were recurring in nature and could be captured by laws, the historical sciences, by contrast, tended to explain what he called 'individual non-recurring events.'[167] This distinction, between 'lawfully recurring nature' and 'individualistic nature', pointed out something fundamental in respect to the methods used to explain concrete reality. Rickert stated that the natural sciences explain the empirical world by what he called a 'generalizing' methodology in contrast to the 'individualizing' methodology of the historical sciences. To understand fully his distinction, it will be helpful to look briefly at Rickert's conception of empirical reality.

By and large, Rickert maintained that the nature of empirical reality was such as to be inherently infinite and, in fact, so extensive in scope and nature that it would be impossible to 'know' in any complete or comprehensive way. He reasoned that, because reality was so 'fundamentally boundless,' no science could claim to describe the totality of subject matter, and the classification of subject matter in the sciences could never

---

165 Ibid., p. 143.
166 Robert Anchor, 'Heinrich Rickert,' *The Encyclopedia of Philosophy*, Vol. 7, pp. 192–4.
167 Ibid., pp. 192–4.

be complete.[168] He maintained that, in order to overcome the vastness of the empirical world, the natural sciences deal with the problem in two ways: first, they generalize by essentially focusing away from the mass of particulars in order to concentrate on 'wholes,' and in doing so look for common properties among individual phenomena. Second, they employ concepts in order to contend with large parts of the empirical world, and in so doing they bring as many particulars as possible under one precise descriptive term. Empirical reality, reasoned Rickert, is thus dealt with by the process of summary activity in which traits common to objects are found and are captured by procedures called concepts.[169] This process, thought Rickert, was essentially abstracting in that it classified individual objects under broad conceptual categories, thus abstracting from their individual character. In the end, only general features are retrieved under concepts, and individual phenomena are eliminated altogether. In addition, these concepts are related to a framework of regularities which yield general laws of nature.[170] The natural sciences, therefore, can be characterized as an infinitely extended process of abstraction that entirely overlooks the element of individuality. From this perspective, one of the major limitations of the methodology of the natural sciences is that it is given to a generalizing tendency that overlooks the existence of individual objects which are part of concrete reality. In showing that the natural sciences depend on a generalizing methodology, Rickert was able to point up a major deficiency in method.

(iii) On a third front, Rickert looked at the nature of concept formation in both the natural and historical sciences. He maintained that each employ concepts in different ways and this causes them to relate to reality differently. In order to understand Rickert's meaning, we must look at the nature of concepts. Concepts, first and foremost, are the means by which all sciences surmount the extensive nature of reality. Empirical reality simply cannot be dealt with except by organizing segments of it in terms of concepts which narrow down the phenomena of the natural world. But in the natural sciences, concepts are fundamentally reductive of empirical reality and in the last instance completely disqualify 'the element of individuality and can in fact be said to lead away from empirical reality' itself.[171] Concepts do this to the extent that they search for common features among individuals and constantly relate individual phenomena to a framework of generality. Thus, while concepts form reality into coherent wholes which can be grasped by the mind, they are also 'formative' of reality and in this sense represent it.[172] In the historical sciences, by contrast, concept formation attempts to relate as closely as possible to

168 H.H. Bruun, *Science, Values and Politics in Max Weber's Methodology*, Copenhagen: Munksgaard, 1972, p. 85.
169 Ibid., p. 85.
170 Ibid., p. 86.
171 Ibid., p. 86.
172 Burger, *Max Weber's Theory of Concept Formation*, p. 19.

reality and it does this, according to Rickert, by selecting individual phenomena. Selection of these phenomena is linked to the individual aspects of concrete reality and selection appropriates 'elements' of it rather than representing reality as such.

Next, Rickert turned his attention to showing that history qualifies as a science. Up to this point, the primary criterion of a science had been its claim to objective knowledge – that is, it makes observations about phenomena that can be confirmed by universal laws. With respect to the historical sciences, many had stated that history had no claim to being a science since it provides no account of the laws of historical development. According to this view, if history eludes laws, it can only mean that the foundations of its logic and method are unsettled. Without lawful assumptions, nothing can be explained and thus history has no scientific status. While it can furnish a description of facts, it cannot search for laws and thus its status as a science is unfounded.[173]

Rickert set out to solve the problem of objective knowledge by looking at what 'knowledge' is. The natural science view asserted that knowledge is the result of a straightforward encounter with nature and that visual sensations from the natural world are transferred directly to the mind in the form of facts. Rickert doubted this. He stated that knowledge is not the direct apprehension or grasp of nature, but could only be developed by means of concepts which select and abstract individual features from the whole. According to this view, the natural sciences form concepts by abstracting from the whole and, in doing so, eliminate individual features of the phenomenon under investigation. This method of abstraction underlies the law-giving nomothetic sciences. In addition, Rickert thought that concepts in the natural sciences shape reality by selecting out certain elements of the empirical world. In selecting only particular aspects of reality, we are not only exercising a physical grasp over it, but are making judgments about the nature of the things or objects examined. One of Rickert's insights was that scientific observation is informed by judgments and that, in fact, the sciences are concept forming since they cannot grasp reality directly but instead must conceptualize it by looking for common elements. In the process, however, individual phenomena are overlooked.

(iv) On the fourth front, Rickert turned his attention to showing that a description of society and history using the criteria and the methods of the natural sciences would be of no interest to anyone, and in fact that human beings could not act in a world described by the natural sciences.[174] If the world were made up of generalized phenomena, stated Rickert, the experience of concrete reality would contain no particulars and no individuals, only abstract general processes. The natural sciences thus produce a picture of reality which is made up of such simple elements that the empirical concreteness of the world disappears from experience.

173 Ibid., p. 21.
174 Ibid., p. 21.

According to Rickert, the sciences have thereby oversimplified concrete reality – so much so that an experience of it is not included as part of their description. As far as he was concerned, human experience cannot be lived out in a generalized tendency. Rickert stated that such a world would have no interest to human beings, and, in fact, what gives reality its interest is individual particulars. He reasoned that our relation to this individuality is through what he called 'values.'

Rickert's discussion of the role of values in the description of society highlights a central distinction between the natural and historical sciences. Rickert believed that a unique characteristic of the human historical world is that it reflects 'values.' Human action, Rickert asserted, is guided by practical valuation and this points up the fact that an individual living in society during a historical time and place is always value oriented in some way, and this value orientation always leads to judgments and evaluations with respect to society and the world. Human beings, according to this view, act in relation to ends which they value. In contrast to the social world, things in the natural world do not act with respect to values. In fact, objects of the natural sciences are things which act in reference to the laws of nature; the objects of the historical and social world are things which act in reference to valued social ends. Examples of these values, according to Rickert, are laws, customs, language, economy and religion. Rickert went on to reason that social institutions embody these values, and human beings recognize them and act in relation to ends which they value. From this position emerged a fundamental distinction between the sciences of value and the sciences of fact. In sciences of fact, values are irrelevant because they do not enter into the laws of nature. But the sciences of value, such as history and social sciences, must concern themselves with human beings who, unlike natural phenomena, live in societies and engage in activities which compel them to act in reference to ends which are valued. Hence, the products of their actions always reflect values.[175]

To summarize: human beings are value-conferring by nature. Rickert thought that the products of nature were thus devoid of values, whereas the products of human society are value-relevant – that is to say, they always embody values. Products of society, according to this view, are always unique because they have been valued by conscious knowing subjects. 'The presence or absence of values,' Rickert reasoned, 'thus must serve as a reliable criterion for distinguishing between two kinds of scientific objects' and two kinds of science.[176] The first set of objects are those belonging to the natural world and these exist independently of human agency and have a life, or lawfulness, of their own. A second set of objects, however, are the objects of the social and cultural world. These are produced directly by human agents acting in relation to valued ends.

---

175 Ibid., pp. 36–7.
176 Heinrich Rickert, *Science and History: A Critique of Postivist Epistemology* (trans. George Reisman), Princeton: D. Van Nostrand, 1962, pp. 18–19.

These objects belong to a social realm so far as they are produced by human beings acting on the basis of what is valued.

The Methodenstreit *of the 1880s: Controversy over Method*

During the latter part of the 1890s, Weber turned his attention to resolving theoretical issues in the social sciences and to responding to arguments which challenged the validity of the social sciences. In order completely to understand the direction that Weber took in his methodology, we must turn our attention to the historical context of the *Methodenstreit*.[177] *Methodenstreit*, is a German term referring to a methodological controversy which emerged out of the framework of German social thought in the last quarter of the nineteenth century.[178] The central issues of the *Methodenstreit* originated in the conflict over which methods were appropriate to the social sciences. The *Methodenstreit* involved three points of disagreement: the subject matter of the social sciences, the investigative methods pursued in the social sciences, and the purpose or aim of the social sciences.[179]

First and foremost, the controversy began to take shape in the 1880s and was largely centered on the University of Heidelberg, primarily in economics. The dispute focused on whether historical economics could, in fact, be considered a valid science of society. The dispute reached its peak when Gustav Schmoller, the foremost proponent of the historical school of economics, reviewed a work by Carl Menger, the leading advocate of the classical school.[180] Menger, in his work, had asserted that if economics was to be a science, its purpose would have to be to discover laws of society and to do this it must be generalizing in its methodology, since only a generalizing science is able to draw conclusions about the laws governing economic behavior. For economics to be a science, according to this view, social life must be subject to the laws of nature and investigated using the methods of the natural sciences. Menger found support for his contention in the work of John Stuart Mill whose utilitarian doctrine took the position that all human economic acts could be reduced to motives of utility and self-interest. According to Menger, this meant that all human action was reducible to the simple motive of economic exchange.

Schmoller, in his review of Menger's argument, criticized his thesis as being a short-sighted scientific view of human action and proceeded to call into question the philosophical foundations of scientific methodology

---

177 For a discussion of the *Methodenstreit* of the 1880s see Burger, *Max Weber's Theory of Concept Formation*, pp. 140–53.

178 For a good general discussion of the *Methodenstreit*, see Dirk Kasler, *Max Weber: An Introduction to his Life and Work*, Chicago: University of Chicago Press, 1988, pp. 174–96; and Burger, *Max Weber's Theory of Concept Formation*, pp. 140–53.

179 Hughes, *Consciousness and Society*, pp. 296–314.

180 Ibid., pp. 303–4; Toby E. Huff, *Max Weber and the Methodology of the Social Sciences*, London: Transaction, 1984, pp. 27–42.

itself.[181] Schmoller believed that a new method had to be devised for the social sciences which would take into account the historical character of social phenomena. Along with other members of the historical school, Schmoller took the position that, because societies tend to develop in historical stages and are fundamentally different from one another in their social forms, a generalizing methodology in search of causal laws would not be able to take individual differences between societies into account, let alone capture the complex nature of social action represented in economic behavior. Taking these issues into consideration, we find that there are five key points of disagreement between the classical and historical schools. First, the historical school believed that the generalizing methodology of the natural sciences could not explain the complex social nature of economic interchange since it made no distinction between the natural and social world.[182] Second, Schmoller and his colleagues took the view that causal statements about social phenomena were out of the question because science had not yet recognized that societies were products of human social action. According to Schmoller, before economic theory could discover general laws about society it had to be made historical, and this involved a shift from the natural to the social world. Once this shift is undertaken, laws could be obtained in an inductive fashion after detailed observation of human behavior in society. Third, so far as a generalizing methodology looks for laws, it overlooks non-recurring individual phenomena. According to Schmoller, because each society is unique, concepts must accommodate the individualizing character of human social action and the different social values which act as motives of social action. It was Schmoller's view that societies were the result of historical development, and that the nature of social behavior could only be grasped by a theory which understood that societies develop in relation to human agents acting on the basis of what is valued.[183] This brought values and ethics into the picture, since values were seen to be a product of human social action. Fourth was the issue centering on the question of human motives and behavior. Menger's law-giving position asserted that all human behavior was the same and could be reduced to the pursuit of rational self-interest and utility. This led to the view that all individual acts have as their basis a rational economic motive which may be studied by science. The historical school disagreed, stating that no single rational motive underlies human action since it is bound up with various political, religious and social beliefs – many of which are irrational in nature. The fifth issue separating the historical school from the classical tradition of economics was the view that because economics is an 'objective' science, its purpose is to search for underlying laws that are subject to observation. In direct opposition to this, the historical school

181 Hughes, *Consciousness and Society*, p. 30.
182 Ibid., p. 30.
183 Bruun, *Science, Values and Politics*, p. 85.

asserted that because social and economic life involves human beings acting on the basis of what they value, economics is a science which has to take into account the 'subjective' basis of human values and the relation of values to the realm of ethical conduct.

Weber's Contribution to the Methodenstreit: Concept Formation, Values and Social Science

While the *Methodenstreit* debate in economics eventually diminished, Weber took up some of the issues raised by Menger and Schmoller in order to develop his own methodological position. Between 1903 and 1906, Weber wrote a series of essays underlining problems in the *Methodenstreit* debate.[184] His response is confined to two writings in particular. First is an essay written in 1903, entitled 'Objectivity in Social Science and Social Policy.'[185] Second is a work entitled *Roscher and Knies: The Logical Problems of Historical Economics.*[186]

In his discussion of *Roscher and Knies*, both of whom were economic historians, Weber turned his attention to methodological questions. He attempted to outline the methodological foundations of the social sciences by showing how they were different from other disciplines, including the natural sciences. In this work, Weber took five important steps beyond the controversies of the *Methodenstreit*. First, he wanted to demonstrate that a search for law-like regularities was not possible in the social sciences. Second, he wanted to show that the phenomena studied by the social sciences have definite properties which mark them off from other disciplines and that this difference rules out the possibility of establishing a natural science of society. Third, he wanted to demonstrate that the subject matter of the social sciences was made up of individuals whose social action was based on values. This led Weber to assert that the social sciences must begin the process of understanding how these values act as a basis of social action. Fourth, Weber sought to demonstrate that in all the disciplines, including the natural sciences, the facts never speak for themselves – that is, they neither identify themselves nor how they fit into the scheme of description, since this requires interpretation.[187] In Weber's view, no science, not even the natural sciences, is fundamentally neutral and its observation language is never theoretically independent of the way individuals see the phenomena and the questions they ask about them.[188] Fifth, Weber went on to show that the social sciences must arrive at a methodology which encompasses both general and individual aspects of historical reality, a procedure he referred to as the 'ideal type.' Let us look more closely at these issues.

184 For a discussion of the *Methodenstreit* debate focusing on epistemological questions, see S. Hekman, *Weber, the Ideal Type and Contemporary Social Theory*, pp. 18–27.

185 Weber, 'Objectivity,' 1949.

186 Weber, *Roscher and Knies*.

187 Guy Oakes, 'Introductory Essay,' in ibid., pp. 19–37.

188 Ibid., pp. 19–37.

In *Roscher and Knies*, Weber first turned his attention toward the question of subject matter and considered the social sciences in relation to the natural sciences. In order to understand how Weber resolves some of the problems of the *Methodenstreit*, we have to go back to Rickert and a concept used by Rickert called 'value relevance.'[189] Essentially, Weber drew on Rickert's discussion of value relevance and, therefore, our understanding of the term hinges on Rickert's theory of knowledge in the historical sciences.

In contrast to the view held by scholars in the field of the natural sciences, Rickert believed that knowledge of the empirical world does not derive from observation and sense perception because, he insisted, judgment always precedes the act of observation. Rickert thought that because knowing is preceded by judgment and judgment is a form of selection, knowing itself was seen as a kind of valuing and this meant that knowledge itself had a basis in human values. If, as Rickert reasoned, all knowing has a basis in values and values derive from the social historical context, then our interest in and knowledge of scientific objects must derive from our relation to values. If this is true, what was the reasoning behind Rickert's assertion?

In his theory of knowledge, Rickert treated as a problem the idea that empirical reality presents itself as an 'infinite multiplicity' of events and objects.[190] If there is to be knowledge of the empirical world, he stated, then this infinite multiplicity has to be overcome in some way. According to Rickert, the scientific observer overcomes the problem of the infinite array of objects in the empirical world by a process of selection that narrows empirical reality to manageable elements. This process, Rickert thought, was carried out by means of concept formation, since concepts act in such as way as to frame empirical reality and 'reduce the mass of facts in the empirical world.'[191] 'Without concepts,' therefore, 'knowledge of the empirical world would be impossible.'[192] Rickert went on to reason that concept formation was essential to scientific activity since any judgment about reality was impossible without concepts.

Rickert went on to focus his attention on the process of selection and the criteria by which a phenomenon comes to the attention of the observer. He reasoned that when something is isolated as worthy of attention, this attention is not the property of the object but must instead point to the observer's process of selection. There are, according to Rickert, two main principles of selection.[193] The first concerns a criterion of selection which searches for properties common to all phenomena. In this principle, what is essential are the common properties of the object

189 Burger, *Max Weber's Theory of Concept Formation*, pp. 37–43.
190 Ibid., p. 21.
191 Ibid., p. 21.
192 Rickert, quoted from ibid., p. 21.
193 Burger, *Max Weber's Theory of Concept Formation*, p. 22.

and, subsequently, what is individual is left out of analysis or set aside. The second principle of selection referred to by Rickert, is a criterion which selects individual phenomena. This principle selects individual objects which are unique to the extent that they can be distinguished from other objects and have properties which are not common to other phenomena.

The first set of methods and principles of selection leads to 'general concepts' and is a practice common to the natural sciences. The second set of methods and principles leads to 'historical individuals' which are key to describing unique historical configurations such as capitalism, feudalism or charismatic domination.[194] General concepts provide objective knowledge, whereas individual concepts provide knowledge of specific features of social and historical events. Since concept formation is a means by which objects are singled out from empirical reality, Rickert thought that value relevance operates in both cases as the standard against which a selection is made. 'Every individual,' wrote Rickert, 'is guided by a conception of the world by which they separate everything existing into essential and inessential.'[195] Hence describing and observing is impossible without valuing what is of interest and, in this sense, selection always embodies cultural values.

Rickert went on to suggest that the objects of empirical reality must be of interest to us only because they are value relevant, not because they have intrinsic scientific merit. In fact, what interests us must be a part of the universal values of society, originating in society and the social context within which the individual lives and shares with others. Here, then, is the point of Rickert's reasoning: the principle by means of which specific aspects of reality are brought to our attention is the principle of value relevance. Rickert thought that the principle of value relevance comes into play when scientists use concepts, since it is by means of concepts that we are able to reduce the mass of facts in the empirical world. Without concept formation, there is no understanding; thus concepts act as a means of separating the essential from the inessential. Hence the historical sciences are dependent upon the process of selection from empirical reality in order to arrive at their subject matter.

As far as Rickert was concerned, the operation of selection was central to the investigative process. He thought that the criteria of selection in the natural and social sciences were essentially the same since each pursue aspects of empirical reality by separating out elements which are essential from those which are inessential. Considered in this light, an 'interest' always reflects its origin in the value framework of the society and the ongoing social and historical scheme contemporaneous with the lives of others.

194 Ibid., p. 22.
195 Rickert quoted from ibid., p. 35.

This orientation to values became the center of Rickert's theory of history. Essentially, by value relation Rickert was referring to the fact that individuals live their lives within the context of a historical age which is marked by an orientation to specific values. 'A person who is really living is by definition value oriented in the sense that they are judging and evaluating the surrounding world. Thus defined, human beings cannot be interested solely in the general regularities of life, but must to a certain extent pay attention to things in their individual aspect and this individual aspect constitutes reality as such.'[196] The historian thus selects material by means of a value relation; that is, by means of criteria of values that are in part based on the phenomenon's relation to a system of values in a wider society that is shared in common by others. Simply stated, the value relation refers to the idea that a certain phenomenon is 'worthy of interest' on the basis of the scheme of values current in society.[197]

To summarize: using the criterion of value relevance, Rickert could claim that 'knowledge was not the grasp, so much as the construction of the object.'[198] Viewed in these terms, the value relation and value relevance became a form of constituting reality. This was important because the entire scope of scientific thinking was governed by a relation to values.

Ideal Types

It is not surprising that Weber's ideal type construction is premised on Rickert's theory of concept formation. Initially, the ideal type was first put forward by Weber in 'Objectivity in Social Science and Social Policy,' which he published in 1905.[199] As a methodological construction, the ideal type is neither a typology in the conventional sociological sense of the term, nor a dichotomous list of contrasting elements. Neither is it a list of comparative characteristics. Rather, Weber defines the ideal type as a 'conceptual pattern which brings together certain relationships and events of historical life into a complex which is conceived of as an internally consistent system.'[200]

Historical ideal types are the main category of type formation. These may be described as ideal types which are formed by selecting out general concepts common to a range of phenomena. Historical ideal types form concepts by selecting phenomena on the basis of common characteristics and employ a criterion of selection of only those general concepts 'which are precisely and unambiguously definable, such as individualism, feudalism' and capitalism.[201] In this sense, the ideal type is designed to capture features of empirical reality by arriving at what Weber referred to as the

196 Bruun, *Science, Values and Politics*, pp. 88–9.
197 Ibid., pp. 88–9.
198 Willey, *Back To Kant*, p. 37.
199 Weber, 'Objectivity,' pp. 50–112.
200 Ibid., p. 90.
201 Ibid., p. 92.

'analytical accentuation' of certain aspects of social historical reality. For example, when we attempt to understand the development of a city economy, asserted Weber, we compare a craft-based economy with a capitalistic city economy. When we engage in these ideal type operations we 'construct a concept of a city economy' and thus get closer to it.[202] In this sense, an ideal type is a 'picture of events' which approximates the reality of a given society under certain conditions of its organization.[203] For instance, we can take the concept of a 'city economy' and construct a type. The general concept, 'city economy,' thus lends itself to type construction by an extraction of traits. The essential traits of a city economy may include such elements as a system of law based on statutes, decline of magic and a system of private property. Other traits related to a city economy may include the concept of a citizen, a municipal organization and a bureaucracy created by political office holders. All this may presuppose a municipal environment with a civil life which is distinctive of a 'city economy' in Western society, and this stands in contrast to the city economy of the Greek city states.[204]

Though the type 'city economy' has been abstracted from concrete reality, we are able to formulate the concept of a city economy only by isolating what is essential from what is inessential. The ideal type does not serve as a description of concrete historical reality, but is a construct used to elucidate the features of historical reality. This is done by extracting essential 'traits' which elaborate concepts by comparing them with concrete phenomena. These traits are then compared to an ideal picture of social reality and from this a workable type is formed. The type is created by providing a 'one-sided accentuation of one or more points of view and by the synthesis of a great many diffuse, discrete, concrete individual phenomena arranged according to a one-sided emphasis into a unified analytical construct.'[205] When applied to reality, ideal types are useful in research and exposition. It functions, according to Weber, by arranging certain traits actually found in society in an unclear and even confused state, and develops these into a consistent ideal construct by an elucidation of their essential elements.

Another category of ideal types which Weber looked at are those which can be used to form an 'ideal picture of a shift' occurring in society by reason of certain historical factors.[206] This is carried out, stated Weber, by introducing a 'developmental sequence' into a type construction in order to capture the shift taking place and the conditions leading to it. Developmental sequences introduced into types lead in the direction of theoretical conclusions about the prevailing conditions of society. When a

202 Ibid., p. 90.
203 Ibid., p. 90.
204 Weber, *General Economic History*, p. 238.
205 Weber, 'Objectivity,' p. 90.
206 Ibid., p. 101.

'developmental sequence is constructed into the type' it gives rise to considerable 'heuristic value.'[207] An example of this kind of type construction can be found in Weber's comparison of the shift from a system of administration by notables to a modern system of bureaucratic administration. This type is constructed by forming the general concept of administration by notables and by isolating common elements such as their means of legitimacy, type of administration, degree of calculation in decisions, and the characteristics of a system of law. The 'shift' from such a system to a modern bureaucratic administration may be conditioned by specific factors such as a system of legal authority, the dominance of formal rationality, a hierarchy of offices and decision makers, and a reliance upon written documentation and record keeping. All this pre-supposes the 'rationalization of the conduct of life,' and the adherence to patterns of social action oriented to social rules. In this case, the type offers an 'ideal picture of the shift' from a patriarchal form of admin-istration to a modern bureaucratic type.[208]

A second criterion of ideal type construction is a capacity to draw connections and interrelations between divergent condensed elements. In this respect, it functions as a shorthand medium of concept formation, the goal of which is to extract the essential elements and formulate the type. The purpose of the ideal type, in this sense, is that it constructs rather than describes historical types and 'the construct here is no more than the means of explicitly and validly imputing an historical event to its real cause while eliminating those which on the basis of present knowledge seem impossible.'[209] The most common are economic ideal types. These function to differentiate societies in terms of their economic systems by comparing characteristics that are associated with the historical systems of production. One example might be the formulation of a capitalist economy.[210] To illustrate the general concept of 'modern capitalism,' for example, certain traits may be included such as a market, a system of rationality, a method of producing an exact balance rather than making estimates, a legal system, the concept of the citizen, and a framework of social action based on earning profits. These elements are added progressively, by selecting what is essential from what is inessential and by comparing these elements with other economic systems in other historical contexts.

The goal of the ideal type is to make explicit both the general and individual characteristics of empirical reality. Here, Weber is reliant on Windelband's nomothetic–ideographic distinction and the generalizing–individualizing distinction of Rickert. Under these circumstances, the goal of the ideal type is to 'frame out' the empirical characteristics of reality

207 Ibid., p. 101.
208 Ibid., p. 101.
209 Ibid., p. 102.
210 Ibid., p. 101.

while at the same time retaining the focus on historical individuals. Weber, like Rickert, knew that empirical reality could not be described in any complete factual sense, but he did believe it could be 'framed out' by means of criteria of selection. At the outer limits of the frame are generalizing concepts such as capitalism, feudalism or a city economy. At the inner limits of the frame, there can be a reference to subjective meaning. Weber referred to the subjective meaning of individuals in three ways: in relation to (i) values, (ii) types of social action, and (iii) types of rationality.

According to Weber, the ideal type serves several distinct investigative purposes. First, it can discover relationships of the types referred to in concrete reality by seeing if the types actually exist in reality and whether their characteristics can be made clear and understandable.[211] Second, it is indispensable for heuristic and expository purposes since it helps develop an understanding of the kinds of activities which can be assigned to different societies during research. Third, while it is not a hypothesis, it offers constructive help in forming hypotheses.[212] Fourth, while an ideal type is not a description of reality, it can assist in reducing ambiguity about empirical reality by providing the means to foster adequate descriptions of it. Fifth, the ideal type leads to the formation of concepts about societies by holding ideas of historically given types of societies within its conceptual understanding of reality.

Weber's Theory of Social Action

Weber first developed his theory of social action in *Economy and Society*, which he wrote between 1911 and 1920. The term 'social action' derives from the body of Weber's work which concerned itself with developing a theory for making valid judgments about the decisions individuals make in their actions with others in a social environment. The theory of social action proposed by Weber eventually embraced the question of 'meaningful' social action and attempted to incorporate the relevance of values in a theory of human action. Because Weber's theory of action is the product of the *Methodenstreit*, it will be useful to summarize some of the points of disagreement Weber had regarding the distinction between the natural and social sciences which led to him to put forward a theory of social action.

Weber's comparison of the natural and social sciences focused on three distinct issues. First he stated that the subject matter studied by the two sciences was distinctly different. The natural sciences study physical and natural events, while the social sciences study human social action. Second, each seeks to obtain different kinds of knowledge. In the natural sciences, knowledge is of the external world which can be explained in terms of valid laws. In the social sciences, knowledge must be 'internal' or

211 Ibid., p. 90.
212 Ibid., p. 90.

'subjective' in the sense that human beings have an inner nature that must be understood in order to explain outward events. Third, investigations in the natural and social sciences take up different orientations and attitudes to their subject matter. In the natural sciences it is sufficient to observe events in the natural world and to report relationships between things observed. In the social sciences, however, investigations must go beyond observation to look at how individuals act on their understanding, and how this 'understanding' may be related to their social action.[213]

Working from Rickert's methodological innovations, Weber made two fundamental assertions: first, that sociology must concern itself with the interpretation of social action; and second, that it must devise a social theory of values since the acts of valuing and judging are a precondition of social action. Weber's theory of social action may then be defined as that body of social theory devised by him in order to make valid judgments about the 'inner states' of actors in their actions. By 'inner states' Weber was referring to the capacity of the actor to choose between the means and ends of action and to exercise 'rational' choice. He believed that individuals act in, and come to understand, the social world only through these rational acts. At the most fundamental level, this involves the process of assigning 'meanings' to the given factual states in the outer world and thus involves subjective processes. Weber reasoned that because these meanings do not already come 'attached' to experience, they must be products of the meaning states of actors. Weber's theory of social action involves four central concepts: (i) the concept of understanding or *Verstehen*; (ii) the concept of interpretive understanding; (iii) the concept of subjective meaning; and (iv) the concept of social action.

Let us begin by looking at Weber's central thesis which is put forward in *Economy and Society*. Weber stated:

> Sociology is a science which attempts the interpretive understanding of social action in order to arrive at a causal explanation of its course and effects. In action is included all human behavior when and insofar as the acting individual attaches a subjective meaning to it. Action in this sense may be either overt or purely inward or subjective; it may consist of positive intervention in a situation or of deliberately refraining from such intervention or passively acquiescing in the situation. Action is social insofar as, by virtue of the subjective meaning attached to it by the acting individual, it takes account of the behavior of others and is thereby oriented in its course.[214]

Social action, for Weber, can be defined as occurring 'when the acting individual attaches a subjective meaning to an act and when it takes account of the behavior of others and is thereby oriented in its course.'[215] What is central to Weber's discussion of social action is the idea of

213 The most developed discussion of Weber's theory of social action can be found in Weber, *Economy and Society*, pp. 3–26.
   214 Ibid., p. 4.
   215 Ibid., p. 4.

'interpretive understanding' and this takes us directly to the concept of *Verstehen*.

In methodological works written between 1903 and 1906, Weber claimed that the social sciences were essentially 'subjectifying' in the sense that they concerned themselves with the 'inner states' of actors in contrast to the sciences of objective fact which concerned themselves with the 'outer states' of the natural world.[216] 'History and other "subjectifying" sciences,' stated Weber, 'have as their object a variety of things which in principle are different from the objects of the sciences like physics, chemistry, biology.'[217] What sets the subject matter of social sciences apart from the subject matter of the natural sciences, according to Weber, is that human beings have 'inner states' in terms of which they 'understand' the events of the world in which they act. Because of this 'understanding,' Weber reasoned, 'individual human conduct is in principle' distinct from a 'natural event,' such as, for example, the movement of cells within the body.[218] This distinction refers precisely to the fact that human individuals 'understand' the actions of others and depend on this understanding in order to act. This suggests that their actions involve 'meaningful interpretations,' whereas the actions of the 'cells' are not based on the 'understanding' of their acts. Weber used the term 'understanding' or *Verstehen* to identify this difference in subject matter between the social and natural sciences.

Literally the term *Verstehen* translates as 'human understanding,' and Weber used it to signify what was unique about the subject matter of the social sciences. In Weber's view, the social sciences are concerned with the actions of human beings that presuppose they have an 'inner state' in which they constantly make judgments and evaluations that lead them to understand and interpret their environments. In direct opposition to this is the subject matter of the natural sciences. Since the subject matter of the natural sciences does not possess 'understanding' – *Verstehen* – it stands to reason that the methods employed in the natural sciences must be disqualified or ruled out as inadequate to the study of human social action. Weber drew the conclusion that any form of investigation which reduced human action to its simple external characteristics would be meaningless since it would not capture human interpretive understanding. 'If human conduct cannot be interpreted in this way, it is no different from the fall of a boulder from the cliff.'[219]

As we stated earlier, the term *Verstehen* translates from the German as 'human understanding'.[220] But what exactly was the role of 'understanding' in the social sciences? Weber believed that the job of the social

216 Weber, *Roscher and Knies*, pp. 129–30.
217 Ibid., pp. 129–30.
218 Ibid., p. 125.
219 Ibid., p. 125.
220 Guy Oakes, 'The *Verstehen* Thesis and the Foundations of Max Weber's Methodology,' *History and Theory*, 16, 1977, 11–29.

sciences was to examine the processes related to 'meaning' or 'under-standing' in society. He thought that the central distinction regarding the subject matter of the social sciences was the human capacity for 'meaningful acts.' Human beings in contrast to the objects of nature always rely on their 'understanding' of each other's actions and on the 'meanings' they assign to what they and others do. However precise or logical the natural sciences, their subject matter always confines itself to the study of external characteristics of things which have no 'under-standing' as such.[221] This fundamental distinction between the 'inner states' of human actors and the 'outer states' of the natural world led Weber to assert that the subject matters studied by the natural and the social sciences were fundamentally different. The basic presupposition is that physical phenomena do not have 'understanding;' only human beings make judgments and evaluations which lead them to interpret their environments. This led Weber to assert that social phenomena are identified not by their external characteristics but by their dependence on 'understanding' or *Verstehen*.

Two Types of Understanding: Weber's Interpretive Sociology

A second concept in Weber's theory of social action is 'interpretive understanding.' Weber discusses interpretive understanding in *Economy and Society* where he makes the distinction between two types of under-standing: direct and explanatory or interpretive understanding.[222]

(i) Direct understanding, according to Weber, comprehends an action by virtue of the physical characteristics of the act and by focusing attention to what is going on in the external world. In this instance, the meaning of the act is discernible from 'direct observation' of the physical characteristics of the act.[223] As such, direct understanding relies on observation to obtain the meaning of an act and confirm what has taken place. Weber would say that direct understanding refers to the means by which individuals confirm actions in the world through observation. A home run in baseball, for instance, can be directly understood by the sequence of physical occur-rences, such as the hit and tour of bases. An example Weber used to illustrate direct understanding is the formula $2 \times 2 = 4$. This, he stated, involves direct understanding 'when we hear or read it.'[224] Another example used by Weber is that of chopping wood or an outburst of anger. These actions can be grasped by their visible characteristics and we may discern directly what is going on.

(ii) Explanatory understanding, by contrast, understands the meaning of an act only by placing the action in a complex of meaning and by attaching a motive to the act – chopping wood to sell in the market or

221 Burger, *Max Weber's Theory of Concept Formation*, pp. 102–15.
222 Weber, *Economy and Society*, pp. 8–12.
223 Ibid., pp. 8–12.
224 Ibid., pp. 8–12.

writing the expression 2 × 2 = 4 in a scientific demonstration. Explanatory understanding places the act within a context and assigns a motive to it. While explanatory understanding apprehends an action by its physical characteristics, what makes it different from direct understanding is the actor's attempt to lodge it in a complex of meaning in order to provide a motive. Thus, whereas direct understanding grasps the physical characteristics of an act, explanatory or motive understanding constructs reasons and assigns motives. This type of understanding entails contextualizing the action in order to discern a motive, for example, chopping wood to burn in the fireplace or sell in the market, etc. Motive understanding, in contrast to the understanding of direct observation, differs by virtue of the fact that it is able to 'place the act' within a context of motivation and to this extent is interpretive.[225]

Inasmuch as explanatory understanding is a form of social action which engages in judgments about motives, Weber believed that it takes place within the 'inner states' of the actor. Weber called this 'subjective meaning' in order to denote that it occurs in the actor's inner state and therefore out of range of the observation of others. Along with understanding external patterns of events, motive meaning makes assumptions about the inner states of the actor. For Weber this involves interpretative activity since the meaning of an act is obtained only in the light of judgments about the varieties of motives sustainable with respect to a given act. To discern a motive, the actor must exercise 'interpretive understanding' by attaching a meaning to the act. What is unique about the investigation of interpretive understanding, according to Weber, is that it accomplishes:

> something which is never attainable in the natural sciences, namely the subjective understanding of the action of the component individuals. The natural sciences on the other hand cannot do this, being limited to the formulation of causal uniformity in objects and events and the explanation of individual facts by applying them. The additional achievement of explanation by interpretive understanding, as distinguished from external observation, is of course attained only at a price – the more hypothetical and fragmentary character of results. Nevertheless, subjective understanding is the specific characteristic of sociological knowledge.[226]

Weber made some of his most explicit assertions about 'interpretive understanding' in relation to the *Methodenstreit* debate. He reasoned that the general and individual elements of phenomena should be stressed in an empirical social science. One of the key statements capturing Weber's stress on the objective and subjective elements for developing a theory of social action, appeared in his criticism of Rudolf Stammler.[227] Stammler was an economic theorist who, in 1896, had described the state of the social sciences. In his writing, Stammler had set out what he thought could

225 Ibid., pp. 8–12.

226 Ibid., p. 15.

227 Max Weber, *Critique of Stammler* (trans. Guy Oakes), New York: The Free Press, 1977.

be described within the context of the social sciences. Stammler argued that a central element of social life was its regulation by external rules, and had insisted that rules are the constituent properties of society. Stammler asserted that the principal feature setting the social sciences apart from the physical sciences was their rule-governed nature. Rules, according to Stammler, constitute the empirical regularities of the social sciences and, as such, define their central subject matter.

Weber's response to Stammler is key to understanding the methodological precepts of his theory of social action and his central premise regarding interpretive understanding in the social sciences. The argument revolves around one central problematic: social phenomena, asserted Weber, are identified not by their lawful nature or by their external physical properties alone, but by their dependence on 'interpretive understanding' and meaning conferring activity. Weber's response to Stammler began by stating that the criteria of meaning precede the criteria of regulation by rule. This can be captured in the following statement:

> Let us suppose that two men who otherwise engage in no social relation – for example, two uncivilized men of different races, or a European who encounters a native in darkest Africa – meet and exchange objects. We are inclined to think that a mere description of what can be observed during this exchange – muscular movements and, if some words were spoken, the sound which, so to say, constitute the 'matter' or 'material' of the behavior – would in no sense comprehend the 'essence' of what happens. The 'essence' of what happens is constituted by the meaning which the two parties ascribe to their observable behavior, a meaning which regulates the course of their future conduct. Without this meaning, we are inclined to say, an exchange is neither empirically possible nor conceptually imaginable.[228]

In this brief paragraph, Weber makes it clear that the social nature of what takes place between two actors resides not in its physical compliance to external rules but in the meaning which they assign to each other's acts. These meanings reside in the subjective viewpoints of the actors. For Weber, that which regulates what they do is the meaning they confer on each other's actions, not the facts which set constraints from without. Without these meanings, no exchange – empirical or otherwise – is possible. Hence, to qualify as an exchange, interpretation must take place and this occurs as the parties 'ascribe meaning to their observable behavior.'[229] This is one of the key issues in Weber's concept of *Verstehen*. Stated simply, the *Verstehen* thesis is based on the idea that meaning precedes action; or more specifically, meaning is a causal component of action since we cannot act unless we know the meaning of other acts. This meaning, Weber thought, constitutes a positive basis to make distinctions between the natural and social sciences, since the objects studied by the physical sciences do not have 'understanding.'

Weber believed that the 'facts' for social sciences were constituted by the

228 Ibid., p. 109.
229 See Oakes, 'The Verstehen Thesis,' pp. 21–2.

meaning which actors bestow on each other's acts. This, he thought, gave rise to two different categories of facts: facts related to physical phenomena of the natural sciences and facts related to human acts in the social sciences. In the first case, facts related to physical phenomena can be confirmed only by observation and description, but they cannot be experienced or understood directly. In the second case, facts can be confirmed through experience because they can be 'understood' within the situation of action. Since for Weber action is social – (i) by virtue of the subjective meaning attached to it, and (ii) when it takes account of the behavior of others – he reasoned that the differences in subject matter disqualified the social sciences from copying the forms of the natural sciences. The name Weber gave to this analysis is the study of 'meaningful conduct,' which was most fully developed in his theory of social action.

Types of Social Action

At the heart of Weber's theory is an outline of four distinct types of social action. Since it was his purpose to make distinctions regarding the degree of rationality and meaningfulness inherent in different types of social action, it will be useful to outline briefly what Weber meant by the term 'rationality.' Generally speaking, Weber used the term to describe an orientation to reality which systematically weighs up means and ends for purposes of efficacy. To the extent that action is rational, therefore, it weighs up means and ends and relies on calculations. Weber believed that different types of rationality become dominant at different periods of social development and, as they do, they tend to eliminate other orientations to reality, such as magic or prayer. Rationality, then, replaces earlier orientations to reality by a straightforward practical application of means and ends. As far as Weber was concerned, rationality can be of two types: (i) subjective rationality, referring to the degree of inner evaluation which the actor engages in cognitively before the act; and (ii) objective rationality, which refers to the degree that action embodies rational principles by adhering either to formal rules or to specific means–ends calculations.[230]

Weber began by distinguishing between four types of social action and by focusing on their different rational orientations. The first type of action Weber describes is traditional action. In this type of action the actor reacts 'automatically to habitual stimuli which guide behavior in a course which has been repeatedly followed.'[231] To act in this way, according to Weber, the actor need not imagine a goal, picture an outcome or be conscious of specific commitments to values. Action of this type is patterned by an orientation to a fixed body of traditional beliefs which act as moral imperatives upon the actor's judgment. According to Weber, the great

230 For a discussion of the distinction between subjective and objective rationality, see Donald N. Levine, 'Rationality and Freedom: Weber and Beyond,' pp. 11–13.

231 Weber, *Economy and Society*, p. 25.

bulk of everyday action approaches this type, so far as both ends and means are fixed by custom. To the extent that traditional action lacks a specific orientation to rationality, it lies close to the 'borderline of what can be justifiably called meaningfully oriented action.'[232] The lack of rational orientation in traditional actions exists because of the actor's habitual responses to the outside world and the degree to which these responses act as guides for future behavior. Traditional action lacks evaluative criteria and is not rationally oriented to ends and means. Clergy abiding by church doctrine would be an example of this type of action.

The second form of action referred to by Weber is the affectual type. Action is affectual if it 'satisfies a need for revenge, sensual gratification, devotion, contemplative bliss, or the working off of emotional tensions.'[233] In this type of action, the actor is directly motivated by an emotional response dictated by the state of mind of the actor. Like traditional action, affectual action is not oriented to a specific goal or values but is an expression of the emotional state of the actor in a given circumstance. It lacks a rational orientation and forgoes the weighing up of means and ends. Like traditional action, 'purely affectual behavior is on the borderline of what is considered meaningful' action and is irrational because it is uncontrolled, is not oriented to weighing up of means and ends, and forgoes inner evaluation.[234]

A third type of action discussed by Weber is value rational action or *Wertrational.* While the first two types of action are characterized by their non-rationality, both value rational and instrumentally rational action exemplify a rational orientation. Weber describes value rational action as a straightforward orientation to an absolute value. Under these circumstances, actors seek to 'put into practice their convictions of what seems to them to be required by duty, honor, the pursuit of beauty, a religious call, personal loyalty or the importance of some cause no matter in what it consists, regardless of possible cost to themselves.'[235]

In this case, the meaning of the action 'does not lie in the achievement of a result ulterior to it, but in carrying out the specific type of action for its own sake,' and, therefore, the sole aim of value rational action is the realization of the value. While value rational action undertakes considerations with respect to the efficacy of the means of action, there is no weighing up of the ends against other ends, since the value pursued is paramount. The actor, in this respect, feels obliged to follow 'commands' or 'demands' which are 'binding' on the actor.[236] This may vary depending on how much 'value' the actor attaches to the action. Since value rational action holds out valued ends as paramount, it may be considered irrational

232 Ibid., p. 25.
233 Ibid., p. 25.
234 Ibid., p. 25.
235 Ibid., p. 25.
236 Ibid., p. 25.

to the extent that ends are pursued without evaluation of 'possible costs' and hence without 'rational consideration' of other ends.

The fourth type of action discussed by Weber is instrumentally rational action or *Zweckrational*. This type differs from value rational action by virtue of the fact that 'the ends, the means and the secondary results are all rationally taken into account and weighed.'[237] To the degree that the efficacy of this type of action entails a systematic rational orientation to means and ends, it is the most rational type of action. In instrumentally rational action, the actor is free to choose the means of action purely in terms of their rational efficacy. Acting in accord with traditional or an affectual orientation runs completely counter to action of the instrumental type and, from the point of view of instrumental rationality, value rational action is specifically irrational. Action of the instrumental type represents the greatest degree of rational orientation inasmuch as it systematically weighs up means and ends in relation to outcomes. But in addition to this, it is also oriented to subjective rationality in a manner distinct from the other types of action. Actors may choose to treat 'ends' as a given set of 'subjective wants and arrange them in a scale of consciously assessed urgency.'[238] To the extent that instrumental action orients itself to the 'rational achievement of ends' it may, 'in limiting cases,' be without relation to values, and in this respect the actor may not be bound by specific values or value scales. In addition to its rational orientation, instrumentally oriented action is broader in scope and in rationality than the other action types. This is evident in the considerations it chooses to weigh up. The actor systematically takes into account the behavior of others and acknowledges these actions as conditions to be considered in the 'attainment of the actor's rationally pursued ends.'[239] The most significant characteristic of instrumentally rational action is the weighing up of means and ends, including the systematic taking into account of 'alternative means to the ends, of the relations of the end to the secondary consequences, and of the relative importance of different possible ends.'[240]

Weber's action types invite various comparisons. Differences between instrumental and traditional action exist when the actor is free to choose the means purely in terms of the efficiency or success that an action may bring about. Traditional action is bound by a set of means which are often determined by regulatory rules existing outside the actor's evaluations. In instrumentally rational action, the meaning of an act is based neither on duty nor obligation, but on the technical use of means and ends as instruments to perfect the attainment of goals. In action of the instrumental type, the actor takes into account those conditions of knowledge calculated to produce the best possible outcomes. In value rational action,

237 Ibid., p. 26.
238 Ibid., p. 26.
239 Ibid., p. 25.
240 Ibid., p. 26.

however, action is undertaken for its own sake, in the light of values that are meaningful to the actor, independent of its chance of success. Value rational action always involves a moral code to which the actor feels bound despite chances of loss. Instrumental rational action, on the other hand, differs from the other types by virtue of its stress on the calculation of available means and the tendency to take into account outcomes based on knowledge of the situation.

Weber's Political Writings and the Theory of Legitimate Domination

Weber's political works were written between 1914 and 1920 and appear in the first volume of *Economy and Society*. The body of political writings, many of which are unpublished, covers a wide range of themes relating to state development, expression of political power, the organization of political communities, democracy and administration, the emergence of a system of law, and the historical comparison of forms of domination.[241] In these works, Weber concerned himself explicitly with two issues of social and historical development: first, he wanted to trace the pattern of development leading to the decline of empires and the rise of the modern state; and second, he wanted to look at the changes taking place in the manifestation of political authority as the modern state developed. He believed that, as the state changes in its political organization, power is altered as the state becomes dependent on bureaucratic administration. Weber's political writings explore the interrelation between three distinct spheres in society: the political, legal and religious spheres. At the center of Weber's political work is his theory of legitimate domination.

Between 1914 and 1920, Weber's work reflected a number of historical shifts which had taken place in society as a whole. One of the major developments discussed by Weber was the emergence of the modern nation state with its complex legal and political structure. He believed that the dominance of the political and legal spheres, which only became a reality at the turn of the century, signified major changes in the way the state was governed. Gone were the impoverished social classes of antiquity who were dominated by a traditional land owning aristocracy; gone were the empires with their absolute monarchies and dominant leaders who were not themselves subject to laws. Replacing the empire was the democratic nation state with its parliamentary system, bodies of rational law, world markets and enfranchised individuals. Democratic states also replaced the old system of absolute monarchy, aristocratic classes, economic monopolies, and laws favoring one group or class. As the modern state formed around these considerations, its authority became centralized, markets and economies broadened, legal and political rights were allotted, and the

---

241 Ibid., pp. 212–301.

conduct of everyday life was rationalized. The rise of the new state system led to new forms of political authority, and it is to this that Weber turned his attention in developing a theory of legitimate domination.

Weber's theory of domination is one of the most coherent discussions in his work. He began to outline the rudiments of the theory of domination in *Economy and Society* in 1914. In focusing on the change in political institutions of modern societies, Weber became interested in how political power manifested itself in different historical contexts. This called for a comparative analysis of the systems of legitimate domination which existed during various historical periods. Generally he used the terms 'domination' and 'authority' interchangeably in his discussion. Both derive from the German term *herrschaft*, which indicates leadership, political authority and domination. Technically, the term *herrschaft* encompasses an entire system of dominance and subordination supported by a means of enforcement.[242]

Weber began by making a distinction between power and domination. Power is the ability of individuals to carry out their will in a given situation, despite resistance.[243] Domination, by contrast, refers to the right of a ruler within an 'established order' to issue commands to others and expect them to obey.[244] In a given historical situation, the ruler has the right to exercise commands and to expect compliance from others. This combination of 'ruler' and 'command' forms a legitimate system of authority which applies to the state, to large-scale organizations, to large families and administrative situations.

Weber's primary aim was to focus on various systems of domination rather than on power itself and so his approach focused primarily on the structure of domination. In the light of this, he began with the assumption that different systems of domination vary in the way commands are issued and in the expectation of obedience by individuals who are subject to such commands. Each system of domination may be viewed as a total 'apparatus of authority' since each system reflects the relationship between ruler, administrative officials and groups or persons existing within the 'established order.'[245]

In looking at the historical types of authority, Weber focused on two central elements which are key to any system of domination. First is the concern for legitimacy, and the perception that authority is legitimate among those who are subject to it. Second is the development of an administrative staff. Essentially, by the term legitimacy Weber was referring to the extent to which officials, groups and individuals actively acknowledge the validity of the ruler in an established order, and the right of the ruler to issue commands. Accompanying each established order,

---

242 See, Guenther Roth's introduction to Weber, *Economy and Society*, pp. xc. For further discussion of the term *herrschaft* and the debate related to its interpretation, see ibid., p. 61, n. 31.

243 Weber, *Economy and Society*, p. 53.

244 Ibid., p. 53.

245 Bendix, *Max Weber*.

stated Weber, are beliefs about the 'legitimacy' of a given system of domination. Every system of domination is based on some corresponding belief of people in the legitimacy or right of the ruler to issue commands and rule over individuals. The second component, the formation of an administrative staff, is essential to any system of domination and its means of enforcement. In modern societies with large populations, for example, those who lead require a large staff to administer and enforce rules and commands. While the administrative staff serves as a link between the leader and the people, Weber thought that the means of administration alter the nature of power.

Having established the importance of the concepts of legitimacy and administration, Weber went on to point out that each system of domination varies in terms of four characteristics: first is the claim it makes to legitimacy; second is in the type of obedience it elicits in individuals; third is in the kind of administrative staff designed to carry out commands; and fourth is in the way a given system exercises authority.[246] Given the difference in these characteristics, various systems of domination have existed in societies at various times. There are, for example, societies based on military dominance, others on centralized monarchical powers, others on a system of laws, and still others that are based on the direct use of physical force. This led Weber to look at the question of the social and historical conditions leading to long-lasting systems of domination and the mechanisms by means of which they maintain themselves.

In his theory of authority Weber put forward three types of legitimate domination: (i) charismatic domination; (ii) traditional domination; (iii) rational–legal domination. Each of these types give rise to a corresponding form of legitimacy, type of obedience, administrative apparatus and mode of exercising power. While existing societies and forms of domination incorporate elements of charisma, tradition and legal rationality, Weber examined each of the structures of domination as 'pure types.'

Charismatic Domination

The first type of domination discussed by Weber is charismatic domination. The term charisma has its origins in religious history and essentially means the 'gift of grace.' Weber used the term to refer to 'a certain quality of an individual's personality which is considered extraordinary and treated as endowed with supernatural, superhuman, or exceptional powers and qualities.'[247] Charismatic leaders are believed to have capabilities which are not accessible to ordinary individuals, and their powers 'are regarded as having a divine origin, and on this basis the individual is treated as a leader.'[248] Such individuals can be prophets, persons with reputations, or heroes in war. The powers manifested in these leaders are

246 Weber, *Economy and Society*, pp. 212–16.
247 Ibid., p. 241.
248 Ibid., p. 241.

thought to transcend the routines of everyday life and are believed to rest on magical or oracular qualities. Leaders may emerge from the ordinary population, they may announce themselves as saviors, or they may be persons with heroic reputations. What is of key importance is that the individual's powers are regarded by followers to be valid and true. Proofs of validity may require demonstrations to believers that the leader's claims are legitimate by virtue of having undergone some extraordinary experiences, having had some revelation, or having claims to special inspiration or vision. Under certain circumstances, 'proofs' of the charismatic quality of the leader consist in the belief by followers that the leader's revelations constitute 'miracles.' Proofs of claims to charisma bring recognition by followers that the leader is in some way chosen and their devotion to the leader is unquestioned.[249]

In charismatic domination, the leader's claim to legitimacy originates from two related levels of belief. First is the level which derives legitimacy from people's belief that the leader is to be followed because of extraordinary capacities or powers of personal inspiration. Second is the level which derives legitimacy from the degree of 'felt duty' which the followers believe is put upon them to carry out the demand or commands of the leader. This 'recognition of duty' is key to the followers' felt belief that they should undertake to put into practice the vision of the charismatic leader.[250] In such circumstances, believers adhere to the authority of the leader on the basis of an inner devotion, which they expect will resolve long-standing inner conflicts and suffering from which they hope to be emancipated. This psychological connection to the leader increases the followers' inner commitment, and may induce them to suspend any critical judgments regarding the abilities of the leader.

Weber maintained that one of the characteristic qualities of charismatic leadership is its tendency to become unstable if the proof of a valid claim to legitimacy should fail. If success eludes leaders or if leaders fail in their promises, they may lose their power in the eyes of followers or they may suddenly be exposed as 'ordinary' or 'vulnerable'. In circumstances where charismatic leaders appear to lose their powers, are defeated in their mission or appear to be thwarted by natural misfortunes, Weber stated that they may appear to their followers as having been 'deserted by God.'[251]

A second characteristic of charisma is its ability to mobilize legitimacy by a 'renunciation of the past.'[252] In this respect it may be associated with revolutionary force for change. This places the leader squarely within the tradition of rejecting the past on the basis of some unacceptable inequality, suffering or wrong committed against the people. Thus, in its pure form,

249 Ibid., p. 242.
250 Ibid., p. 244.
251 Ibid., p. 242.
252 Ibid., p. 244.

charisma constitutes legitimate authority to obtain compliance in persons by virtue of an authentic 'call' to a particular mission or to some 'spiritual duty.'[253] This led Weber to suggest that one of the central features of charismatic domination is its tendency to reject the desires and needs of everyday life. He reasoned that the charismatic leader obtains legitimacy by rejecting attachments to the routines of everyday life and argued that such a rejection creates a necessity of the ruler to transcend everyday activity by emotional indifference, renunciation of desire or repudiation of worldly pleasure and material property.[254] This serves to create the appearance that the leader is 'above' everyday needs and routines and adopts an ascetic way of life.

Because of these characteristics, Weber believed that charismatic authority often emerges in times of social crisis. This occurs especially when established ways of solving problems are seen as inadequate and when a 'nation' or a 'people' is thought to be on the brink of a political or economic crisis. In such circumstances, the charismatic leader consolidates power by mobilizing national symbols rather than dealing with issues of historical or social substance. In this sense, charismatic authority presupposes a people's renunciation of the past in favor of pursuing a direction founded on the leader's divine inspiration. Because of these volatile qualities, charisma is thought to be incompatible with legal and traditional domination in three important respects: first, charisma is unable to accommodate demands arising from the pragmatic sphere of everyday life and routine; second, charisma dislikes specified rules and procedures; and third, charisma resists the development of a bureaucratic means of administration.[255]

A third characteristic of charisma is the tendency to undergo transformation in its orientation to power. This transformation may be forced on charisma by the necessity to change in some manner or become rationalized in ways which alter its administrative staff. When this occurs, it forces charisma to be constitutionally changed and Weber referred to this transformation as the 'routinization of charisma.'[256] By the term 'routinization' Weber essentially meant the demands placed on a charismatic system of domination (including its legitimacy, administrative apparatus, and commands to obedience) that would cause it to adjust to 'the normal, everyday needs and conditions of carrying on administration.'[257] Routinization can be defined as any external demand which would cause charisma to adjust its means of administration to the practical routines of everyday life and practical economic conditions.

Weber largely confined the problems of routinization to two key areas

---

253 Ibid., p. 244.
254 Ibid., p. 244.
255 Ibid., p. 245.
256 Ibid., p. 246.
257 Ibid., p. 252.

of adjustment: first is the adjustment which comes with succession to the charismatic leader. He thought that charismatic leadership led to problems of succession, since a new leadership would be obliged to demonstrate that it possesses the same extraordinary qualities as the previous leader. Second is the problem of adjustment in the transition from charismatic administration to an administrative situation which is 'adapted to everyday conditions.'[258]

In charismatic domination, if the leader dies or becomes unable to lead there is always the potential of a crisis in belief and leadership. Weber thought that there are three ways of resolving the problem. First is to execute a search for a new leader on the basis of matching the existing qualities of the original leader. In this way the selection of a new leader is 'bound' to search for distinguishing marks or characteristics which most resemble the original leader. Second is to bring about succession by revelation. This relies on a method of selection based on 'oracles, lots, divine judgments or a combination of such techniques.' In this case the legitimacy of the newly-selected leader hinges on the legitimacy of the 'techniques of selection.'[259] Third is succession by designation, in which the original leader chooses a successor and the personal endorsement of the leader functions as the means of legitimacy.

Weber took the view that the process of routinization places a structural strain on charismatic domination that tends to transform it in the direction of traditional or rational authority. This transformation is based on the following set of precautions: (i) charismatic authority must ensure that it retains its focus on the ideal rather than the material. This is carried out by separating the 'ideal' core of the doctrine from the demands of everyday life to ensure that the doctrine is not compromised by the material world. (ii) To ensure that charismatic revelations attesting to the leader's powers and accomplishments are preserved, they should be set into texts or received doctrines and made available to different legitimizing rationalities. This helps make the original inspiration of the leader available to theological processes. (iii) To ensure transmission of the original charismatic concepts, the separation of the charismatic power from the individual may be required in order to effect its repersonalization in some other form or entity. In this way, legitimacy is no longer focused upon the personal qualities of the leader, but rather on the words, utterances and commands of the doctrine.[260]

Charismatic Domination and Administration The administrative organization of charismatic domination varies considerably in comparison with traditional and legal forms of domination. First and foremost, the administrative staff of the charismatic leader has no appointed officials or

258 Ibid., p. 253.
259 Ibid., p. 247.
260 Ibid., pp. 246–8.

a hierarchy of offices, and its members are not technically trained.[261] Appointments to offices or positions are not made on the basis of social privilege or the dependency of individuals on the leader's movement. Rather, the leader 'selects' disciples or followers who commit themselves to 'serve' the leader because of their beliefs in the leader's powers. Their service to the leader may function in the form of sacrifice based on renunciation of their own interests for those of the master. Under these circumstances, the administrative functions are carried out by disciples rather than autonomous office holders. For this reason, decision-making functions and other necessary judgments may be made by the leader personally, on a case by case basis, at the leader's discretion. In such circumstances, decision making occurs in the form of intervention by the leader.[262] Often the leader's judgments take on the quality of revelation or divine inspiration.[263] From this position, the leader obtains compliance by placing demands on followers and by exhorting them through personal revelation and the force of his or her personal will. Because charismatic domination tends to reject specific rules of procedure and the development of an autonomous administrative apparatus, Weber believed that charismatic authority does not adhere to norms of rational decision making and therefore resists the tendency to bureaucratic administration.

Traditional Domination

The second system of domination discussed by Weber is traditional domination. Authority is traditional when its legitimacy is based on tradition and custom, on the 'sanctity of age-old rules and powers.'[264] Compliance to traditional authority is owed not to an objective system of legal rules but to the framework of obligations that bind individuals to leaders by personal loyalties. Obligation to obey commands derives from the traditional status of the ruler. In traditional forms of domination, leaders obtain their powers from inherited right and are seen as legitimate in the light of customary rights and traditional norms. Monarchies and lords of feudal estates are historical examples of traditional systems of domination. In societies where traditional authority is dominant, obedience is owed not to the enacted rules as such, but to the individual. The authority of the leader is obtained in two ways. First, by the prestige conferred by tradition and by the belief that the ruler's commands are valid because of the authority inherent in the office or status of the ruler. Second, rulers have authority by virtue of the discretionary powers which are conferred upon them by titles or hereditary claims to power.[265] Powers exist in the form of traditional prerogatives, privileges and rights which

261 Weber says 'that the administrative staff of a charismatic leader does not consist of "officials," and least of all are its members technically trained,' ibid., p. 243.

262 Ibid., p. 243.

263 Ibid., p. 243.

264 Ibid., p. 226.

265 Ibid., p. 227.

tend to confer almost unlimited authority upon the leaders. Inasmuch as the ruler is considered to be a 'personal master' over those who are within the established order, followers are formally 'subject' to the ruler and 'obedience is owed not to enacted rules but to the person who occupies the position of authority.'[266] Similarly, the relationship between subject and ruler is defined by the personal loyalty owed to the ruler by subjects, rather than being defined by impersonal legal precepts. The relationship between subject and ruler is governed by traditional norms which extend to the lifetime of the subject rather than by contractual arrangements.

A second characteristic of traditional domination is that commands are conceived to be legitimate within two spheres of action. In the first, a command is believed to be valid or legitimate in terms of the specific weight of customary rules which may apply in a situation. In the second sphere, however, the ruler's commands are perceived to be valid by virtue of the leader's right to exercise personal discretion, in which case prerogatives are relied upon as a legitimating source of a command. In such circumstances, the ruler is not bound by specific rules but rather acts on the basis of 'good will' even though it may not be legally binding on the ruler as such.[267]

Patrimonial and Patriarchal Forms of Administration Another characteristic of traditional domination focused on by Weber is the nature of the administrative apparatus. There are two formal types of traditional administrative authorities, patrimonial and patriarchal. Patrimonial administration is common in feudal societies where traditional authority is prevalent, and where the landlord may rule entirely without administrative staff. In this system of domination, rulers may rely on family members, on dependents or, in some cases, on slaves to perform specific functions for the master. Patrimonial forms of administration tend to be based on a 'system of favorites' who perform functions for rulers out of loyalty or obligation.[268] Individuals who occupy official positions are invariably personal followers of the master. This form of administration leads to arbitrary decision making which follows the personal discretion of the master, rather than to a strict set of administrative rules which apply equally to everyone.

Weber believed that traditional systems of domination tend to resist bureaucratic development. The main features of bureaucratic organization lacking in patrimonial forms of administration are rationally established hierarchies of offices, technical training for functionaries and a clearly delineated jurisdiction of powers and responsibilities.[269] In a patrimonial form of administration, tasks are assigned on the discretion of the master

266 Ibid., p. 227.
267 Ibid., p. 229.
268 Ibid., pp. 231–6.
269 Ibid., p. 229.

and roles are performed by individuals who are often tied to household positions to which they revert after the performance of the function. In such circumstances, masters may find themselves compromised between their own interests and the pressure from outside interests who constantly seek favors, incomes, privileges, the 'granting of grace' or other forms of remuneration and advantage.[270] As a result, decision making is always at the discretionary right of the master and is based on the master's right to seek legal opinion in disputes – although this may not be binding on the final decision made. For this reason, Weber believed patrimonial forms of authority do not develop fully-formed bureaucratic administrations.

A second type of administration identified in traditional systems of domination is patriarchalism. This is a variation of traditional domination which develops no clearly defined administrative staff. Typically, this form of administration is found in households in which the master obtains legitimacy and governs by rule of inheritance. The central characteristic of patriarchalism is the belief that authority is exercised by 'joint right' and in the interest of all members.[271] In order for this system to sustain itself there should be no personal staff retained from family members, since this would create a conflict of interests. In such circumstances, the master's power remains tied to the 'consent' of the other members of the household and compliance to authority is not dependent on a formal apparatus of enforced rules. These associations differ from others insofar as they are entirely dependent on traditional norms and exist by force of obligatory entitlements rather than by formal enactments.[272] Under these conditions, obedience is owed directly to the master rather than to the enacted regulations or laws.[273] In this sense, members would not be subjects as much as they would be 'co-consenters.'

The empirical type of this system may be found in European forms of feudal societies such as in France or Germany. Where the size of lands and households eventually leads to large administrations and administrative staff, they typically develop only in the form of 'benefices,' which allow members to draw from the lord's treasury, obtain land rights and appropriate taxes, dues and fees.[274] Benefices lead to autonomous authorities which function as subsidiaries. In addition, Weber pointed out that the monopolistic practices arising from patriarchal authority tend to obstruct the development of capitalism because their economic monopolies do not produce enough freedom to encourage private enterprise, and because the absence of contracts and binding legal norms discourages the development of calculation in the means and ends of action.

270 Ibid., p. 232.
271 ibid., p. 231.
272 Ibid., p. 231.
273 Ibid., p. 232.
274 Ibid., p. 232.

Patriarchal Authority and the Edict In traditional systems of domination, obedience is owed to the ruler rather than to objective legal rules. Traditional domination thus issues commands on the basis of what Weber called the 'edict.' This may be defined as a personal decree issued by a leader that tends to reflect the 'arbitrary' nature of traditional powers. Because the power of the ruler is based on custom rather than an explicit system of legal rules, there is no separation between the power of the ruler and the political office. This element of traditional authority thus reflects cultural values and patterns of social action that have been stable for long periods of time.

Legal Domination

The third type of political authority discussed by Weber is legal domination. In a system of domination characterized by legal authority, legitimacy rests on 'rational grounds' and on the belief in the inherent 'legality of enacted rules and the right of those elevated to authority under these rules to issue commands.'[275] In this system, compliance is owed to those issuing commands on the basis of principles of law rather than the personal authority of the leader, and individuals owe their obedience to an impersonal legal order. Authority in legal domination, therefore, rests in a system of rationally-determined judicial rules. Individuals pursue their interests within limits established by legal precepts and follow norms approved by the group governing them. A key characteristic of legal domination is that officials in power are themselves subject to laws and must orient their action to an impersonal order of legal rules in their disposition of commands. In societies based on legal domination, individuals comply only in their capacity as members of society and the authority which they obey resides not in the person of the leader, but in a framework of legal rules. Claims to legitimacy in a system of legal domination rest on the belief in the inherent legality of the enacted rules and the rights of those in authority to issue commands.[276] Accordingly, a key characteristic of legal domination is that persons elevated to the office of leader are subject to the rules of law and must orient their action to these rules in the disposition of commands.

Since the operation and organization of this system of domination takes the form of legality, the total system of laws and judicial framework leads to a form of administrative organization which grows out of the principle of legality. Weber took the view that legal domination, therefore, tends to a form of administrative apparatus which is bureaucratic in orientation and this orientation is reflected in the organization of offices, staff and official files.

The connection between legal authority or legality *per se* and a bureaucratically organized means of administration is central to Weber's

275 Ibid., p. 215.
276 Ibid., p. 219.

reasoning in a number of ways. First, he believed that bureaucracy and the bureaucratic organization were technically the most rational means of exercising authority over people, and that its development was at the basis of the Western democratic state. Second, he thought that in a system essentially defined by legal precepts, the organization of offices necessarily followed a pattern of official hierarchy related to offices in terms of rank, and related to functions in terms of specified jurisdictions.[277] Each of these, in turn, would be governed by a system of supervision and control. This meant that the conduct of offices and officials would be regulated by technical rules and norms to such a degree that it would formally eliminate individual will or personal say-so. More than any other system of domination, legal authority decreases arbitrariness in power and eliminates forms of authority in which individuals wield power by virtue of status privilege or by the appropriation of power through sheer physical force.

In addition, the conduct of officials is guided by enacted rules, and officials act as functionaries only within the context of a given sphere of competence that is explicitly defined by a framework based on a division of labor. Under these conditions, the means of obtaining the compliance of functionaries must be clearly set out and the use of any force is subject to definite conditions and procedures. Offices which are governed in this way function as administrative agencies with clearly defined limits imposed upon their powers and decision making. Members of the administrative staff are required to obtain certified technical training and act as functionaries within the administration. In this sense, officials occupy positions not as outright owners of the means of production nor as owners of their offices, but as administrative officials who are either 'appointed' or 'elected' to a term of office.[278] Notwithstanding the various structural developments related to bureaucracy and legal domination, rational norms dictate that all administrative acts be put in writing. This not only made the 'document' part and parcel of the legal order as well as the system of legitimacy and compliance, but it also acted as a means of verifying procedural considerations since the retention of documents serves as a method to warrant that all procedural requirements have been met.

Statute vs the Edict   Weber maintained that legal domination exists and creates legitimacy by virtue of the statute. The statute, in contrast to the edict, is a formal regulation lawfully passed by a legislative body and is based on principles grounded in lawful decision making rather than on the arbitrary judgment of a ruler. The efficacy of the statute resides in its lawfulness and adherence to objective legal rules. In Weber's view, legal authority implies a change in the way power is exercised, since it replaces the arbitrary judgment of the ruler with a system of rational law. Laws are

277 Ibid., p. 218.
278 Ibid., p. 218.

seen as legitimate by people only when they are seen to be enforced by reliance upon fair procedure and due process. In rational legal domination, both ruler and ruled are constrained by laws, and leaders who propagate laws are seen as having the right to act only when they have obtained their positions in accordance with what are perceived as procedurally correct elections. These can be created and changed only by procedurally correct enactments.[279] Rational legal forms of domination are based on correct legal procedure and consequently require a large administrative apparatus.

Weber felt that the operation and organization of the system of legal rules was reflected in the form of administrative organization which tended to grow around systems of domination based on the principle of legality. He took the view that legal domination tends to form an administrative apparatus he called bureaucracy which is ultimately reflected in its organization of officials and staff. The connection between legal authority and a bureaucratically organized means of administration is central to Weber's reasoning in a number of ways. First, he believed that bureaucracy and bureaucratic organization were technically the most efficient means of exercising authority over people and that bureaucratic development was at the basis of the Western democratic state.[280] Second, he thought that in a system defined by legal precepts, the organization of offices necessarily followed a pattern of official hierarchy related to offices in terms of rank, and related to functions in terms of specified official jurisdictions. Each of these, in turn, would be governed by a system of supervision and control. This meant that the conduct of offices and officials would be regulated by technical rules and norms to such a degree that individual power would be formally eliminated. More than any other system of domination, Weber believed that legal authority eliminates arbitrariness in the exercise of power and replaces forms of authority in which individuals wield power by virtue of status privilege or by physical force.

Weber's Study of Bureaucracy

Historical Context of Bureaucracy

Weber first wrote on the subject of bureaucracy as early as 1908 in his study on the *Economies of Antiquity*.[281] Later, in *Economy and Society*, he included a much larger section on bureaucracy in which he looked more extensively into the question of the development and growth of the modern administrative apparatus. Formally, Weber's study of bureaucracy is part of a much larger study of the theory of domination which appeared

---

279 Ibid., p. 219.
280 Ibid., p. 223.
281 For references to this early work of Weber's, see Guenther Roth's introduction in ibid., p. L.

in Part One of *Economy and Society*.[282] Nevertheless, his discussion stands alone as an independent investigation into the historical determinants of bureaucratic administration in society.

Weber began by tracing the development of the modern means of administration. He believed that a bureaucratic type of organization began in societies whose political organization tended toward an officialdom. Early examples of societies with large political administrations include the Germanic and Mongolian empires, and feudal estates of the twelfth and thirteenth centuries. Among these societies, Weber cited the cases of emperors and feudal lords who, when making known their decrees and pronouncements, would appoint commissioners whose powers were exercised within the lord's jurisdiction. Weber identified six basic types of bureaucratic structure: (i) states which tend to control policy and policing functions; (ii) ecclesiastical communities which are required to administer to large populations of believers; (iii) economies whose main function is to distribute goods and coordinate functions; (iv) the modern agency; (v) the military; and (vi) the judiciary.

Distinction between Administratively Oriented Societies and Bureaucratic Societies

One of the chief interests which Weber had in developing a historical understanding of bureaucratization was to show that it was a development of modern society. In order to demonstrate this, he drew on several historical comparisons of administratively oriented societies. He looked at the administration of early Egypt and Rome, at the administration of the Catholic Church, at Asiatic societies and at feudal economies of central Europe.[283] While these societies develop administrative staff and trained decision makers, they are, in Weber's view, formally pre-bureaucratic in their administrative organization. This restricts the development of bureaucracy to modern society. For instance, in looking at early Egypt, Weber made it clear that while a large staff of 'scribes and officials' arose from the public necessity to administer water resources, 'Egypt was not a bureaucratically organized society.'[284] Nor, stated Weber, were the large households of the European feudal economies which had extensive administrations and large staffs. Since these administratively oriented societies constitute the first rudiments of bureaucratic administration, let us look more closely at their characteristics.

In European feudal societies, the system of organization was in the form of 'patrimonial administration' with several basic administrative characteristics. First was the estate household, which acted as the center of administrative activity. At its head was the lord who required a large administrative staff. Business and administrative dealings were conducted

---

282 Weber, *Economy and Society*, pp. 956–1003.
283 Ibid., pp. 964–70.
284 Ibid., pp. 271–2.

according to the discretion of the lord, and there was no official separation between household and office.[285] The administrative authority of the feudal household was concentrated in the patrimonial ruler. Powers were defined by customary right rather than by written law, and few restrictions were placed on the leader's authority except those imposed by customary rules not written into law.[286] The head of the household observed customary restrictions and traditional norms, but was not bound by legal rules in the execution of administrative acts. This, of course, gave the widest latitude to the lord's discretionary powers. All administrative acts were the private prerogative of the master and were carried out on the basis of personal say-so. In this respect, the administrative rationality of the bureaucratic type was lacking. Relations between the head of the household and the official staff were based on personal loyalty, and recruitment was carried out by the lord in terms of prerogatives associated with title and position. Officers performing administrative functions were part of the lord's personal staff, and payment and supervision of functionaries was the personal responsibility of the lord. All offices, in this case, were considered 'part of the ruler's personal household and private property' and officers functioned as personal retainers who pledged loyalty through oaths.[287] The business and administration of the household was conducted by personal communication rather than by written documentation, which is the opposite of the principle of modern bureaucracy.

In direct contrast to the administratively oriented feudal household of traditional societies is the type of administration which develops under legal domination. Two important changes occur in legal domination which favor the development of bureaucracy. First, administrative activities are carried out under procedurally correct legal enactments and the legitimacy of rules rests on legal authority. Second, with modern society comes the 'quantitative extension' of administrative tasks, and these tend to increase to such an extent that there is a need for a large bureaucratic organization.[288] Under these circumstances, bureaucracy intensifies as the administrative tasks of the state expand. Mass populations and an extensive political apparatus are thus the 'classical' starting place of bureaucratic development.[289]

A second causal component of bureaucratic development is the emergence of a modern economy, the rise of civil politics, a rational political sphere and the need for police regulation.[290] The larger the population and the bigger the state, the greater the bureaucratic development. Societies of this type give rise to a bureaucratic form of administration which contrasts sharply with the patrimonial type found in feudal society in several

285 Ibid., p. 1028.
286 For a discussion of these characteristics, see Bendix, *Max Weber*, p. 425.
287 Weber, *Economy and Society*, pp. 1028–9.
288 Ibid., p. 969.
289 Ibid., p. 969.
290 Ibid., p. 972.

respects. First, the seat of administrative activity shifts from the household to the office, and this is clearly demarcated and set aside. Administrative activity is subject to principles of office management, and authority is distributed hierarchically according to offices. Second, in contrast to feudal households, administrative authority is strictly bound by legal rules and the activity of the 'official' is governed by jurisdictional authority circumscribed by legal rules. This serves to narrow the scope of discretionary powers that once belonged to the official. Administrative acts are carried out on the basis of 'procedurally correct enactments' rather than the personal say-so of the official. Third, heads of offices observe legal limitations to their authority and are bound by rules which circumscribe their sphere of social action.[291] Under these circumstances, the business of the bureaucracy is conducted in accordance with strict regard for official rules and technical procedures, and authority is strictly impersonal. Consistent with the development of bureaucratically organized administration is the growth of an 'administrative rationality' which informs all decision making and maintains a rational orientation to problem solving. Fourth, the relation between heads of offices and subordinates is governed by procedural rules which regulate interaction between incumbents. Staff are recruited on the basis of technical qualifications rather than personal loyalty to the head of the office. Officials are not obligated to those who are over them, but owe their allegiance to an impersonal legal order. Fifth, the implementation of rules is regulated by law and lawful enactments, and official rules govern the conduct of those within the bureaucracy. Offices are divided by jurisdictions which are organized into separate hierarchies of offices that function as spheres of authority linked by a chain of command. Sixth, all business and communication of the bureau is conducted on the basis of written documentation, and a system of file keeping based on the retention of records becomes part of everyday bureaucratic activity.[292]

Factors Leading to Bureaucratization

Weber believed that several historical factors led to the development of the bureaucratic means of administration under legal domination. These, he thought, could be divided into two distinct categories of change: (i) changes occurring in the conditions and organization of society; and (ii) changes occurring in the system of rationality and decision making. Among the first category is the process of industrialization in which machines were able to perform work previously performed by humans. This reduced repetitive labor and increased control over the environment by creating free time in order to plan activities. These changes motivated social innovation and the rational planning of activities, making know-how and ingenuity prominent. Second, as these changes took place there

291 Ibid., p. 957.
292 Ibid., p. 957.

was a greater need for the use of rational accounting methods in industrial and commercial enterprises, leading to the rationalization of the conduct of everyday life and industrial production.[293] This promoted the decline of the old economic monopolies and their replacement by rational markets governed by universalistic legal norms. Third, was the development and gradual imposition of a system of 'calculable law' and legislation.[294] This brought about the rationalization of commercial and business techniques through greater reliance upon written records, eventually giving rise to a system of accounting, file keeping and administration. Fourth, was the recognition of the utility of technical rules leading to greater efficiency in the means of administration. Eventually, this led to the separation of homeplace and workplace, and the emergence of a rational means for dealing with the work day. This gave rise to the sphere of the office, the concerns of which were official business and record keeping. With the rise of the technical means of administration and the appearance of the official, asserted Weber, the work day was subject to norms of efficiency and technical control could be exerted outside the home.

Key Concepts in Weber's Study of Bureaucracy

In order completely to understand how Weber used the term bureaucracy, we have to look at two additional questions: how is bureaucracy a form of administrative rationality and how is bureaucracy a form of domination? To examine these questions we must look at two additional concepts: (i) means and ends; and (ii) formal and substantive rationality. Let us look at how Weber used the concept of means and ends. Simply stated, the 'means' of action refers to the methods individuals use to obtain goals and reach desired ends or outcomes. Means therefore refers to methods or techniques. 'Ends', on the other hand, refers to the goals, results or desired outcomes of action. Weber took the view that, while all human action is governed by what he called a 'means–ends rationality,' this rationality is subject to change. During earlier periods, the means and ends of action were governed by ethical or value standards. At one time, these standards in the West were largely regulated by Christian ethical injunctions and were to some extent fixed. As societies became more modern, however, the means and ends of action became less and less regulated by ethical mores, since these were replaced by technical means and ends. One of the consequences of this, Weber believed, is that the 'ends' themselves become subject to technical criteria, and become so important that people seek to attain them at all costs.

In addition to change in the means and ends of action there is a subsequent change in the system of rationality, which is key to the development of bureaucracy. Weber, in fact, saw bureaucracy as a triumph of one form of rationality over another. For Weber, rationality describes

293 Weber, *General Economic History*, p. 208.
294 Ibid., p. 208.

an orientation to reality which weighs up the means and ends of action in a staightforward and pragmatic manner.[295] To the extent that bureaucracy stresses 'technique' and technical requirements in decision making, the means are always converted into 'techniques,' which act as tried and true procedures in administrative situations. This implies that the boundaries of decision making are fundamentally altered by bureaucratic rationality since a technical orientation to means and ends always rules out decision making in terms of values. Weber thought that the distinctive feature of technical rationality was its systematic consideration of means, in which case he thought that the ends are always treated as beyond doubt.

Weber went on to suggest that the development and success of bureaucratic administration was an indication of the triumph of one form of rationality over another, specifically of formal over substantive rationality.[296] Weber used the term 'formal rationality' to refer to a type of decision making which is subject to calculation in means and ends. Formal rationality signifies to the amount of calculation that goes into an action to increase its chance of success, and its decisive feature is that it eliminates an orientation to values because of their non-technical character. Rationality is formal, therefore, when there is a view to solving problems by a straightforward application of technical criteria.[297]

In contrast to formal rationality, substantive rationality is a term Weber used to refer to a type of decision making that is shaped by a criterion of values which involves an appeal to ethical norms, independent of the nature of outcomes.[298] Weber reasoned that the operation of modern society is largely based on formal rationality which is evident in the increased bureaucratization. At the heart of bureaucratic development, therefore, is formal rationality with its technical guidelines and formalized decision making.

The Technical Superiority of Bureaucracy

One of the main concerns Weber had in looking at the historical roots of bureaucratic development was to examine its technical superiority over other forms of administration. A bureaucratic apparatus compares, stated Weber, with other administratively organized societies exactly as does the development of machine with non-mechanical means of production.[299] The network of functions, coordinated offices, rules of procedure and technical means of administration associated with bureaucracy form an 'apparatus' of administration whose 'precision, speed, knowledge of files and cases,' leads to the subordination of everyday life to norms of procedure.[300] This reduction to functional norms and an emphasis on technical procedure

295 Weber, *Economy and Society*, pp. 65–8.
296 Ibid., pp. 85–6; 225–6.
297 Ibid., pp. 85–6; 225–6.
298 Ibid., pp. 85–6; 225–6.
299 Ibid., p. 973.
300 Ibid., p. 973.

plays a decisive role in promoting the superiority of bureaucracy over other means of decision making and administration. To illustrate the nature of bureaucratic efficiency, Weber compared it with two earlier types of decision making – administration by notables and by collegiate bodies.[301] Administration by notables and collegiate bodies, according to Weber, is always less efficient because their interests inevitably conflict and bring about compromises between views. This creates delays which slow down progress and make decision making less precise and less reliable. In a bureaucracy, by contrast, 'official business is discharged precisely and with as much speed as possible.' Accordingly, the degree of control afforded by the use of procedural rules alters the performance of individuals so that they are less likely to enter into conflict over personal interests.[302] In this way bureaucracy changes the nature of cooperation and decision making between people because it requires the 'objective discharge of business according to calculable rules without regard for persons.'[303]

Another illustration of the technical superiority of bureaucracy is in its tendency to promote the development of capitalism. Weber pointed out that bureaucracy develops only in a money economy and only where authority is under legal domination. The technical superiority of bureaucracy promotes capitalism in four broad ways. First, insofar as capitalism requires a market economy in which official business can be executed effectively in accordance with rules of procedure, bureaucracy enhances the speed of business operations by promoting the regulation of work and a chain of command. Once in place, bureaucracy carries out administrative functions with maximum objective consideration and efficiency. Second, capitalism presupposes the rapid discharge of business activity and adherence to calculable rules. Stress on the 'calculability' of rules is decisive since the more bureaucracy develops calculation, the more rational are its decisions and the more effective are its operations.[304] Third, the more perfectly bureaucracy develops, the more it tends to 'dehumanize,' and the more it does this the more it eliminates decision making based on love, hatred and personal or irrational considerations. When fully developed, bureaucracy adheres to the principle of *sine ira et studio* – without hatred or passion.[305] Fourth, to the extent bureaucracy is associated with the emergence of rational law, the specialization of business and commerce tends to develop in relation to it. This acts effectively to replace the old patriarchal administrator with the trained expert, leading to greater efficiency. 'The more complicated and specialized modern culture becomes, the more its external supporting apparatus demands the personally detached and strictly objective expert, in lieu of the lord of older social structures who was moved

301 Ibid., p. 974.
302 Ibid., p. 974.
303 Ibid., p. 975.
304 Ibid., p. 975.
305 Ibid., p. 225.

to act on sympathy, grace and personal gratitude.'[306] Only bureaucracy has provided the foundation for the means of administration based on rational law 'systematized on the basis of statutes,' eliminating irrational considerations in the application of expediency.[307]

Characteristics of Bureaucracy

Weber went on to outline a number of key characteristics related to bureaucratic administration.[308] Among these are the following characteristics. (i) A bureaucratic administration presupposes a chain of command that is hierarchically organized. This organization follows a clearly defined structure of offices and positions, with duly assigned responsibilities. It is reliant on procedurally-correct decision making based on consideration of levels of authority, jurisdiction, due process and correct rulings. (ii) In a bureaucracy, a system of impersonal rules governs the rites and duties of positional incumbents and the adherence to rules prevails over sentiment. (iii) The rights and duties of officials are explicitly prescribed and proscribed in written regulations which have been properly 'enacted.' This results in staff members owing their allegiance to the system of impersonal legal rules rather than to the caprice of superiors.[309] (iv) Officials receive contractually-fixed salaries and do not own their positions or the means of production. This creates an official separation between the administrative sphere of responsibility and the private affairs of the official. (v) A bureaucracy presupposes a system of impersonal guidelines for dealing with and defining work responsibilities. Rules are designed for typical cases and officials deal with them effectively by applying uniform rules and procedures. Decision making is carried out with regard to a reliance on technical knowledge and the concept of the expert prevails. (vi) A bureaucracy is predicated on a clearly defined division of labor based upon functional specialization of tasks and a well-defined hierarchy of authority. Authority is strictly defined and officials take orders only from those immediately above them in rank. (vii) Within the bureaucracy, norms of impersonality govern interpersonal relations. Employees act within their roles as incumbents of offices rather than in terms of personal ties. (viii) Officials treat people in terms of 'cases' rather than as individuals and remain impersonal in their contacts with the public. Officials interact with members of the public only in their capacity as incumbents of offices and roles. (ix) Written documentation and orientation to files is a precondition to legitimate decision making. (x) In a bureaucratic administration, the discharge of responsibilities is based on calculable rules which are carried out 'without regard for persons.'[310]

306 Ibid., p. 975.
307 Ibid., p. 975.
308 Ibid., pp. 956–8.
309 Ibid., pp. 956–8.
310 Ibid., p. 975.

Concept of the 'Office' in Bureaucratic Organization

One of the most important characteristics of bureaucracy is the concept of the office. By 'office,' Weber meant a sphere of legal authority that is granted to an area of work which is under the administrative jurisdiction of an official and his or her directives.[311] Bureaucratic office holders obtain their position by appointment to public service that is in accord with the vocation of the office holder. Office holders are required to undergo 'prescribed courses of training which require their total attention for a long period of time.'[312] They are required to take special examinations which function as preconditions to employment and service. In this context, officials perform their responsibilities as 'duties' which are executed as administrative functions. Tasks and duties of office holders are defined according to a set of legal precepts. In this sense, office holding stands formally outside the ownership over the means of production and access to gratuities which may be exchanged for services.[313] Officials exchanging services or granting favors for gratuities break legal rules which trigger removal from office and indictment. Loyalty to the office owes allegiance to the framework of legal rules which are contractually enforced. Weber pointed out that it is of key importance that the system of loyalty converges around the office and the system of legal rules rather than attaching to persons or personal relationships within the bureau. Slippage in the direction of patrimonial authority or a widening of the sphere of personal discretion reduces stress on objective rules and is seen as an abuse of the office.

Weber went on to reason that so far as the bureaucratic official functions within a sphere of legal authority, a degree of social respectability is associated with the holding of offices.[314] Where this status is high, such as the officers' corps of the German Army, there is 'guild-like closure of officialdom' that carries with it the connotation of patrimonial authority.[315] On the other hand, where esteem is low, the demand for expertise is diminished and the authority of the official is weakened.

Next, Weber considered the difference between election and appointment of the office holder.[316] He stated that it is the norm for bureaucratic officials to be appointed to their positions by superiors. As soon as officials are elected by those they govern, they immediately lose their bureaucratic characteristics. One obvious consequence of this is the procedure of elections, which immediately alters the hierarchical structure of bureaucratic authority because elected officials tend to be autonomous *vis-à-vis* their superiors, and are directly accountable to the people who

---

311 Ibid., pp. 958–9.
312 Ibid., pp. 958–9.
313 Ibid., pp. 958–9.
314 Ibid., p. 959.
315 Ibid., p. 960.
316 Ibid., p. 960.

elected them. In Weber's view, the procedure of election tends to impair the bureaucratic mechanism and weakens the hierarchy of authority and subordination. To illustrate this, Weber cited the example of the practices used in American municipal elections in which officials working with local bureaucrats use their power in what he calls a 'caesarist' manner.[317] The inclination to 'caesarism,' according to Weber, grows out of the tendency of democracy to encourage the position of the 'caesar' as a freely-elected trustee of the masses who, on the one hand, is unfettered by tradition and, on the other, able to consolidate powers in the office in a monopolistic way. Weber believed that this type of rule by individuals works against formal democracy and the legal principle of officialdom.

Bureaucracy and Law

Next, Weber turned his attention to the relationship between bureaucratic decision making and the development of branches of law. He pointed out that the decision-making apparatus of bureaucracy is preceded by earlier forms which have been based on tradition, revelation, oracle or informal judgments rendered in terms of ethical considerations. Other such decision-making practices have rested on formal judgments rendered by drawing on analogies and even, in some cases, on assigning causal agency to forces outside individuals – such as those found in medieval legal judgments which were based on theological intervention by God.

In the discussion of bureaucracy and law, Weber made the distinction between two different kinds of decision making: (i) empirical decision making; and (ii) rational adjudication by precedent.[318] Empirical decision making tends rigorously to exclude all considerations based on ethical or moral norms and looks instead for factual consistencies between preceding cases. The primary principle of empirical decision making is its straightforward reduction to the facts and its ability to convert factual similarities into 'techniques.' Adjudication by precedent, on the other hand, tends to resist standards of equity and democratic fairness by working towards the principle of preserving the status position of élites and by controlling dominant interests. Adjudication by precedent is based on the aim of retaining closure on decision-making practices, and in this sense it procedurally adheres to formal requirements and is 'bound to hallowed tradition.'[319] For this reason, it is less rational and less universalistic. The use of Roman law, according to Weber, was far more rational. It introduced objective procedure into decision making and put an emphasis on procedural consideration by trained experts. Generally speaking, English jurisprudence was slow to accept Roman law because it emphasized universal procedure which tended to conflict with a decision making that favoured élites. This led to the situation of justice by notables, which

317 Ibid., p. 961.
318 Ibid., p. 978.
319 Ibid., p. 976.

was less rational and less bureaucratic in its development of legal decision making. Weber pointed out that the general tendency toward the principle of fact pleading in law, in contrast to universal appeal to concepts, has made decision making more empirical.

This matter of factness in decision making and the tendency to develop a technical attitude towards trial procedure, made law more rational. Weber believed that rational law and bureaucratic decision making go hand in hand because it is important that arbitrary judgment and individual discretion are eliminated from decision making. It is always a bureaucratic ideal that a 'system of rationally debatable reasons' can be drawn on in bureaucratic administration to warrant decision making.[320] This places stress on legal guarantees against arbitrariness and ensures equality before the law. In addition, it marks the transition from ethics to formalism and to rule-bound matter of factness in bureaucratic administration.

The Leveling of Social Differences

Next, Weber turned his attention to a process he referred to as the 'leveling effect' of bureaucratic administration. This 'leveling' is a result of the dominant role of bureaucracy in modern society. By 'leveling,' Weber meant the process of conforming to norms which emphasize standard procedure, and the effects this standardization has on society and culture as a whole. He traced this leveling to the democratic process itself. This comes about with the appearance of mass democracy, which ultimately leads to the disappearance of élites and the social privileges of rank that go with élites. Insofar as democracy requires complete equality before the law, it regularizes authority in its abstract form, and leads to what Weber called the 'horror of privilege.'[321] Leveling in bureaucratic society, according to Weber, is always to the lowest common denominator; the result being a disdain for rank, for honorific preferences and a removal of all social levels and distinctions.[322] He pointed out that the development of bureaucratization runs parallel to the development of state administration, which he thought arises in democratically inclined societies such as France, England and North America. In North American society, for instance, the norm of public opinion has replaced rank and privilege. In addition to this, there are two principles that go hand in hand with democracy: (i) intolerance for closed status groups in favor of universal accessibility; and (ii) the containment of the authority of officialdom so that 'public opinion' can be expressed to the widest extent and used to serve the public in establishing consensus. The social leveling that occurs as a result of bureaucracy brings with it a political and legal leveling as well.

320 Ibid., p. 979.
321 Ibid., p. 983.
322 Ibid., p. 983.

Consequences of Bureaucracy

In the final section of Weber's investigation, he examined the social consequences of bureaucratization. He outlined two broad categories of consequence. The first is the incompatibility of democracy with bureaucratic development. As soon as bureaucracy develops, the governed tend to accept the authority of bureaucratic decision making without question and thus give up the right to accountable government.[323] Underlying this problem is the influence of moneyed élites, who tend to wield power over bureaucratic agencies through political donations in exchange for patronage positions. This gives rise to economic interest groups who lobby state officials to advance their interests by manipulating the structure of power. A second consequence of bureaucracy is the tendency to develop secrecy. All bureaucracies tend to foster secrecy with regard to their knowledge and their intentions. This leads to the exclusion of the public from decision making and from participation in the production of consensus.[324] Bureaucratic institutions thus become closed, and this entails a loss of democracy.

323 Ibid., p. 989.
324 Ibid., p. 1002.

5
Conclusion

Sociological Theory in America

Throughout this book, we have examined the influences leading to the development of sociological theory during the nineteenth century. By and large, there are four central themes which define this period of development: revolution, industrialization, capitalism and modernism. In response to these large-scale social changes, two broad theoretical perspectives emerged: Marx's materialist perspective, based on economic determinants and class analysis of societies; and Durkheim's consensus perspective, based on the discovery of the normative patterning of society and group life. What these sociological theories share is their 'structural' orientation to the formation of society. In contemporary social thought, the term 'structural theory' is used to describe a way of looking at society which is characteristic of nineteenth-century sociological investigation. These theories may be defined as broad-based theoretical perspectives which examine the nature of social life by searching for an underlying pattern or reality whose internal logic acts to bring about, shape or cause the dominant pattern of social life. Viewed in this way, we can state that Marx described the underlying pattern of social life in terms of the historical tendency of societies to divide themselves into classes on the basis of economic production. Durkheim, on the other hand, described the underlying tendency of social life to produce normatively patterned social environments so that individuals emerge from the group differently than they would have been had they lived alone in isolation. In both these cases, the internal logic of the underlying pattern is believed to affect the prevailing structure of reality and social life. Both these theories identified the underlying class historical elements of social life and the normatively patterned environment of the group.

However, one of the shortcomings of structural theories is that all the major sociological categories generally focus on the description of the pattern in the objective world, with varying degrees of emphasis on either the class historical pattern or the normative social pattern. In focusing exclusively on the objective world as such, structural theory tends to squeeze out all the subjective categories.[1]

---

1 Talcott Parsons, 'Weber's Methodology of Social Science,' in *Max Weber: The Theory of Social and Economic Organization*, New York: Free Press, 1947, p. 10.

In this concluding chapter, we turn our attention to the twentieth century, where the developments of sociological theory in America make a shift in the structural theories of Marx and Durkheim.

While Weber did not play a major role in forming the grand perspectives of European social theory, his work had a profound effect on the formation of sociological theory in America between 1945 and 1970. Where Weber was most influential was in putting forward the rudiments of a theory of social action, a development which later came to be called interpretive theory. This may be defined as a body of social theorizing initially devised by Weber and elaborated by thinkers in America, particularly Talcott Parsons and Robert Merton. Weber's dramatic point of departure from structural theory is his focus on the normative pattern from the point of view of subjective categories. While structural theory had described society from the perspective of the objective concepts of history, society, class and social institutions, it left out what the normative pattern meant to the person whose action is being studied. Weber's sociological categories allowed individual action to be treated not merely as a response to outside constraints, but as an orientation to the normative pattern in terms of the subjective motives and judgments of the individual actor. This shift gave a decisive action orientation to social life.

Weber's theory of social action was the product of the methodological controversy in Germany in the early part of the twentieth century. Because he believed that individuals act in and come to understand the social world only through interpretive acts, Weber devised a methodology for making judgments about the 'inner states' of actors in their actions with others in society. At the most fundamental level, these acts were seen to involve the process of assigning meanings to the given factual states in the outer world. Weber believed that the 'inner' rather than the 'outer' state of the actor should be the key investigative focus of the social sciences.

Developments in American Sociology

After Weber's death in 1920, the growth of sociological theory was centered at the University of Chicago and at Harvard University. Work carried on in Chicago during the 1920s and 1930s led directly to the shift in sociology from macro-level to micro-level social theory. This perspective, called social interactionism, derived its conceptual and theoretical focus from Max Weber, Georg Simmel and its American proponent, G.H. Mead. Its central argument was that human beings act toward society and each other in terms of meanings they attribute to their situations.

A second development in America was that of modern consensus theory pioneered by Talcott Parsons and Robert Merton during the 1940s and 1950s. Both Parsons and Merton advocated a synthesis of the works of Durkheim and Weber which led to the development of social action theory in America, stemming largely from the work of Weber. The underlying premise of a theory of social action was that human beings make judgments in their acts. These acts are therefore seen to be the products of 'considerations' and 'choices' which are social in nature and which point up 'strategies' used by actors to make decisions. In writings such as *The Structure of Social Action* and *Toward a General Theory of Social Action* published in 1947 and 1951 respectively, Parsons' work reflected the need in sociological theory to describe individual intention and the relationship between intention and social action. The basic insight, however, was Weberian. It was Weber who explicitly argued that sociology must be a science which attempts the interpretive understanding of social action.

It is noteworthy that, while Weber did not play a major role in the formation of the grand theoretical perspectives of the nineteenth century as had Marx and Durkheim, he nevertheless provided an important contribution to those of the twentieth century.

Glossary of Concepts

Marx

Abstract labor A term used to describe the change that takes place in capitalist social relations when all labor is treated as having an element in common so that it can be remunerated at the same rate regardless of the differences in the skills of the laborer. To illustrate how this process takes place, Marx makes the distinction between 'useful labour' and 'abstract labour'. Useful labor refers to the capacity of labor to confer use value on a commodity. A coat, for instance, has use value only so far as the skill of the laborer confers value upon it, and this use value is capable of satisfying some distinct human need. Marx maintained that the capacity of labor to produce these utilities in commodities is qualitatively different in each of the different kinds of labor, as is evident in the skills that it takes to produce linen, coats, shoes etc. 'Useful labour' is therefore qualitatively distinct and is a product of human nerve, muscle and skill. Abstract labor, however, arises in capitalism when all useful labor is treated as having an element in common, so that all labor can be viewed as the same and remunerated at the same hourly rate. When labor is conceived in this way it is abstract because it is measured in 'a temporal duration of labour time' rather than as a unique skill conferring use value. Marx believed that this central shift from a qualitative to quantitative framework yields what he calls 'abstract labour.' From this point of view, all labor is but the quantitative expression of what was a qualitative social relation.

Abstraction The concept of abstraction is central to Marx's thinking and generally describes a lapse or break which occurs in the system of social relations when individuals no longer see themselves as connected to society or to the productive power of their labor. Marx believed that human beings were once connected to society by a system of social relations which existed in concrete ties to the land, estates and guilds. As soon as modern capitalism began to develop, however, these links were severed and replaced by abstract ties to the political state in the form of rights and freedoms. As these former ties to society became fragmented, the new system of links only resembled the earlier links in the abstract. The process is especially evident in alienation and reification, where the individual's connection to the larger system of social relations does not reflect his or her human nature, but only resembles it in the abstract.

Alienation A central concept in Marx describing a state of disruption taking place in the laboring process leading to a loss of control by laborers over their labor and the self-defining characteristics of laboring activity. The concept was first used by Hegel to pinpoint the moment when human beings experience their own activity as something external to them and he described this as self-estrangement. Later, Feuerbach developed the term by arguing that, in making religion, human beings project their own essence onto an image and make this image into God by assigning qualities to it that are distinctly non-human. Alienation occurs, according to Feuerbach, at the moment when this image is reimposed on the life of human beings in the form of unwanted rules and prescriptions. After Feuerbach, Marx expanded the concept by looking at the effects of capitalism on the human labor process. Central to his reasoning is the role played by labor in human self-definition and identity. Labor, for Marx, is central in that it serves to connect individuals to themselves through the products of their labor and to others through the products they produce. For Marx, alienation takes place in four broad ways. First, when human beings lose control over the product of their labor as a result of the means of production falling into private hands and as a result of their product entering into the medium of exchange. Second, alienation occurs when individuals lose control over the self-defining nature of their productive activity because they are required to sell their labor in exchange for a wage, and their labor is thus owned by another. This loss of productive activity leads to what Marx calls a fundamental 'reversal' of what is 'human to what is animal.' This reversal takes place in the sense that the worker is only free in those functions he or she shares with animals, such as eating, sleeping, drinking and procreating, since it is only in these functions that the worker is alone and unsupervised. Third, alienation takes place when human beings lose the connections they have to their own species since, under capitalism, labor is turned into a physical rather than a creative act. Like animals, human beings are required to perform their laboring functions only to fill their immediate physical needs, and in doing this they relinquish their conscious being. Fourth, alienation occurs when human beings are estranged from their fellow humans as a result of the fact that their labor under capitalism has turned them into individual beings who compete alone against others in the pursuit of private gain. This disruption of the labor process estranges individuals from the human community since, at one time, their labor was cooperative and collective, whereas now it is individual.

Ancient Mode of Production   This term is used to refer to a stage of economic development in which the ownership of the means of production is concentrated in the hands of a small élite. The productive system is essentially agrarian with developed private property, rudimentary industry, trade and commerce. Growing directly from the productive system is the division of society into a class system of patrician and slave. Relations of production are between élites and slave laborers, with élites obtaining their wealth and economic existence through the exploitation of a class of slaves who act as the direct producers. An example of a productive system of this type was the Graeco-Roman world.

Appearance–Reality   This term is used by Marx to draw attention to the distinction between the way things 'appear' on the surface and an underlying essence or reality. The term was initially used in Greek philosophy to draw attention to the idea that the perceptible world is often contradictory to some underlying pattern, truth or reality. While Marx believed that appearance and reality never really coincide, he stated that 'appearances' grow out of our social relations which, in turn, arise from economic production. In a key passage, Marx put forward the idea that reality is shaped by how people use the means of production. In this sense, economic activity constitutes the structure of appearances since it shapes human social relations. At the center of the distinction is the idea that the material world is not a 'true' reflection of reality and that reality itself lies beneath appearances. An example is found in feudal society where religious directives justify the serfs' unequal relation to the lord. It is Marx's contention that this inequality 'appears' to be acceptable only because it masks an underlying reality, making what is actual invisible. Marx thought that it was in the nature of 'appearances' to present to the eye the exact opposite of the underlying reality. The questions for Marx are, to what extent do appearances dominate, what sustains appearance in the light of the underlying reality, and what mechanisms can be used to reinstate reality over appearances?

Bonapartism   This is a term used in *The Eighteenth Brumaire of Louis Bonaparte* to describe the emergence of the modern state apparatus during the period of crisis which took place in France during the class struggle of 1849–51, when Louis Bonaparte ruled France and constitutional powers were suspended. By various political maneuvers Bonaparte was able to detach the controlling offices of the state from the parliament and convert them into organs of state executive power. At that moment the state became separate from society and its powers were independent or autonomous of the interests of the dominant classes. The term 'Bonapartism' gained significance because it identified the actual creation of the modern political state and the powers used to relieve the bourgeoisie of their claim to political dominance. By such maneuvers Louis Bonaparte: (i) weakened the political power of all the classes; (ii) claimed to represent the classes (peasants, workers and bourgeoisie) equally; and (iii) rendered the bourgeoisie incapable of realizing their own political interests. Though Marx felt that Bonaparte himself was unimportant historically, he thought that the Bonapartist period was significant in that it marked the development of the capitalist state by pointing to the political vacuum that is created at the moment when all classes lie 'prostrate' before the state machine.

Capitalism   Marx defined capitalism as a system of social relations. He believed that neither money nor commodities alone were sufficient to make capitalism. For a society to be capitalistic, money and commodities had to be transformed into a system of social relations and this takes place only when: (i) the worker is forcibly separated from the means of production; (ii) ownership is in private hands; and (iii) a system of exchange emerges which governs the buying and selling of commodities. Marx identified the advent of capitalism with a process called 'primitive accumulation,' in which feudal land is coercively transformed into private property and the direct producer is divorced from the means of production. The process began in the fourteenth and fifteenth centuries, leading to worldwide commerce, markets and trade by the eighteenth century. As capitalist production became established, it altered the labor process found in feudal society where laborers had direct access to the means of production, owned the product of labor and directly produced their livelihoods. In capitalism, by contrast, the laborer is separate from the means of production, work is directly under the control of the capitalist and the product of labor belongs to the owners of the means of production. The basis of capitalist production is exchange.

Capitalist Mode of Production   Marx used the term 'mode of production' to show how economic production shapes the system of social relations and the class system arising from it. Since the way people produce governs the form of their social relations, a capitalist mode of production presupposes the development of private ownership of the means of production, a class system of capitalist and laborer, and a system of exchange which governs social relations. Historically a capitalist mode of production arose during the break-up of the feudal economy and the shift in production from the countryside to the town. As the feudal economy began to dissolve, serfs were coercively separated from the land and turned into a class of wage laborers (proletarianization) who sold their labor on the market to satisfy their economic needs. In a capitalist society, there is widespread emergence of private property, a developed class system of laborer and capitalist, and an advanced division of labor with trade and commercial activity. Capitalist classes draw their wealth from the class of wage laborers and surplus labor is the prevailing form of exploitation.

Civil Society   A central political concept in Marx used to identify the emergence of a new realm of social action separate from the old political categories of the state and monarch. The term serves to describe the political changes taking place in society during the development of the modern state. It came into use with the work of Adam Smith and Georg Hegel who first used it to describe the birth of a civil realm which arose after the dissolution of the old political order and the demise of the monarchy as the center of the state. In Marx, the term is used to pinpoint the precise historical moment when there is a development of an independent economic realm in society which emerges as a consequence of the centralization of the political state. With the emergence of civil society, there is a shift in the center of gravity from the state to the economy. At the end of the process of civil society stands the 'free individual' who is stripped of various ties to communal bodies and who is the possessor of political rights and freedoms based on the private pursuit of economic gain.

Class   A central concept in Marx referring to groups whose 'economic conditions of existence compel them to live separately from one another' and who have a 'mode of life' different from each other. Marx links the existence of social class to the development of property relations in society, and defines a class in terms of its relationship to the means of production. Class is also used in Marx to refer to a historical principle evident in the laws of economic development and the repetition of class relations throughout history. Class is a historical social relation in which the principle of production manifests itself.

Class Consciousness A term used by Marx to designate the development of conscious awareness among the working classes that takes place as a result of the increase in class antagonism occurring during the rise of modern capitalism. A full understanding of the term depends upon the distinction between the 'objective' conditions of a social class and the 'subjective' realization of these conditions. Marx believed that, with the rise of capitalism, the objective situation of the working class worsened as ownership of the means of production fell into private hands and the growth of industry intensified the labor of the worker. The decline in objective conditions led to the crystallization of a political and economic struggle which increased the overall unity of the proletariat. Marx believed that the change in the objective conditions created conscious awareness among the working classes in: (i) their realization that the class of capitalists constitutes a 'permanent opponent' whose interests conflict with their own; (ii) that this opposition promotes the cohesion of the working class which, in turn, (iii) leads to an understanding that the situation in which they find themselves is a result of social inequalities inherent in social classes. As this conscious awareness increases, they are transformed from a 'class in itself' to a 'class for itself,' with full awareness of their historical position.

Commodity A key concept in Marx's theory of capitalism which derives its significance from its early use by classical political economy to designate a category of production and a thing bearing value. Marx thought that the analysis of the commodity by classical political economy was incomplete and needed to be singled out for systematic treatment since it was so closely linked to capitalist development. Marx thought that commodity production was a central way of understanding capitalist society and often compared it to feudal society where there were no commodities, no system of exchange and all production was directly for use. Marx claimed that one of the distinguishing characteristics of commodity production in capitalism is that commodities are subject to buying and selling, and in this sense, enter into the medium of 'exchange.' It was this 'system of exchange' which had not been seen before and it had the effect of reducing all social relations to acts of buying and selling. According to Marx, commodities essentially have two distinct properties: (i) use value which is capable of satisfying human needs; and (ii) exchange value in which quantities of one commodity can be expressed in the value of quantities of another commodity. Marx thought that exchange value is found only in capitalist society and his criticism of it centered on its dominance in social relations.

Consciousness A term used by Marx to differentiate human existence from the existence of animals. Marx believed that human beings are distinct from animals because they have conscious being, in contrast to animals who only have physical being. Marx reasoned that individuals distinguish themselves from animals to the extent that their existence requires them to produce their physical environment in order to satisfy the primary economic needs. In this respect, human beings are distinct because: (i) they produce their means of subsistence; (ii) they enter into a conscious relation with nature in order to survive; and (iii) they have consciousness and are capable of reflecting on their own situations. This suggests that individuals reflect continually on their own circumstances, think about themselves in relation to others and to society, and are impelled to act on behalf of their needs.

Contradiction A philosophical term initially used by Hegel to denote the presence of the principles of affirmation and negation existing at the same time. Hegel took the view that contradiction is rooted in reality and believed that it was reflected in the existence of opposing elements which bring about the process of change and development. Later, Marx used the term to identify contradictory elements in historical social relations which manifest themselves in the appearance of social class and class conflict. Historically, capitalism entails two contradictory principles in its relations of workers and capitalists. Both these principles are contradictory since each class does not have the same aim or interest and their activity develops along contradictory lines. For Marx, contradictions have their roots in class inequalities and always reflect the fact that social relations are based on unequal class divisions. It is the job of ideology to manage the contradictions by: (i) making them appear as legitimate; (ii) by resolving them in favor of the dominant classes; and (iii) by explaining the contradictions away by assigning their causes to sources other than social inequalities and class differences.

Dialectic The term originates in Greek philosophy where it was used as a method to get at underlying truths which could not be obtained using techniques of observation or sense perception. In the eighteenth and nineteenth centuries, dialectics reached its highest stage of development in the work of Georg Hegel who employed the method to show the inter-connections between various categories of experience such as history, spirit, and conscious-ness. Hegel's dialectic propounded a theory of development by stating that all things are in a continuous state of motion and change, and that the general laws of motion are intrinsic to the development of the individual and history. The importance of Hegel's observation is that it viewed the world, existence and being in terms of interconnected processes rather than seeing persons and things as separate by themselves. The doctrine that all things are interconnected later became the theoretical basis for the dialectical view of reality and history. Central to Hegel's theory of the dialectic is the principle of 'contradiction' which expresses itself in the wider struggle of existence having three main stages: first is the stage called 'affirmation' or thesis, referring to the capacity of an existing thing to affirm itself in the world actively rather than passively. Second is the stage of the dialectic called the 'negation' or antithesis, which refers to the principle which acts to thwart or restrict the capacity of an existing thing to develop its own being. Third is the principle of 'negation of the negation' or synthesis, which denotes the capacity of the negation to be reconstituted and fundamentally altered. Since negation itself stands for limit, then 'negation of the negation' is that principle of development which surpasses boundaries and reconstitutes limits. After Hegel, Marx took the dialectic in a different direction, developing the material side by looking at historical and economic growth. Marx's doctrine of development is called the materialist dialectic to indicate the shift from the dominance of ideas to the dominance of economic conditions. Marx took the view that the principle of change was manifest in economic production and, in taking this step, he placed a decisive materialist emphasis on the process of development. He thought that the principle of contradiction manifested itself in the form of the coercive class structure of society and found the concept of social class to be a material expression of the law of contradiction expressed at the level of economic relations. For Marx, the stages of develop-ment were related to economic production and the system of social classes. In the first stage, called primitive community, class relations are not crystallized and private ownership is not developed. In the second stage, called ancient society, a system of ownership emerges leading to the crystallization of social classes and the structuring of historical social relations based on the dominance of one class over the others. In the third stage, called feudal society, class relations are embedded in property relations, from which emerges a class of producers subject to those who are dominant over them. In the fourth stage, called capitalism, classes are in direct opposition and conflict and this leads to the development of a revolutionary class who are conscious of the conditions that oppress them. In this sense, Marx's historical con-figuration of successive societies and class structures made the dialectic historically real.

Doctrine of Increasing Misery This is a term Marx used to convey the essential connection between the constant growth of capital, the accumulation of wealth and the growing social distress of the working class. Marx believed that the connection between the growth of capital and the growing misery of the worker is fundamental to capitalism and can be seen to play itself out as the productivity of capitalism increases. He argued that, as the productive capacity of capitalism improves, it concentrates its resources on innovative techniques which result in a reduction in the amount of labor required for production. This acts to increase the population of unemployed, which in turn adds to the mass of the industrial reserve army. At the same time there is an increasing demand for labor. As a result, the conditions of the worker become more impoverished and the worker is reduced to the status of a pauper. The greater the accumulation of wealth at one end of society, the greater the accumulation of misery at the other.

Dual Character of Labor   This term refers to a central discovery by Marx relating to the claim by political economists that labor imparts exchange value alone to commodities. Marx insisted that there are two elements that labor puts into the commodity, and he called this the 'dual character of labour.' The two characteristics of labor identified by Marx are 'useful labour' and 'abstract labour.' Useful labor refers to the precise ability of the worker to add utility to a commodity by conferring a use value upon it. A tailor, for instance, brings the utility of a coat into existence as a function of the labor that is put into it. Labor in its useful form is thus a condition of human existence since it serves a specific material purpose which is to sustain life. Marx goes on to state that this capacity of labor to produce use values is qualitatively different in each of the different kinds of labor, as is evident in the different skills that it takes to produce different commodities. In these terms, labor is always 'heterogeneous,' or qualitatively distinct, since if it were not, different commodities could not meet in the market with different exchange values. Thus, useful labor is the actual activity which adds exchange value to a commodity. Abstract labor, on the other hand, refers to the process of abstraction which 'heterogeneous' labor undergoes in capitalism when all useful labor is treated as having an element in common so it can be remunerated at the same hourly rate. When labor is conceived in this way, it is abstract, since it is measured in 'a temporal duration of labour time' rather than as a qualitative skill conferring use value. Marx drew attention to the 'dual character' of labor in order to show the mechanism of exploitation in capitalist society which ensures that labor is never remunerated at a rate equivalent to the value it creates.

Economic Base   Marx used this term to demonstrate how the system of social relations is derived from economic production. He reasoned that since human beings must produce to satisfy their material needs, the first act of all societies is economic and this leads to the formation of subsequent social relations. The economic base may be thought of as the underlying historical force propelling human beings to produce the means of their survival. Marx thought that since all societies are founded on the need to produce, society itself tends to take the shape of the social forces of production. Marx believed that the evidence for this exists in the class structure of society which reflects economic relations of production. In contrast to the base, the term 'superstructure' is used by Marx to refer to the social institutions which arise on top of the economic base. Chief among these are the legal and political institutions which, in Marx's view, are not separate from the economy and in this sense are determined by it. Using the concepts of base and superstructure, Marx was able to show: (i) that economic production shapes social relations and hence the structure of society; and (ii) that economic production shapes the class structure and the corresponding ideas related to the roles which people play in production.

Equivalent Form of Value   This is a term Marx used in conjunction with the concept of relative form of value to solve the problem posed by political economy concerning the value of commodities. Political economists had asserted that commodities were bearers of value and believed that value was a substance found in a commodity. Marx refuted this by showing that no commodity has value in itself (except as use value), but has value only in relation to other commodities, a phenomenon he referred to as relative value. This issue is central to his theory of value because it was Marx's aim to show that exchange value is the product of a social framework and a set of social relations specific to capitalism rather than a 'substance' which inheres in a commodity. Marx introduced the term 'equivalent value' to complete his discussion of the origin of value by putting forward the formula that value occurs when the relative and equivalent forms of value confront each other. Relative and equivalent forms of value constitute 'two poles of the expression of value' and, therefore, in order for value to occur, commodities must confront each other in these two forms. For example, the value of linen could not be determined until it was brought into comparison with the value of a coat. In this sense, linen does not know its own value until it is reflected in the mirror provided by the value of the coat. 'The whole mystery of value,' wrote Marx, 'lies hidden in this simple form.'

Exchange Value   Marx used this concept to pinpoint the change taking place in the form of value as a result of the development of capitalism and the emergence of a market as a medium of exchange. Marx believed that, before capitalism, value was in the form of use or utility which served directly as a means of existence. This was evident in feudal society where production was entirely for use and what was produced was consumed directly to satisfy human needs. Under these circumstances, the products of labor do not become commodities since there are no markets and no buying and selling. Exchange value, by contrast, arises in capitalist society as a result of the development of a medium of exchange called the market, and the dominance of buying and selling. What is produced becomes a 'commodity,' since its value is determined by its ability to enter into exchange. Exchange value thus denotes the dominance of one form of value over the other, and the resulting change which occurs in social relations. Marx's criticism of exchange centers on how all social relations in society come to be determined by it.

False Consciousness   This term was never used by Marx. It originates from Frederick Engels, who first used the term in a letter to Franz Mehring in 1893 to describe a situation in which the proletariat are unable to grasp the 'true' nature of their interests or their historical role as a subordinate class. Engels ascribed 'false consciousness' to outside forces which he believed impel individuals to impute false motives to the causes of their hardship and suffering. Later the term was adopted by Georg Lukács who took the view that false consciousness could be traced to structural relations in society. However, because of the ambiguity created in the idea of 'true' vs 'false' consciousness, the term became misleading and theoretically imprecise. When describing ideological functions, Marx preferred the more active term of the 'camera obscura' or 'inverted image', in which reality appears to be upside down. By this he implied that the ideological distortion appears in reality first and consciousness later. What is important to notice here is that Marx shifts the emphasis to locate the material origin of the ideological distortion in the productive relations, and it is these relations which become reflected in consciousness rather than the other way round. Hence, 'social being determines consciousness.'

Fetishism   A concept used by Marx to refer to the stage in the development of capitalism when commodities are assigned powers which they do not have in reality. Marx believed that commodities have simple use values, are capable of satisfying human needs and serve the purpose of sustaining existence. The fetishism of commodities occurs only when commodities are believed to have powers which surpass their simple use values. The prototype of fetishism is found in tribal societies where magical powers are assigned to objects which people believe grow out of the nature of the object. Marx thought that, by themselves, objects have no powers and believed that the hidden source of this power was the individual's active relation to the object. This relationship was shaped by none other than the system of social relations in which beliefs about objects are imbedded in society. Marx thought that fetishism could be historically understood since it refers to a stage of economic development when commodities become bearers of certain powers which are conferred upon them when they enter into exchange. This does not occur in feudal societies where the products of labor never become commodities and never obtain powers beyond their simple use value. In capitalism, as soon as commodities enter into a system of exchange, they appear to have values beyond their mere use. It is at this point that the transactions between material things (e.g., commodities) take on the fetish form. Commodities appear to have a life of their own and enter into social relations with one another (exchange, buying and selling, etc.), and as such appear to have human qualities. As a direct consequence, human social relations become thing-like so far as individuals confront each other as the possessors of commodities.

Feudal Mode of Production A term used by Marx to refer to a stage of economic development in which production is based on a class of landholders who derive their wealth by relying on an enserfed peasantry who work the land to the advantage of the landholder. A feudal mode of production is entirely agrarian, has little town life and no industry. The class system is crystallized into serfs and landholders who have powers of coercion over the class of serfs. The central economic unit is the feudal estate encompassing large bodies of agricultural land, with social and political power residing in the landholder. Landholders have rights over the labor of the serf, the serf's agricultural production and the right to impose economic exactions on serfs in the form of free labor service, dues and taxes. Serfs have direct access to the means of production and use these to produce their own economic livelihoods.

Feudal Society A term used to refer to a type of society based on a system of land holding for purposes of production and economic maintenance. In the early stages of feudal society the rural way of life was universal, there was an absence of towns and the production of a food supply dominated everyday life. Landholders drew their social and political powers from links to aristocratic classes which conferred rights centering upon land holdings and economic prerogatives. At the center of feudal society was the relation between lord and serf, a relationship which formed the basis of the class system. Serfs were attached to the land by obligations resting on customary rights rather than explicit legal rules. Obligations set out the social relations between lord and serf and formed a system of privilege which defined the feudal way of life. Serfs occupied agricultural holdings, cultivated land and produced their own economic livelihood. The system of customary rights linking the serf to the lord took the form of: (i) economic obligations consisting of the right of the lord to compel unpaid labor service from the serf; (ii) social distinctions in which serfs were legitimately subordinated to the lord; and (iii) economic exactions including taxes, dues, and fees which were levied by the lord upon the serf. Feudal societies as a whole began to decline during the sixteenth and seventeenth centuries after capitalist development led to the dissolution of the feudal economy, giving way to a system of exchange, commodity production and wage labor.

Forces of Production A term used by Marx to outline one of the major components of the materialist theory of history. The forces of production may be defined as capacities in things and persons to be set into use for purposes of production. Specifically, the forces of production refers to the available techniques existing in the means of production and includes instruments, equipment, knowledge, persons, tools and the prevailing means of production. According to Marx, societies always operate at the limits of the productive forces, so that new productive forces may effect a transition to a new mode of production. By themselves, the productive forces do not create inequalities or social classes since they have to be put to use by persons and by the prevailing ideas and social relations. In themselves, the productive forces only create activities. New productive forces often engender transition points leading to the development of a new mode of production. The transition from the productive forces of feudalism (land, tools, plough, techniques of cultivation, etc.) to the productive forces of capitalism (industrial technique, science, machine technology, etc.) is an example of the shift in the prevailing forces of production.

Free Labor Marx used this term to describe the social and political condition of the working class after the dissolution of slavery and serfdom. It is Marx's contention that, in order for capitalism to develop, labor must be 'free' in the sense that it be subject to buying and selling so that it can be purchased as a commodity. In order for the capitalist to find labor on the market as a commodity, certain essential conditions must be met: (i) the possessors of labor power must be in a position to sell their labor as a commodity; and (ii) laborers must be seen to be 'free proprietors' of their own labor and thus 'free' to dispose of it as they see fit. This very precise condition of being able to dispose of one's own labor on the market is called 'free labour' and is fundamental to capitalism, since it makes the buying and selling of labor possible. Marx pointed out that, while it appears as if buyers and sellers meet in the market on an equal basis, it is obvious that the advantage is conferred on the buyer of labor power.

Guild System   The guild system can be defined as a professional association of craftsmen whose main function was to protect and regulate work relating to trades and crafts. Guilds were commonplace in Europe between the eleventh and eighteenth centuries and included all goods and services produced by persons skilled in a trade who had served the appropriate period of training and apprenticeship. The guild system involved all aspects of economic life including the work of weavers, carpenters, wheelwrights, etc., and had the central function of regulating access to trades and controlling prices of goods and services. During the seventeenth and eighteenth centuries, the guild system prohibited the expansion of workshops and restricted the development of capitalism by placing limitations on the number of workers a master could employ and by prohibiting the purchase of labor as a commodity. By the eighteenth century, the guild system began to decline, opening up the way for capitalist development.

Hegel   Best known as the originator of German idealism, Hegel's work is key to the development of social and political thought and to the work of Marx. Initially, Hegel was influenced by Aristotle who believed that Plato's separation of the material and ideal realms was unnecessary and, instead of situating absolutes above human existence as Plato had, Aristotle thought that the material and ideal realms were fused together. This was a key philosophic step since it took the view that the principles of human and social development were implicit in all matter. Hegel's contribution was in pioneering a system of thinking which attempted to explain history and existence as a process of development. One of Hegel's central concepts was the 'spirit,' a term he used to refer to a 'unifying pattern' which confers order and meaning on the material and ethical world. Marx criticized Hegel for: (i) asserting that ideas were real and had purposes of their own rather than seeing that they arise from economic production and class relations; and (ii) for putting forward the view that ideas rather than economic production shape the material world.

Human Essence   This is a term Marx used to describe a characteristic of human beings which is realized through their labor and productive activity. Distinct from Hegel's and Feuerbach's understanding of human essence as 'contemplative,' Marx thought that labor was the ultimate category of being, self-definition and existence. He believed that, because laboring comes first, it is essential to human material well-being and self-realization. Marx thought that human beings are defined by their labor in three specific senses: (i) by exerting control over nature they feel themselves to be active rather than passive in history; (ii) by producing the material necessities of food, shelter and clothing they maintain their physical existence; (iii) by controlling their circumstances, they provide self-definition and feel confirmed in their activity. Alienation robs individuals of their laboring essence since, in making the means of production the property of one class, labor is experienced as external and outside human control.

Idealism   A philosophic term used to identify a tradition of social theory which takes the view that the fundamental task of philosophy is to investigate the existence of a realm of ideas thought to be beyond the physical world. Plato was among the first to set out principles of thought asserting that the material world is constantly changing and that nothing can be known except a realm of 'universals' or 'absolutes.' This dimension gets its name from a set of ideas which the Greeks believed were permanent and unchanging because they could be applied universally to all social and historical circumstances. Plato took the view that the ideal realm included concepts such as equality, justice and virtue which he thought could be considered to be 'absolute' to the extent that they (i) were universally valid for all human societies, (ii) gave purpose and meaning to existence, and (iii) structured human action along standards on which was founded the political good of society. In the early nineteenth century, Georg Hegel pioneered a form of idealist philosophy which endeavored to explain history and existence as a process of development. Unlike Plato, who had believed the material and ideal spheres were separate, Hegel argued that they belonged together and were fundamentally rooted in the structure of reality and history. Hegel's theory put forward the idea that all things are in a continuous state of motion and change, and that the general laws of motion are intrinsic to the development of the individual and history. The importance of Hegel's observation was that it viewed the world, existence and being in terms of interrelated processes rather than seeing individuals and history as separate by themselves. The doctrine that all things are interconnected later became the theoretical basis for the dialectical view of reality and history. The terms Hegel used to denote the interconnection between the material and ideal realms were spirit, reason, history, consciousness, etc. Central to Hegel's philosophy was the focus on building a system which would show how our various experiences of past, present and future are, in fact, linked together to form totalities or meaningful wholes which can be explained by philosophical analysis. Marx criticized idealist philosophy for its mis-representation of reality and for its failure to come to terms with the basic material reality of satisfying everyday economic needs. Historically, idealism is opposed to materialism which takes the view that economic production and the satisfaction of material needs is the primary reality.

Ideology Marx developed his general theory of ideology in 1845–6 in order to break with the Hegelian view of ideology as an abstract representation of ideas. Marx wanted to show that ideas have a material origin and arise from economic activity. To do this, he put forward two central premises which provided the framework for a theory of ideology: (i) economic production shapes social relations and therefore the structure of society; and (ii) from this production, a system of ideas arises which comes to represent the productive relations and these stand as 'conscious images in mental life.' Marx maintained that the system of ideas arises from the way people produce and that these ideas always reflect the dominant material relationships and class interests in society. In general, Marx took the view that ideology was diffused throughout society, embodied in social institutions and reflected the existing social relations of production. Ideology can be defined as a system of attitudes, conceptions, ideas and beliefs which: (i) shape reality; and (ii) alter the perception of reality. The theoretical basis underlying this view derives its authority from Marx's assertion that we do not perceive reality directly but rather through the filters of prevailing ideas and beliefs which tend to act as distorting lenses which reflect the dominant economic relationships and ideas. This happens when the ideas and beliefs reflect only the wills and interests of the dominant classes and have the power to rule over material reality. Marx thought that ideology performs three specific functions: (i) legitimates the existing class system in which one class dominates over the material means of production; (ii) makes the subordinate classes politically passive and quiescent; and (iii) conceals contradictions between the classes and the ultimate coercive nature of society. In his theory of ideology, Marx was able to show the material origins of ideas.

Individual Marx used the term individual to denote a social and political entity which made its appearance in civil society at the end of the eighteenth century as a result of historical and economic changes. For Marx, the individual was a legal construct denoting a social person who is the bearer of certain rights and freedoms, while at the same time being separate from society. Marx put forward a theory of the development of the individual which begins with the process of the break-up of the old political bodies of estate, caste and guild, resulting in the individual becoming a sphere of autonomous social and economic action. As action became a 'private affair' of the individual rather than part of the wider community, the satisfaction of all wants was through the pursuit of private economic gain. At the end of this process, said Marx, is the isolated individual, whose private autonomy is a political and social absurdity.

Industrial Revolution Marx conceived of the Industrial Revolution as a shift which took place in the material conditions of society and in the social relations between persons. So far as material relations were concerned, the Industrial Revolution began with a shift in property from landlords to capitalists, beginning with the dissolution of the feudal economy, the rise of town manufacture and industrial production. This sparked an economic surplus leading to world markets, the development of trade, and the production of commodities. In conjunction with this was the change which took place in the system of social relations beginning with the break-up of all 'natural relationships' in favor of economic relationships, the creation of universal competition, and the emergence of a capitalist class whose primary activity was material acquisition. As a consequence, a laboring class was created which 'bore all the burdens of society without enjoying the advantages.'

Labor   This is a term used in Marx's writings to describe the activity by which human beings produce the means of their existence and their economic survival. Marx took the position that human labor is self-actualizing, because it is through labor that human beings create use values, maintain their existence, and confirm themselves in society and history. The term gained key theoretical prominence when Marx called into question the way political economists used it as an economic category by describing labor as a commodity which the worker sells to the capitalist. Marx refused to think of labor in this way, arguing that labor was not a commodity but, rather, an activity which defines individuals in nature and history. Marx thought that there was both a material and conscious element to human labor.

Labor Power   A key term in Marx's economic works which enabled him to make a central distinction between 'labour' as a human activity and 'labour power' as a capacity to add use values to commodities. Political economists believed that it was simply 'labour' that was exchanged and purchased by the capitalist. Marx thought that political economists had erred in their understanding of the term and went on to make the distinction between 'human labour' and 'labour power' in order to show that there existed an intervening category of labor. Human labor, in contrast to labor power, is the actual work and physical activity carried out when an individual works. Labor power, on the other hand, is what is sold to the capitalist at a value less than the value it creates. This distinction between 'labour' and 'labour power' allowed Marx to pinpoint the precise mechanism creating surplus value in capitalist society. In order for capitalists to profit, they must be able to find a commodity on the market which has the property of creating more value than it costs to purchase. The only commodity which answers to this demand is human labor. Marx points out that what the capitalist actually buys is not 'labour' outright, since if it were, slavery would be reintroduced. Rather, the name Marx gives to the commodity which the capitalist buys is 'labour power'. Labor power has two essential attributes: (i) it is found on the market and purchased as if it were a commodity; and (ii) it produces more value than the price at which it is purchased.

Labor Theory of Value   Essentially derived from classical political economy, this theory holds that the value of any commodity is created by the labor that is put into it. While Marx adopted the rudiments of a theory of value from Smith and Ricardo, he took two additional steps beyond their naive view that labor was the sole source of value inherent in the commodity: (i) he argued that political economy had completely overlooked the question of how use value is transformed into exchange value; and (ii) he rejected the view that value is a substance which inheres in a commodity by asserting that no commodity has exchange value in itself. Marx was able to demonstrate that value does not reside in a commodity by showing that it is arrived at 'relatively' when one commodity is brought into relation with another commodity. Marx's logic consists in the fact that the value of any commodity cannot be expressed in isolation, but only in relation to other commodities. To illustrate, the value of linen, said Marx, cannot be expressed in linen: you cannot say '20 yards of linen is worth 20 yards of linen.' But as soon as linen is set into comparison with another commodity, such as a linen coat, value emerges. This is called the 'relative form of value' and, with this concept, Marx was able to show that value is the product of a social framework rather than a substance which inheres in a commodity. This assertion immediately shifted the underlying basis of value theory from the level of the economy to the level of a social construct.

Law of Capitalist Accumulation   This law states that the greater the accumulation of wealth by one class, the more there is an accumulation of poverty, misery and degradation of another class. Marx used the term to demonstrate the doctrine of internal relations by showing that accumulation of wealth was not an economic category by itself but took place at the expense of a class whose labor produced this wealth. 'Accumulation of wealth at one pole is at the same time an accumulation of misery and moral degradation at the opposite pole.'

Materialism A term used by Marx and Engels to refer to a theoretical perspective which holds the view that the satisfaction of everyday economic needs is the primary reality. Opposed to German idealism, materialism takes the position that society and reality originate from simple economic acts which human beings carry out in order to provide the necessities of food, shelter and clothing. Materialism takes as its starting place the view that, before anything else, human beings must produce their everyday economic needs through their physical labor and practical productive activity. This single economic act, Marx believed, gives rise to a system of social relations which include the political, legal and religious structures of society. What is of central importance about this perspective is that it attempts to found a theory of society and existence from the starting place of human productive acts. It is the most basic premise of materialism that society and history are created from productive acts designed to fulfill human needs. The shift from philosophical idealism to materialism marked the point in the history of thought in which theory turned its attention to the material conditions of human experience.

Materialist Theory of History This is a term used to describe Marx's central theoretical perspective which explains the laws of historical development and the economic roots of social class and class inequality. The perspective holds that society and history develop in stages marked by distinct economic epochs in which social inequality is reproduced in existing class relations. It explains the origins of this process by looking for the laws of historical and economic development which tend to give rise to social classes and the dominance of one class throughout history. The main precept of the theory states that history is governed by underlying laws of economic development which are expressed in a series of productive acts. The guiding presupposition is that the very first act of all human societies is economic, in that human beings must produce in order to live. From this simple act of production, there arise social classes, one of which comprises the owners of the means of production; the other, the non-owners who are subject to the class who are dominant over them. Eventually the political structure of society takes the shape of the productive relations and on top of these 'arises a legal and political superstructure.' Using the materialist theory of history, Marx was able to assert that: (i) economic production shapes social relations and hence the political structure of society; and (ii) economic production gives rise to a legal and political structure which comes to represent the productive relations. This fundamental law of development is expressed in all societies by the fact that they tend to divide themselves into unequal social classes in which the labor of one class is to the economic benefit and maintenance of another. Conceived of in this way, history can be divided into three great economic epochs or modes of production: ancient, feudal and capitalistic.

Means of Production One of the three central concepts in Marx's materialist theory of history, referring to any physical or material thing used to produce the main economic needs of food, shelter and clothing. The means of production can be defined as anything in the external world which is put to use to sustain existence and satisfy material needs. The way jobs are used to produce wages and land to produce food and fuel constitutes the means of production. It is important to note that material needs and economic necessities cannot be produced privately on one's own, but rather only when we employ the means of production. Marx believed that the condition of ownership over the means of production was the most fundamental historical fact leading to the division of society into economic classes. Ancient and feudal societies reflected this monopolization of the means of production by a ruling class which directly exploited a class of workers to perform physical labor. The means of production take on different technological identities in various periods of economic history. In the first two historical epochs – ancient and feudal societies – the means of production were concentrated in land and constituted the major economic resources. It is the monopolization of the means of production that is the source of class conflict. In capitalist societies, the means of production are more diversified and become concentrated in technologies, resources and knowledge.

Mode of Production   This term is used by Marx to identify the primary elements of a given historical age by showing how its system of production and productive techniques shape its social relations. Marx believed that the 'way people produce' determines how they enter into social relationships with one another, and, that a mode of production comprises the total way of life of society. A mode of production is made up of both 'forces' and 'relations' of production. Forces of production refer to the instruments, equipment, land and tools which are put to work for purposes of production. These may include existing productive technologies and the way these technologies define work roles and social relations. The forces of production can only be put into operation when people in society enter into the 'relations of production' which are the roles allotted to individuals in the production process. However, because of the tendency for ownership to reside in one class, there are only two roles in production: producers and non-producers of physical labor. Relations of production thus constitute coercion and constraint for one class and an economic advantage for another. Marx identified three distinct modes of production – ancient, feudal and capitalistic – and each of these produced economic goods in ways which developed different systems of social and class relations. In each mode of production, there are class divisions arising from property relations which give rights to the owners of the means of production to control both the product and the labor of the producer.

Objectification   This is a term used by Marx to refer to the capacity of human beings to positively 'duplicate' themselves in the world they create. According to Marx, this duplication in society takes place through human labor so far as it is the realization of human aims. It is through their labor that human beings can 'contemplate themselves in the world they have created.' By producing things, in this sense, an individual becomes an object for others within the structure of social relations. For Marx, objectification is necessary if individuals are to humanize nature and transform it into an expression having human qualities. By making the distinction between alienation and objectification, Marx grasped the historical character of labor and argued that the end of alienation will emancipate the species by rehumanizing labor.

Political Economy   A term referring to a nineteenth-century economic doctrine espoused by Adam Smith and David Ricardo holding that the primary economic categories of production, exchange, value and labor can be studied as if they were independent economic phenomena that operate above human social and historical relations. Its central assumptions state that the laws of economic activity (production, exchange, consumption, labor, value, etc.) are analogous to the laws of nature and apply to all societies irrespective of their historical and social development. Marx rejected these views by showing that the economic categories (value, exchange, production, etc.) were not universally valid for all societies but only have validity under certain historical conditions. The theory of value became one of the most contentious battlegrounds between Marx and political economists. Smith asserted that exchange value was an attribute of a commodity which he believed had been conferred on it by acts of labor (the labor theory of value). Marx rejected this view by stating that value is not a universal phenomenon, but is related to a whole set of historical circumstances which come into play only in a capitalist society. Marx was able to show that the concept of 'value' arises only in societies which develop a system of exchange (a market) and when commodity production is exclusively for exchange. Marx believed that this system of exchange comes into being only in capitalist society and was able to link the concept of value to a specific mode of production rather than it being a general category of economic activity. Marx thought that political economy was a bourgeois science because it failed to look beneath appearances to underlying social relations, and because it mistakenly took production, consumption and exchange as the reality of economic life when, as far as Marx was concerned, the essence of capitalism was the system of unequal social relations.

Primitive Accumulation   A term used to refer to a central process during capitalist development when there was coercive acquisition of feudal lands and a transformation of these lands into private property. The result of primitive accumulation was the divorce of the producer from the means of production. Marx sees this accumulation as 'primitive' so far as it forms the historical basis of capitalism and the historical moment when the direct producer is transformed into the wage-laborer of capitalist society. The process takes place in two distinct historical stages, the first beginning with the expropriation of the agricultural laborer from the land. This stage began during the fifteenth century when large populations of agricultural workers were 'forcibly' thrown from the land by eviction and foreclosure leading to the dissolution of a whole way of life. The second stage was marked by the legal transfer of feudal lands into private hands by direct seizure and expropriation. This took place by means of the bills of enclosure which, by the middle of the nineteenth century, had created the industrial worker, the wage laborer, the factory system and private ownership of the means of production.

Reification   A term used to denote a stage of social and economic development when human beings experience society as if it were independent of their actions and indifferent to their purposes. Marx used the concept to define the process by which society appears to be an objective production while all along being a product of human labor. Though Marx believed that human beings create society in their economic and productive activity, reification can be defined as the stage in the development of society when it no longer reflects human origins but appears to have a life of its own disconnected from human aims. Reification takes place when purposes and functions are attached to economic forces (the 'needs' of capital or of 'production') and human activity becomes passive and thing-like. Under such circumstances, individuals appear to be components of social functions and economic forces rather than active agents in history. As components of these functions, human beings appear as if 'they arose from them' and 'belonged to them' in the first place. Reification reverses the process by which human beings create society by making it appear as if society gives birth to human beings.

Relation   A term used throughout Marx's writings to describe the interconnection between the major economic categories of production, exchange, consumption and human social activity. Marx used the concept of 'relation' as a methodological tool in his confrontation with classical political economists whom he criticized for their tendency to treat economic activities as if they were independent acts which could be thought of as operating above social and political life. Marx showed that when political economists considered economic phenomena, they did so only from the standpoint of a one-sided theoretical perspective in which they looked at economic questions from the point of view of capital, rather than capital and labor. Drawing on the concept of the social relation, Marx argued that economic categories were not separate but interrelated and believed that there are always two sides in any social relation. Viewed from this perspective, money, capital and profit are not independent categories produced outside of a mode of production but rather are inherent in the activity of human labor. Using this technique, Marx was able to show that wealth was not a product of capital but a product of the relation between capital and labor.

Relations of Production   This is a pivotal concept in Marx's materialist theory of history which he used in conjunction with the means of production, forces of production and mode of production. Essentially, the term refers to the coercive bond which exists between the owners of the means of production and those who provide their labor. More broadly, Marx used the term to indicate the connection between the way a society produces and the social roles allotted to individuals in production. Marx believed that the roles individuals assume in production are related to the system of social class arising from the fact that ownership tends to be concentrated only in one class of society. Ownership over the means of production tends to create two distinct social roles in production: producers and non-producers of physical labor. The role played by the relations of production becomes clear when we look at the result of class relations in historical terms: (i) non-owners are compelled to enter into relations of production in order to satisfy their own economic needs and, as a result, they are subordinated to the class which is dominant over them; and (ii) 'relations' of production constitute 'fetters' to non-owners who are compelled to perform the economic maintenance of the dominant class. Marx thought that the relations of production were key to the development of society because of their ability to be transformed into relations of domination. He maintained that different relations of production manifest themselves at different stages of economic development and these always seem to coincide with the way societies produce. Slavery, serfdom and wage labor are the names given to the relations of production in ancient, feudal and capitalistic societies respectively. Owners of the means of production obtain rights to control both the product and the labor of producers.

Relations of Subordination   In its classical form, relations of subordination refers to the way in which individuals are subordinated to others within an existing social framework. Historically, subordination is expressed in relations such as slavery and serfdom which are largely derived from economic, social and political distinctions between persons. Classically, relations of subordination occur in economic contexts, as between laborer and employer, but they are also present in the family, in gender relations, and in the political and economic relations in society. Characteristically, they involve some means of compulsion, either by direct physical force or indirectly through coercion.

Relative Form of Value   Used in conjunction with 'equivalent form of value,' this concept plays a central role in Marx's theory of value. Simply stated, political economy had taken the view that value is a natural property of a commodity and inheres in it as a substance. Marx broke with this tradition by stating that no commodity has value in itself except as use value. Using the concept 'relative value,' Marx was able to show that a commodity has exchange value only in relation to some other commodity. For example, the value of linen cannot be determined until it is brought into comparison with another commodity, such as a coat, in which the linen is worked up. In this case, said Marx, the value of linen is determined in relation to the value of the coat. Marx believed that the value of a commodity emerges only in comparison with some other commodity and the term he used to describe this phenomenon is 'relative value.' After being able to demonstrate that value was established 'relatively,' Marx wanted to show that value was a product of a social framework rather than a substance which inheres in commodities.

Relative Surplus Population   Marx used this term to challenge the theory of population proposed by Thomas Malthus, who put forward a general law of population growth which applied to all societies. Malthus proposed that, as the population increases, it creates a 'surplus' or redundant population relative to the available food supply. Malthus went on to draw controversial conclusions about the relationship between a population surplus, poverty rates and what he called 'positive checks' on the surplus population. Marx, by contrast, argued that there are no general laws of population, but only laws 'relative' to specific societies and given historical modes of production. He went on to show that the formation of a surplus population of unemployed poor was not a product of the rates of population growth in the abstract, but was a specific product of operations of modern industry and capitalist development. Marx believed that capitalism and modern industry set into motion laws which create a population surplus and this population is always 'relative' to the cycle of requirements of capital and is thus a necessary condition of it.

Reserve Army   This is a term used by Marx to describe the tendency of industrial capitalism to create a population of unemployed workers who are held in reserve for purposes of labor. He believed that the reserve army was created by two simultaneous demands of the capitalist system. On the one hand, there is the constant demand for refinements and productivity in the capitalist system, producing labor saving techniques which create a decrease in the demand for labor. This creates a decrease in the number of jobs and, consequently, a population of unemployed who become a permanent floating surplus collectivity. On the other hand, there are increased demands for labor as the requirements of capitalism become refined and developed. This creates an excess of jobs which cannot be filled and a greater demand on labor. Marx believed that it was in the nature of capitalist society to produce a reserve army of unemployed, since the more productive capitalism becomes, the greater the amount of 'workers it throws out into the streets.' Marx referred to the reserve army as the 'Lazarus layer' of labor, to be brought back to life when the supply of labor becomes low.

Serfdom   A term used to describe the form of labor and a relation of production in feudal society. Serfdom may be defined as a social institution existing within the framework of a feudal economy in which the wealth and economic maintenance of a class of landholders is derived from the labor of the serf. Technically, the serf is a peasant cultivator who works on the land to produce an economic livelihood. Serfdom is historically significant for the reason that it economically 'binds' the serf to the lord through compulsory obligation owed to the lord by the serf. The lord has legal jurisdiction over the serf's labor and the serf's agricultural product.

Slavery   A term used by Marx to denote an extreme form of economic compulsion existing in societies whose mode of production was commonplace during early periods of history and economic formation. Technically, 'slavery' is the name Marx gives to the form of labor in ancient societies and to a relation of production resulting in a complete absence of freedom. An individual can only become a slave, in Marx's view, in a certain mode of production and under certain historical conditions. In Marx's writings the slave is one of the most dramatic expressions of the economic relationships and of the dominance and subordination resulting from the exploitation of labor. Slaves have neither control over their own labor nor the means of production, and their product is forcibly appropriated by the dominant classes. Slaves are outside society, have no political or legal rights and are subject to the direct physical coercion of their masters. Slaves are the most dramatic expression of the labor relationship since, in the strict sense, they are treated as an object, defined as the property of others and are privately owned as a commodity. While there are different types of societies where slavery existed, the Graeco-Roman world exemplified the most dramatic expression of slave societies, where the slave was at the center of the production process.

Socially Necessary Labor   Marx used this term to identify the exact mechanism giving rise to the profits realized by the capitalist and to solve the problem of why the worker becomes poorer as the capitalist accumulates more wealth. Socially necessary labor can be defined as the portion of the workday it takes for workers to produce in wages the cost of their own maintenance in food, shelter and clothing. Marx reasoned that it takes approximately six hours of the workday for the workers to produce the cost of their own maintenance. However, during the remaining portion of the workday, which includes an additional six hours of labor, the labor of the worker is no longer necessary and does not furnish the maintenance of the worker at all. This Marx calls 'surplus labour'. In direct contrast to necessary labor, 'surplus labour' refers to the time during the working day where the labor of the worker creates value for the capitalist. Marx believed that he had discovered the origin of profit since in this reasoning the worker obtains only 6 hours of pay for 12 hours of labor. For Marx, necessary labor identifies the mechanism by which workers create more wealth than they are remunerated for in wages.

Socially Productive Power of Labor   This is a term Marx used to describe the economic benefit which accrues to the capitalist by reason of making separate contracts with many individual workers. Marx stated that insofar as the capitalist enters into contracts with 100 unconnected individuals, he pays them the value of 100 separate wages, but not for the combined labor power that is produced from their cooperative labor and activity. This 'combined' result is a free gift to the capitalist when workers are placed under conditions of cooperation and this combined power costs the capitalist nothing.

State   This is a key concept in Marx's writings, referring to a central political apparatus which arises at a certain stage in the economic development of society and whose purpose it is to maintain and defend the interests and dominance of one class over another. Marx's theory of the state departs from earlier political thinkers (Aristotle, St. Augustine, Hegel) who believed that the state was a political abstraction standing over and above society. Marx showed that the state arises only at a certain stage in the economic development of society and this allowed him to link state development with material activity. In his political writings, Marx set out to trace the development of the state by looking at the historical conditions leading to state formation in eighteenth-century France. This process begins with: (i) the breakup of feudal economies and their separate political jurisdictions; and (ii) the centralization of the political and economic spheres which took place during the transfer of power from landlords to capitalists. Marx's emphasis on the material nature of political functions led him to assert that the state arises out of the productive relations of society and is not independent of the economic realm. In this sense, the state reflects the prevailing class structure of society and acts as an instrument of the ruling classes. This consolidation of the material and historical made Marx's theory of political society distinct from previous political thinking in its assertion that: (i) economic production shapes social relations and hence the political structure of society; and (ii) that economic production gives rise to a legal and political structure which comes to represent the productive relations. Marx believed that the appearance of the state coincides with the development of 'civil society' which protects private property, promotes individual pursuit of private interest and gives the illusion that private competition can be carried on humanely even though the means of production have fallen into private hands.

Surplus Labor   This is a term Marx used to refer to the portion of the workday which exceeds the amount of labor required for workers to maintain their own physical existence and reproduce themselves in necessary food, shelter and clothing. Marx believed that surplus labor existed throughout history, describing it as part of the workday which is worked without economic compensation to the worker to the advantage of the capitalist. According to Marx, surplus labor is extracted from the worker and directly creates wealth for the dominant classes. In ancient and feudal societies, surplus labor existed in the form of the forced labor of the slave and the unpaid labor of the serf. In capitalism, this surplus labor creates surplus value for the capitalist but not for the worker.

Surplus Value   A central concept used by Marx to identify the form of profit enjoyed by capitalists that was created from the surplus labor of the worker. Marx's theory of surplus value is a key theoretical discovery and can best be understood in the light of the concept of surplus labor. In all societies, according to Marx, productive relations are structured to extract excess work or surplus labor from the producer. In ancient societies, slaves were compelled to perform surplus labor in exchange for minimal subsistence and, in feudal societies, serfs were obliged to perform free labor service on the lord's estate. In both these cases, surplus labor confers an advantage to the dominant classes and identifies the specific mechanism of exploitation in ancient and feudal societies. 'Surplus value' is the name Marx gave to the specific form of exploitation in capitalist society occurring as a result of the surplus labor extracted from the worker. To show how the mechanism of surplus labor operates, Marx made the distinction between necessary and surplus labor. Necessary labor refers to the part of the workday it takes for the workers to produce in wages the cost of their own maintenance. Marx reasoned that if the workday is 12 hours, it takes approximately 6 hours of labor to produce the cost of maintaining the worker in food, fuel and clothing. Surplus labor, by contrast, refers to the part of the working day in which laborers expend labor power but create no value for themselves. The labor expended by the worker adds value to the product and the value the worker creates during this part of the day benefits the capitalist alone. Marx stated that the laborer is paid only for one part of the workday and that the unpaid part constitutes the 'surplus,' and it is this part which produces the value for the capitalist. Surplus value has four central attributes: (i) it is the value created by the surplus labor of the worker; (ii) it is unpaid and, therefore, creates value for the capitalist but not the worker; (iii) it presents a deception since it claims to be paid labor; (iv) it is the recognized form of overwork and thus goes to the heart of exploitation since the worker is not paid for the wealth created by producing surplus labor.

Theory of Value A central body of Marx's work which is based on the assumption that exchange value is a product of a social framework rather than a substance which inheres in a commodity or is found in a commodity naturally. Devised essentially to refute the assumption by classical political economy that value is a substance found in a commodity, Marx's theory looks at the question of value from the standpoint of the existing social relations. He believed that one of the mysteries of capitalist society lies in the puzzle of how commodities come to be bearers of value. For the answer to this question Marx looked behind the 'value form' itself. The origin of value, he believed, lies not in the laws of the exchange of commodities or in the price they obtain in the market, but rather in the system of social relations. To demonstrate, Marx drew on the concept of 'relative value' which states that no commodity has value in isolation and that the value of any commodity is expressed relatively in relation to some other commodity. To illustrate, Marx used the example of linen and coats. The value of linen, said Marx, cannot be expressed in linen; we cannot say 20 yards of linen has the value of 20 yards of linen. However, as soon as linen is set into comparison with another commodity, such as a coat, value can be established relatively. Marx reasoned that if no commodity has value in relation to itself, then no commodity is valuable by itself and, if this is true, then value does not belong to a commodity naturally. Value therefore must be a product of social relations which exist within an ongoing framework of society. Hence 'exchange value' emerges only at a historically given epoch, precisely at the moment when the value of one commodity is brought into a relation of exchange with another. By showing that no commodity has value in itself and that commodities are not bearers of value, Marx was able to contradict the law of value established by political economy.

Use Value A central term used by Marx in his discussion of capitalism which can be defined as the particular quality a commodity has to satisfy human needs. Understood in this sense, use value refers to the ability of a commodity to render a particular service to an individual by satisfying some need or want and by sustaining life. A coat, for instance, provides warmth, and this serves directly as a means of existence. In addition, the use value of a commodity is capable of filling only one particular function which is not interchangeable with other commodities. For example, the use value of bread cannot be substituted with the use value of coal, and so on. Because each commodity has a unique use value and serves a particular human function, use values of commodities cannot be compared. What happens in exchange value is that a common element is found between commodities which has to do with their quantitative 'value' in exchange. As soon one commodity is compared to another in terms of value, the qualitative element of use drops out of the equation.

Durkheim

Abnormal Forms A term used by Durkheim to identify a deviation in the division of labor resulting in its failure to produce social solidarity. For Durkheim, the normal function of the division of labor is to produce social solidarity linking individuals and institutions in a manner that serves the overall purposes of society. But as large-scale industry develops and there is a rapid rise in specialization and the division labor, certain social functions 'are not adjusted' to one another and conflict rather than solidarity becomes more prevalent. Durkheim identified three abnormal forms which resulted from the lack of adjustment in the division of labor: (i) the anomic division of labor where there is a breakdown in the body of social rules regulating relations between employer and workers, and where restraint preventing disputes in the past readily gives way to conflict; (ii) the forced division of labor where constraint rather than occupational aptitude links individuals to their social functions as a result of one class taking control of the division of labor; and (iii) the insufficient coordination of the division of labor resulting in the misallotment of social and occupational roles.

Altruistic Suicide   A term used by Durkheim to describe a type of suicide which occurs when individuals' attachment to society exceeds their loyalty to themselves. Altruistic suicide is best understood in the context of social integration, a term used by Durkheim to describe the extent to which individuals are linked to social groups outside themselves. In relation to egoistic suicide, Durkheim had claimed that individuals take their lives when social integration to larger groups is either absent or not well developed. At the opposite end of the integrative pole is altruistic suicide, and it is this term Durkheim used to describe the form of suicide which occurs when there is an excessive degree of social integration. Altruistic suicide is the clearest case of suicide that is imposed by social ends. Durkheim first made his observations about altruistic suicide by looking at the customs of tribal societies. He found that they conferred honor on individuals who take their own lives in the name of social purposes greater than themselves. In this case, people take their own lives not because they assume the personal right to do so, but because of a social duty imposed upon them. There are three forms of altruistic suicide identified by Durkheim: (i) obligatory altruistic suicide; (ii) optional altruistic suicide; and (iii) acute altruistic or mystical suicide. Each differs in terms of the degree of obligation placed upon individuals to take their own life.

Anomic Division of Labor   A term Durkheim used to describe a type of deviation in the division of labor which occurs when there is a loss of social solidarity due to excessive occupational specialization. Under normal circumstances, the division of labor produces solidarity among workers and employers. This serves the purpose of adjusting social relations between groups and maintaining the spirit of cooperativeness. However, during the rapid development in the division of labor brought about by industrial society, a lack of adjustment between groups leads to a more frequent occurrence of conflict and revolt. In small-scale societies where the division of labor is not as developed, social relations between employers and workers show greater solidarity, and conflicts and disputes rarely arise. Where organic solidarity develops, however, work is divided, employer and worker exist apart, and the social links between them diminish. The ties between employer and worker become weak, leading to more frequent conflict and dispute, undermining the 'spirit of togetherness.' As a consequence, individuals form greater attachments to their occupations, and pursue their private interests more readily. Thus the more separate and specialized labor becomes, the less solidarity there is. In addition, as social relations are governed by contracts, groups tend to treat one another as adversaries rather than as cooperators. Industrial crises and commercial failures are more frequent because discipline breaks down and the ties binding groups become dispersed, giving way to a reduction in consensus.

Anomic Suicide   A form of suicide resulting from the overall decline in the regulatory powers of society. Durkheim believed that one of the most important functions of society was to set restraints and limitations on individuals so that social wants of wealth, power and prestige would not become conscious material desires. Durkheim thought that, in comparison with animal needs which are adjusted to bodily wants, human needs are unlimited and therefore restraint must be set by society. In modern society, however, the limitation imposed by social institutions is replaced by a 'spirit of free pursuit' of individual goals and the system of restraint begins to break down. As a result, material desires begin to increase and social wants exceed the possible means for attaining them. Durkheim thought that this led to disappointment and feelings of individual failure, and even to despair. When social wants exceed limitations imposed by society, disappointment with life and the feeling of failure increases. Durkheim thought that this circumstance was compounded in modern society where the economy becomes the dominant social institution and where restraint and limitation are incompatible with economic competition. When the forces of society fail to set limitations on wants, individuals continually exceed the means at their disposal, and their desires, by definition, become frustrated and out of reach. This can only happen, Durkheim maintained, when individuals constantly aspire to reach ends or goals which are beyond their capacity to obtain. To pursue goals which are unattainable ensures repeated disappointment, and when goals are set which have no end or conclusion, individuals become despondent, and anomie ensues.

Anomie A term first used by Durkheim in 1893 to describe the deterioration of moral restraint which occurs in industrial society when the division of labor fails to produce social solidarity and when the regulatory restraints of society are unable to set limits on social wants so that needs begin to exceed the means to attain them, and disappointment and despair follow. Later in 1897, Durkheim used the term to put forward a theory of anomie in relation to suicide by pinpointing the decline of the regulatory mechanism of society which takes place when the economy and industry are dominant. As the economy develops, markets are extended and social wants are freed from previous limitation. As a result, the 'capacity for social wants became insatiable and the more one has, the more one wants.' The stress on economic activity increases individual desires to such an extent that discomfort and restraint that were tolerable in previous societies become less acceptable. Durkheim believed that it is in the economically related functions of society where anomie creates the largest category of suicide in contrast to other spheres of society in which the 'old regulatory forces' still prevail. Looked at in this way, anomie can be defined as the decline which takes place in the regulatory force of society brought about by unchecked economic progress. This decline occurs as society is unable to regulate social wants which develop in large industrial societies.

Categories of Thought This term is used by Durkheim in his discussion of religion to dispute the claim by philosophers that knowledge is a product of human reason. At the root of Western thinking about human beings lies the view that the human mind alone has the capacity to reason and comprehend the characteristics of the external world. Immanuel Kant, one of the foremost proponents of this view, reasoned that the categories of space, time and cause were not only innate to human reason but were categories which made it possible to understand spatial and temporal relationships and to form knowledge of the outside world. Durkheim, by contrast, took the position that the 'categories of thought' were social in origin and derived from the fact that human beings live in groups, and because of this, they tend to group their ideas and their categories. According to Durkheim, group categories come first, then come cognitive intellectual categories. Durkheim based this reasoning on investigations into the origin of concepts such as space, time and cause showing that they spring from the social activity of groups and therefore are not a priori in nature. Concepts of class and category, according to Durkheim, are categories of thought derived from the fact that human beings live in groups and employ principles of classification which are later incorporated into mental categories.

Clan This is a term used by Durkheim in the context of classifying different types of society according to their structural complexity and level of development. A clan denotes a type of society which is at the earliest stage of development and may be defined as a group or aggregate which has no additional social segments and no clear political divisions. Clans develop from simple societies called hordes which are the least complex form of social organization. Durkheim reasoned that the horde must be the social species from which all other social types develop. Clans were once hordes and therefore possessed the morphology of hordes. This morphology, however, has been altered because their structural characteristics have been rearranged. In this classification, hordes are distinct so far as they constitute single segment societies. As they become more complex, they become compounded into segments and these segments combine to give a more complex group structure. Hordes are the simplest of sociological types, whereas clans are compounded segmental societies that do not develop distinct segments.

Classification of Social Types This is a term Durkheim used to establish a system of classification of types of society. Generally, this system is referred to as a 'social morphology' which denotes the relationship between the complexity of a society and its structural characteristics such as the size of the group and its institutional components. Durkheim identified three types of society, each of which has a distinct social morphology and a distinct type of social cohesion and dynamic density. These are: (i) a horde, which is the most elementary social form characterized by an absence of parts; (ii) a clan, which is formed by the combination of various groups leading to a more complex social structure; and (iii) polysegmentals, which are societies made up of the combination of various aggregates which together form a confederated group or common tribe.

Collective Representations This concept was used by Durkheim to identify the existence of social phenomena and the characteristics which make these phenomena distinct from psychological facts. They can be defined as any subject matter into which the collective practices of society have been condensed so that they come to 'represent' the beliefs and ideas prevalent in society. Examples of the collective representations into which social subject matter is concentrated are religious doctrine, legal rules, myths, legends, proverbs, customs, and social traditions. Durkheim believed that collective representations reflect social subject matter in four central ways: (i) they reflect a reality different from that of the individual; (ii) they have characteristics of their own which are autonomous from individuals; (iii) they can be investigated in their own right without being subsumed under psychological or biological laws; and (iv) they arise from the collective activity of group life. Collective representations exercise a coercive influence upon individuals which is due not to individual disposition but to the 'prestige with which these representations are invested.'

Common Conscience A central concept used by Durkheim to refer to a body of collective beliefs and social practices which are held in common by all members of society and which determine the relations of individuals to one another and to society. The common conscience is diffused throughout the society, functions as a basis of collective action and generally structures the pattern of social life. It may be thought of as a determinate system of ideas, attitudes and beliefs which create social likenesses among individuals in society. Durkheim took the view that these beliefs evolve according to their own laws, have an independent existence and can be studied according to the methods of science. He outlined four characteristics of the common conscience: (i) volume, which refers to the extent of the reach of collective beliefs to all parts of society; (ii) intensity, referring to the degree of leverage collective values and beliefs have on individual attitudes and behavior; (iii) determinateness, referring to how well the common beliefs and social practices are defined and the extent of resistance these beliefs have to change, transgression or violation; and (iv) content of the common conscience, which refers to the dominant characteristics of the society and to its collective nature. Content can be religious, in which case the primary form of collective sentiments originates from religious law and exerts a hold over individuals through religious expiation; or it can be secular, in which case the primary form of collective sentiments is divested of its religious content.

Constraint A term used by Durkheim to refer to the capacity of social rules and conventions to exert leverage on individuals and to impel them to act in accordance with social expectations and the prescriptions of society. Technically speaking, constraint is the force exerted by social rules on individuals and involves the point at which social conventions and customs in society act on individuals to secure their compliance. Social constraints are always external to the individual, originate from society and precede the individual historically. Constraints are properties of social facts and collective representations, and denote the power of social rules to act coercively on individual behavior.

Contract Law Sometimes called 'written law' by Durkheim, this term refers to a system of judicial rules and legal sanctions which arises in large-scale societies as a result of the development of the division of labor. Contract law is a derivative of industrial society and has essentially two central characteristics: (i) it prescribes obligations and expectations by binding contracting parties; and (ii) it defines sanctions as they relate to offenses and breaches against contracts. In contrast with small-scale societies, industrial society leads to the development of various social organs which become increasingly specialized. In this context, the law functions through specialized institutions such as the courts, arbitration councils, tribunals and administrative bodies. The authority of the legal rules is exercised through specific functionaries such as judges, magistrates and lawyers who possess specialized credentials. In contrast to penal law, the function of contract law is to regulate relations between particular individuals rather than acting in the name of the collective norms of the group. The purpose of contract law is to develop rules which bind individuals to each other by regulating contractual obligations. Durkheim took the view that this system of law did little for social solidarity since it does not regulate the bond between the individual and society but restricts itself to regulating only contractual links between individuals.

Division of Labor   This is a central concept in Durkheim's work, referring to the process of dividing up labor into specialized functions and the system of social links resulting from the fact that individuals are more reliant on others when their occupational and productive functions become more specialized. Used primarily to designate the development of industrial society and the shift from mechanical to organic solidarity, the term describes the effects on social cohesion which result when work is divided into minutely specialized functions. Used in its economic sense, the division of labor refers to the process of dividing labor into separate and specialized operations with the purpose of increasing production. Used in its sociological sense, however, the division of labor refers to the principle of social cohesion which develops in societies whose social bonds result from the way individuals relate when their occupational functions are separate and specialized. The division of labor facilitates the rise of contract law, autonomous social institutions, and creates social bonds by contract rather than by sentiment.

Dynamic Density   A term used by Durkheim to describe the degree of social activity created by populations interacting with one another. Durkheim employed the term to look at the relationship between the types of society and the extent of interaction created among populations. The 'dynamic density' determines the degree of 'concentration of aggregates' and the ways in which the concentrations of aggregates lead to economic and social interchange. Two kinds of facts act on the dynamic density of society: (i) those related to the size of the society and its structural organization; and (ii) those related to the proximity of individuals to each other. Measurements of dynamic density may determine how intense social life is and the 'horizon of thought and action of the individual.'

Egoism   The term 'egoism' originated in the nineteenth century and was widely used by Durkheim and others to indicate a breakdown in the links tying individuals to society. Egoism can be described as the process by which individuals detach themselves from society by turning their activity inward and retreating into themselves. Egoism is characterized by excessive self-reflection on personal matters and a withdrawal from the outside world. In this state, the 'springs of action' are relaxed and individuals turn inward and away from society. Egoism occurs when the tie binding 'the individual to others is slackened and not sufficiently integrated at the points where the individual is in contact with society.' It results from an excess of individualism and from the 'weakening of the social fabric.' In a state of egoism, social bonds break down and individual ends are more important than the common ends of society. Under these circumstances, egoism constitutes a threat to society, to aggregate social maintenance and to collective authority. Durkheim believed that there is a direct connection between suicide and the degree of integration of the individual to various social groups. Egoism is the result of prolonged and unchecked individualism which is a consequence of industrial society.

Egoistic Suicide   This is a type of suicide which results from a radical change in the levels of social integration serving to tie individuals to groups outside themselves. Durkheim pointed out that social ties to religious, familial and national groups have a moderating effect on egoistic suicide because these groups share the property of being strongly integrated and constitute links to society. Durkheim found that in industrial society, group attachments grow weak due to excessive individualism. The weaker the bonds attaching individuals to social groups, the less they depend upon them and the more they depend on themselves. Durkheim asserted that the degree of integration could be measured by looking at the individual's attachment to the religious group, family group and the social community at large. He found that the suicide rates were higher when the links binding individuals to religious groups were weak and social cohesion was low. In one case he demonstrated that, because Protestants tend to be more autonomous than Catholics in matters of religous doctrine, this leads to greater self-sufficiency and egoism among Protestants, and therefore a higher rate of suicide.

Fatalistic Suicide A category of suicide which is the polar opposite of anomic suicide and results from an excess of social regulation. Fatalistic suicide occurs when the prospects, goals and aspirations of individuals become blocked due to an excess of social regulation imposed by another individual or by society. Durkheim cites the example of slaves who, suffering severe restraint and deprivation, take their own lives due to restrictions in their social horizons.

Forced Division of Labor This is a term used by Durkheim to refer to a form of deviation which occurs in large-scale industry when classes and castes gain control over the division of labor. In this case, labor is not divided by merit or ability but is forcibly constrained by the activities of one class or caste. In order for the division of labor to produce solidarity, it must assign tasks to individuals that 'fit their aptitude.' When this process is blocked by one class, individuals are allotted functions solely on the basis of constraint and to the advantage of their employer. Under these circumstances, disputes arise more readily, social cohesion diminishes, and individuals have little stake in the production process. The forced division of labor is manifest: (i) when there is hereditary transmission of occupations, (ii) when inequalities arise in contracts; and (iii) when groups monopolize opportunities and close off avenues to occupations.

Individual A term used by Durkheim to draw attention to the fact that the proper subject matter of the sociological sciences are realities external to the individual. Insofar as social realities exist in the form of social rules, customs and beliefs, Durkheim thought that these phenomena can only be studied by focusing on social facts rather than on individuals. This is evident in his assertion that 'society cannot exist if there are only individuals.' Anti-individualist doctrines of this type summed up Durkheim's investigative stance in the social sciences and his criticism of social thinkers such as Hobbes and Rousseau who erred, he believed, when they deduced society from the individual. According to Durkheim, to focus on the individual is to ignore the larger system of social rules which forms the basis of society. He thought that it was scientifically defensible to focus on society without taking the individual's separate attitudes and dispositions into account.

Individualism A term first used by social thinkers of the early nineteenth century to describe the shift which takes place when the individual becomes the central social and political unit of society. It identifies a period which formally began after the French Revolution, when political and legal freedoms were assigned to individuals as a function of their new social status and freedoms. Later, with the work of Durkheim and Tonnies, the term referred to the glorification of the individual which came about as a result of industrial development and the emergence of large-scale society. In early societies, individuals were thought to participate only as members of larger social groups. Individuals were absorbed into collective life, links to society were direct, and social control repressive. As ties began to weaken due to the division of labor, individuals became the recipients of rights and freedoms in which their ties to society were expressed indirectly. Adjustments in social solidarity freed individuals from the claims which society exerted upon them. Durkheim used the term individualism largely to designate the themes of egoism and autonomy which were thought to have been brought about as the links connecting individuals to larger groups began to dissolve. Many believed that the focus on the individual jeopardized the greater collective interests of society and, for some, the progress of individualism meant the collapse of social unity and the dissolution of society into autonomous individuals. In nineteenth-century France, individualism was seen as a crisis which threatened to atomize society and destroy collective unity.

Integration   This is a major theme in Durkheim's work, used to stress the nature of social links attaching individuals to groups outside themselves. Social integration can be defined as the extent to which individuals are linked to and feel allegiance for social groups to which they are attached. Durkheim believed that individuals do not exist by themselves autonomously and are therefore not separate from society. He thought that social integration serves several key functions: (i) it operates to connect individuals to society by ensuring a high degree of attachment to commonly held values and beliefs, thus promoting bonds between the individual and the group; (ii) it acts as a check against individualism by imposing restraints on needs and wants and by focusing interests outside the self; and (iii) it serves connective functions insofar as it propels individuals out into the wider society by creating links to larger social groups and by promoting the perception that they are part of a larger social whole.

Interdiction   A term used in the context of Durkheim's study of religion to denote a special class of social rules that has the power to prohibit activity construed as threatening to the sacred character of the totem or any class of sacred things or persons. Used synonymously with taboo and prohibition in maintaining the sacred nature of the totem, interdictions may arise in a variety of spheres related to rules governing contact with the totem including the rules related to eye contact, food intake or sexual activity prior to approaching the totem. Interdictions set requirements about what must be observed when approaching the totem, handling the totem or in some way avoiding bodily contact with it. Interdictions place moral restraints upon individuals to comply due to perceived dangers inherent in defiling the totem if the interdictions are not observed. One of the key characteristics of interdictions is the perception that their non-observance implies extreme danger. Interdictions are mainly enacted during religious ritual and express themselves in the form of observances regarding the performance of acts related to sacred things. Some interdicts are categorical, whereas others function as maxims.

Mechanical Solidarity   A term used by Durkheim to describe a type of social cohesion which is characterized by a strong system of social links between individuals and society based on obligation, custom and sentiment. The force of these links is such as to discourage individual autonomy, and society as a whole envelops the individual completely. Collective rules and social practices are predominantly religious in nature and a strong common conscience pervades all aspects of social life. The kinship group is the dominant social institution and domestic activity forms the basis of social cohesion. Social rules are based on penal law and offenses against society are penalized by repressive sanctions which act to reaffirm beliefs by severe punishment. The individual's relation to society is an indistinguishable part of the collective whole, with individual differences being subordinated to the group. The degree of proliferation of common values and beliefs is diffused throughout the entire society and social cohesion is strong and unified. Societies of this type are characterized by: (i) a homogeneous population which is small and isolated; (ii) a division of labor based on social cooperation with little specialization; (iii) a system of social institutions in which religion is dominant; (iv) a system of beliefs which is uniformly diffused throughout the society, creating uniformity in attitudes and actions; (v) a low degree of individual autonomy; (vi) a system of penal law based on repressive sanctions that punish individual transgressions violently and repressively; (vii) a system of social links between individuals based on custom, obligation and sentiment; and (viii) a common conscience that is rooted in religious law.

Moral Rules   Durkheim used this term to refer to the nature of social rules and the extent to which they can be studied as an objective reality external to the individual. These rules ultimately have the force of moral imperatives in that they place duties on individuals to comply to social expectations independent of their wills. The term 'moral' is used to denote the coercive 'force' of social rules rather than to refer to a religious doctrine. Generally, moral rules constitute a class of rules which have coercive powers over individuals. Durkheim was interested in the way these rules were capable of overriding individual discretion. He believed that social rules are moral in that they originate from collective norms and sentiments, imposing 'moral imperatives' on individual actions.

Organic Solidarity   A term used by Durkheim to denote a type of social cohesion in which the links between individuals and society are affected by acute alterations in the division of labor. In societies whose solidarity is organic, individuals are linked more to each other than to society as a whole, but their dependence on society becomes greater as their occupational functions become more specialized. The nature of these links stems from the development of the division of labor, where individuals are dependent on others to perform economic and productive functions which they are not able to carry out themselves. The force of social bonds integrates individuals in their economic and occupational functions, and the ties to the society become indirect and operate through the division of labor. Social bonds between individuals are enforced by contracts rather than by prevailing customs or religious beliefs. The individual's place in society is determined by occupational functions rather than by kinship affiliation. The system of law is based on restitutive sanctions in which judicial rules redress social wrongs by restoring things to their original state. The individual has greater autonomy and becomes the object of legal rights and freedoms. Autonomous social organs develop in which political, economic and legal functions become specialized and there is a minimum of shared understandings between members of the group. The main characteristics of organic solidarity are: (i) larger populations spread over broader geographic areas; (ii) an increased complexity of division of labor leading to occupational specialization in which individuals are more dependent on others to carry out functions which they cannot perform themselves; (iii) a system of social relations in which individuals are linked by contracts rather than by sentiment or obligation; (iv) increased autonomy of the individual based on legal rights and political freedoms; and (v) the development of contract law in which judicial rules and sanctions redress social wrongs by restoring things to their original state.

Penal Law   Prevalent in small-scale societies, penal law can be distinguished from other forms of law by its repressive sanctions and its straightforward intention of imposing harm on the offender. It does this either by reducing the social honor of the offender or by depriving offenders of their freedom or their life. In a system of penal law, punishment is severe, often bringing physical harm to the offender, and sanctions against offenders are 'repressive.' It is the function of repressive sanctions to maintain social cohesion by setting examples which act to maintain the vitality of the common conscience. Penal law and repressive sanctions are found in societies in which solidarity is mechanical. Penal law is distinct from contract law in that no criterion of justice operates to ensure that the 'punishment' fits the crime.

Profane   This term is used by Durkheim to point to the tendency of all religions to separate the world into two realms, the sacred and profane. The division between these two realms forms one of the central principles of a social theory of religion, and is the most distinctive element of religious life. The profane may be defined as anything which is subordinated in dignity to the sacred and radically opposite to it. In this sense, the profane is the principle which has the capacity to contaminate the sacred. In all religions, rules exist which regulate the separation between the two realms and precautions must always be taken when they come into contact since profane things carry the potential to defile, contaminate or inspire disgust or horror. Profane things are set apart from sacred things and are regulated by a special class of religious prohibitions called interdictions. It is Durkheim's view that the division of the world into sacred and profane spheres led to the first system of classification regarding physical boundaries in societies, since the profane is always kept distinct from the sacred, thus forming boundaries which separate the two in all societies.

Religion Durkheim defined religion as a set of beliefs, rites and practices relative to sacred things. He thought that all religions could be identified by three elementary forms: (i) the tendency to divide the world into sacred and profane spheres; (ii) the formation of beliefs relative to sacred things; and (iii) the development of a system of rites specifying the duties and obligations owed to sacred objects. Durkheim's point of departure in the study of religion is his assertion that religion originates from the social activities of groups and the tendency of groups to form beliefs relative to sacred objects. In this respect, Durkheim differed from those who believed that religion is derived from nature, from the universe or from the experience of the divine. Religion exists, according to Durkheim, because it serves the function of representing the collective realities of society to those who live within it.

Religious Force This concept is used by Durkheim in his study of religion to describe the force of religious rules which believers feel compelled to obey. Durkheim believed that the 'religious force' is the definitive characteristic of religion in that it: (i) compels individuals to render pious duties toward it; (ii) creates moral obligations which cannot be canceled out; (iii) remains continuous over time while individuals are constantly being replaced; (iv) is protected by a system of interdicts or prohibitions; (v) is at the foundation of the principle of the sacred; and (vi) takes the form of society.

Repressive Sanctions This term is used by Durkheim to refer to a form of punishment found in societies where solidarity is mechanical and whose law is penal in nature. The central characteristic of repressive sanctions is their tendency to punish individual transgressions swiftly and violently, serving the purpose of repairing the damage done to collective sentiments. The rules which these wrongdoings offend are so central to the well-being of the group that they are endowed with a sacred authority. Punishment therefore has a religious character and takes the form of expiation which refers to the process of making things right through atonement. Repressive sanctions are social responses to transgressions which are perceived to be an offense against society and the common conscience. The purpose of repressive sanctions is to punish the offender rather than to determine the nature of the offense or arrive at a just punishment. Durkheim believed that penal law always seeks public vindication and therefore acts without fully weighing the circumstances of the crime.

Restitutive Sanctions This is a term used by Durkheim to describe a system of redressing social wrongs in large-scale society by restoring things to the state existing prior to the offense. Restitutive sanctions originate from a system of judicial rules in which solidarity is organic and law is contractual. Under this system of laws, sanctions are restitutive rather than repressive and legal rules become a specialized function of an advanced division of labor. A central characteristic of restitutive sanctions is their concern to establish a criterion of justice by ensuring that the punishment adequately fits the crime. In contrast to repressive sanctions, restitutive sanctions have the job of restoring things to the way they were prior to the offense and of reconciling interests between special parties. These may be exercised through various agents such as lawyers, magistrates and quasi-legal officials. Unlike repressive sanctions, restitutive sanctions do not directly involve the organs of society but only specialized parts or segments.

Sacred A term used to denote the principle of division between sacred and profane things which occurs in all societies and is at the foundation of all religions and religious experience. Sacred things embody gods, spirits and natural objects and embrace beliefs and social practices. A belief, practice or rite can have a sacred character and carries the tendency to be viewed by others as a 'consecrated' thing. Certain words and expressions can be sacred as well. In situations where this is the case, they can be uttered only by consecrated persons and involve gestures and movements which only appointed persons can perform. Formally, the sacred refers to a system of rites, beliefs and social practices which emerge from sacred things and radiate around them. The sacred: (i) is separate from all other objects and therefore constitutes things set apart; (ii) constitutes a system of rites and social practices which set out how the sacred is to be approached and how members of the group are to conduct themselves in regard to it; (iii) is protected by interdictions which have the force of prohibitions or taboos; (iv) is segregated from profane things and is thought to be superior in dignity; (v) represents a unifying principle which separates the natural from the spiritual world and provides society with a model of opposites such as good and evil, clean and dirty, holy and defiled etc.; and (vi) must be accompanied by rites of initiation or rebirth when a profane state is 'transformed' into a sacred state.

Segmental Societies   A term used to describe a type of society the organization of which is based on a series of separate clans who are united together as a common people, such as the North American Indian tribes. All the members of the group are linked together by kinship and blood ties and a series of social relations link them to common beliefs, sentiments and social practices. They have a common religion, collective political functions and their solidarity is mechanical. Durkheim refers to these societies as segmental because their social organization is based on a formation of groups whose segments are like the 'rings of an earthworm.' Durkheim used the concept to illustrate the process of the division of labor and believed that the growth of the division of labor was based on the tendency of segments to lose their individuality and develop functions which became specialized. As soon as interrelated functions emerged, segments were replaced by new organs creating attitudes and beliefs which gave rise to a central authority, a system of administrative and judicial functions, contract law and a modern economy.

Social Facts   A term used by Durkheim to describe elements of society which can be studied independently of individual disposition. Durkheim believed that the primary task of sociology was the description and observation of social facts. The study of social facts is the first step in the program of scientific sociology because they: (i) identify collective phenomena separate from individuals; (ii) are not part of individual psychological motivations; (iii) are subject to observation; (iv) are diffused throughout the society; and (v) exist in their own right independent of the individual. Social facts are: (i) external to the individual; (ii) have the power of external coercion; (iii) exert constraints on individuals which are backed up by sanctions; and (iv) are expressed through social rules, customs, religious doctrines, legal codes, etc.

Social Morphology   This is a term used by Durkheim to describe a system of classifying societies according to the number of structural components and the mode of combination of these components. For Durkheim, social morphology was the first step in devising a system of classification of types of societies since it examines the elementary parts which enter into their structure. According to Durkheim there are two broad classifications: (i) classifications of simple societies; and (ii) classification of complex societies. The first type is found in societies called 'hordes', the second type in societies called 'clans.' Durkheim believed that the procedures for classifying societies begin with the step of understanding how simple societies 'form compounds,' and how these compound societies become complex. In beginning with simple societies and progressing to complex ones, Durkheim believed that sociologists could examine the morphological changes from one type to another.

Social Pathology   This is a term used by Durkheim to draw a comparison between healthy societies and non-healthy societies, and between normal and pathological states. Drawn from physiology, pathology refers to the degree of disease present in an organism. Durkheim believed that certain social states can be considered as a form of disease and the name he gave to these developments is 'social pathology.' Durkheim reasoned that all phenomena, including social ones, assume two distinct forms: (i) a 'normal' state, in which the social conditions are most widely distributed and occur in other societies under general conditions; and (ii) a 'morbid or pathological' state, which occurs when social phenomena depart from what is widespread or normative. A phenomenon is to be considered morbid or unhealthy only if it does not maintain its proper relationship to the dominant social institutions.To illustrate, Durkheim drew upon the example of crime and criminal activity in society. He pointed out that while many tend to assume crime is pathological in nature, the opposite is true because it appears in all societies and no society is exempted from the problem of crime. In classifying crime as normal, Durkheim is not confirming anything about the criminal nature of individuals, but only that crime is a factor in 'social health' and, therefore, an integral part of healthy societies.

Social Suicide Rate A central concept in Durkheim's study of suicide arrived at after studying the mortality data of different societies. Durkheim inferred from the data that each society had a 'suicide rate' and that the 'rate' could be studied independently of individual suicides. This established a basis for looking at the 'social causes' of suicide independent of individual motives or psychological states. After studying the rates, Durkheim observed that they varied from society to society and that the number of suicidal deaths in each of the countries did not change dramatically and were considered to be stable. The stability of the rates within a given society indicated that social forces were operating to produce the 'yearly precision of rates.' This led Durkheim to reason that the predisposing cause of suicide lay not within the psychological motives of the individual, but within the social framework of the society. He took the position that the suicide rate must represent a 'factual order' that is separate from individual disposition and, therefore, presents a regularity which can be studied in its own right. Durkheim thought that because the 'social suicide rate' is independent of individual suicide, it should be the subject of a special study, the purpose of which would be to discover the social causes leading to a definite number of people that take their own lives in a given society.

Solidarity A concept used by Durkheim to form the basis of the study of society. Initially, solidarity can be defined as the system of social relations linking individuals to each other and to society as a whole. Durkheim tended to use the term in several different ways. In one context he used the term interchangeably with social integration to describe the degree to which individuals are connected to social groups existing outside themselves. In another, he used the term to refer to the system of social interchanges which go beyond the brief transactions that occur during economic exchange in society. This system of interchange forms a vast network of social solidarity that extends to the whole range of social relations and acts to link individuals together to form a common social unity based on similar beliefs, values and customs. In yet another context, he asserted that solidarity takes two principal forms: mechanical and organic. Each provides a system of links in which the bonds between individuals and social groups vary according to the division of labor in society. In drawing attention to the solidarity existing in society, Durkheim was able to focus on the system of social rules and related social practices which develop as individuals form social groups.

Theory of Knowledge Durkheim's theory of knowledge derives from his study of religion in which he found that the general tendency of all religions is to classify the natural and social world into distinct categories. This led him to conclude that intellectual categories must be products of social activity having their origins in society. In making these assertions, Durkheim challenged the prevailing philosophical view of knowledge by maintaining that the categories of thought do not spring from human reason or individual minds. He took two important steps beyond the prevailing view. First, he claimed that intellectual categories leading to complex systems of thought such as science, logic and philosophy, derive their classificatory frameworks from the fact that human beings live in groups and thereby tend to group their ideas. Second, he took the view that intellectual categories are originally derivatives of group categories, which is contrary to Kant's contention that internal mental categories are primary in the apprehension of the external world. Durkheim drew on the categories of space, time and cause to illustrate this relationship. He reasoned that these concepts not only appear to be universal across societies but also find their origin in categories based on how groups divide themselves into classes and clans. Beginning with the concept of space, Durkheim showed that the first framework for understanding the physical world derives from spatial relationships. This concept has its origins in the social group from which the individual perception of spatial relationships develops. We come to understand spatial relations by first conceptualizing a 'center' from which everything else radiates. Durkheim reasoned that the fixed territory of the group becomes the standard of the spatial organization which provides a model for the mental organization of space, thus creating the point of spatial direction. Australian tribal societies, for instance, tend to conceptualize space in the form of a circle, and when asked to draw a circle they draw the exact physical shape of the camp. Regarding the category of time, Durkheim shows that the concept of time finds its origins in the nature of social life and in the tendency of societies to mark off social occasions such as feasts, rituals and harvests from work routines. All groups, he said, organize their social experience on the celebration of rituals and rites which establish periodic cycles by moving from work to ritual. These practices form themselves into yearly rhythms, the essential constituents of which are evident in the cycle of feasts which return regularly at determined periods. The perception of time thus corresponds to the cycle of assembly between feasts, ceremonies and collective rites. The concept of time is not something that uniquely emerges from the human mind, but rather arises from the rhythmic nature of social life and the tendency of societies to divide experience into temporal bits marked off by ritual.

Theory of Suicide   Durkheim's theory of suicide is founded upon the central assumption that the 'social suicide rate' in a given society can be studied independently of the personal motives that lead people to take their own lives. The 'social suicide rate' refers to the population of suicidal deaths in a given society and the patterns which can be inferred as a result of studying the 'rates' as an independent factual order. By focusing attention on the 'rates' within a given society, Durkheim found that they varied according to social factors such as religion, marital status, occupation and military service. Durkheim reasoned that since the rates were stable within a given social environment, they demonstrated that the predisposing cause of suicide lay not within the psychological motives of individuals but within the social framework of the society. Durkheim's theory of suicide is divided into two explanatory parts. In the first, he explained the phenomenon by drawing on the concept of social integration, referring to the strength of the social bonds which tie individuals to the religious group, the family group, and the political or national group. This social integration serves connective functions by propelling individuals out into the wider society and by promoting the perception that they are part of a larger social whole. When these connective links are weakened by excessive individualism of the sort found in industrial society, low social integration produces suicide of the egoistic type. Conversely, when connective links are over-developed, as is the case with tribal society, suicide is imposed on the individual by the group as a 'duty,' leading to the altruistic type. In the second part of the theory, Durkheim explained suicide by examining the regulatory functions of society and their capacity to impose restraints on individual social needs and wants, such as wealth and prestige. Durkheim argued that, when the regulatory mechanisms are disrupted as in industrial society, the absence of restraint gives rise to an increase in social wants, to a point which exceeds the means for attaining them. When wants are not fulfilled, disappointment results and suicide is of the anomic type. Conversely, in societies where the regulatory mechanisms are excessive, suicide occurs because of too great a degree of regulation and, in this case, is of the fatalistic type.

Totemism   Formally, this is a term referring to a system of religious beliefs found among Australian tribes which Durkheim studied in order to identify the central characteristics of religious life. Totemism may be defined as a tribal religion which represents the group as descending from a mythical being or object, which is subsequently treated as sacred and pious duties are rendered toward it. Durkheim found that the totem requires all members of the group to: (i) refer to themselves by a common tribal name with a common ancestry; (ii) recognize duties and obligations toward each other that are on the level of blood obligations; and (iii) treat as sacred all prohibitions and interdictions which keep the totem apart as a sacred thing and which maintain it as an object of worship. Durkheim thought that in this way totemism links the natural world to religious experience and religion to society.

Weber

Action, Affectual   One of the four types of social action discussed by Weber to demonstrate the degree of rationality inherent in social acts. From this perspective, action is affectual if it 'satisfies a need for revenge, sensual gratification, devotion, contemplative bliss, or the working off of emotional tensions.' In this type of action, the actor is motivated by an emotional response dictated by the state of mind of the actor. Like traditional action, affectual action is not oriented to specific goals or values, but is an expression of the emotional state of the actor in a given situation. Affectual action lacks a rational orientation and forgoes weighing up of means and ends. Like traditional action, 'purely affectual behavior is on the borderline of what is considered meaningful' action, and is irrational because it does not weigh up ends and means and forgoes inner evaluation.

Action, Social   The term 'social action' derives from the body of Weber's methodological work which concerns itself with developing a theory for making valid judgments about the decisions individuals make in their actions with others in a social environment. In contrast to behavior, action is the name Weber gives to a form of activity in which the actor: (i) attaches a subjective meaning to an act; (ii) interprets the actions and acts of others in the social environment; and (iii) acts only after having understood the actions and acts of others. Weber also used the term to denote a central distinction in the subject matter of the natural and social sciences. While in the exact sciences it is sufficient to observe events in the natural world and to report relationships between things observed, in the social sciences investigation must go beyond observation to look at how individuals act on their understanding, and how this 'understanding' may be related to their social action. Weber concluded that the natural and social sciences seek to obtain different kinds of knowledge. In the natural sciences, knowledge is of the external world which can be explained only in terms of valid laws, whereas in the social sciences knowledge must be 'internal' or 'subjective' in the sense that human beings have an inner nature that must be understood in order to explain outward events. Since social action is the product of the 'inner states' of the actor, Weber sought to devise methods to show how these 'inner states' enter into the social acts of individuals. The primary assumption of social action theory is that individuals act on their understanding (*Verstehen*), and that this understanding reflects motives, judgments and evaluations of acts. Weber's aim was to develop a way of elucidating how these judgments were evident in the social acts of individuals.

Action, Instrumental Rational (Zweck)   Weber used this term to refer to a type of social action in which 'the ends, the means and the secondary results are all rationally taken into account and weighed.' In instrumental action, the actor is free to choose the means of action purely in terms of rational efficacy. In this case, the actor systematically takes into account the behavior of others and uses this 'knowledge' as conditions to be considered in the 'attainment of the actor's rationally pursued ends.' The most significant characteristic of instrumental action is the weighing up of means and ends and the systematic taking into account of 'alternative means to the ends, of the relations of the end to the secondary consequences, and of the relative importance of different possible ends.' The actor takes into account those conditions of knowledge that are: (i) based on an understanding of the circumstances as they may lead to alternative means; and (ii) the likely behavior of relevant others in their effect on secondary consequences and the extent to which these conditions affect the attainment of particular ends.

Action, Traditional   A term used by Weber to refer to a type of social action which is patterned on the basis of a fixed body of traditional beliefs which act as moral imperatives upon the actor's judgment. To act according to tradition, the actor need not imagine a goal, picture an outcome or be conscious of specific commitments to values. Weber believed that the great bulk of everyday action conforms to this type so far as both ends and means are fixed by custom. To the extent that traditional action lacks a specific orientation to rationality, it lies close to the 'borderline of what can be justifiably called meaningfully oriented action.' The lack of rational orientation in traditional actions exists because of the actor's habitual responses to the outside world and the degree to which these responses act as guides for future behavior. Traditional action lacks evaluative criteria and is not rationally oriented to ends and means. Clergy abiding by church doctrine would be an example of this type of action.

Action, Value Rational (Wert)   A term used to describe a type of social action which is guided by reference to ultimate values. Value rational action is undertaken in the pursuit of values independent of its chances of success. Actors pursue these values regardless of the possible cost to themselves, and act to put into practice their convictions of what seems to them to be required by 'duty, honor, the pursuit of beauty or the importance of some cause no matter in what it consists.' Value rational action always involves commands or demands which are binding on the actor. In this case, the orientation of the actor is distinct from the affectual type by its 'self-conscious formulation of ultimate values' governing the action and the constantly planned orientation of the actor's values. Value rational action places 'demands' on the actor to put into practice a moral code to which the actor feels bound. While value rational action undertakes considerations regarding the efficacy of the means of action, there is no weighing up of the ends against other ends, since the values pursued are paramount.

Asceticism   A term used by Weber in his study of capitalism to denote a form of self-denial which arises in everyday life to prohibit spontaneous enjoyment and worldly pleasure. Historically, the term originates from religious piety when self-denial was expressed through renunciation of enjoyment with the purpose of diminishing sin and obtaining salvation. As a religious doctrine, asceticism holds that one can achieve a higher state through self-discipline and denial, and that the deferral of enjoyment brings reward. Weber used the concept to establish a connection between modern capitalism and self-denial by showing how self-control becomes a category of social action in societies where capitalism flourishes and where self-denial is linked to industry and achievement. Weber identified two types of asceticism: (i) world-rejecting and (ii) 'innerworldly.' While both seek the path of salvation by involving the believer in formal withdrawal from the world, the first requires the believer to renounce the world because it is corrupt and because its material pleasures offer temptation; the second requires believers to focus their activities in the world undertaking the responsibility to 'transform it in accordance with an ascetic ideal.'

Authority   This term is used by Weber to refer to the power a political leader has to issue commands and obtain compliance from others. While there are many kinds of authority, Weber focuses primarily on political authority and its various historical expressions and determinants. Included in his description are: (i) legal authority, whose right to issue commands and obtain compliance from others rests on the inherent legality of the system of rules; (ii) traditional authority, whose right to issue commands and obtain compliance rests on the sanctity of age-old rules and inherited traditions; and (iii) charismatic authority, whose right to obtain compliance and issue commands rests on the exceptional powers of revelation the leader is perceived to have by followers.

Authority, Charismatic   One of the three types of legitimate domination discussed by Weber in his theory of political authority. Charisma refers to a form of authority whose claim to legitimacy lies in the people's belief that the charismatic leader has oracular or divine powers and is able to galvanize followers by virtue of seeing into the future. Often based on the promise of the leader to emancipate oppressed peoples by fusing their purposes to the realization of a 'true' social destiny or rightful national place, charismatic authority is seen as legitimate only so far as the powers possessed by the leader are not accessible to the ordinary person and are, therefore, perceived as extraordinary. Weber believed that charismatic domination was inherently unstable, not amenable to the development of an administrative apparatus, and had the potential to lose legitimacy when discredited by the failure to realize goals or promises.

Authority, Rational-legal Weber used this term in his political theory to describe a form of legitimate domination resting on the belief that rules are enacted by due process and founded upon basic legal precepts. The overriding characteristic of legal authority is its basis in a system of rational law. Legal authority rests on a belief in the legitimacy of enacted rules and the right of those elevated to office to issue commands. In states whose domination is by legal authority, leaders and their officials are subject to the rule of law and must orient their action to the law in their disposition of power. Officials exercising power are themselves subject to the rule of law and must orient their action to the lawfully enacted rules. Those obeying rules owe their allegiance not to individuals but to an impersonal legal order. Rational-legal authority arises in societies with a developed system of industry, markets and a bureaucratic means of administration. Based on the statute as opposed to the edict, laws are developed through legislative acts rather than the personal say-so of the ruler.

Authority, Traditional A term used by Weber to denote a system of domination whose claim to legitimacy is based on the 'sanctity of age-old rules' and customs. In societies in which traditional forms of domination prevail, leaders obtain their positions and justify their power in the light of custom and customary rights. Power resides in the ability of the ruler to issue commands by virtue of the authority inherent in the person. Sovereigns, monarchs and lords of feudal estates are examples of traditional systems of domination. Persons obey traditional authority out of the recognition of the ruler's inherited claim to the position and the respect engendered by it. Obligations to the leader are owed to the person rather than to objective legal rules and the execution of authority relies on a rudimentary administrative staff. Traditional authority issues commands on the basis of what Weber called the edict. These are personal decrees issued by heads of state reflecting the 'arbitrary' nature of traditional powers. Because the power of the leader is based on custom rather than an explicit system of legal norms, there is no separation between the power of the leader and the political office. The elements of traditional authority thus reflect cultural values and patterns of social action that have been stable for long periods of time.

Bureaucracy Weber used this term to denote the development of a modern means of administration, and believed that bureaucracy was an outcome of historical and social processes. Beyond the formal characteristics of bureaucracy, Weber put forward a theory of bureaucratic development in which he linked the rise of bureaucracy with the emergence of legal domination. In a system of legal domination, authority is derived from rules which are legally and rationally enacted. It was Weber's contention that legal domination develops only in Western society, and only within this system does a full-scale bureaucracy arise. A bureaucractic means of administration includes: (i) the principle of office hierarchy; (ii) a chain of command based on belief in the authority of the office; (iii) a reliance on procedurally correct decision making which presupposes 'correct rulings;' (iv) a reliance on due process; (v) the regulation of offices by impersonal rules; (vi) a form of decision making that is reliant on technical correctness, calculative reasoning, and the ethics of factual consistency; (vii) the tendency to produce the 'leveling' of differences in society and to appeal to the broadest possible interpretation of the 'common interest'; and (viii) a strict orientation to means and ends. Bureaucratic society represents the dominance of formalistic rationality over substantive rationality.

Calculation A term used by Weber to refer to the general process by which the system of money calculation and counting procedure penetrates other spheres of social action and ultimately social values. It was Weber's contention that, at a certain stage of historical development, monetary calculation begins to dominate over other forms of social action, and he saw this as part of the overall process of assigning money values to a system of calculative reasoning. Because it tended to increase efficiency and control, calculative reasoning extended its scope to other activities in social life. According to Weber, the practice of calculation begins with monetary mechanisms and becomes fully established when goods and services come to be manipulated by a standard of evaluation and accounting. Ultimately, accounting rationality extends itself into other spheres of social action including the sphere of values.

Calvinism A branch of Protestantism which began with the theological teaching of John Calvin, a sixteenth-century Swiss cleric. In 1534, Calvin severed his ties with the Catholic Church because it refused to stress the rejection of worldly pleasures. Calvin is best known for his restrictive regulations on worldly enjoyment and for his salvation theology. Chief among these is his doctrine of predestination, which took the view that God had divided all humanity into two classes of persons: the saved and the damned. To those whom God had elected to be saved, he gave everlasting life, salvation and eternal grace; to those from whom he had withheld salvation, he gave everlasting death and dishonor. Calvin decreed that no believer could know to which group he or she belonged until it was revealed at death and nothing could be done to relieve, forgive or reverse the decision. This created a 'feeling of unprecedented inner loneliness' among Protestants, since it placed into jeopardy their hope of eternal salvation. It was Weber's contention that, as a substitute, Protestants threw themselves into commercial activity and eventually viewed their 'success' in business as a 'sign' that they had been 'elected' to be saved.

Capitalism, Ascetic This is a term Weber used to denote the point at which Puritan religious doctrine transformed economic practices and money making by infusing them with ascetic conduct. Since the aim of asceticism is to reject the material pleasures of everyday life, Weber wanted to show that a religious ethic had entered the commercial sphere and affected the development of capitalism. The use of money for personal enjoyment had to be spontaneously avoided in the name of rigorous self-denial.

Capitalism, Modern Weber defined modern capitalism as distinct from other types of money economies by its straightforward introduction of rational methods of accounting and accounting procedure in 'industrial undertakings.' Such procedures are capable of coordinating and mobilizing physical resources such as land, machinery and tools that may be required to be placed at the disposal of private operations for purposes of production. These undertakings, Weber believed, led to the emergence of 'rational' markets which replaced the 'irrational limitations' once imposed on commerce and trade by feudal restrictions and aristocratic classes. The 'rationalization' of industry and trade eventually led to the development of 'calculable law' which ensured the rational operation of economic life by universally applied rules and the *de facto* elimination of privilege and privileged classes. For Weber, modern capitalism is distinctive for its development of the 'gain spirit' which arose in commercial practices and work attitudes. Modern capitalism presupposes the reliance on methods of capitalist accounting, rational technology and the application of calculable law.

Capitalism, Traditional Distinct from modern capitalism, traditional capitalism may be defined as a form of economic activity which refuses opportunities for gain in favor of traditional norms of work. In traditional capitalism, the ethical motive for gain is absent and individuals reject the opportunity to earn more in favor of working less. Weber believed that ascetic capitalism replaced traditional capitalism as soon as the Protestant ethic began to equate the pursuit of economic gain with religious virtue and moral duty. Weber argued that the elevation of economic gain to a 'moral duty' was historically new and had not been seen in traditional forms of capitalism.

Class Weber used the term social class to refer to groups who 'share the same causal component of life chances.' In this, he differentiated himself from Marx who thought that social class was defined by ownership of the means of production. Weber went beyond Marx by identifying two distinct categories of social class. In the first category, class situation is determined by the ownership of usable property which creates life chances in the form of rents and returns on investments. In the second category, class situation is determined by the kinds of skills and services that can be put up for sale in the market, and which are the direct result of training and education. The latter group constitute class formations whose life chances and economic opportunities are not dependent on property or the ownership of the means of production. This class situation is determined by the market for services and may include 'technicians, civil servants and various levels of white-collar workers.' While these classes lack the specific life chances of property, they are able to obtain incomes in the form of salaries as a result of selling their skills. As far as Weber was concerned, Marx considered only the class situation of the first kind. This shift in the class composition described by Weber alters 'the effect of the naked possession' of property, suggesting that the possession of property itself must have been only a 'forerunner' of the class situation. The transition to the class situation of modern times creates expanding political rights for workers and a reduction in class antagonism. In Weber's view, the class struggle is thereby altered in the later stages of capitalism and the tendency for revolution minimized.

Formal Rationality A term used by Weber to indicate the amount of calculation and accounting procedure that goes into an action to increase its efficacy. Though essentially used to refer to a system of reasoning, rationality may be termed 'formal' when there is a view to expressing a situation, solving problems or conceptualizing actions by a 'straightforward, unambiguous application of numerical, calculable standards'. In this sense, formal rationality designates the amount of quantitative reasoning and accounting procedure which is technically possible and can be applied to an action or situation to insure consistency of outcome and the assurance that goals will be obtained. Formal rationality imposes order on the world through a system of measurement and calculable activity. To the extent that formal rationality adheres to norms of accounting procedure, it conflicts with the criterion of values found in substantive rationality.

Historical Explanation This is a term used in Weber's methodological studies to draw a distinction between explanation in the exact sciences and explanation in the social sciences. Weber believed that explanation in the social sciences had to be historical so far as it: (i) attempts to explain concrete reality rather than search for general laws; (ii) takes recourse to 'interpretive understanding' rather than relying on methods of observation; (iii) focuses on human social action rather than on events in the natural world; and (iv) bases its knowledge on 'subjective' criteria that must be understood in order to explain outward events.

History Weber used the term 'history' to refer to the tendency of social action to bring about change and development. Generally, Weber conceived of historical change in terms of 'rationalization processes' in which the economic, political and legal spheres of society act as determinants of historical change by an increased reliance on technique and procedure. The capability inherent in these spheres to bring about change led Weber to look for various causes of social development such as the decline of magic and the rise of prophecy, the replacement of medieval with rational law and the substitution of traditional modes of social action with forms of action based on a means–ends orientation to reality. Many of Weber's studies emphasize this process of history by their focus on the shift to modern capitalism, religious prophecy, legal domination and bureaucracy.

Ideal Type The ideal type is a methodological procedure used by Weber to overcome some of the limitations of investigation in the social sciences. Because social subject matter cannot be directly observed, Weber thought that ideal types could be used as a means of discovering common properties of social phenomena. It is designed to show that social phenomena can be studied when social scientists engage in 'concept formation' which functions to select aspects of empirical reality that are worth knowing. The ideal type is thus designed to capture empirical reality by arriving at the 'analytical accentuation' of certain aspects of society. In Weber, the main category of type formation is the historical ideal type. These may be described as types formed by selecting out general concepts common to a range of phenomena which employ a criterion of selection by means of general concepts. It functions to elucidate the features of historical reality by extracting essential 'traits' which elaborate concepts by comparing them with concrete phenomena. Traits are then compared to an ideal picture of social reality and from this a workable type is formed. For example, to understand the development of a city economy, a comparison can be made between aspects of modern industrial society and those of a medieval society. In this sense, an ideal type is a picture of events which approximates the reality of a given society under certain conditions of its organization. The traits of a city economy may include such elements as a system of law based on statutes, the concept of a citizen, a municipal organization, bureaucracy and political office holders.

Interpretive Sociology   This term is used to define a body of social theory devised by Weber in order to make valid judgments about the 'inner states' of actors in their actions with others in a constituted social environment. Weber believed that individuals act in and come to understand the social world only through interpretive acts. At the most fundamental level, these acts involve the process of assigning meanings to the given factual states in the outer world, and since these meanings do not already come 'attached' to the socio-cultural facts of the world, Weber took the position that they must be products of the meaning states of actors. He believed that the processes of assigning meaning to the factual states of the outer world are evidence of the 'inner states' of actors who rely on their understanding (*Verstehen)* of the acts of others.

Legitimacy   This is a term used by Weber in his theory of legitimate domination to indicate the extent to which officials, groups and individuals actively acknowledge the validity of a ruler in an established order and the right of a ruler to issue commands. Accompanying each established order are beliefs about the 'legitimacy' of a given system of domination. Every system of domination is based on some corresponding belief by people in the legitimacy and right of the ruler to issue commands and rule over individuals. In modern society, law is a basis of political legitimacy.

Legitimate Domination   Weber used this term to refer to the right of a ruler in an 'established order' to issue commands and to expect that these commands will be obeyed. Weber thought that the right of a ruler to exercise commands and expect compliance forms a legitimate system of authority. The two central elements to any system of domination are: (i) the perception that authority is legitimate for those who are subject to it, and (ii) the development of an administrative staff to act as a barrier between the leader and the people. Weber identified three types of legitimate domination: (i) charismatic; (ii) traditional; and (iii) rational-legal. Each system encompasses a total 'apparatus of authority' reflecting the relation between ruler, administrative officials, groups or persons existing within the 'established order' and a means of enforcement. In his political sociology, Weber looked at the social and historical conditions leading to long-lasting systems of domination and the mechanisms which maintain them.

Magic, Emancipation from   Weber uses this term in the context of the study of religion but it has wide application to Weber's theory of the development of rational law, the growth of the modern city and the rationalization of Western economies. Weber took the view that, in early societies, magic creates priestly classes which develop monopolies over bodies of knowledge and control over spiritual and commercial resources. Under these circumstances, the hold by magic over everyday life leads to an absence of social change and the dominance of religion in the interpretation of experience. In Weber's view, the development of modern civilization proceeds directly in relation to the decline of magic in social life. This is evident in his discussion of the growth of the city as a rational institution and the development of a prophecy religion. Weber thought that prophecy brought about an end to magic because it situated the miraculous outside the collective camp and this 'destroyed magical procedure because it was viewed as devilish rather than divine.' It is the decline of magic, Weber believed, which leads to world markets, rational commerce and science.

Means and Ends of Action   This term is used throughout Weber's writings to indicate the various degrees of rationality of social action and the extent to which these rationalities serve as guides to the realization of goals. Weber took the view that human action could be understood in terms of a 'means–ends' rationality. The 'means' in this case refer to the methods or procedures individuals use to attain goals and achieve tasks whereas 'ends' refer to the aims or purposes of action. At one time, the 'means' of action were governed by moral, ethical or value standards leading to demands upon actors to pursue goals in the light of prescribed means. In modern societies, however, the means of action are freed from given ethical standards and ends are pursued strictly in terms of the practical efficacy of specific means. As societies become more modern, human action becomes less regulated by ethical standards, and means and ends are subject to rational calculation. Modern society effects change in the means–ends scheme.

Methodenstreit   This term is used by Weber to refer to the methodological debate carried on in Germany in the latter half of the nineteenth century concerning which methods were appropriate for the study of society. Literally, the term means 'methodological controversy' and indicates the growing tension between the methodologies of the natural and social sciences which developed as a consequence of the pressure put upon the social sciences to adopt the methods of the natural sciences. The focus of the debate was on two distinct fronts: on issues of subject matter and on a theory of knowledge. With respect to subject matter, Weber, following Heinrich Rickert, rejected the methods of the natural sciences stating that the subject matter of the social sciences differed by its focus on the inner states of individuals in contrast to the scientific focus on the outer states of the natural world. This fundamental distinction between the 'inner states' of human actors and the 'outer states' of nature led Weber to assert that the subject matters studied by the natural and the social sciences were fundamentally different. On a second front were issues related to a theory of knowledge. In the scientific view, knowledge was seen to be the accumulation of facts drawn from the physical world, facts which could only be obtained by observation. Rickert's work was central here because he called into question the scientific certainty of observation as the basis of all knowledge by arguing that observation was a form of judgment. Judgment was thus placed before knowing, leading the way to asserting that judgment is, in fact, prior to observation. This was central because Rickert could claim that physical reality had substance only through the act of human judgment. Rickert went on to reason that the characteristics of history and reality were thus made up of human valuing and judging, and that observation methods would not be adequate to the social sciences whose concern it was to grasp the relationship between values and human social action. He asserted that, since the elements of reality comprising human judgment cannot ever be grasped by the generalizing, law-giving perspective of the natural sciences, new methods had to be devised to capture the products of human social acts.

Party   This term is used in the context of Weber's political sociology to refer to the sphere of activities appropriate to political parties. For Weber, the development of political parties forms the third dimension of social adjustment, along with class and status, which takes place in the later stages of capitalist development. In contrast to class and status, the place of political parties is in the sphere of political power. Political parties are oriented toward the acquisition of power and the influencing of the actions of others for political purposes. In Weber's view, parties must maintain their separation from the economic and status spheres of society and take the electorate into account, since their neglect would upset future election. Weber believed that modern political parties alter the class structure of society by absorbing elements of the class struggle in their representation of all social groups.

Power   A term used by Weber to describe the state of affairs in which individuals are in a position to carry out their own will over others 'despite resistance.' Power is defined by Weber as the likelihood that an individual will realize his or her will in a situation of social action. By contrast, domination refers to the 'probability' that a specific command will be 'obeyed by a given group of persons' by virtue of the legitimate right of a ruler to issue commands.

Predestination This term is used by Weber to denote a religious doctrine propagated by John Calvin in the sixteenth century. Calvin's central doctrine of predestination was based on four precepts: (i) that God had divided all humanity into two classes of persons – the saved and the damned – each being assigned an eternal fate which they were powerless to change. To those who had been elected to be saved, God gave everlasting salvation, whereas those who were condemned were given everlasting death and dishonor; (ii) that no believers could know their fate until death; (iii) that nothing could be done to relieve, forgive or reverse the decrees – no priest, no prayer, no sacrament and no worldly forgiveness by confession or communion; and (iv) that God abandoned all but the elect since, in Calvin's view, Christ had endured suffering only for the elect. Weber believed that the withdrawal of salvation created tremendous anxiety among Protestants, and in order to overcome it, they threw themselves into worldly work and sought to reinterpret their relationship to God by practicing discipline and self-denial.

Protestantism A sixteenth-century religious doctrine espoused first by Martin Luther and then by John Calvin. Weber believed that Calvin's teachings were so influential that they penetrated everyday life and commercial activity with Protestant religious maxims. Three key elements of Calvinist doctrine were definitive: (i) asceticism and self-denial in daily life; (ii) the doctrine of predestination stating that God had divided all humanity into two classes of persons, the saved and the damned; (iii) the doctrine of *sola fide*, which made religious faith a private matter and placed the individual on his or her own in spiritual concerns.

Puritanism Weber used this term in his study of capitalism to identify an attitude which Protestants develop toward life that is largely based on the self-denial of and antagonism toward sensuous experience. In addition, puritanism presupposes individual autonomy in spiritual matters and the commitment to purge the church of Catholic influences.

Rational Weber used the term rational to refer to (i) types of social order, and (ii) orientations to social action. In the first case, rational societies demonstrate the development of calculable law, rational commerce, a practical orientation to reality. With respect to an orientation to social action, rational refers to various means–ends calculations which increase the attainment of practical outcomes and social goals.

Rationality This is a key concept in Weber's work used to refer to a standard of action whose substance lies in its weighing up of means and ends. Weber essentially used the term to describe an orientation to reality which systematically weighs up means and ends for purposes of efficacy and the practical attainment of goals. To the extent that action is rational, therefore, it weighs up means and ends and relies on calculations. Weber believed that different types of rationality become dominant at different stages of social development and this, he thought, tends to eliminate other orientations to reality such as magic, prayer or oracular considerations. Rationality replaces earlier orientations to reality by a straight-forward orientation to means and ends. With respect to social action, rationality can be of two types: (i) subjective rationality, referring to the degree of inner evaluation which the actor engages in cognitively before an act; (ii) objective rationality, which refers to the degree to which action embodies rational principles by adhering to formal norms or to specific means–ends calculations. Weber identified four distinct types of rationality: (i) instrumental; (ii) technical; (iii) formal; and (iv) substantive. The four types of rationality differ in the stress placed on the degree of consideration given to the means and degree of calculation in the attainment of ends.

Rationalization A central theme in Weber's work encompassing his general theory of history, change and social development. Weber used the term rationalization to describe the process by which nature, society and individual action are increasingly mastered by an orientation to planning, technical procedure and rational action. Western societies reflect this tendency in their systems of law, science, medicine, and commercial practices. Several fundamental principles of rationalization link it to central themes in Weber's overall approach to historical development. These include: (i) the principle of development inherent in the process of civilization and Western society; (ii) the stress on the rational containment of everyday life; (iii) the widespread use of calculation as a strategy of social action; (iv) the freeing of social action from all magical thought; (v) the emphasis on a practical orientation to empirical reality; and (vi) the reliance on technical procedure as a way of controlling practical outcomes and mastering everyday life. Rationalization depends on strategies of social action and adjustments to the means and ends of action in the attainment of goals.

Sola fide This is a term used by Weber to describe the particular feature of Protestant religious doctrine which advocates private solitude in the practice of religious faith. Weber took the view that the principle of *sola fide* put forward a new doctrine of religious action since it diverged sharply from the Catholic concept of *consilia evangelica*, in which religious faith took place collectively and was communal in nature. Weber believed that the practice led to inner calculation and self-conscious planning.

Social Spheres Weber used the term social sphere to indicate different realms in society whose existence, activities, ideas and rationality: (i) create orientations for social action; and (ii) impart influences and modes of development to other social realms. Chief among these spheres are the legal, political, religious, and economic realms of society. These may be thought of as analogous to social institutions whose combined structure is made up of actions, activities and techniques which influence other spheres in society. Weber's differentiation of social spheres is important for the connections he deduced between diverse realms of society and the role these play in the patterning of social change and the structure of social action. Weber showed that no single sphere was dominant historically, but that spheres overlap and intersect one another to bring about change. Examples of the interconnection between social spheres is found in his study of capitalism where there is a link between the economic and religious spheres, and in his theory of political domination were there is a connection between the legal, religious and political spheres of society.

Spirit of Capitalism A term used to identify the unique characteristics of capitalist society which arise when religious doctrine becomes linked to economic practices. Weber believed that, when compared to other systems of money making, Western capitalism was alone in developing a central philosophy or 'spirit.' He thought that the spirit of capitalism was unique in two respects: (i) it developed only in modern Western capitalism and was lacking in other societies where capitalism had existed; and (ii) it brought about the appearance of ethical demands in economic activity and implied the presence of religious doctrine. He reasoned that the spirit of capitalism can be identified by three overriding imperatives: (i) the devotion to amassing wealth and profit beyond the personal needs of the individual; (ii) the commitment to unrelieved toil and work coupled with self-denial; and (iii) the avoidance of the use of wealth for purposes of personal enjoyment.

State Weber defined the state as a rational institution characterized by a system of law, a rational economy and a bureaucratic means of administration. The modern state is distinct from other political entities by: (i) its monopoly of the legitimate use of violence; (ii) its system of domination based on legal authority; and (iii) its legitimating relations founded on duly enacted legal rules. At the center of Weber's theory of the state is the connection between legal authority and a bureaucratically organized means of administration. Bureaucratic organization affects the state in two ways. First, it ensures that the legal and political spheres are separate from the economic realm and that the economy is governed by rational legal norms. Second, it ensures that all groups are enfranchised by political rights and freedoms advocating universalism and equality. As a bureaucratic norm, universalism offsets the power of the capitalist classes by mobilizing the consensus of groups within society and by promoting equitable social policy. In contrast to Marx, who reduced state activities to sheer economic domination of one class and to judicial and police functions, Weber believed that the state was concerned with the practical and technical exercise of power and the active construction of consensus.

Status Group   This is a term used by Weber in conjunction with his theory of social class to refer to the form of social adjustment taking place in the structure of social groups in late capitalism. Weber drew the distinction between class and status in order to look into the question of whether or not groups formed on the basis of status considerations and whether these were distinct from the formation of social classes in the economic sphere. A status group may be defined as a group whose members share the same component of 'life fate' as determined by a positive or negative estimation of honor or social worth. In contrast to class, status groups involve: (i) the activities by means of which groups set themselves apart from other groups; and (ii) the badges and insignia employed in defining the status group in relation to other groups. As communities, status groups share common perspectives such as lifestyle and a common criterion of evaluation. Social differentiation by 'strata' involves 'strict submission' to codes of dress, habits of taste and monopolies over certain goods and professions. Submissions to these codes are indications that individuals put forward a claim to qualify as members of a status group. Weber sees class and status as separate dimensions of the stratification system. While class is defined by the market situation and related to the 'acquisition' of incomes and opportunities, status operates outside the market order and is defined by patterns of 'consumption.' Class and status thus occupy different social spheres and engage different levels of the stratification system.

Subjective   Weber used the term to identify an order of events related to human social action, particularly the inner judgments and evaluations preceding a social act. Technically speaking, the term 'subjective' refers to human 'inner states' and is intended to demarcate itself from the purely outward behavior of individuals. Weber believed that the social sciences are distinct from the natural sciences because: (i) they study human social action which involves reference to the 'cognitive' states of actors; and (ii) because human beings, unlike the objects of nature, attach meaning to their acts and engage in subjective judgment in the effort to evaluate their social environments. This evaluation occurs in the subjective dimension as opposed to the objective world of physical nature. For Weber, a theory of social action had to be based on human subjective processes in order to devise a complete theory of society.

Substantive Rationality   Weber used this term to refer to the degree to which action is shaped by an orientation to 'ultimate values,' in contrast to action which is shaped by purely formal or practical ends and calculations. According to Weber, substantive rationality is not restricted to the straightforward attainment of goals, but applies values which are shaped by ethical, utilitarian or egalitarian standards. Substantive rationality always upholds 'value scales' and adheres to principles of social justice, ethics and equality. Weber contrasted 'substantive rationality' with 'formal rationality,' and believed that the operation of modern Western society is largely based on formal rationality, evident in the increased bureaucratization and the practical orientation to means and ends. Whereas formal rationality entails an orientation to decisions which rely on norms of efficiency, substantive rationality relies on qualitative judgments which may be bound by ethical or aesthetic criteria. Weber believed that formal and substantive rationality are opposed, and that ultimately, formal rationality views substantive rationality as inimical to its own purpose.

Technical Rationality   Weber used the term to indicate an orientation to reality stressing a systematic evaluation and consideration of the means and ends of action for specific outcomes. In technical rationality the means are converted into 'techniques' which act as tried and true procedures in attaining goals, whether administrative or political. The distinctive feature of technical rationality is its systematic consideration of means, in which case the ends are treated as beyond doubt. The highest form of technical rationality is the scientific experiment which leads to a calculated stress on the means in order to achieve specific ends or outcomes. To the extent that action is technical, it is functionally oriented to the selection of means.

Value Orientation   Weber used the term to pinpoint one of the differences between the subject matter of the social sciences and the subject matter of the natural sciences. Weber believed that one of the major characteristics setting the subject matter of the social sciences apart from the exact sciences was that human social action reflects an orientation to 'values.' Human beings, according to this view, always act in relation to ends which they value whereas objects of the exact sciences act only in reference to the laws of nature. Examples of these values are to be found in laws, customs, language, economy and religion. From this standpoint there emerged a fundamental distinction between the sciences of value and the sciences of fact. In sciences of fact, values are irrelevant because they do not enter into the laws of nature, whereas in the social sciences such as history and sociology, values are central because they concern themselves with human individuals whose actions reflect the judgments and evaluations of a surrounding social world. In this sense, the products of their actions always reflect an orientation to values and the social sciences must undertake to study these values.

Value Neutrality   This is a term Weber used in his methodological studies to: (i) indicate the necessary objectivity required by researchers in solving problems in the social sciences; and (ii) the caution investigators should exercise against making 'value judgments' which coincide with the particular orientation or motives of the researcher. What is important to note is that while Weber believed that value neutrality was the aim of research, he thought that the social sciences must engage in the interpretation of values and attempt to understand the value orientation of social actors.

Value Relevance   This is a term used by Weber to refer to the means by which specific aspects of reality are brought to the attention of scientific observers and isolated as a matter of investigative interest. Weber used the term in relation to Heinrich Rickert, who believed that the principle of value relevance comes into play when scientists use concepts, since it is by means of concepts that individuals are able to reduce the mass of facts in the empirical world and make them comprehensible. The principle of value relevance is a way of dealing with the claim that the natural sciences select what is of research interest solely on the basis of its objective scientific merit. It was Rickert who suggested that the objects of empirical reality must be of interest to us only because they are 'value relevant,' not because they have intrinsic scientific merit. According to this view, what interests human beings must be related to the universal values of society.

Verstehen   Literally translated as 'human understanding,' this term is used by Weber in the context of a theory of social action. Weber employed the term to convey what he thought was unique about the subject matter of the social sciences in contrast to the natural sciences. Weber believed that however precise the natural sciences were, their subject matter confined them to the study of the external characteristics of the natural world and the outer states of things. By contrast, the social sciences are 'subjectifying,' in that they concern themselves with the 'inner states' of actors who act on their 'understanding' (*Verstehen*) of the acts of others and on their interpretation of the social environment. Since the subject matter of the natural sciences does not possess 'understanding' (*Verstehen*), it stands to reason that their methods must be disqualified or ruled out as inadequate to the study of human social action. It is this dependence on 'understanding' which made social phenomena, distinct from physical phenomena, and the methods of the natural sciences inadequate for the study of society.

Bibliography

Primary Texts

Marx, Karl. *Capital: A Critique of Political Economy* Vol. 1. Middlesex, England: Penguin, [1867] 1976.

Marx, Karl. *Capital: A Critique of Political Economy* Vol. 2. Moscow: Foreign Languages Publications, [1885] 1957.

Marx, Karl. *Capital: A Critique of Political Economy* Vol. 3. Chicago: Charles H. Kerr, [1894] 1909.

Marx, Karl. *The Civil War in France*. Peking: Foreign Languages Press, [1871] 1970.

Marx, Karl. *A Contribution to the Critique of Political Economy*. Moscow: Progress Publishers, [1859] 1977.

Marx, Karl. *A Critique of Hegel's Philosophy of Right*. J. O'Malley (ed.), Cambridge: Cambridge University Press, [1843] 1970.

Marx, Karl. *The Economic and Philosophic Manuscripts of 1844*. New York: International Publishers, [1932] 1964.

Marx, Karl. *The Eighteenth Brumaire of Louis Bonaparte*. Moscow: Progress, [1852] 1977.

Marx, Karl. *Grundrisse: Foundations of the Critique of Political Economy*. Middlesex, England: Penguin, [1953] 1973.

Marx, Karl. 'On the Jewish Question', pp. 26–52 in R.C. Tucker (ed.), *The Marx–Engels Reader*, (2nd edn), New York: Norton, [1843] 1978.

Marx, Karl. *The Poverty of Philosophy*. New York: International Publishers, [1847] 1982.

Marx, Karl. *Pre-Capitalist Economic Formations*. New York: International Publishers, [1857–58] 1984.

Marx, Karl. 'Value, Price and Profit,' *Collected Works* Vol. 20. London: Lawrence & Wishart, [1865] 1985.

Marx, Karl and Engels, Frederick. *The Communist Manifesto*. F.L. Bender (ed.), New York: W.W. Norton & Company, [1848] 1988.

Marx, Karl and Engels, Frederick. *The German Ideology*. New York: International Publishers, [1845] 1947.

Marx, Karl and Engels, Frederick. *The German Ideology: Collected Works*, Vol. 5, New York: International Publishers, [1846] 1975.

Marx, Karl and Engels, Frederick. *The Holy Family, or Critique of Critical Criticism*. Moscow: Progress Publishers, [1846] 1956.

Engels, Frederick. *Anti-Dühring*. Peking: Foreign Languages Press, [1878] 1976.

Engels, Frederick. *The Condition of the Working Class in England*. Oxford: Basil Blackwell, [1845] 1958.

Durkheim, Emile. *The Division of Labor in Society*. New York: The Free Press, [1893] 1933.

Durkheim, Emile. 'The Dualism of Human Nature and Its Social Conditions,' [1914] pp. 325–40, in Kurt H. Wolff (ed.), *Essays on Sociology and Philosophy*. New York: Harper, 1960.

Durkheim, Emile. *The Elementary Forms of the Religious Life*. London: Allen & Unwin, [1912] 1915.

Durkheim, Emile. 'Individualism and the Intellectuals' (trans. S. and J. Lukes) [1898], *Political Studies*, 17, 1969, 14–30.

Durkheim, Emile. 'Emile Durkheim's Inaugural Lecture at Bordeaux,' (trans. Neville Layne) in *Sociological Inquiry*, 44, 1974, 189–204.
Durkheim, Emile. 'On Totemism,' *The History of Sociology*, 5, [1902], (Spring) 1985, 91–122.
Durkheim, Emile. *The Rules of Sociological Method*. New York: The Free Press, [1895] 1938.
Durkheim, Emile. *Suicide*. New York: The Free Press, [1897] 1951.
Durkheim, Emile and Mauss, Marcel. *Primitive Classification*. Chicago: University of Chicago Press, [1903] 1963.
Weber, Max. *Critique of Stammler* (trans. Guy Oakes). New York: The Free Press, 1977.
Weber, Max. *Economy and Society* Volumes 1 & 2. G. Roth and C. Wittich (eds), Berkeley: University of California Press, 1978.
Weber, Max. *From Max Weber: Essays in Sociology*. H. Gerth and C.W. Mills (eds), New York: Oxford University Press, 1967.
Weber, Max. *General Economic History*. New York: Collier Books, [1922] 1961.
Weber, Max. *The Methodology of the Social Sciences*. E.A. Shils and H.A. Finch (eds), New York: The Free Press, 1949.
Weber, Max. 'Objectivity in Social Science and Social Policy,' in E.A. Shils and H.A. Finch (eds), *The Methodology of the Social Sciences*. New York: The Free Press, 1949.
Weber, Max. *The Protestant Ethic and The Spirit of Capitalism*. New York: Scribner's Press, [1904–5] 1958.
Weber, Max. *Roscher and Knies: The Logical Problems of Historical Economics* (trans. Guy Oakes). New York: The Free Press, 1975.
Weber, Max. *The Sociology of Religion*. Boston: Beacon Press, [1922] 1964.

Secondary Texts

Abel, Theodore. 'The Operation Called Verstehen,' *The American Journal of Sociology*, 54, 1948, 211–18.
Abel, Theodore. 'A Reply to Professor Wax,' *Sociology and Sociological Research*, 51, 1967, 323–33.
Abercromie, N., Hill, S. and Turner, B.S. *The Dominant Ideology Thesis*. London: George Allen & Unwin, 1980.
Acton, H.B. 'The Materialist Conception of History,' *Proceedings of the Aristotelian Society*, 1951–52, 205–24.
Alpert, H. 'France's First University Course in Sociology,' *American Sociological Review*, 2, 1937, 311–17.
Althusser, Louis and Balibar, E. *Reading Capital*. London: Verso NLB, 1979.
Althusser, Louis. *Lenin and Philosophy*. New York: Monthly Review Press, 1971.
Anchor, Robert. 'Heinrich Rickert,' *The Encyclopedia of Philosophy*, Vol. 7, New York: Macmillan, 1967, pp. 192–4.
Anderson, Perry. *Lineages of the Absolutist State*. London: Verso, 1979.
Anderson, Perry. *Passages from Antiquity to Feudalism*. London: Verso, 1978.
Arendt, Hannah. *On Revolution*. New York: Viking, 1963.
Aron, Raymond. *Main Currents in Sociological Thought*. (2 Vols). New York: Doubleday, 1970.
Barbalet, J.M. *Marx's Construction of Social Theory*. London: Routledge, 1983.
Barker, Ernest. *Greek Political Theory: Plato and His Predecessors*. London: Methuen, 1918.
Barnes, J.A. 'Durkheim's Division of Labour in Society,' *Man*, 1, 1966, 158–75.
Beck, Lewis White. 'Neo-Kantianism,' *The Encyclopedia of Philosophy*, Vol. 5, New York: Macmillan, 1967, pp. 468–73.
Bellah, Robert. 'Durkheim and History,' *American Sociological Review*, 24, 1959, 446–61.
Bendix, Reinhard. *Max Weber: An Intellectual Portrait*. New York: Doubleday, 1960.
Bendix, Reinhard. 'Max Weber's Sociology Today,' *International Social Science Journal*, 17, 1965, 9–22.

Berger, Peter and Pullberg, S. 'Reification and the Sociological Critique of Consciousness,' *New Left Review*, 35, 1966, 56–71.

Braverman, Harry. *Labor and Monopoly Capital: The Degradation of Work in the Twentieth Century*. New York: Monthly Review Press, 1974.

Black, Antony. *Guilds and Civil Society in European Political Thought from the Twelfth Century to the Present*. London: Methuen and Co., 1984.

Blackburn, Robin (ed.). *Ideology in Social Science: Readings in Critical Social Theory*. New York: Pantheon, 1972.

Blum, Jerome, 'The Rise of Serfdom in Eastern Europe,' *The American Historical Review*, 62, 1957, 807–36.

Bottomore, Tom (ed.). *A Dictionary of Marxist Thought*. Cambridge, Mass.: Harvard University Press, 1983.

Bottomore, Tom and Nisbet, R. (eds). *A History of Sociological Analysis*. New York: Basic Books, 1978.

Brubaker, Roger. *The Limits of Rationality: An Essay on the Social and Moral Thought of Max Weber*. London: George Allen & Unwin, 1984.

Bruun, H.H. *Science, Values and Politics in Max Weber's Methodology*, Copenhagen: Munksgaard, 1972.

Burger, Thomas. *Max Weber's Theory of Concept Formation: History, Laws, and Ideal Types*. Durham: Duke University Press, 1976.

Carling, Alan. 'Forms of Value and the Logic of Capital,' *Science and Society*, 50, 1986, 52–80.

Chambers, J.D. 'Enclosure and the Labour Supply in the Industrial Revolution,' *Economic History Review 2nd Series*, Vol. V, 1953, 319–43.

Chambers, J.D. and Mingay, Gordon E. *The Agricultural Revolution, 1750–1880*. London: Batsford, 1966.

Charlton, D.G. *Secular Religions in France 1815-1870*. London: Oxford University Press, 1963.

Charlton, D.G. *Positive Thought in France*. London: Verso, 1979.

Charlton, D.G. *Positivist Thought in France During the Second Empire: 1852–70*. Oxford: Clarendon Press, 1959.

Claeys, Gregory. 'Individualism, Socialism and Social Science: Further Notes on a Process of Conceptual Formation 1800–1850,' *Journal of the History of Ideas*, 33, 1986, 81–93.

Cohen, G.A. *Karl Marx's Theory of History*. New Jersey: Princeton University Press, 1978.

Colletti, Lucio. *Marxism and Hegel*. London: Verso, 1979.

Collins, Randall. 'Weber's Last Theory of Capitalism: A Systematization,' *American Sociological Review*, 45, 1980, 925–42.

Comte, Auguste. *Cours de Philosophie Positive*. Paris: Bachelier, 1830–1842.

Comte, Auguste. *A General View of Positivism*. London: Routledge, 1908.

Cornforth, Maurice. *Dialectical Materialism: An Introduction*. London: Lawrence & Wishart, 1953.

Cornforth, Maurice. *Historical Materialism*. London: Lawrence and Wishart, 1962.

Cropsey, Joseph. 'Karl Marx,' pp. 697–723 in Leo Strauss and Joseph Cropsey (eds), *History of Political Philosophy*. Chicago: Rand McNally & Co., 1963.

Dawe, Alan. 'The Relevance of Values in Weber's Sociology,' pp. 37–66 in A. Sahay (ed.), *Max Weber and Modern Sociology*. London: Routledge & Kegan Paul, 1971.

De Tocqueville, Alexis. *The Old Régime and the French Revolution*. New York: Anchor Books, [1856] 1955.

Di Quattro, Arthur. 'Verstehen as an Empirical Concept,' *Sociology and Social Research*, 57, 1972, 32–42.

Dobb, Maurice. *Studies in the Development of Capitalism*. New York: International Publishers, 1947.

Dohrenwend, B.P. 'Egoism, Altruism, Anomie and Fatalism: A Conceptual Analysis of Durkheim's Types,' *American Sociological Review*, 24, 1959, 466–72.

Douglas, Jack. 'The Sociological Analysis of Social Meanings of Suicide,' *European Journal of Sociology*, 7, 1966, 249–75.

Draper, Hal. *Karl Marx's Theory of Revolution*. New York: Monthly Review Press, 1977.

Driver, Cecil. *Tory Radical: The Life of Richard Oastler*. New York: Oxford University Press, 1946.

Duby, Georges. *Rural Economy and Country Life in the Medieval West*. Columbia, S.C.: University of South Carolina Press, 1968.

Dumont, Louis. 'The Modern Conception of the Individual,' *Contributions to Indian Sociology*, 8, 1965, 13–61.

Dunayevskaya, Raya. *Marxism and Freedom*. London: Pluto Press, 1971.

Eisenstadt, S.N. (ed.). 'Declaration of the Rights of Man and Citizen,' in *Political Sociology: A Reader*. New York: Basic Books, Inc., 1971, p. 341.

Eisenstadt, S.N. (ed.). *The Protestant Ethic and Modernization*. New York: Basic Books, 1968.

Fenton, Steve. *Durkheim and Modern Sociology*. Cambridge: Cambridge University Press, 1984.

Feuerbach, L. *The Essence of Christianity*. Buffalo, N.Y.: Prometheus, 1989.

Feyerabend, Paul K. *Problems of Empiricism*. London: Cambridge University Press, 1981.

Fielden, John. *The Curse of the Factory System*. New York: Augustus Kelley, [1836] 1969.

Findlay, J.N. *Hegel: A Re-Examination*. London: George Allen & Unwin, 1958.

Finley, M.I. *The Ancient Economy*. London: Chatto & Windus, 1973.

Finley, M.I. *Slavery in Classical Antiquity*. Cambridge: Heffer, 1968.

Geras, Norman. 'Essence and Appearance: Aspects of Fetishism in Marx's *Capital*,' *New Left Review*, 65, 1971, 69–85.

Giddens, Anthony. *Capitalism and Modern Social Theory*. Cambridge: Cambridge University Press, 1971.

Giddens, Anthony. 'The "individual" in the Writings of Emile Durkheim,' *European Journal of Sociology*, 12, 1971, 210–28.

Giddens, Anthony. 'A Typology of Suicide,' *European Journal of Sociology*, 7, 1966, 276–95.

Gilbert, Michael, 'Neo-Durkheimian Analysis of Economic Life and Strife: From Durkheim to the Social Contract,' *Sociological Review*, New Series, 26, 1978, 729–54.

Gordon, Marshall. *In Search of the Spirit of Capitalism*. New York: Columbia University Press, 1982.

Gordon, Marshall. *Presbyteries and Profits: Calvinism and the Development of Capitalism in Scotland, 1560–1707*. Oxford: Clarendon Press, 1980.

Green, R.W. (ed.). *Protestantism and Capitalism: The Weber Thesis and its Critics*, Boston: Heath & Co., 1959.

Halevy, Elie. *The Growth of Philosophic Radicalism*. Boston: Beacon Press, 1955.

Hamilton, E. and Huntington, C. (eds). *The Collected Dialogues of Plato*. Princeton: The University Press, 1961.

Hegel, G.W.F. *The Phenomenology of Mind*. New York: Harper & Row Publishers, [1807] 1967.

Hegel, G.W.F. *Phenomenology of Spirit*. Oxford: Oxford University Press, [1806] 1977.

Hegel, G.W.F. *Philosophy of Right*. Oxford: Clarendon Press, [1843] 1958.

Hegel, G.W.F. *The Science of Logic*, Vol. 2, London: Allen & Unwin, [1812] 1929.

Hekman, Susan. 'Weber's Concept of Causality and the Modern Critique,' *Sociological Inquiry*, 49, 1979, 67–76.

Hekman, Susan. *Weber, the Ideal Type, and Contemporary Social Theory*. Notre Dame, Indiana: University of Notre Dame Press, 1983.

Henderson, W.O. *The Industrial Revolution on the Continent 1800–1914*. London: Frank Cass, 1947.

Hibbert, A.B. 'The Origins of the Medieval Town Patriciate,' *Past and Present*, 3, Feb. 1953, 15–27.

Hilton, Rodney. 'Capitalism: What's in a Name?', *Past and Present*, 1, Feb. 1952, 32–43.

Hilton, Rodney. *The Decline of Serfdom in Medieval England*. London: St. Martin's Press, 1969.

Hilton, Rodney. *The English Peasantry in the Later Middle Ages.* Oxford: Clarendon, 1975.

Hilton, Rodney. 'Introduction,' *Transition from Feudalism to Capitalism,* London: NLB, 1976.

Hilton, Rodney. *The Transition from Feudalism to Capitalism.* London: NLB Humanities Press, 1976.

Hobbes, Thomas. *Leviathan.* Middlesex, England: Penguin, [1651] 1968.

Hobsbawm. E.J. *The Age of Revolution.* New York: Dover, 1938.

Hook, Sidney. *From Hegel to Marx.* London: Victor Gollancz, 1936.

Huff, Toby E. *Max Weber and the Methodology of the Social Sciences.* London: Transaction, 1984.

Hughes, H. Stuart. *Consciousness and Society: The Reorientation of European Social Thought 1890–1930,* New York: Vintage Books, 1958.

Jones, G.S. 'History: The Poverty of Empiricism,' pp. 96–118 in Robin Blackburn (ed.), *Ideology in Social Science: Readings in Critical Social Theory.* New York: Pantheon, 1972.

Jones, Robert Alun. 'Durkheim, Totemism and the Intichiuma,' *History of Sociology,* 5, 2, 1985, 79–89.

Jordan, Z.A. *The Evolution of Dialectical Materialism.* New York: St. Martin's Press, 1967.

Kalberg, Stephen. 'Max Weber's Types of Rationality: Cornerstones for the Analysis of Rationalization Processes in History,' *American Journal of Sociology,* 85, 1980, 1145–79.

Kalberg, Stephen. 'The Search for Thematic Orientations in a Fragmented Oeuvre: The Discussion of Max Weber in Recent German Sociological Literature,' *Sociology,* 13, 1979, 127–39.

Kant, Immanuel. *Critique of Pure Reason.* New York: St. Martin's Press, [1781] 1965.

Kasler, Dirk. *Max Weber: An Introduction to his Life and Work.* Chicago: University of Chicago Press, 1988.

Kerridge, Eric. *The Agricultural Revolution.* New York: Augustus Kelly, 1968.

Kerridge, Eric. 'The Movement of Rent, 1540–1640,' *Economic History Review 2nd Series,* Vol. VI, 1953, pp. 17–34.

Kohachiro Takahashi. 'A Contribution to the Discussion,' in Paul Sweezey (ed.), *Transition from Feudalism to Capitalism,* London, NLB, 1976.

Korner, S. *Kant.* Harmondsworth: Penguin, 1955.

Korsch, Karl. *Karl Marx.* New York: Russell & Russell, 1963.

Laclau, Ernesto. *Politics and Ideology in Marxist Theory.* London: NLB, Verso, 1977.

Laclau, Ernesto and Mouffe, Chantal. *Hegemony and Socialist Strategy.* London: Verso, 1985.

Laibman, David. 'Modes of Production and Theories of Transition,' *Science and Society,* XLVIII, 1984, 257–94.

Larrain, Jorge. *The Concept of Ideology.* Athens, Georgia: University of Georgia Press, 1979.

Larrain, Jorge. *Marxism and Ideology.* London: Macmillan Press, 1983.

Lazonick, William. 'Karl Marx and Enclosures in England,' *Review of Radical Political Economics,* Vol. 6, 2, 1974, 1–58.

Lefebvre, Georges. *The French Revolution From its Origins to 1793.* London: Routledge, 1962.

Levine, Donald N. 'Rationality and Freedom: Weber and Beyond,' *Sociological Inquiry,* 51, 1981, 5–25.

Lindsay, A.D. 'Individualism,' *Encyclopedia of the Social Sciences,* 7, 1930–33, 674–80.

Locke, John. *Two Treatises of Government.* New York: Mentor Books, 1963.

Lukács, Georg. *History and Class Consciousness.* London: Merlin Press, 1968.

Lukes, Steven. *Emile Durkheim: His life and Work.* Stanford: Stanford University Press. 1973.

Lukes, Steven. *Individualism.* Oxford: Basil Blackwell, 1973.

Lukes, Steven. 'Prolegomena to the Interpretation of Durkheim,' *European Journal of Sociology,* 12, 1971, 183–209.

McLellan, David. *Karl Marx: His Life and Thought.* New York: Harper & Row, 1973.

Macpherson, C.B. *The Political Theory of Possessive Individualism.* London: Oxford University Press, 1962.

Malthus, Thomas. *An Essay on the Principle of Population.* London: Ward Lock, [1798] 1890.

Mantoux, Paul. *The Industrial Revolution in the Eighteenth Century.* London: Methuen, 1907.

Marcuse, Herbert. *Reason and Revolution: Hegel and the Rise of Social Theory.* New York: Humanities Press, 1954.

Meek, Ronald L. *Economics and Ideology and Other Essays.* London: Chapman and Hall, 1967.

Meek, Ronald L. (ed.). *Marx and Engels on Malthus.* New York: International Publishers, 1954.

Meek, Ronald L. *Studies in the Labour Theory of Value.* London: Lawrence & Wishart, 1973.

Merton, Robert. 'Durkheim's Division of Labor in Society,' *American Journal of Sociology*, 40, 1934, 319–28.

Mill, John Stuart. *Utilitarianism, Liberty, Representative Government.* London: Dent & Sons, [1846] 1910.

Muller, Max. 'Comparative Mythology,' in *Introduction to the Science of Religion: Four Lectures.* Varanasi: Bharuta Manisha, [1870] 1972.

Nelson, Benjamin. 'Max Weber's Author's Introduction: A Master Clue to his Main Aims,' *Sociological Inquiry*, 44, 1974, 269–77.

Nettleship, Richard. *Lectures on the Republic of Plato.* London: Macmillan, 1958.

Oakes, Guy. 'The Verstehen Thesis and the Foundations of Max Weber's Methodology,' *History and Theory*, 16, 1977, 11–29.

Ollman, Bertell. *Alienation: Marx's Conception of Man in Capitalist Society.* London: Cambridge University Press, 1971.

O'Neill, John. 'The Concept of Estrangement in the Early and Late Writings of Karl Marx,' *Philosophy and Phenomenological Research*, 25, 1, 1964, 64–84.

Padgug, Robert A. 'Problems in the Theory of Slavery and Slave Society,' *Science and Society*, 40, 1976, 3–27.

Palmer, R.R. 'Man and Citizen: Applications of Individualism in the French Revolution,' pp. 130–52 in Milton R. Konvitz and Arthur E. Murphy (eds), *Essays in Political Theory.* New York: Kennikat Press, 1972.

Parsons, Talcott. 'Weber's Methodology of Social Science,' in *Max Weber: The Theory of Social and Economic Organization.* New York: Free Press, 1947.

Parsons, Talcott. *The Structure of Social Action.* New York: The Free Press, [1947] 1968.

Parsons, Talcott. *Toward a General Theory of Social Action.* Cambridge, Mass.: Harvard University Press, [1951] 1959.

Patterson, Orlando. 'On Slavery and Slave Formations,' *New Left Review*, 117, (Sept.–Oct.), 1979, 31–67.

Patterson, Orlando. *Slavery and Social Death: A Comparative Study.* Cambridge Mass.: Harvard University Press, 1982.

Plummer, Alfred. *The London Weavers' Company 1600–1970.* London: Routledge & Kegan Paul, 1972.

Poggi, Gianfranco. *Calvinism and the Capitalist Spirit: Max Weber's Protestant Ethic.* London: Macmillian Press, 1983.

Poggi, Gianfranco. 'The Place of Religion in Durkheim's Theory of Institutions,' *European Journal of Sociology*, 12, 1971, 229–60.

Polanyi, Karl. *The Great Transformation: The Political and Economic Origins of our Time.* Boston: Beacon, 1957.

Pollard, Sidney, 'Factory Discipline in the Industrial Revolution,' *Economic Historical Review*, 2nd Series, 16, 1963–64, 254–71.

Ricardo, David. *On the Principles of Political Economy and Taxation.* London, Dent & Sons, [1817] 1973.

Rickert, Heinrich. *Science and History: A Critique of Postivist Epistemology.* (trans. George Reisman) Princeton: Van Nostrand, [1916] 1962.

Rickert, Heinrich. *The Limits of Concept Formation in the Natural Sciences: A Logical Introduction to Historical Sciences.* New York: Cambridge University Press, [1896] 1986.

Richardson, Ruth. *Death, Dissection and the Destitute.* London: Routledge & Kegan Paul, 1987.

Rotenstreich, Nathan. *Basic Problems of Marx's Philosophy.* Indianapolis: Bobbs-Merrill, 1965.

Rousseau, Jean-Jacques. *The Social Contract and Discourse on the Origin of Inequality.* New York: Simon & Schuster, [1762] 1967.

Rubel, M. and Manale, M. *Marx Without Myth: A Chronological Study of His Life and Work.* New York: Harper & Row, 1975.

Rubin, Isaak Illich. *Essays on Marx's Theory of Value.* Montreal: Black Rose, [1928] 1973.

Samuelsson, Kurt. *Religion and Economic Action: A Critique of Max Weber.* New York: Harper & Row, 1957.

Schluchter, Wolfgang. *The Rise of Western Rationalism.* Berkeley: University of California Press, 1981.

Schluchter, Wolfgang. 'Weber's Sociology of Rationalism and Typology of Religous Rejection of the World,' pp. 92–115 in S. Whimster and S. Lash, (eds), *Max Weber, Rationality and Modernity.* London: Allen & Unwin, 1987.

Shaw, William H. *Marx's Theory of History.* Stanford: Stanford Universtiy Press, 1978.

Simon, W.M. *European Positivism in the Nineteenth Century.* New York: Cornell, 1963.

Smith, Adam. *The Wealth of Nations.* London: Dent & Sons, [1776] 1910.

Smith, Dorothy. 'The Ideological Practice of Sociology,' *Catalyst,* 8, 1974, 39–54.

Smith, Dorothy. 'A Sociology for Women' in J.A. Sherman and E.T. Beck (eds), *The Prism of Sex: Essays in the Sociology of Knowledge.* Wisconsin: University of Wisconsin Press, 1976.

Soboul, Albert. *The French Revolution 1787–1799.* Vol. 1. London: NLB, 1974.

Sohn-Rethel, Alfred. *Intellectual and Manual Labour.* London: Macmillan, 1978.

Spencer, B. and Gillen, F.J. *The Native Tribes of Central Australia.* New York: Dover Publications, [1899] 1968.

Stepelevich, L.S. *The Young Hegelians: An Anthology.* Cambridge: University Press, 1983.

Strauss, Leo and Cropsey, Joseph (eds). *History of Political Philosophy.* Chicago: Rand McNally & Co., 1963.

Swart, K.W. 'Individualism in the Mid-Nineteenth Century (1826–1860),' *Journal of the History of Ideas,* 23, 1962, 77–90.

Swingewood, Alan. *Marx and Modern Social Theory.* London: Macmillan, 1975.

Tawney, R.H. *The Agrarian Problem in the Sixteenth Century,* New York: Harper & Row, [1912] 1967.

Tawney, R.H. *Religion and the Rise of Capitalism.* Harmondsworth England: Penguin, [1947] 1984.

Taylor, A.E. *Elements of Metaphysics.* London: Methuen, 1956.

Tenbruck, Friedrich H. 'The Problem of Thematic Unity in the Works of Max Weber,' *The British Journal of Sociology,* 31, 1980, 316–51.

Thompson, E.P. *The Making of the English Working Class.* Harmondsworth: Penguin, 1968.

Thompson, Kenneth. *Auguste Comte: The Foundation of Sociology.* London: Thomas Nelson & Sons, 1976.

Toynbee, Arnold. *The Industrial Revolution.* Boston: Beacon Press, [1877] 1956.

Tribe, Keith (ed.). *Reading Weber.* London: Routledge, 1989.

Troeltsch, Ernst. *The Social Teaching of the Christian Churches.* London: Allen & Unwin, 1956.

Tucker, R.C. *The Marx–Engels Reader.* (2nd edn), New York: Norton, 1978.

Turner, S.P. and Factor, R.A. *Max Weber and the Dispute over Reason and Value.* London: Routledge & Kegan Paul, 1984.

Tylor, Edward. *Primitive Culture: Research into the Development of Mythology, Philosophy, Religion, Art and Custom.* London: J. Murray, 1871.

Versenyi, Laszlo. *Socratic Humanism.* New Haven: Yale University, 1963.

Viner, Jacob. *Religious Thought and Economic Society.* Durham, North Carolina: Duke University Press, 1978.

Viner, Jacob. 'Adam Smith and Laissez Faire,' in J.M. Clark, P.H. Douglas, J.H. Hollander and G.R. Morrow (eds), *Adam Smith 1776—1926.* New York: Augustus Kelly, 1966.

Ward, J.T. *The Factory Movement 1830–1855.* London: Macmillan, 1962.

Wax, Murry. 'On Misunderstanding Verstehen: A Reply to Abel,' *Sociology and Sociological Research*, 51, 1967, 323–33.

Weber, Marianne. *Max Weber: A Biography*. New York: John Wiley & Sons, 1975.

Weber, Max. 'Politics as a Vocation,' pp. 77–128 in H.H. Gerth and C. Wright Mills (eds), *From Max Weber: Essays in Sociology*. New York: Oxford University Press, 1967.

Weber, Max. 'Science as a Vocation,' pp. 129–59 in H.H. Gerth and C. Wright Mills (eds), *From Max Weber: Essays in Sociology*. New York: Oxford University Press, 1967.

Weber, Max. 'The Social Psychology of the World Religions,' pp. 267–301 in H.H. Gerth and C. Wright Mills (eds), *From Max Weber: Essays in Sociology*. New York: Oxford University Press, 1967.

Willey, Thomas E. *Back to Kant: The Revival of Kantianism in German Social and Historical Thought, 1860–1914*. Detroit: Wayne State University Press, 1978.

Windelband, Wilhelm. *A History of Philosophy: With Especial Reference to the Formation and Development of its Problems and Conceptions*. New York: Macmillan, 1901.

Wolff, Kurt H. (ed.). *Essays on Sociology and Philosophy*. New York: Harper, 1960.

Wolin, Sheldon. *Politics and Vision: Continuity and Innovation in Western Political Thought*. Boston: Little Brown, 1960.

Worsley, P.M. 'Emile Durkheim's Theory of Knowledge,' *Sociological Review*, New Series, 4, 1956, 47–62.

Index